D0746240

Gender

on Campus

Gender

on Campus

Issues for College Women

SHARON BOHN GMELCH

With the Assistance of
MARCIE HEFFERNAN STOFFER
 and
JODY LYNN YETZER

RUTGERS UNIVERSITY PRESS
New Brunswick, New Jersey, and London

Library of Congress Cataloging-in-Publication Data

Gmelch, Sharon.
    Gender on campus : issues for college women / Sharon Bohn Gmelch
with the assistance of Marcie Heffernan Stoffer and Jody Lynn Yetzer.
      p. cm.
    Includes index.
    ISBN 0–8135–2521–7 (alk. paper)—ISBN 0–8135–2522–5
(pbk. : alk. paper)
    1. Women college students—United States.   2. College student
orientation—United States.   3. Feminism and education—United
States.   4. Sexism in higher education—United States.
I. Stoffer, Marcie Heffernan   II. Yetzer, Jody Lynn.   III. Title.
LC1757.G65 1998
378.1'9822—dc21   97–49861
                                                         CIP

British Cataloging-in-Publication data for this book is available from the British Library

Manufactured in the United States of America

CONTENTS

GENDER ISSUES ON CAMPUS

DEALING WITH DIVERSITY

SEXUALITY AND THE BODY

COLLEGE AND BEYOND

ACKNOWLEDGMENTS

I AM VERY grateful to two former students, Marcie Heffernan Stoffer and Jody Lynn Yetzer, who assisted me as summer research fellows in the beginning stages of this book. Both have long since graduated from Union College. Marcie obtained a Master's in Social Work and is now a family counselor in upstate New York. Jody went on to Yale Law School, served on the *Yale Journal of Law and Feminism*, and now works with the American Civil Liberties Union. Other students also helped in significant ways; Carianne Bishop, Kathy Blackburn, Autumn Cohen, Allison Hirschman, Sarah Israel, and Raquel Millman commented on chapters and directed me to some valuable resources.

The many students—both women and men—who have taken my Gender and Society course over the years stimulated me to write this book. The topics I have chosen to discuss in large measure reflect their concerns, and I have quoted anonymously from several of their journals. Although I cannot thank every student by name, Frank Attah, Marisol Agreda, Tracy Bush, Tonda Clark, Rebecca Danchik, Kate Durocher, Nolan Farris, Susan Flehinger, Fran Goldstein, Alyson Heller, Beth Isenberg, Amy Joslin, Cora Junowicz, Christa Kelleher, Rachel Kraus, Naomi Krupa, Farah Lalani, Elaine Lee, Carolyn Levy, Melissa Murphy, Molly Pearsall, Nadine Pendley, Jeffrey Quinn, Betsy Robinson, Kristen

Ruckstuhl, Jill Schuck, Adina Stonberg, and Elizabeth Willis deserve special mention. I am also grateful to the women who answered a questionnaire on what it means to be a "nontraditional" student.

Many professionals provided me with information on their programs, answered questions in their areas of expertise, or reviewed chapters. I especially wish to thank Geneva Walker Johnson, Edgar Letriz-Nunez, Paul Mantica, Connie Ostrowski, Donna Perry, Kate Schurick, and Trish Williams for their helpful comments. My good friend and colleague, the late Miriam Lee Kaprow, assisted me in clarifying several points even while she was ill with cancer.

The manuscript was prepared with the calm and very capable assistance of Janet McQuade, Mary McKay, Autumn Proemm, and Danette Slevinski who proofread and corrected it, and willingly served as last-minute consultants. The librarians at Union College, especially Dave Gerhan, Donna Burton, and Bruce Connelly, tracked down references with speed and good humor for which I am very grateful. Adaya Henis copyedited the final manuscript with care, intelligence, and wit. Finally, I wish to thank Leslie Mitchner, my editor at Rutgers University Press, for recognizing the value of this project and for wise counsel during its long gestation.

GENDER

ISSUES ON

CAMPUS

CHAPTER 1

What Is

Feminism?

I myself, have never been able to find out precisely what feminism is.
I only know that people call me a feminist whenever I express
sentiments that differentiate me from a doormat. . . .

—Rebecca West, 1913[1]

Am I a feminist? It's a question that I have dodged many times. This
avoidance only adds to the reasons I should become more aware. I
know the stereotype that goes along with the "feminist" label. It's the
one that makes my dad grunt at the dinner table. Visions of lesbian,
man-hating, sloppy, forceful, womyn-spelling women dance in the back
of my mind. I am not an extreme person, but I realize that gender
seems to play an unnecessary role in too many facets of life. It angers
and then confuses me when I think of this and all the cues that are so
ingrained into our culture for me to notice.

—Union College student, 1995

ALTHOUGH IT MAY surprise you, most students support feminism. In one
survey, 71 percent of the more than 350 male and female students at Michigan
State University who were asked to define "feminism" defined it favorably.[2]

"Some kids at school called you a feminist, Mom, but I punched them out."

Drawing by Donnelly; © 1996 The New Yorker Magazine, Inc.

Only 6 percent gave an unfavorable definition; the rest were mixed. But when the same students were asked to define a "feminist," fewer responses were favorable, and far fewer students were willing to attach the label to themselves. This finding is supported by other research and probably by your own experience. At the University of Michigan, for example, only 40 percent of the nearly 250 women students participating in another study identified themselves as feminists.[3] National polls of American women have found that while a large majority support feminism and believe that the women's movement has improved women's lives, only a third call themselves feminists.

Some students regard the label as "too harsh" to describe their support for women's rights. Given widespread stereotypes of feminists as radical "feminazis" or angry "male-bashers" and lesbians, it is not terribly surprising that many students do not readily apply the label to themselves. I have found that students in the introductory women's studies course I teach are much more willing to say they "advocate feminism" than to call themselves feminists. This reluctance distresses many young feminists.

It really disturbs me to hear a woman say something like, "Oh, don't worry, I'm not into the *feminism* thing" when talking to a man (or other women for that matter). I see this as a woman conveniently removing the "threat" for the man's sake. . . . I really hate the assumption that the search for equality and removal of old destructive customs has to be seen as radicalism—especially in the eyes of so many women. I don't understand the motive behind their words. Perhaps it's the fear. I guess that is something everyone will have to deal with in their own way, but, personally, I would be much more afraid of continued male dominance over women than of some of the serious measures that must be taken in order to break the age-old pattern. My advice to women who "hate feminists" would be for them to step outside of their comfort zone and take in the big picture. . . .[4]

Many African-American women use the term "womanist" instead of "feminist." According to Alice Walker in *In Search of Our Mothers' Gardens*, "womanism" derives from the expressions some black mothers use with female children as in you're "acting womanish" (i.e., courageously).[5] "Womanism" was also a nineteenth-century term for the support of women's rights. Many African-American women reject the label "feminist" because they associate it with a white woman's movement that has in the past ignored or slighted their concerns. "You see, it's like this," explained one student. "I know that all these white women want black women to jump on the feminist bandwagon. That's all good, but where are they when we are fighting for the erasure of racism? Maybe you'll see a handful. But utter the word 'feminism,' and they're up in arms." According to another student, "I don't deal with it [feminism] at all because as a black woman I'm always being forced to choose sides. Well, I have made up my mind, and that's to fight against racial oppression. . . . I don't know, the whole thing is just fucked up, you know?"

According to African-American feminist and scholar bell hooks, "From the mass media and such unlikely sources as black male rap stars, they [young black women] learn that feminism only serves white women and that 'dissin'' it will win them points with just about anybody, particularly sexist black men. . . . some young black females feel that they finally can one-up white girls by insisting that they are already 'real' women, taking care of business, with no need of feminism."[6]

Students who do not advocate feminism—and you may be one of them—are not necessarily unaware of sexism. Nor are they necessarily conservative or traditional in their attitudes about appropriate gender roles and gender relations, although there is a correlation. Students who frequently tell antifeminist jokes, who ridicule campus speakers and entertainers who present feminist

views, and who make fun of women's studies courses and majors ("What about *men's* studies?" or "What are you going to do with *that*?") tend to hold stereotyped views of men and women. How supportive the students on your campus are of feminism and concerned about the campus climate for women will depend on many factors, including the location and type of school you go to, the diversity and political views of its student body and faculty, the nature of its curriculum, and its student culture. Some schools, especially if they are small, can be heavily influenced by the Greek system, which tends to promote stereotyped thinking about gender roles and gender relations.[7]

Sororities provide many college women with a group of close friends and opportunities to work with and to appreciate the skills of other women. Individual sorority women often support feminist goals, and some consider themselves feminists (and even major in women's studies). Nevertheless, the sisterhood formed in sororities is fundamentally different from the sisterhood conceived of by feminist women. According to sociologist Lisa Handler, sorority sisterhood is based on an idealized notion of female friendship ("Sisters are always there for you") that operates primarily to help women deal with the "male-dominated culture of romance" on college campuses.[8] Although sororities differ depending on the size, type, and geographical location of the school as well as their racial composition and other factors, men are still the "focal point" of sorority life.[9] Sorority women, unless they are also feminists, seldom challenge the prevailing asymmetry of gender relations. Few challenge, for example, fraternity men's use of them as the "currency" that helps establish a fraternity's prestige on campus. Many sorority sisters regard this use of women as flattering evidence of their desirability. During pledging, sisters also end up evaluating other women—at least partially—on the basis of how well they will contribute (e.g., by virtue of their good looks) to the sorority's reputation, which is based largely on its ability to attract male attention.

Sisterhood in feminist terms, in contrast, is a socially transformative experience built on the recognition that women as a category have been subjugated because of their gender. Feminists as a group do not hate men—although some individuals may—but they do hate being belittled and hindered just because they are women. This assertion is confirmed by research by sociologists Donna Henderson-King and Abigail Stewart, who compared the attitudes of college women who identify themselves as feminists with those who do not.[10] They found that neither group of students—feminists nor nonfeminists—was more or less positive than the other in their attitudes toward men. Furthermore, both felt a strong sense of "being women." Only feminists, however, felt a sense of "commonality" or shared identity with other women; that is, only the feminists saw other women as having similar goals, beliefs, and fate as a result of their gender. While sorority sisters value each other's friendships and may also value some traditionally "masculine" traits—brains (i.e., high GPAs) and athletic ability—sororities as social institutions support stereotyped notions of femininity that imply a sexual and dependent relationship with men. "For women to be feminine is *not* to recognize connections with other women; rather, it means to define themselves *in terms of their relationships with men* and, sometimes, to see other women as rivals for the attention of men [emphasis added]."[11]

Despite many women's ambivalence about being feminists, feminism as a social movement has changed women's lives for the better. It has opened up many opportunities for women and has made both men and women more flexible in their conceptions of appropriate gender roles. Recent research has found that when college students of both genders describe their "ideal" woman, they describe a mixture of stereotypically "masculine" traits (e.g., intellect) and "feminine" traits (e.g., compassion). This reflects a real change in student attitudes about gender. Twenty years ago, women and men both idealized masculine gender traits. Today they also idealize some feminine ones, and their ideal woman is more androgynous (a mixture of masculine and feminine psychological traits).[12] When students in the study were asked to describe what most women and most men are actually like (rather than their "ideal"), however, they still described each in terms of "feminine" and "masculine" gender stereotypes.

Defining Feminism

In academia—the world of higher education and scientific research—feminism refers to scholarship and theoretical perspectives that place gender at the center of analysis and usually seek to explain the persistence of gender inequality. For most people, including many academics, feminism also involves a personal commitment to political activism on behalf of women's rights and an end to patriarchal privilege. Beyond these broad definitions, a range of views and interpretations exists. When scholars have tried to categorize the complex diversity of contemporary feminist thought, they have used terms like "liberal," "socialist," "Marxist," "radical," "separatist," "ecofeminism," "spiritual," "reform," "conservative," "cultural," and "difference," which sometimes overlap and confuse more than they clarify. Other recent labels, like the dichotomy between "power feminists" and "victim feminists" and between "equity feminists" and "gender feminists," often reflect the user's own politics as much as anything else.

Feminism is one of humanity's basic social movements for equality and liberty. Its activists are leaders in every positive sense of the word. Theorist bell hooks has defined feminism as the "struggle to eradicate the ideology of domination that permeates Western culture on various levels as well as a commitment to reorganizing society so that the self-development of people can take precedence over imperialism, economic expansion, and material desires."[13] "Feminism is not just about women's rights," says Patricia Ireland, president of the National Organization for Women. "[As] a feminist organization [we are] concerned with ending discrimination based on race, class, and other issues of oppression that come from a patriarchal structure."[14]

The "first wave" of Western feminism is usually considered to span the period from 1792, when British feminist Mary Wollstonecraft wrote *A Vindication of the Rights of Women*, to 1929. Wollstonecraft defined and identified male oppression and wrote about the fallacy of male supremacy; the need for comprehensive women's education; the correctness of opening up the professions and wider world to women; and the need to develop a society in which women and men were truly free and equal. In the 1800s, feminists like Elizabeth Cady Stanton, Susan B. Anthony, Lucretia Mott, Frederick Douglass, Matilda Gage, Lucy Stone, and Sarah and Angelina Grimké fought to end slavery, reform discriminatory laws (e.g., inheritance, divorce), and obtain the right to vote.

Feminist activists (i.e., the "suffragists") achieved one major goal in 1920 with ratification of the Nineteenth Amendment, which extended the right to vote to women. Following this, the movement splintered between those feminists who focused on individual rights and those who fought for group protections. In the public's eye, the flapper era of the 1920s seemed to signify that women were now free; they could cut their hair, smoke cigarettes, dispense with corsets, and dance the night away. For several decades, feminism virtually disappeared from public view, its flames practically extinguished by the Depression, World War II, and the postwar prosperity of the 1950s.

With the publication of Betty Friedan's *The Feminine Mystique* in 1963, the fire was rekindled. Although many women had worked for wages during World War II, once the troops returned, middle-class women retreated into the home. Aided by new wealth and technology, they became professional wives and mothers who managed efficient households, making it possible for husbands to go to work and children to go to school. Friedan gave voice to "the problem that has no name"—the boredom, depression, and unspoken yearning for something more that many of these women felt. She urged them to reach beyond the "comfortable concentration camp" of their homes to find fulfillment in work. Her book did not, however, address the reality of working-class and poor women, including many women of color, who from necessity did work outside the home and saw it not as a prison but as a sanctuary.

During the 1960s many activist women involved in the civil rights movement, the antiwar movement, and organizations like Students for a Democratic Society were also beginning to think and talk about what was then called "women's liberation." They encountered indifference or hostility from most of the men they marched with, many of whom "argued that gender issues were secondary because they were subsumable under more basic modes of oppression, namely, class and race."[15] Many women felt they were treated like second-class citizens and sex objects. In 1970 activist Robin Morgan published an essay entitled "Goodbye to All That," in which she denounced male domination and the sexist attitudes and behavior characteristic of most men in the "counterfeit" Left and announced that "Women are the real Left."[16] At the same time, women were sharing their personal experiences with each other and exploring the reasons for sexism in women's "consciousness-raising" or "rap" groups. One of the conclusions they reached was that patriarchy oppressed women in society in the same way that many individual men dominated women in the home. The expression "The personal is political"—coined by Carol Hanisch in *Notes from the Second Year*—became the main slogan of the women's movement.[17]

Much of the theoretical basis for "second wave" feminism was provided by Kate Millett's *Sexual Politics*, published in 1970. In this and later writing, she showed how patriarchal power creates a sexist society that oppresses women at both the institutional and private level. Much of this work developed out of her literary criticism of authors like D. H. Lawrence and Norman Mailer, whose work she linked to antiwoman Freudian psychology. Many powerful American feminist voices were heard during the late 1960s and 1970s: Shulamith Firestone (*The Dialectic of Sex: The Case for Feminist Revolution*, 1970), Robin Morgan (*Sisterhood Is Powerful*, 1970, and *Going Too Far*, 1973), Mary Daly (*The Church and the Second Sex*, 1968, and *Gyn/Ecology: The Metaethics of Radical Feminism*, 1978), Gerda Lerner (*The Woman in American History*, 1971), and Barbara Smith (*Toward a Black Feminist Criticism*, 1977), to name a few.

Rallying under the slogan "Sisterhood is powerful," these second-wave white and black feminists worked to change society's thinking about women by insisting that they were equal to men in intelligence, strength of character, emotional stability, and the capacity to exercise power.[18] They made significant strides in achieving legal equality and reproductive freedom for women. In fact, the women's movement seemed so successful that after the passage of affirmative action legislation, a Supreme Court ruling guaranteeing women's right to an abortion, and the development of greater pay equity, many young women growing up in the 1980s took gender equality for granted. A media-supported backlash against feminists during the 1980s—and continuing today—caused other young women to conceal their interest in feminism. Researcher Carol Sternhell discovered women in campus libraries in the early 1980s hiding copies of *Ms.* inside issues of *Cosmopolitan* in order not to draw attention to themselves. She has characterized their attitude as: "It's okay to beat the boys in tennis, particularly if you look cute in shorts, but whatever you do, don't let them know you're a feminist."[19] Journalist Paula Kamen remembers the reaction she received as a student in the late 1980s writing feminist-oriented columns for the University of Illinois newspaper: "I was branded. People I met began to treat me like a radical separatist Marxist; a co-columnist labeled me 'feminist fatale.' A friend alerted me that when she mentioned my name in conversation to her fellow engineering majors they recoiled in horror. . . . There was no public dialogue—by, for or about young feminists; during our 'coming of age' years from 1980 to 1990, young feminists didn't seem to exist."[20]

Several events in the 1990s helped relegitimize many young women's interest in feminism. In 1991, Susan Faludi published *Backlash: The Undeclared War Against American Women*, which documented the many myths disseminated by the media and individual writers that amounted to an attack on feminism. Anita Hill's testimony during Clarence Thomas's confirmation hearings for the Supreme Court publicized the issue of sexual harassment and also highlighted the male domination of the U.S. Senate and the insensitivity of many political leaders to women. These hearings radicalized many women who decided it was time to pay attention to feminism again; some decided to run for public office. Successful court challenges by conservative "right to life" groups to *Roe v. Wade* and women's guaranteed right to an abortion—a right most prochoice women had come to take for granted, whether or not they would ever choose it for themselves—alerted many women to the dangers of complacency.

When Rebecca Walker, daughter of author Alice Walker and godchild of activist Gloria Steinem, published an article in *Ms.* entitled "I Am The Third Wave," it drew a surprising response.[21] Young women from all over the country wrote letters informing the magazine of the activist work they were quietly engaged in and encouraging older feminists and leaders of the women's movement not to write them off. According to Barbara Findlen, an executive editor of *Ms.*, young feminists

> have been shaped by the unique events and circumstances of our time:
> AIDS, the erosion of reproductive rights, the materialism and cynicism
> of the Reagan and Bush years, the backlash against women, the erosion
> of civil rights, the skyrocketing divorce rate, the movement toward
> multiculturalism and greater global awareness, the emergence of the
> lesbian and gay rights movement, a greater overall awareness of sexual-
> ity—and the feminist movement itself. . . . But even those of us not lucky
> enough to be raised by feminists have found other avenues to discover
> and integrate feminism into our lives: women's studies, a huge body of
> feminist fiction and nonfiction, community- and school-based activist

groups, the occasional sitcom. . . . [Many] of us have integrated feminist values into our lives, whether or not we choose the label "feminist." This is an important barometer of the impact of feminism, since
feminism is a movement for social change—not an organization doing a
membership drive.[22]

Feminism has many voices. It has meant and always will mean different
things to different people. Even within a single society at a single point in
time, women are divided by age, class, race, sexual orientation, and individual
experience. These group memberships, as well as individual views, produce
different feminist analyses and concerns. Women with disabilities often take a
different stance on "choice"—a core feminist issue—because abortion has been
used to "root out those whom society deems imperfect and unworthy of life."[23]
Some lesbian feminists—not all—believe that women cannot have heterosexual
relationships with men and still be feminists. Many poor women and women
of color are more interested in fighting for decent housing, safe communities,
and the right to a proper education for their children than for more publicized
feminist issues like reproductive rights. As bell hooks has pointed out, many
of these women have felt that "child care rather than abortion or lesbian rights;
economic survival rather than political equality; and a sticky floor rather than
a glass ceiling should be given attention."[24] Nor do young women have exactly
the same concerns as older women.[25]

Even within categories there are differences. In the words of one young
feminist, "Generation X, thirteenth generation, twenty something—whatever
package you buy this age group in—one of the characteristics we're known for
is our disunity . . . [but] what may appear to be a splintering in this generation
often comes from an honest assessment of our differences as each of us defines
her place and role in feminism."[26]

In the 1980s, a lively debate took place between antipornography feminists, who believe that pornography is the embodiment of misogyny (hatred of
women) and promotes violence against women, and those feminists who believe that it is a legitimate form of expression or "speech" that is fully protected by the First Amendment.

Many early feminist scholars sought to identify the one key factor that
would explain the persistence of sexism historically and across cultures. Today, most recognize that the diversity of women's lives makes this impossible
and have changed the focus of their research and theorizing. Nevertheless, a
persistent and fundamental disagreement within feminism, among scholars
and activists alike, is related to this issue. Some feminists—sometimes referred
to as difference feminists—believe that there are essential (i.e., biologically
based) differences between men and women, and that all women possess a

unique female nature (e.g., they are spiritual, nurturing, natural pacifists). Ecofeminists, for example, hold patriarchy responsible for devaluing and damaging the environment, and many believe that women's biologically based nurturance makes them more nature-oriented and life-affirming. They argue, therefore, that women have a special relationship to and responsibility for the planet. This view essentializes the differences between men and women and gives the impression that women across cultures and time share certain innate characteristics. The reality among feminists is that "while some women share some common interests and face some common enemies, such commonalities are by no means universal; rather, they are interlaced with differences, even with conflicts."[27]

Some of the most insightful critiques of feminism have come from women of color. Many are highly critical of the women's movement because they associate it with white women who have in the past been insensitive to their concerns and slighted their input. "Even though Black women intellectuals have long expressed a unique feminist consciousness about the intersection of race and class in structuring gender, historically we have not been full participants in white feminist organizations," writes African-American scholar Patricia Hill Collins. "Even today African-American, Hispanic, Native American, and Asian-American women criticize the feminist movement and its scholarship for being racist and overly concerned with white, middle class women's issues."[28] The National Organization for Women is still sometimes criticized for ignoring race, a claim its leadership refutes today, while acknowledging that NOW's past agendas have disproportionately reflected the interests of white feminists.

Much feminist scholarship also has had a white, middle-class bias. Patricia Hill Collins cites Nancy Chodorow's groundbreaking work on gender identity and psychologist Carol Gilligan's work on women's moral development as examples of mainstream feminist theory and research that has taken white, middle-class women to be the norm. "The absence of Black feminist ideas from these and other studies," she says, "places them in a much more tenuous position to challenge the hegemony of mainstream scholarship on behalf of *all* women [emphasis added]."[29] Although many recent works by white feminist scholars incorporate the insights of women of color, others do not, just as some women's studies courses still fail to assign writings by feminist women of color.

If you are white, you may never have thought about the privileges your color automatically confers on you. "I did not see myself as a racist because I was taught to recognize racism only in individual acts of meanness by members of my group, never in invisible systems conferring unsought racial dominance on my group from birth," writes Peggy McIntosh of Wellesley's Center for Research on Women. "I think whites are carefully taught not to recognize white privilege, as males are taught not to recognize male privilege. I have come to see white privilege as an invisible package of unearned assets which I can count on cashing in each day, but about which I was 'meant' to remain oblivious."[30] This unrecognized privilege helps explain many white feminists' presumption that their ideas and actions pertain equally to all women. To the list of "unearned assets" that—like white skin color—give their possessors automatic privileges, we can add ablebodiedness, middle- and upper-class socioeconomic status, heterosexuality, and Western cultural membership. As a cultural anthropologist, I am continually struck by the ethnocentrism or cultural bias of scholarship—feminist and otherwise—that purports to theorize about all "women" (or some other group or condition) on the basis of North American or European experience.

Another critique of contemporary feminism comes from women on the political right who claim that "orthodox" feminism vilifies men and that things aren't as bad as feminists make out. In *The Morning After: Sex, Fear and Feminism on Campus*, for example, Katie Roiphe accuses feminists of intentionally exaggerating issues like the prevalence of date rape in order to get their agenda across.[31] Christine Hoff Summers paints all feminists as extremists who deliberately set out to dupe the public with misinformation about women in order to portray them as victims.[32] To her credit, she traced the source of an often-cited but erroneous statistic about the high number of women who die each year from anorexia nervosa and discovered that an early mistake had been carelessly repeated. Such writers—many of whom also call themselves feminists—accuse other feminists of portraying women only as passive victims in need of protective laws and codes of behavior. Camille Paglia claims that "rape has become a joke" and asserts that women need to take responsbility for their actions and that by going to a man's room alone they are "in effect consenting to sex."[33] Antifeminist writer Mary Matalin once quipped, "Get these moody girls [feminists] a prescription of Motrin and a water pill, quick" and "Mainstream feminists, get a grip."[34]

The more thoughtful of these critics (as opposed to those who lambaste feminism to grab the media spotlight) underestimate the real hurdles still facing many women in American society and the need for women to take group political action rather than relying on individual solutions. Ironically, while they dismiss mainstream feminism as "victimology" and feminists as "whiners" or "humorless prudes," these successful women at the same time embody and enjoy many of the reforms the women's movement has brought.

Pulitzer Prize–winning author Susan Faludi and others have effectively countered such accusations about feminism. Faludi reminds us that the victimhood argument first appeared in conservative journals in articles written by men. One of the first articles was written by Norman Podhoretz and concerned date rape. In it he claimed that a "brazen campaign" by feminists will deny men the privilege of "normal seduction" and the "male initiative" in sexual matters. He also asserted that feminism emasculates men; "the number of whimps . . . will multiply apace" as will the incidence of "male impotence." "Just who's spouting hype?" Faludi asks, feminists or their detractors?[35]

The early 1990s also saw the emergence of a men's movement, which was signaled by the publication of such books as poet Robert Bly's *Iron John* and writer Sam Keen's *Fire in the Belly*.[36] Much like women's consciousness-raising groups in the 1960s, men's groups formed around the country to discuss the meaning of manhood, fatherhood, communication, and relationships with women. They have been praised by many because participants challenge stereotypical male gender roles, but according to sociologists Nijole Benokraitis and Joe Feagin, much of the movement represents a backlash against feminism by privileged white men.[37] Serious scholarship on men, masculinity, and male-female relationships, however, is also being written by feminist-inspired writers such as John Stoltenberg (*Refusing to Be a Man* and *End of Manhood*). Courses on masculinity are becoming more common on campus. Male feminists like Jackson Katz, founder of the Boston-based group Real Men, have become popular campus speakers on sexism and violence against women. Feminist bell hooks prefers not to use the term "women's movement" because "men must be part of the feminist movement, and they must feel that they have a major role to play in the eradication of sexism."[38]

Despite the diversity of views and challenges to feminism, the center of feminism still holds. According to Sheila Tobias, in *Faces of Feminism: An Activist's Reflections on the Women's Movement*, feminists can still unite around the goal of ending the subtle and persistent allocation of economic, social, and political advantages to men.[39] Furthermore, many specific feminist issues such as violence against women affect (or potentially affect) virtually every woman. The changes brought by feminism also affect all our lives and have filtered even into more conservative campus organizations.[40] Most national sororities, for example, now recognize the importance of women's health care concerns, campus date rape, and career networking.[41]

In academia, feminist research and scholarship has profoundly influenced many areas of knowledge. It has uncovered the androcentrism (male bias) of much previous research and many of the "truths" we once held dear. It has rediscovered women of achievement whose work has long been ignored. Feminists have also suggested tantalizing new ways of understanding and analyzing old questions about human nature. Their work has transformed most disciplines in the humanities and social sciences and has had an important impact in sciences like biology and psychology. In my own field of anthropology, feminist scholarship has led to new interpretations of the archaeological record, new ideas about human evolution, and a more sophisticated understanding of the social construction of women's roles in other cultures and of the gendered impact of global processes like international development.

Since 1970, when the first women's studies program was established, the number of American colleges and universities offering undergraduate and graduate courses in women's studies has grown steadily. These courses challenge sexist and androcentric assumptions, provide information about women that is missing from the traditional curricula, and make gender the focus of study. One of their main goals is to bring about an understanding of the political, economic, and social forces that shape the lives of women and men globally. College provides you with a unique opportunity to discard outmoded ideas about gender, to learn about the history and goals of feminism, and to explore the findings of feminist scholarship.

Are You a Feminist?

Essayist Katha Pollitt believes that

> to be a feminist is to answer the question "Are women human?" with a yes. It is not about whether women are better than, worse than, or identical with men. . . . It's about justice, fairness, and access to the broad range of human experience. It's about women consulting their own well-being and being judged as individuals rather than as members of a class with one personality, one social function, one road to happiness. It's about women having intrinsic value as persons rather than contingent value as a means to an end for others: fetuses, children, the "family," men.[42]

If you want women to have full equality, to earn the same (not *nearly* the same) pay, and to have the same opportunities and life choices as men—then you are a feminist. If you deplore sexism—being devalued just because you are a woman and being patronized, harassed, or discriminated against because of your gender—and speak out against it—then you are a feminist. If you want a world in which women and men are equally valued as is the "feminine" within men and the "masculine" within women—then you are a feminist. In the words of one student,

> I don't understand how women can *not* be feminists. Why wouldn't they want to be treated as equals to men? I think it's because the word "feminist" has taken on such negative connotations. Women are scared to be perceived this way because it puts men off, and heterosexual women are afraid of being thought a lesbian. Feminists are stereotyped as tough, manly, and radical. This is far from the true range of feminists in age, color, and beliefs on every band of the spectrum. I think a woman

_____ *Books by Women Whose Words Have Changed the World* _____

Jane Addams, *Twenty Years at Hull House*
Louisa May Alcott, *Little Women*
Isabel Allende, *The House of the Spirits*
Maya Angelou, *I Know Why the Caged Bird Sings*
Hannah Arendt, *The Human Condition*
Jane Austen, *Pride and Prejudice*
Simone de Beauvoir, *The Second Sex*
Ruth Benedict, *Patterns of Culture*
Boston Women's Health Book Collective Staff, *Our Bodies, Ourselves*
Charlotte Brontë, *Jane Eyre*
Emily Brontë, *Wuthering Heights*
Susan Brownmiller, *Against Our Will: Men, Women, and Rape*
Pearl S. Buck, *The Good Earth*
Rachel Carson, *Silent Spring*
Willa Cather, *My Ántonia*
Mary Boykin Chesnut, *A Diary from Dixie*
Kate Chopin, *The Awakening*
Agatha Christie, *The Murder of Roger Ackroyd*
Emily Dickinson, *The Complete Poems of Emily Dickinson*
Mary Baker Eddy, *Science and Health*
George Eliot [Mary Ann or Marian Evans], *Middlemarch*
Fannie Farmer, *The Boston Cooking-School Cook Book*
Frances FitzGerald, *Fire in the Lake*
Dian Fossey, *Gorillas in the Mist*
Anne Frank, *Diary of a Young Girl*
Emma Goldman, *Living My Life*
Germaine Greer, *The Female Eunuch*
Radclyffe Hall, *The Well of Loneliness*
Edith Hamilton, *Mythology*
Betty Lehan Harragan, *Games Mother Never Taught You*
Karen Horney, *Our Inner Conflicts*
Zora Neale Hurston, *Their Eyes Were Watching God*
Helen Keller, *The Story of My Life*
Maxine Hong Kingston, *The Woman Warrior*
Elisabeth Kubler-Ross, *On Death and Dying*

Frances Moore Lappé, *Diet for a Small Planet*
Harper Lee, *To Kill a Mockingbird*
Doris Lessing, *The Golden Notebook*
Anne Morrow Lindbergh, *Gift from the Sea*
Audre Lorde, *The Cancer Journals*
Carson McCullers, *The Heart Is a Lonely Hunter*
Katherine Mansfield, *The Garden Party*
Beryl Markham, *West with the Night*
Margaret Mead, *Coming of Age in Samoa*
Golda Meir, *My Life*
Edna St. Vincent Millay, *Collected Poems*
Margaret Mitchell, *Gone With the Wind*
Marianne Moore, *Complete Poems of Marianne Moore*
Toni Morrison, *Song of Solomon*
Lady Shikibu Murasaki, *The Tale of Genji*
Anaïs Nin, *The Early Diary of Anaïs Nin*
Flannery O'Connor, *The Complete Stories*
Zoé Oldenbourg, *The World Is Not Enough*
Tillie Olsen, *Silences*
Elaine Pagels, *The Gnostic Gospels*
Emmeline Pankhurst, *My Own Story*
Sylvia Plath, *The Bell Jar*
Katherine Anne Porter, *Ship of Fools*
Adrienne Rich, *Of Woman Born*
Margaret Sanger, *Margaret Sanger: An Autobiography*
Sappho, *Sappho: A New Translation*
May Sarton, *Journal of a Solitude*
Mary Shelley, *Frankenstein*
Susan Sontag, *Illness as Metaphor*
Gertrude Stein, *The Autobiography of Alice B. Toklas*
Harriet Beecher Stowe, *Uncle Tom's Cabin*
Barbara Tuchman, *A Distant Mirror*
Sigrid Undset, *Kristin Lavransdatter*
Alice Walker, *The Color Purple*
Eudora Welty, *Delta Wedding*
Edith Wharton, *Ethan Frome*
Phillis Wheatley, *The Collected Works of Phillis Wheatley*
Mary Wollstonecraft, *A Vindication of the Rights of Women*
Virginia Woolf, *A Room of One's Own*

Reprinted with permission of the Women's National Book Association (WNBA).

who says she is not a feminist is contributing to the injustices against our gender, by being ashamed to exert her power. I do not fully understand what women are afraid of. Perhaps realizing their power means having to face issues in society and recognize the rampant sexism. It's hard, I think, but in order for change to come, every woman should be able to state, "I am a feminist" with pride.

DID YOU KNOW?

- The first organized political movement for the freedom of women was founded in the United States; the first woman's rights conference was held in Seneca Falls, New York, on July 19, 1848.
- Feminist Alice Paul wrote the first version of the Equal Rights Amendment in 1923. Fifty years later, the ERA finally passed both houses of Congress in 1972, although it failed to be ratified by enough states to become law.
- According to the National Council for Research on Women, 78 percent of poor people in the United States are women and girls, but fewer than 6 percent of philanthropic dollars are spent on programs for this group.
- Do you know the significance of March 8? On this day in 1857, women from the garment and textile industry in New York City protested their low wages and poor working conditions. Their demonstration was broken up by police; some women were arrested, and others were trampled in the confusion. On March 8, 1908, thousands of women from the industry again demonstrated, demanding better wages and working conditions as well as the right to vote. To honor their struggle, Clare Zetkin, a German labor leader, proposed the establishment of International Women's Day. For the next sixty years, it was celebrated, mainly in socialist countries. The first celebration in the United States took place in 1967. Today, International Women's Day is celebrated by women's groups around the world.
- A 1986 *Newsweek*/Gallup poll found that 71 percent of the women surveyed believed that the women's movement had improved their lives. A *Time* magazine poll three years later found that 81 percent thought the women's movement was still improving their lives.

WHAT YOU CAN DO

- You don't have to major in women's studies in order to take advantage of the program. You can take courses, listen to guest speakers, participate in workshops and other special events, read and discuss gender issues with your friends and faculty, and join women's groups. You owe it to yourself to learn something about feminism and about how gender influences your life and the lives of women and men around the globe.

- Enjoy some feminist fiction, including: Louisa May Alcott's *Little Women*, Charlotte Perkins Gilman's *The Yellow Wallpaper* and *Herland*, Margaret Atwood's *The Handmaid's Tale*, Doris Lessing's *The Golden Notebook*, Lillian Hellman's *Toys in the Attic*, Joanna Russ's *The Female Man*, Marge Piercy's *Woman on the Edge of Time*, Sylvia Plath's *The Bell Jar*, and Alice Walker's *The Color Purple*.

- To celebrate its seventy-fifth anniversary in 1992, the Women's National Book Association prepared a list of seventy-five books "by women whose words have changed the world" and "brought insight, awe, and pleasure to countless readers over the years." It is reproduced here.

- Don't buy into the "sexual correctness" myth. Feminists are frequently attacked as part of the campaign against so-called political correctness, which often includes attacks on women's studies. Rather than being a powerful force suppressing dissent on campus, women's studies encourages students to listen to ideas and voices that are neglected in other parts of the curriculum. Keep an open mind, and learn about feminist thought. You don't have to agree with every view expressed, but you should listen and read carefully, discuss the issues involved, and arrive at your own opinion.

- You may find that you become interested in working to improve women's lives. Explore the opportunities available to you as a member of a campus organization, through internships, or volunteer work off campus. Many campus women's groups volunteer time at rape crisis centers and participate in events like Take Back the Night marches, organized to demonstrate that women will not be intimidated by the threat of violence and rape. Activism needs constant rekindling; you can add the needed fuel.

- Adopt a cause. Many possibilities exist, from the activities of a local Planned Parenthood office or rape crisis center to an organization working on the national or international scene. The Women's Environment & Development Organization (WEDO) is a nonprofit educational organization that works to make women equal participants, experts, and leaders in policy-making, from the local to the international level. Its president is feminist and former member of Congress Bella Abzug (see Resources).

- Join a women's group on campus. If none is available, start your own. Belonging to a small group of women brings many rewards. (Groups known as consciousness-raising, rap, or just women's groups in the late 1960s and 1970s offered women a support system and personally meaningful insights about women's lives.) To attract interested people, place an advertisement in the student newspaper, post signs in residence halls and around campus, ask your friends and the women you live near.

- Don't be afraid to call yourself a feminist if you consider yourself one. If

someone criticizes you for doing so, explain what feminism actually is. Help
dispel the myths.

 If people make sexist comments that offend you, speak up and let them
know why you find them offensive. If you read an article, watch a television
show, or attend a program presented by a speaker that you feel is sexist,
write to the individual and to his or her agent and sponsors to point out why
you were offended.

 Support individuals and groups who bring informative and positive speakers
and programs to campus. Join the student speakers' forum or other campus
groups responsible for organizing events. Contribute your time and ideas.

 Organize a women's history field trip. Learn more about what women have
done and are doing to promote the cause of gender equity. If your campus is
near enough, visit the National Women's Hall of Fame in Seneca Falls, New
York. Join with other women on campus to attend the National Organization
for Women's Young Feminist Summit, an exciting conference and rally held
each spring in Washington, D.C.

----------------------------- *RESOURCES* -----------------------------

Books

The books listed below provide a sampling of feminist thought and writings
about the women's movement and issues in women's studies. Many more are
available. Two journals produced by the University of Wisconsin are particularly useful: *Feminist Collections* contains review articles on new books, and
New Books on Women & Feminism indexes by topic all new publications on
women and feminism. If these journals are unavailable on campus, suggest that
your library, women's studies program, or multicultural center subscribe to them.
Contact the Women's Studies Librarian, 430 Memorial Library, University of
Wisconsin, 728 State Street, Madison, WI 53706.

Anderson, Margaret, and Patricia Hill Collins (eds.). 1995. *Race, Class and Gender: An Anthology.* Belmont, Calif.: Wadsworth.

Anzaldúa, Gloria (ed.). 1990. *Making Face, Making Soul (Haciendo Caras): Creative and Critical Perspectives by Women of Color.* San Francisco: Aunt Lute.

Ashworth, Georgina (ed.). 1994. *A Diplomacy of the Oppressed: New Directions
in International Feminism.* New York: Humanities.

Baker, Christina Looper, and Christina Baker Kline (eds.). 1996. *The Conversation Begins: Mothers and Daughters Talk about Living Feminism.* New York:
Bantam.

Collins, Patricia Hill. 1990. *Black Feminist Thought: Knowledge, Consciousness,
and the Politics of Empowerment.* Boston: Unwin Hyman.

Cott, Nancy. 1987. *The Grounding of Modern Feminism.* New Haven, Conn.: Yale
University Press.

Daly, Mary. 1968. *The Church and the Second Sex.* New York: Harper & Row.

———. 1978. *Gyn/Ecology:The Metaethics of Radical Feminism.* Boston: Beacon Press.

Donovan, Josephine. 1992. *Feminist Theory: The Intellectual Traditions of American Feminism.* New York: Continuum.

DuBois, Ellen Carol, and Vicki Ruiz (eds.). 1990. *Unequal Sisters: A Multi-Cultural Reader in U.S. Women's History.* New York: Routledge.

Elam, Diane, and Robyn Wiegman (eds.). 1995. *Feminism Beside Itself.* New York: Routledge.

Faludi, Susan. 1991. *Backlash: The Undeclared War Against American Women.* New York: Crown.

Findlen, Barbara (ed.). 1995. *Listen Up: Voices from the Next Feminist Generation.* Seattle: Seal.

Firestone, Shulamith. 1970. *The Dialectic of Sex: The Case for Feminist Revolution.* New York: Morrow.

Friedan, Betty. 1984, rev. ed. (1963). *The Feminine Mystique.* New York: Dell.

———. 1991. *The Second Stage.* New York: Dell.

Hanisch, Carol. 1970. *Notes from the Second Year: Women's Liberation: Major Writings of the Radical Feminists.* New York: Radical Feminism.

Hewitt, Nancy, and Suzanne Lebsock (eds.). 1993. *Visible Women: New Essays on American Activism.* Champaign: Illinois University Press.

hooks, bell. 1981. *Ain't I a Woman: Black Women and Feminism.* Boston: South End.

———. 1984. *Feminist Theory: From Margin to Center.* Boston: South End.

———. 1989. *Talking Back: Thinking Feminist, Thinking Black.* Boston: South End.

Humm, Maggie. 1995. *The Dictionary of Feminist Theory.* Columbus: Ohio State University Press.

Kamen, Paula. 1991. *Feminist Fatale: Voices from the "Twentysomething" Generation Explore the Future of the "Women's Movement."* New York: Donald I. Fine.

Kaminer, Wendy. 1990. *A Fearful Freedom: Women's Flight from Equality.* Reading, Mass.: Addison-Wesley.

Kerber, Linda, Alice Kessler-Harris, and Kathryn Kish Sklar (eds.). 1995. *U.S. History as Women's History: New Feminist Essays.* Chapel Hill: North Carolina University Press.

Kesselmann, Amy, Lily McNair, and Nancy Schniedewind (eds.). 1995. *Women, Images and Realities: A Multicultural Anthology.* Mountain View, Calif.: Mayfield.

Lerner, Gerda. 1971. *The Woman in American History.* Menlo Park, Calif.: Addison-Wesley.

Melich, Tanya. 1996. *The Republican War Against Women.* New York: Bantam.

Miles, Angela. 1993. *Integrative Feminisms: Global Perspectives on North American Feminism.* London: Routledge.

Miller, Page Putnam (ed.). 1992. *Reclaiming the Past: Landmarks of Women's History.* Bloomington: Indiana University Press.

Millett, Kate. 1970. *Sexual Politics.* Garden City, N.Y.: Doubleday.

Moraga, Cherríe, and Gloria Anzaldúa (eds.). 1983. *This Bridge Called My Back: Writings by Radical Women of Color.* 2nd ed. New York: Kitchen Table/Women of Color.

Morgan, Robin (ed.). 1970. *Sisterhood Is Powerful: An Anthology of Writings from the Women's Liberation Movement.* New York: Random House.

Morgan, Robin. 1973. *Going Too Far: The Personal Chronicle of a Feminist.* New York: Random House.

O'Barr, Jean, and Mary Wyer (eds.). 1992. *Engaging Feminism: Students Speak Up and Speak Out.* Charlottesville: University Press of Virginia.

Offen, Karen, Ruth Roach Pierson, and Jane Rendall (eds.). 1991. *Writing Women's History: International Perspectives.* Bloomington: Indiana University Press.

Perry, Linda, and Patricia Geist (eds.). 1997. *Courage of Conviction: Women's Words, Women's Wisdom.* Mountain View, Calif.: Mayfield.

Putnam, Dana, et al. (eds.). 1995. *The Journal Project: Dialogues and Conversations inside Women's Studies.* Toronto: Second Story.

Rendall, Jane. 1984 *The Origins of Modern Feminism: Women in Britain, France and the United States, 1780–1860.* New York: Schocken.

Richardson, Diane, and Victoria Robinson (eds.). 1993. *Thinking Feminist: Key Concepts in Women's Studies.* New York: Guilford.

Rothenberg, Paula. 1992. *Race, Class and Gender in the United States: An Integrated Study.* New York: St. Martin's.

Schneir, Miriam. 1972. *Feminism: The Essential Historical Writings.* New York: Vintage.

Scott, Anne Firor. 1991. *Natural Allies: Women's Associations in American History.* Champaign: Illinois University Press.

Smith, Barbara. 1977. *Toward a Black Feminist Criticism.* Freedom, Calif.: Crossing.

Smith, Barbara (ed.). 1983. *Home Girls: A Black Feminist Anthology.* New York: Kitchen Table/Women of Color.

Stoltenberg, John. 1993. *End of Manhood: A Book for Men of Conscience.* New York: Dutton.

Tobias, Sheila. 1997. *Faces of Feminism: An Activist's Reflections on the Women's Movement.* Boulder, Colo.: Westview.

United Nations. 1997. *The United Nations and the Advancement of Women, 1945–1996.* New York: United Nations.

Walker, Rebecca (ed.). 1995. *To Be Real: Telling the Truth and Changing the Face of Feminism*. New York: Anchor.

Wilson, John K. 1995. *The Myth of Political Correctness: The Conservative Attack on Higher Education*. Durham, N.C.: Duke University Press.

Wollstonecraft, Mary. 1995 (1792). *The Vindication of the Rights of Women*. Boston: Charles E. Tuttle.

Videos

Dear Lisa: A Letter to My Sister. In this forty-five-minute video by J. Clements, the filmmaker asks her sister, herself, and others about the dreams they had growing up and contrasts them to the reality they face as women in the 1990s. Topics include sports, careers, motherhood, body image, sexual assault, and self-esteem. New Day Films, Department WM, 22–D Hollywood Avenue, Hohokus, NJ 07423. Phone: (201) 652–6590.

The F-Word: A Video About Feminism. This ten-minute short by Marcia Jarmel and Erin Gallagher takes a look at the power of the word "feminism" in American culture. Why does it mean so many things to different people? Pithy interviews with women and men from diverse walks of life are rhythmically intercut with computer-animated quotes and set to a rap beat. Discussion and study guide are available. Women Make Movies, 462 Broadway, Suite 500–E, New York, NY 10013. Phone: (212) 925–0606.

Growing Up Female. This was one of the first films of the modern women's movement. Produced in 1971 by Julia Reichert and James Klein, this fifty-minute video looks at female socialization through the lives of six women and girls. It was widely used in the 1970s by consciousness-raising groups to generate interest and help explain feminism. Today, it shows us how much has changed and how much stays the same. New Day Films, 22–D Hollywood Avenue, Hohokus, NJ 07423. Phone: (201) 652–6590.

Hearts and Hands. Pat Ferrero produced this sixty-minute historical film chronicling the nineteenth century's great social movements and events, including women's suffrage. The video presents the lives of many anonymous women as well as important historical figures like Harriet Tubman, Frances Willard, and Abigail Scott Duniway. Winner of numerous awards. New Day Films, 22–D Hollywood Avenue, Hohokus, NJ 07423. Phone: (201) 652–6590.

Some American Feminists. This fifty-six-minute video was made in 1980 by Luce Guilbeault, Nicole Brossard, and Margaret Wescott and was produced by the National Film Board of Canada. It looks at the second wave of feminism, and includes interviews with many of its leading figures, including Rita Mae Brown, Betty Friedan, and Kate Millett. Also contains newsreel footage of the tumultuous 1960s and early 1970s. Critical viewing for anyone interested in the history of modern feminism. Women Make Movies, 462 Broadway, Suite 500–E, New York, NY 10013. Phone: (212) 925–0606.

Organizations

Clearinghouse on Women's Issues (CWI), PO Box 70603, Friendship Heights, MD 20813. Phone: (202) 362–3789. CWI is a nonpartisan clearinghouse for national, regional, state, and local women's and civil rights organizations, focusing on public policies that affect the economic and educational status of women. It disseminates information on issues related to discrimination based on gender, race, age, or marital status. The CWI publishes a newsletter nine times a year.

Ms. Foundation for Women (MFW), 120 Wall Street, 33rd Floor, New York, NY 10005. Phone: (212) 742–2300. The Ms. Foundation seeks to improve the status of women of all ages and to eliminate sex discrimination as well as barriers based on race, age, disability, sexual orientation, and culture. It provides funding and assistance for community-based self-help feminist projects. It also sponsors the annual Take Our Daughters to Work Day, held the fourth Thursday in April.

National Council for Research on Women (NCRW), 530 Broadway, 10th Floor, New York, NY 10012–3920. Phone: (212) 274–0730. The NCRW is a national network of organizations interested in women's issues. It supports feminist research, policy analysis, and educational programs addressing legal, economic, and social inequalities based on gender. It also operates the National Council Database for Work-in-Progress with the Schlesinger Library at Radcliffe and the Research Libraries Group. The Council also produces many reports and directories. A good source of information.

National Organization for Women (NOW), 1000 16th Street NW, Suite 700, Washington, DC 20036. Phone: (202) 331–0066. NOW is a feminist organization for women and men that has been working since 1966 to gain full equality for women and end gender bias and discrimination. (Its first president was Betty Friedan.) It is engaged in many activities, including education, lobbying, and litigation. Its current priorities are preserving reproductive rights, passing the Equal Rights Amendment, stopping violence against women, fighting racism, and supporting lesbian and gay rights. NOW's concerns also include affirmative action, welfare reform, and immigrant rights. It organizes the annual Young Feminist Summit and sponsors other student-oriented activities, including essay contests. It publishes the *National NOW Times*.

National Women's Student Coalition (NWSC), c/o USSA, 1413 K Street NW, 10th Floor, Washington, DC 20006. Phone: (202) 347–8772. This all-women coalition is a branch of the United States Student Association (USSA) that lobbies for women students' issues at the national level. It works to build a national information network for college women to share ideas and resources across campuses. Its goals include addressing gender equity in the classroom. It meets twice yearly at USSA events, including its annual Congress.

Women's Environment & Development Organization (WEDO), 845 Third Avenue, 15th Floor, New York, NY 10022. Phone: (212) 759–7982.

Women's National Book Association, 160 Fifth Avenue, New York, NY 10010. Phone: (212) 675–7805.

CHAPTER 2

Sexism in the

Genderless Classroom

From the academy the boys of my class went to Union College at
Schenectady. When those with whom I had studied and contended for
prizes for five years came to bid me good-by, and I learned of the
barrier that prevented me from following in their footsteps—"no girls
admitted here"—my vexation and mortification knew no bounds. . . .
Again I felt more keenly than ever the humiliation of the distinctions
made on the ground of sex.
                    —Elizabeth Cady Stanton, *Eighty Years and More*, 1831[1]

Being a woman isn't the problem. The problem is being treated
differently.
                    —Student comment, *Radcliffe News*, 1990

IN CONTRAST TO THE SITUATION Elizabeth Cady Stanton faced, women
today make up the majority of college students, and no all-male colleges remain. Does this mean there is equality in the classroom? In 1982, the Association of American Colleges published a disturbing and influential report entitled
"The Classroom Climate: A Chilly One for Women?" which documented wide-

Doonesbury

spread gender bias and sexism in college classrooms. It found, for example, that many faculty called on women less frequently than they called on male students, treated their remarks less seriously, and gave them less feedback on their work. Some faculty were in the habit of speaking to their classes as if no women were present, prefacing hypothetical questions with remarks like "Suppose your wife . . ." or "When you were a boy. . . ." Some routinely used sexist humor and sexual imagery as a teaching device and treated the women in their classes with condescension, calling them "blondie" and the like and sometimes going so far as to suggest that subject matter was too difficult for "girls."

How much have things changed? A follow-up report by the National Association for Women in Education, published in 1996, found that while the classroom climate for women has warmed, gender still makes a difference.[2] Male students are still allowed to dominate most classroom discussions. Some faculty contribute to a "chilly climate" through their own subtle behavior: failing to make eye contact with female students, sounding or looking impatient (e.g., glancing at the clock) when they speak, not responding to their comments. The problems are most pronounced in traditionally male disciplines—certain sciences and engineering. According to a physics graduate student, for example, "countless times I've mentioned an idea for homework or a practice test problem and had it rejected, then seen it accepted as a stroke of genius when mentioned by a man [sic] student."[3]

Many classroom inequalities are not caused by deliberate malice but result from the socialization experiences of students and faculty who have grown up in a male-dominated society. Male students, for example, are more likely than women to have been encouraged to be assertive when they were growing up. Consequently, they are more likely to blurt out an answer to a professor's question and to follow up on other students' comments. Female students are still more likely to collect their thoughts and then raise their hands, especially in coeducational classrooms. A study at Wheaton College, carried out only two years after this former women's school admitted men, found that although men then formed just 10 percent of the student body, they did 25 percent of the speaking in class.[4]

When male students dominate class discussions, resort to gender stereotypes in their arguments, make sexist comments, and mutter or scoff during women's class contributions, they create a hostile environment for women. According to a Harvard/Radcliffe student, the only woman in a twenty-person Psychology of Business course, "I felt compelled to give a different perspective, but every time I started to speak I'd get interrupted. Men feel they have the right to run over you."[5] The problem is not restricted to American classrooms. According to a Canadian student:

I was the only woman in the MBA program last year, and it was very difficult for me. I found the atmosphere so hostile. In one of my first classes, a guy said something like, "I like my women tempura." When I asked him what that meant, he said, "lightly battered." And this was within the course of his presentation. . . . Because the professor didn't seem to understand, I stood up and said: "Are you going to say something or am I?" I think it's the role of the professor to direct the class into productive areas. . . . This kind of thing goes on on a daily basis for women in business classes, engineering classes.[6]

Faculty must take responsibility for creating a gender-neutral classroom environment not only through their own behavior but also by correcting students' inappropriate behavior. One of the recommendations for faculty contained in the National Association for Women in Education's 1996 report is to develop a student handout detailing appropriate class behavior toward other students.

Classroom climate is also affected by the content of course materials. Content analyses done in the 1970s found that history textbooks devoted less than one percent of their coverage to women; the most widely used art history text at the time did not include a single woman artist. From its founding in 1916 to 1970, the *Journal of Negro History* published only five articles devoted exclusively to African-American women.[7] The same situation prevailed in other disciplines. Describing this situation, feminist poet and critic Adrienne Rich once wrote, "If there is any misleading concept, it is that of 'coeducation': that because women and men are sitting in the same classrooms, hearing the same lectures, reading the same books, performing the same laboratory experiments, they are receiving an equal education. They are not, first because the content of education itself validates men even as it invalidates women."[8]

Women's studies developed as an area of scholarly study largely to correct this situation, to write women back into history and tell "herstory." Today, the coverage of women in textbooks and course materials is more equitable, thanks in part to numerous curriculum transformation projects. Nevertheless, the issue is far from resolved. A recent examination of architecture texts and courses, for example, found that women architects and women-designed structures were virtually absent.[9] At the primary and secondary school level, many textbooks that discuss women's accomplishments in effect marginalize them by placing the material in separate boxes or sections rather than incorporating it throughout the main text. Male students often ridicule research projects that deal with women's issues and courses that focus on gender or feminism. A female undergraduate at a small liberal arts school who distributed a one-page survey on sexual harassment received one of the returned forms covered with hostile, sexist remarks. The male respondent ridiculed her project and in a confused melee of epithets called her a "slut," a "fucking feminist lesbian," and a "paranoid nympho." Although this returned survey represented just one out of a hundred, its virulence frightened her. The student who wrote these remarks may have thought he was being funny, but he was actually engaging in misogynistic and harassing behavior.

Male students who take women's studies courses likewise may be ridiculed by peers. Madonne Miner interviewed men who had registered for women's studies courses at the University of Wyoming. Almost all reported receiving "weird looks," being teased by friends, peers, and relatives, and being asked to explain why they had enrolled. Many were discouraged from taking the course by other students who claimed it had a reputation for "male bashing" (a common stereotype of women's studies courses and of feminists generally). Others had male friends who could only understand their behavior by assuming they must be taking the course in order to meet women. According to Miner, they apparently felt that "To take a class with the intention of *understanding* women is to step into suspiciously feminine (and hence, potentially homosexual) territory; but to take the class to *meet* women—that's okay."[10]

The gender of faculty members also has an effect on classroom climate. In recent years, the number of women faculty has grown steadily and rapidly. One-third of college professors are now women; almost 41 percent of all new faculty hired are women.[11] The bad news is that many schools have notably fewer women; less than a fifth of Harvard Law School's faculty, for example, are women.[12] Nationally, female faculty are overrepresented at schools with higher teaching loads and lower pay, and underrepresented at elite colleges and research universities, where teaching loads are typically lighter and pay is higher.

What difference do women faculty make? Many, especially those most influenced by feminist pedagogy, bring new sensibilities and teaching styles to the classroom. Although teaching styles are certainly not gender specific, they are gender related. Women are more likely than men to stress cooperation rather than competition in the classroom. They are more likely to adopt a democratic, give-and-take discussion style rather than using Socratic questioning or a strict lecture format. According to a recent study, many female law students find the Socratic method of questioning (assertive questioning and answering between professor and student), especially in large classes, intimidating and an obstacle to their initiative and problem-solving.[13] The term "decentering the classroom" has been used to describe feminists' attempts to move away from an authoritarian, teacher-centered classroom in order to allow students' voices to be heard and to more actively engage them in learning. At curricular meetings and college-sponsored seminars on teaching, women faculty seem to bring up "chilly climate" issues and to raise questions about *how* subjects are taught more frequently than do men.

Women faculty can face some of the same problems as women students in the classroom. Professor Mary Hart has described what happened to her when a small group of neoconservative male students ganged up on her in class. They made a point of ignoring her, avoided eye contact, and disrupted the class with loud sighs and talk among themselves. Anything she said that could be interpreted as feminist, even something as minor as discussing the use of nonsexist language, was met with eye-rolling, winks, and nods, as if to say, "Here we go again."[14] Once behavior like this gets started in a class, it can escalate, drawing in other students (including some women) and ruining the course. As word spreads on campus, the same thing can be repeated in later courses taught by the same professor. An American Bar Association report entitled "Elusive Equality" found that both female law school students and professors have experienced disrespectful behavior from male professors and students.[15] Other research has found that women faculty receive more negative student evaluations when they teach a course associated with feminism than when they teach a politically neutral subject.[16]

The experiences you have in the classroom and with other students will depend on the school you go to, the discipline you major in, and the specific courses you take. The climate for women in English, for example, is likely to be much warmer than it is in a traditionally male field like engineering or physics. Some institutions and faculties are also much further along than others in recognizing sexism and eliminating it. Sociology professor Anne Constantinople, for example, studied gender bias at Vassar, a former women's college, and found it missing.[17] Critics of "chilly climate" reports claim that the obstacles confronting women students today are overstated. Some recent research supports this view. Researchers Lawrence and Marjorie Nadler, for example, looked at Miami University students' perceptions of classroom communication and climate.[18] They found that male and female students reported no difference in how comfortable they felt in the classroom. Furthermore, female students did not feel that they had experienced more dominance behaviors— like being interrupted in class—than male students. The best advice, therefore, is to be aware of the issues but not to let *expectations* of gender bias or sexism diminish your enjoyment of university life.

Women's Colleges

Fewer than a hundred private women's colleges exist in the United States today. In the 1960s, there were three times as many. Then shrinking college enrollments and the emerging view that single-sex education was outmoded forced many to close and others, like Radcliffe and Vassar, to go coed. Most men's colleges also went coeducational in the 1970s. Over the next generation those women's schools that remained watched enrollments drop and their sterling reputations tarnish. Today, however, interest and enrollments at women's colleges are on the rise, and people have come to recognize the important role single-sex education can play for women.

To begin with, women's colleges provide an environment in which female students can take their studies seriously, free of sexist expectations and gender harassment. Many women students are attracted by what they see as a less competitive classroom atmosphere.[19] The schools also offer "a vision of what a woman can do without the pressure of males in a day-to-day environment. A sisterhood community that supports and encourages you to make your dreams realities," according to a student at Smith. "I didn't think going to a women's college was so important when I started," remarked a Wellesley student, "but the longer I am here, the more I see the importance of a single-sex education for women. At Wellesley, we like to say that women don't receive equal opportunity; they receive every opportunity."[20]

A woman in Mount Holyoke's Frances Perkins program for older or "nontraditional" students told me: "Very few women drop out because other women, on a daily basis, remind them of how intelligent, persistent, strong, and valuable they are. . . . Even outside the program, the school is sensitive to women's issues, educational learning styles—specifically to empower women so they can succeed. For two years I have heard the pronoun 'she' versus 'he' when referring to something in which a gender pronoun is needed. That *affects* women's visibility. I feel like *I* am a part of the thought that is being discussed."

Women's colleges have changed, too. They are not as separatist as they once were. Most have connections with coeducational schools, including some shared classes. Although they were once regarded as places where young women prepared for a successful marriage as much as a successful career, today many women's colleges are recognized as providing strong academic programs even in the sciences. In fact, women from the five remaining "Sisters"—the Eastern colleges of Smith, Bryn Mawr, Mount Holyoke, Barnard, and Wellesley—earn a disproportionate number of the math and engineering doctorates awarded in the United States each year to female liberal arts graduates. Over a quarter of the students at Mount Holyoke and Barnard major in science compared to 7 percent of men and women nationally.[21] These schools provide strong science programs and supportive classroom environments for women. Until coeducational colleges and universities can create similar classroom environments in the sciences (and engineering), some women will be more comfortable learning at single-sex schools. Other opportunities are also easier for women to grasp. They naturally hold all student leadership positions and control campus social life. Many, if not most, administrators, faculty, and staff are also women, providing a wealth of role models.

Politically, the issue of single-sex education is not quite as straightforward. In 1996, the Supreme Court ruled in *United States v. Virginia* that the all-male Virginia Military Institute could not continue to exclude women because doing so violated the Equal Protection Clause of the Fourteenth Amendment. VMI had argued that its rigorous military training and highly disciplined educational program were unsuitable for women, who, it claimed, were more emotional, less aggressive, and more vulnerable to stress and fear of failure than men. The Court's ruling sent a clear message that such stereotypes about women's abilities and interests may not be used to limit their access to educational programs; individual merit must be the only criterion.[22] When Shannon Faulkner sought admission to the only other state-funded college-level military academy in the country—the all-male Citadel, in South Carolina—a few years earlier, the arguments used against her harkened back to 1960s desegregation battles, with Citadel students declaring: "This is our turf. No girls allowed!" If the word "blacks" is substituted for "girls," it is easier to see how untenable their position was. Both VMI and the Citadel are now coeducational.

Does this mean that women's colleges discriminate against men? The short answer is no. An important legal distinction is that all current women's colleges are private, while both VMI and the Citadel are public institutions supported by taxpayer money. The latter also provide a specialized type of education and military training that is not available to women anywhere else. (The Supreme Court decided that the military program VMI helped establish for women at nearby Mary Baldwin College did not provide an equal or equivalent educational experience to that offered at VMI.) In contrast, the liberal arts education women receive at women's liberal arts colleges is widely available to men at a host of other schools. Moreover, women's colleges seek to provide an environment in which women—who form a minority, in terms of their historic lack of economic, legal, and political power—can develop to their full potential without the hindrance of outmoded gender stereotypes and limiting expectations.[23] In this sense, their mission is much like that of historically black colleges. VMI and the Citadel cannot make the same kind of claim for men.

A Classroom of Your Own

If you attend a coeducational institution, as most women do, the courses offered through a women's studies program are probably the closest you will come to having a classroom of your own. Although they are not the only place on campus where you will find your experience reflected in course material, here gender and women occupy center stage. The first women's studies program was established in 1970; today there are over six hundred. Most are interdisciplinary programs that offer courses in cooperation with various academic departments. Such courses challenge sexist and androcentric assumptions, provide information about women that is missing from the traditional curricula, and offer a feminist perspective that treats gender as a focus of study.

The effect that women's studies courses have on students is often dramatic. At the very least, everyday sexist behaviors once accepted as normal or acceptable are now noticed and questioned. A male student wrote the following journal entry:

> Ever since I took this class, I've become a lot more aware of the feminist issues I'm faced with every day. This was the first year I actually noticed (or even thought about) the fact that my mother and three sisters did *everything* for Thanksgiving dinner while my twin brother, father, grandfather, and I sat in the living room and watched the football games. When my grandfather asked one of my sisters to get us all another round of beers, I couldn't help thinking of Thelma's husband from *Thelma and Louise*. So I got up and got the beers. Then I went into the kitchen and offered my services. . . . I learned how to make an apple pie and stuffing, and how to baste the turkey. I even learned how to make a turkey out of the napkins. Then I convinced my brother and my sisters' boyfriends to do the dishes after we finished eating. My mom was quite impressed.

This student's "insight," however, reminds me of a criticism of many women's studies classes that a female women's studies major I know once made.

> One of the problems that I come across often in women's studies classes is that they become self-help and self-actualization groups for women (and sometimes for men) who have never taken a class like this before. In my opinion, this severely detracts from the curriculum offered and belittles the entire class. The classes should focus on the subject matter, which, more often than not, has nothing to do with whose parent does the housework and who worked. This kind of discussion weakens the academic and intellectual rigor of the class. It shouldn't be the responsibility of a women's art history class, for example, to stage a protest about some indirectly related issue. If students get those ideas, that's fantastic, but the focus should stay on the curriculum.

Psychologist Jayne Stake and associates discovered that after taking women's studies courses, students engage in fewer gender-stereotyped behav-

iors, feel more self-confident, and become more politically active on behalf of women's rights.[24] They often become "ambassadors of feminism" on campus, speaking up in other courses, talking to friends outside of class, and introducing a feminist perspective into student organizations.[25] The National Association for Women in Education has recommended that colleges and universities consider requiring all students to take women's studies courses in order to heighten their awareness of sexism and other gender issues on campus. Many of the students that I have taught have suggested the same thing; they think it is important that everyone be exposed to at least some feminist thought in order to become aware of the extent to which gender shapes our lives. A single academic program or required course, however, cannot be expected to carry the whole burden of improving classroom and campus climate. Feminist perspectives and new research on gender and women (as well as race, ethnicity, and age) need to be integrated throughout the curriculum. And, in keeping with the criticism of the women's studies major quoted above, the theory and data being communicated in women's studies courses should not take a backseat to consciousness raising.

Sexual Harassment

Although you may never be subjected to sexual harassment, it is important to be aware that it occurs on campus, just as it does in the workplace.[26] Sexual harassment in academic settings has been defined as "the use of authority to emphasize the sexuality or sexual identity of a student in a manner which prevents or impairs that student's full enjoyment of education's benefits, climate, or opportunities."[27] Researchers like psychologist Michele Paludi have categorized the various forms it takes. "Gender harassment" refers to sexist remarks that convey insulting and degrading attitudes about women. Recent court decisions have found that for classroom speech to constitute harassment, it must be unwelcome, persistent, pervasive, and not germane to the subject matter.[28] "Seductive behavior" refers to inappropriate and unwelcome sexual advances. "Sexual bribery" promises a reward (e.g., good grade, financial aid, prized internship) in exchange for sex, while "sexual coercion" solicits sex using the threat of punishment. "Sexual imposition" describes gross sexual actions (e.g., appearing nude in front of you), sexual assault, and rape.

Sexual harassment can occur in class, the lab, the gym, the cafeteria, a faculty or administrator's office, your dorm, or at a fraternity party.[29] Most harassers are men, but occasionally women are harassers. In one unusual case, a female graduate student accused her doctoral supervisor, a well-known feminist, of pressuring her for sex and grading her poorly after she had rebuffed her superior's advances.[30] Studies have found that men and those in power generally have a narrow definition of what constitutes sexual harassment, while women and people who support gender equality see it as a broader and more serious problem. Unless they are stopped, harassers seldom limit their actions to one person. A recent study of faculty members at six California schools—two community colleges, two private schools, and two state universities—found that most harassers knew that their actions went against school policy but continued their behavior anyway.[31] Two professors at the University of Georgia were belatedly censured and one resigned after repeated accusations of sexual harassment by students and staff spanning more than a decade.[32] A professor at the University of Miami's Graduate School of International Studies was finally fired after being accused of sexual misconduct by seven women, including a female colleague who stated that he had threatened to destroy her career if she did not submit to his sexual advances.[33]

In an essay entitled "Taking Women Students Seriously," Adrienne Rich had this to say about the effects of sexual harassment on students: "Most young women experience a profound mixture of humiliation and intellectual self-doubt over seductive gestures by men who have the power to award grades, open doors to grants and graduate school, or extend special knowledge and training. Even if turned aside, such gestures constitute mental rape, destructive to a woman's ego. They are acts of domination, as despicable as the molestation of the daughter by the father."[34]

Although Rich's description of sexual harassment and the definition given at the beginning of this section describe situations in which there is a power differential between the victim and her harasser, harassment also occurs among peers. According to one report, the students most frequently targeted are African-American women, Asian-Americans, Latinas, Jewish women, lesbians, and feminists.[35] To this list I would add women athletes. The latter three—lesbians, feminists, and athletes—are undoubtedly singled out because they challenge masculinity and traditional male domains. Women who study in male-dominated fields are also likely to experience harassment. A study at the University of Pennsylvania Law School documented widespread peer harassment in law classrooms. One first-year student's male classmates called her "a femi-nazi dyke"; other women who spoke up in class were taunted as "man-hating lesbians."[36]

Much peer harassment takes the form of jokes, comments, and actions thought to be funny. Although jokes about racial and ethnic groups are no longer publicly acceptable, the same cannot be said for jokes about women. This helps explain why JAP (Jewish American Princess) jokes are common on some campuses. To people who think they are funny, the princess part of the joke and the Jewish part defuse each other. The non-Jewish teller can get away with being a misogynist because the subject of the joke is a *Jewish* woman, and he can get away with being anti-Semitic because he is just making fun of a woman. Recently, four male students at Cornell University were charged with sexual harassment for circulating a list of "The Top 75 Reasons Why Women Should Not Have Freedom of Speech" over campus e-mail.[37] Among the reasons they cited: "If my penis is in her mouth, she can't talk anyway" and "If she can't speak, she can't cry rape." A University of Michigan student used the Internet to post sexual fantasies he had written about women and girls being brutally raped, mutilated, and left to die. After he gave one of his victims the name of a real female student in one of his classes, he was arrested and expelled from school.[38] Fraternities are often sites of gender harassment and the verbal abuse of women, and too frequently, sexual assault (as will be discussed in Chapter 12).

Sexual harassment is illegal, and every university and college receiving federal money is required by law to have grievance procedures for students and employees to follow. A Supreme Court ruling in 1992 expanded Title IX of the Educational Amendments of 1972 to allow students who are sexually harassed to sue schools and school officials for monetary damages. This precedent-setting case—*Franklin v. Gwinnett County Schools*—was decided in favor of a high school student who claimed that a sports coach and teacher had repeatedly harassed her and eventually pressured her into having sex. Other court decisions have found that student-to-student harassment is also illegal because it constitutes a hostile environment as defined under Title IX.[39]

Although the odds are in your favor that you will not be sexually harassed, it is important for all women to know how to deal with it effectively. First, keep a record of all incidents (time, place, people present, exactly what occurred) and tell someone else about it. Depending upon the nature of what is happening and who the harasser is, decide on a strategy. According to Mary Rowe, a pioneer in the fields of discrimination and sexual harassment, writing a letter is often the best way to take action with the least cost to you.[40] Many harassers do not fully understand the effect their behavior is having or realize that it constitutes harassment. Seeing their actions described on paper from your point of view may well come as a shock, and the harassment may stop. If their actions have been intentional, your written statement may make harassers worry about their reputation and warn them of the possibility of formal charges.

When you write to your harasser, describe what happened specifically. Next, state what effect these actions have had on you: "This is why I dropped your class"; "I cannot get to sleep at night"; "You have made me change my major." Finally, state what you want to happen next: "Never touch me again"; "Never make remarks about my sexuality again." If you feel you contributed to a misunderstanding, you can acknowledge this: "Although we were dating before, it's important that we now reestablish a professional relationship." If you decide to deliver the letter in person, take a friend for moral support and as a witness. If you send it by mail, use certified or registered mail. (This will let you know that it has been received and provide evidence of that fact later should you need it.) Keep a copy of your letter. In many cases, the behavior will stop. If it doesn't, take a copy of your letter and your record of incidents (and any materials your harasser may have sent you) to the person(s) stipulated in your college's grievance guidelines.

According to Charolette Krolokke, a professor of speech communication at Humboldt State University in California who has studied faculty women's responses to harassment, the most successful way to end recurrent harassment and reduce the likelihood of retaliation is to use a "confrontational communication strategy" that clearly holds the harasser accountable for his or her behavior.[41] Your letter can accomplish this, but so can a meeting. If you choose to speak to your harasser, be firm and specific. Clearly describe what behavior you want stopped: "Stop staring at me and rubbing up against me." If you are reacting to an incident as it occurs, be very direct: "Stop touching me. Move back right now." Make sure your body language and tone of voice support what you are saying: Stand straight, keep your head up, maintain eye contact, don't fidget, and speak in a controlled voice. Be sure to end the interaction on your own terms: "Don't ever do that to me or any other woman again." Then leave the scene, or tell the harasser to leave if he or she is on your turf.

_____ *DID YOU KNOW?* _____

- Women now make up 56 percent of all undergraduates and 53 percent of all graduate students. They also comprise 41 percent of all first-year professional students and earn 39 percent of all PhDs.[42]

- Academic disciplines still tend to be segregated by sex. Women outnumber male undergraduates by an average of four to one in education, communication, health science, and foreign languages, while men far outnumber women in many sciences, math, and engineering.

- A study published in the *Harvard Educational Review*, based on a sample of nearly fifty thousand students, found that women who took the same college math courses and received the same average grades as men had entered college with SAT math scores that were 33 points lower on average. In other words, women do as well in college math as men, despite entering with lower average SAT scores.

- Because National Merit Scholarships are awarded on the basis of SAT scores, two-thirds go to men.

- The number of women presidents of colleges and universities has been growing. In 1996, they made up 16 percent of the top leaders in higher education.

⚗ Beatrix Potter, the much-loved author and illustrator of *The Tale of Peter Rabbit* and other children's stories, was an accomplished mycologist who was the first person to report on the symbiotic properties of lichen and to catalogue the fungi of the British Isles. Yet she was not allowed to join any professional scientific society because she was a woman.

⚗ The U.S. National Academy of Sciences today has fewer than one hundred female members, out of 1,750 living scientists.

⚗ The situation is bound to change, however. Women study in many previously male-dominated fields and now outnumber men in some sciences. They earn three-quarters of all undergraduate psychology degrees, for example, and over half of the biology degrees.[43]

⚗ Many countries—Great Britain, Ireland, South Africa, India, Belgium, Spain, Brazil, Turkey, France, Italy, the Philippines, and Hungary—exceed the United States in the percentage of women earning bachelors' degrees and doctorates in physics.[44] One important reason, many people think, is that students in these countries are required to take more science than American students do before they reach college. Consequently, they cannot opt out of physics early, and more women become interested and pursue it at advanced levels.

_____ *WHAT YOU CAN DO* _____

⊠ Encourage friends (including male friends) to take a women's studies course, and take one yourself if you haven't already.

⊠ Speak to the administration about making a course that deals with gender and race issues a requirement for all students.

⊠ You can make the classroom a friendlier place for women by acknowledging the contributions other women make in class. Preface your own remarks with: "I agree with Myshka's analysis . . . ," "I'd like to return to the point Marisol made earlier . . . ," or "As Autumn said. . . ."

⊠ You can combat generic and stereotypical uses of gender-specific terms. If masculine pronouns are used all the time in class discussions, make an effort to use feminine pronouns in the hypothetical examples you give.

⊠ Encourage male friends to think about campus equity issues and peer harassment. Remind them that harassment can happen to friends like you, a sister, a lover, and possibly someday, a daughter. Some very effective programs to sensitize other campus men have been led by male athletes. Suggest that a coed or men's group bring in a speaker like Jackson Katz ("the feminist football player") who organized the Boston-based Real Men to combat sexism and violence against women.

⊠ If you are faced with sexism or gender bias in the classroom (e.g., frequent sexist humor, comments that put women down, preference given to male students), don't take it. If a faculty member is at fault, speak to him or her during office hours. Calmly but assertively explain what you have observed and how it has made you feel. Many times people are unaware of their gender-biased behavior. If other students in class feel the same way, encourage them to join you or to talk to the faculty member independently. If you are hesitant to speak to your professor, write a note outlining your concerns, and keep a copy. If the behavior or situation does not change noticeably within a couple of weeks, or if the faculty member jokes about your concerns in class, talk to his or her chairperson or the dean of students.

☒ Get a copy of your school's sexual harassment guidelines and read them. Review this chapter to familiarize yourself with the issue and to find out what you can do. (See Resources.)

☒ If a particular department appears to be perpetuating a hostile environment for women students, speak to campus administrators about it. Your school might consider creating a campuswide questionnaire to distribute to students at the end of courses, asking them to think about the way in which women (and minorities) were portrayed in course material and about how fairly the professor treated the men and women in the classroom. The results could be used to discover areas of gender bias and develop guidelines to make the classroom experience more equitable. The administration could also send copies of NAWE's *The Chilly Classroom Climate: A Guide to Improve the Education of Women* (1996) and the AAC&U publications *Teaching Faculty Members to be Better Teachers: A Guide to Equitable and Effective Classroom Techniques* (1992) and *Evaluating Courses for Inclusion of New Scholarship on Women* (1988) to departments for faculty members to consult. (See Organizations.)

☒ If the situation on your campus merits it, join with other students to encourage the president to issue a policy statement reaffirming the institution's commitment to equity on campus, including the need to ensure that women and men are treated fairly in the classroom.

☒ Join or start a campus women's group—a Womyn's Union or Women's Center—and work to heighten student awareness of gender issues and to promote equality for women. Bring speakers to campus. Arrange film showings and discussions. Organize student or student-faculty crosstalks on issues related to campus climate. Write an article for the campus newspaper.

───────────────── *RESOURCES* ─────────────────

Books

Clark, Veve, et al. 1996. *Antifeminism in the Academy.* New York: Routledge.
Dziech, Billie Wright, and Linda Weiner. 1984. *The Lecherous Professor: Sexual Harassment on Campus.* Boston: Beacon.

Gabriel, Susan, and Isaiah Smithson (eds.). 1990. *Gender in the Classroom: Power and Pedagogy*. Urbana: University of Illinois Press.

Gallop, Jane. 1997. *Feminist Accused of Sexual Harassment*. Durham, N.C.: Duke University Press.

Gaskell, Jane. 1991. *Gender Matters from School to Work*. Bristol, Penn.: Taylor & Francis.

Hall, Roberta, et al. 1982. *The Classroom Climate: A Chilly One for Women*. Washington, D.C.: Association of American Colleges.

Hanson, Sandra. 1996. *Lost Talent: Women in the Sciences*. Philadelphia: Temple University Press.

Katz, Montana, and Veronica Vieland. 1988. *Get Smart! What You Should Know (But Won't Learn in Class) About Sexual Harassment and Sex Discrimination*. 2nd ed. New York: Feminist Press.

Maher, Frances, and Mary Kay Tetreault. 1994. *The Feminist Classroom*. New York: Basic.

National Coalition for Women and Girls in Education. 1990. *Education for All: Women and Girls Speak Out on the National Education Goals*. Washington, D.C.: National Women's Law Center.

Orenstein, Peggy. 1994. *Schoolgirls: Young Women, Self-esteem, and the Confidence Gap*. New York: Doubleday.

Paludi, Michele (ed.). 1996. *Sexual Harassment on College Campuses: Abusing the Ivory Power*. Albany: State University of New York Press.

Paludi, Michele, and Richard Barickman. 1991. *Academic and Workplace Harassment: A Resource Manual*. Albany: State University of New York Press.

Rosser, Sue. 1986. *Teaching Science and Health from a Feminist Perspective: A Practical Guide*. New York: Pergamon.

Rothschild, Joan. 1988. *Teaching Technology from a Feminist Perspective: A Practical Guide*. New York: Pergamon.

Sadker, Myra, and David Sadker. 1994. *Failing at Fairness: How America's Schools Cheat Girls*. New York: Scribner's.

Sandler, Bernice, and Robert Shoop. 1997. *Sexual Harassment on Campus: A Guide for Administrators, Faculty, and Students*. Des Moines, Iowa: Longwood/Allyn & Bacon.

Streitmatter, Janice. 1996. *Toward Gender Equity in the Classroom: Everyday Teachers' Beliefs and Practices*. Albany: State University of New York Press.

Von Lowe, Gretchen. 1996. *Forgotten Promise: Race and Gender Wars on a Small College Campus*. New York: Knopf.

Videos

Sexual Harassment: Building Awareness on Campus. This twenty-three-minute video is addressed to both men and women and includes interviews with students, faculty, and experts. Hosted by Jean Kilbourne, it offers a comprehensive, nonthreatening discussion of sexual harassment on campus and what can be done to stop it. Media Education Foundation, 26 Center Street, Northampton, MA 01060. Phone: (800) 897–0089.

Stop It! Students Speak Out About Sexual Harassment. The seventeen-minute video addresses sexual harassment from the students' point of view, both those who have perpetrated it and those who have been victimized by it. It discusses what kinds of behavior are inappropriate, what to do when harassment occurs, and the impact harassment has on victims. Films for the Humanities, PO Box 2053, Princeton, NJ 08543–2053. Phone: (800) 275–5126.

Organizations

American Association for Women in Community Colleges (AAWCC), Amarillo College, PO Box 447, Amarillo, TX 79178–0001. Phone: (806) 371–5175, 353–0568. The organization and its many local chapters disseminate information on women's issues and programs among women in community, junior, and technical colleges and help obtain grants for educational projects for community college women. It produces the *AAWCC Quarterly* newsletter, and an annual, *AAWCC Journal.*

American Association of University Women (AAUW), 1111 16th Street NW, Washington, DC 20036. Phone: (202) 785–7700; AAUWEF (202) 728–7602. The AAUW is an advocacy and research organization that fosters quality education and opportunities for women and girls. It produces the bimonthly magazine *AAUW Outlook,* with articles on gender equity in education and the workplace and updates on legislation affecting women. Among the AAUW's published reports are *Hostile Hallways: The AAUW Survey on Sexual Harassment in America's Schools* (1993) and *How Schools Shortchange Girls* (1994), a report by the Wellesley College Center for Research on Women. Its affiliated Educational Foundation (AAUWEF) sponsors conferences and publishes the quarterly *Outlook* magazine. The AAUW also awards fellowships to women seeking graduate degrees in professional fields such as medicine, business, and law and to women graduate students completing their doctoral and postgraduate study.

Association of American Colleges & Universities (AAC&U), 1818 R Street NW, Washington, DC 20009. Phone: (202) 387–3760. The Association's Project on the Status and Education of Women produced many reports on women in higher education, including *The Classroom Climate: A Chilly One for Women?* (1982), *The Classroom Climate Revisited: Chilly for Women Faculty, Administrators, and Graduate Students* (1986), *Peer Harassment: Hassles for Women on Campus* (1988), and *Teaching Faculty Members to Be Better Teachers: A Guide to Equitable and Effective Classroom Techniques* (1992). The AAC&U

also publishes the quarterly newsletter *On Campus with Women*. Send for a publication list or check with the women's studies program on your campus.

Feminist Teacher Editorial Collective (FTEC), Wheaton College, Norton, MA 02766. Phone: (508) 286–3732. The organization opposes sexism and racism in the classroom and encourages innovative teaching practices that challenge traditional education, disciplinary, and research methodologies. It publishes *Feminist Teacher* three times a year.

National Association for Women in Education (NAWE), 1325 18th Street NW, Suite 210, Washington, DC 20036–6511. Phone: (202) 659–9330. NAWE has produced major reports on women in higher education, including *The Chilly Classroom Climate: A Guide to Improve the Education of Women* (1996) by Bernice Resnick Sandler, Lisa Silverberg, and Roberta Hall. It also publishes the journal *Initiatives*. NAWE also holds an annual conference on women in education.

National Center for Curriculum Transformation Resources on Women, Institute for Teaching and Research on Women, Towson State University, 8000 York Road, 317 Lida Lee Hall, Towson, MD 21252. Phone: (410) 830–3944. The Center publishes directories, manuals, and essays providing the information needed by educators to incorporate new scholarship on women into their courses. The Center also maintains a Web site: http://www.towson.edu/ ncctrw/.

National Coalition for Women and Girls in Education (NCWGE), c/o National Women's Law Center, 11 Dupont Circle NW, Suite 800, Washington, DC 20036. Phone: (202) 588–5180. The organization promotes national policies that will assure educational equity for women and monitors agencies responsible for enforcing civil rights laws. It also produces publications like *Education for All: Women and Girls Speak Out on the National Education Goals*.

National Council for Research on Women (NCRW), 530 Broadway, 10th Floor, New York, NY 10012. Phone: (212) 274–0730. The Council is a coalition of centers and organizations that support and conduct feminist research, policy analysis, and educational programs. It was formed in 1981 to bridge the traditional distinctions between scholarship, policy, and action programs. One of its projects was the Sexual Harassment Information Project. In 1991, it published *Sexual Harassment: Research and Resources*, by Deborah Siegel. It also publishes the *Guide to Federal Funding Opportunities for Women and Girls' Programs and Research Projects*.

National Women's Student Coalition (NWSC), c/o USSA, 1413 K Street NW, 10th Floor, Washington, DC 20006. Phone: (202) 347–8772. This all-women coalition is a subsidiary of the United States Student Association, which lobbies for women students' issues at the national level. It distributes publications like *Affirmative Action*, *Violence Against Women Act*, and *Entitled to IX*, and holds semiannual meetings in conjunction with the USSA March Lobby Conference and the USSA summer congress.

National Women's Studies Association (NWSA), 7100 Baltimore Avenue, Suite 301, College Park, MD 20740. Phone: (301) 403–0525, 403–0524. NWSA supports feminist causes and lobbies for women's studies programs at the elementary, secondary, and college level. It compiles statistics, holds an annual conference, and produces numerous publications including *The Courage to Question: Women's Studies and Student Learning, Guide to Graduate Work in Women's Studies*, and the *National Report on the Women's Studies Major*. It also publishes the quarterly *NWSA Journal* and a newsletter, *NWSAction*. The Association also administers graduate scholarships in women's studies and offers prize money for the best manuscript in women's studies.

CHAPTER 3

Language

and Gender

The limits of my language mean the limits of my world.
—Ludwig Wittgenstein, *Tractatus Logico-Philosophicus*, 1922[1]

Women's Speech?

In 1975, linguist Robin Lakoff introduced the term "women's language" to describe the communication style of American women. She found women to be more indirect, polite, and personal in their conversation than men. Many speech patterns also differed; for example, women used more qualifiers ("I think it's *about* ten minutes to two"), intensifiers ("It was *such* a good party"), and "tag questions" ("John's here, *isn't he*?") than men. These speech patterns have been linked to women's subordination. In our society, men are freer to omit polite expressions and syntax, to forcefully express their opinions, to use strong language and swear, to give commands, and to ask direct yes/no questions without risk of offending others (or at least, without suffering serious consequences). Girls still grow up learning to be more concerned with the feelings of others. This concern often comes across in speech, as when a woman politely asks that something be done rather than giving an instruction: "Will you please close the door?" instead of "Close the door." (Of course, in some communities in the United States, as well as in other English-speaking countries, both men and women would typically say "Close the door.")

When men and women speak to one another, they often misunderstand each other's intentions. When a woman asks a question in order to keep a conversation going, many men interpret this as merely a request for information and also as an acknowledgment of their authority. Similarly, if a personal problem is mentioned during a mixed-sex conversation, men are more likely than women to assume the role of expert and to offer advice rather than sympathy. They are also more likely than women not to follow up on other people's comments, to change the topic of conversation, and to avoid or delay giving responses like "um-hmm" or "right," which show the other person they're listening. Such differences in communication styles can discourage interaction; many also indicate men's greater social power.[2]

Other speech differences also reflect gender socialization. American women use a larger color vocabulary than most men. "The wall is mauve" would sound somewhat peculiar if uttered by a man, unless he is an artist or decorator. Adjectives like "adorable," "charming," "sweet," and "lovely" are largely confined to American women's speech. (In Ireland and Great Britain, however, "lovely" is regularly used by men.) Women also curse less than men (although it may not seem like it in your circle of friends) and tend to use milder expletives and emphatic words. Many other cultures also have gendered speech, with women's speech typically the more polite, cooperative, and indirect. In Japan, where relative social rank (based on age, occupational status, and gender) is very important, the differences between men's and women's speech are dramatic. It is important to remember, however, that as socially accepted roles for women and men change, socialization patterns and speech and communication styles also change.

As linguist Deborah Tannen has pointed out, the "meaning" of any linguistic strategy can vary, depending on the context of a conversation and on the speech styles and strategies of its participants.[3] Tag questions, which generally have been thought to make women's speech less "forceful" than men's, can in fact be a good conversational tool, because they help draw other people out and also can be used to neutralize opposition. In research by social psychologist Linda Carli, women voiced disagreement more tentatively when speaking to men rather than to other women, but this didn't make them any less persuasive. In fact, women who spoke tentatively had more influence with men (who found them more trustworthy and likeable) than did women who voiced their disagreement assertively.[4] (Tentative speakers, however, had less influence with other women, and both men and women regarded them as less competent and knowledgeable than women who spoke assertively.)

Speech patterns differ in formal and informal settings. William O'Barr and Bowman Atkins found that in the formal and somewhat intimidating setting of a trial courtroom, both male and female witnesses used speech patterns (e.g., hedges, hesitation forms, intensifiers) that are typically associated with women.[5] The researchers concluded that language patterns people use reflect their social status and the situation in which they find themselves as much as they do gender. It is also important to remember that the similarities between men's and women's speech far outweigh the differences.

What Words Say About Women

Language is not only a means of communicating; it also expresses a society's values and attitudes. In English, women are often treated as a deviation from or derivation of the basic male form: "poetess" from poet, "actress" from actor, "sculptress" or "lady sculptor" rather than sculptor. Until the widespread adoption of "Ms.," social titles indicated the marital status of women (Mrs. vs. Miss) but not of men (Mr.), symbolizing a wife's status as property.[6] In some circles married women are still referred to by their husband's names, as in Mrs. Ralph Williams. But have you ever met a Mr. Cindy Jones? Dominant people (as determined by social class, age, occupational status, race/ethnicity, and gender) are typically referred to by their last names (often prefaced by titles) rather than their first names. Sociologist Michael Messner and his research associates found that sports commentators refer to female athletes by their first names 53 percent of the time, compared to only 8 percent of the time for male athletes. This practice reflects women's subordinate status relative to men as well as the announcers' own socialization.[7]

Adult females are referred to as "girls" much more frequently than adult males are called "boys." Sports commentators frequently call women athletes "girls," while male athletes are never called "boys."[8] The word "girl" refers to a young woman who has not reached sexual maturity. When used to refer to an adult, it carries connotations of immaturity and dependency. Its actual usage, however, is more complex. Among African Americans, "girl" is often used positively as in "Hey, girl" or "Go girl!" As one black woman explained, "Many black women reject the word 'woman' because when black men say 'You're my woman,' it implies ownership." Many older white women refer to women friends as "girls" and do not feel it demeans them. There is a lot of confusion on campus about the use of the word "girl." At Barnard and Berkeley, it would probably be an insult among most women on campus to call a female student a "girl." On other campuses, female students regularly refer to each other as "girls" because it is customary or because "women" seems too mature and a bit threatening. A transitional term like "guys," for males who are no longer "boys" but not yet ready to assume full adult responsibilities, does not exist for females.

"Gals" certainly does not work as a comparable term, forcing many young women to use "guys" as a generic.

"Lady" is a euphemism for woman with positive connotations for some people, especially the older generation, because it brings to mind someone who is well bred. African-American sorority sisters commonly refer to themselves as ladies. Yet the term also implies being constrained to a narrowly defined range of behavior (e.g., soft-spoken, proper) considered appropriate for a conventionally "feminine" woman. It also suggests a class struggle, since some women are defined by others as ladies, while other women never are. In the military this usage is overt. The word "ladies" is reserved for the wives of officers (when not used as a degrading term for male recruits), while "wives" is commonly used to refer to the women who are married to enlisted men. As befitting her husband's high social rank, the President's wife is referred to as the First Lady.

The word "woman"—meaning an adult female person—stems from the Old English "wifman," derived from "wif" (meaning female) and "mann" (meaning human being). An adult male person was called a "werman" from "wer" (meaning male) and "mann."[9] The changed spelling of "wifman"—dropping the "f" and replacing the "i" with an "o"—had evolved by the fourteenth century. By then, "woman" had come to mean a "ladylove" and later, a kept mistress; the plural "women" referred to females in their capacity as sex partners. By the fifteenth century, "woman" signified a wife. But the word continued to carry sexual and negative connotations, indicated in phrases like "a woman of pleasure" and "woman of the town," both of which referred to a prostitute. By the end of the eighteenth century, it began to be contrasted to "lady," with its opposite connotations of gentility and proper feminine behavior.

Only in the late nineteenth century did "woman" begin to suggest strength and emancipation; the term "new woman" was applied to women with progressive and independent ideas, and "womanism" was used for the advocacy of women's rights. During the campaign for female suffrage, the term "womanist" was used along with "feminist" and "suffragist." "Suffragette" was used as a term of denigration: the diminutive "ette" literally diminished the importance of the women advocating female suffrage. Today womanist is the preferred term among many African-American feminists. "Woman," when used in the context of feminism or the women's movement, means a strong, independent-minded female. According to one student, "'Women' is a *great* word. As part of the X generation of women who are young, ambitious, and even a little (or a lot) rebellious, I find 'woman' to be more than suitable. It has become much more casual, yet assertive; feminine yet not soft. Why should we bother ourselves looking for another word?"

Most dictionary definitions, however, still reveal an ambivalent image of "woman." According to Jane Mills, author of *Womanswords: A Dictionary of Words About Women*,

> she is modest, delicate, tender, compassionate, sympathetic, gentle, affectionate, domesticated but she is also intuitive, changeable, capricious, submissive, prone to tears, fickle, superficial, foolish, and lacking in promptness. Above all, she is weak, subordinate to man, and possesses qualities that have not been highly valued in a society which glorifies the characteristics connoted by manliness, i.e., courage, valor, gallantry, strength, braveness, resoluteness, vigour, maturity, honor, dignity, nobility and authority. The worst that can be said of manliness, as recorded by the OED [*Oxford English Dictionary*], is selfishness and pride.[10]

English words about women can be categorized in a variety of ways. Philosopher Robert Baker finds that synonyms for the word "woman" fall into five categories: neutral terms, animals, playthings, gender, and sex. Many have derogatory connotations. The animals that refer to women are typically those that are subservient to or hunted by humans, such as "chick," "bird," and "fox." According to Baker, none symbolize intelligence or great wisdom. Words that depict women as playthings, such as "doll," "babe," and "baby," associate women with mindless objects or with immaturity and weakness. Baker considers a few words, like "gal" and "sister," to be fairly neutral. Others are anything but, particularly those in the "sexual" category (e.g., snatch, cunt, ass, twat, piece, lay, pussy, hammer). With the exception of "chick," which some women use in reference to each other, Baker finds that all nonneutral terms for woman are used only by men. Not until both men and women find words like "babe," "doll," "chick," and "broad" as paternalistic and objectionable as "boy" or "nigger" are now, maintains Baker, will women be conceived of as independent and equal human beings.

When it comes to metaphors, women are often compared to food (e.g., honey, sugar, cookie, pudding, tomato, cupcake, piece of cake, meat), as if they are available to be sampled or consumed. The imagery is bleak when it comes to terms for the sex act. All the verbs used by men and in reference to men's role in heterosexual intercourse are active, while those used for women are passive constructions: "Dan screwed (laid, fucked, had, banged, humped, balled, etc.) Jane," while "Jane was screwed (laid, etc.) by Dan." Since the late 1960s, feminists have asserted that sexual intercourse is not something men do *to* women in heterosexual relationships, but *with* them. Only phrases like "did it with," "slept with," or "made love to" are considered neutral and reciprocal. The active/passive usage described above isn't a necessary consequence of differences in male and female anatomy. An active role in sex could be given to women by using terms like "engulfing" or "enveloping." Many of the metaphors (screw, poke, shaft) used for sex also suggest harm. According to Baker, American English conceives of the male role in sex as that of hurting the person in the female role.

A lot of abusive language about women is heard on college and university campuses. According to the dean of students at one university, "If we had a [disciplinary] category for abusive language and other kinds of overt disrespect toward women, we could clear this place out, because there's an awful lot of that here."[11] Researchers have discovered that sexist humor is enjoyed more by people who hold traditional views of women's roles than by those with liberated views.[12] The fraternity and male locker room are two strongholds of heterosexual masculinity and sexist put-downs. Fraternity songs often objectify, demean, and degrade women, sometimes in graphic detail (many songs are also racist and homophobic).[13] Athletes often try to avoid being the target of put-downs by their teammates by affirming their "masculinity" through conversation and jokes that ridicule and demean women and gays.[14]

What are the consequences of sexism in our language? It is largely through language that we learn how to view ourselves and others. Many years ago, linguist Edward Sapir, with Benjamin Lee Whorf, proposed that language controls its speakers' perceptions of the world. Today most people acknowledge that language, if it does not control, at least shapes our perceptions of reality. Calling Asians "gooks" and the Japanese "japs" during war helped dehumanize them, making it easier to fight and kill the enemy in battle. Similarly, labeling Native Americans "primitives" and "savages" once made it morally acceptable for European settlers to conquer and "civilize" them. Carol Cohn has analyzed the gendered discourse of contemporary national security discussions. She has found that male policy analysts avoid discussing certain topics—like the human costs of war—because such concerns are considered feminine and weak. In language no better than locker room or fraternity bar talk, they frequently referred to allies who disagreed with them as "limp-dicked wimps," "pussies," and "Euro-fags." Unfortunately, avoiding discussing certain topics and dismissing people with different points of view as weak and unmasculine prevents these analysts from exploring all options and from thinking fully about complex political and national security issues.[15]

The effect of language is often subtle. In 1984, a *Newsweek* article described vice-presidential candidate Geraldine Ferraro as having a "gift for tart political rhetoric, needling Ronald Reagan on the fairness issue and twitting the Reagan-Bush campaign for its reluctance to let Bush debate her." Meant as praise, the words "needling" and "twitting" nevertheless portrayed Ferraro as a minor contender, and it is hard to imagine them being applied to a man. When describing women's strengths in basketball, sports commentators often use words that at the same time undermine or neutralize them, such as "She's a big girl,"

"She's small, but so effective under the boards," and "her little jump hook." They also describe male and female coaches differently; men "yell" at their teams, while women "scream" at theirs. The word "screaming" implies lack of control, even hysteria.[16] As linguist Deborah Cameron reminds us, "Language is part of patriarchy. . . . It is instrumental in maintaining male power, and feminists must study its workings carefully."[17]

A male student's awareness of sexism in language and the attitudes it reflects was heightened on an outing with his sister, which he later wrote about in his class journal. After attending a hockey game, during which he and his sister had exchanged a few words with a group of rowdy fans sitting in front of them, they went to the arena's bar.

> The three guys were there playing pool, and my sister walked over and put her quarters up, claiming the next game. When it was our turn, the guys challenged us to play for a few pitchers of beer. They were winning by about six balls when one of them sank a shot and said, "I ain't losing to no broad." When my sister's turn came, she ran the table. She hit some of the most amazing shots I've ever seen. After she sank the eight ball, she laid down the pool stick, looked at the three guys, and said, "I ain't no broad! And by the way, we're drinking Bud." Pretty cool, huh? I taught her everything she knows! (Just kidding.)

Does "Man" Include Woman?

Despite claims to the contrary and the weight of conventional practice, the words "man," "he," and "his" are not generic terms. Research has demonstrated that people usually visualize men (not women) when they read or hear these words.[18] This is why statements like "the sisterhood of man" and "Man, being a mammal, breast-feeds his young" are so jarring. Words like "chairman," "mailman," "salesman," "fisherman," "policeman," and "councilman" all imply that these jobs should be filled by men. When students at Indiana University were asked to read occupational titles and then write brief descriptions of the "average person" in each occupation, they were much more likely to describe a man when the titles had "man" as a suffix or contained no suffix (e.g., department chair) than when the titles used "person" (e.g., chairperson).[19] Gender-marked language influences not only people's perceptions of the speaker's or referent's gender but also other characteristics about them. When job titles end in "man," their occupants are assumed to have stereotypically masculine personality traits.[20] In another study, when God was described as male in an audiotaped script, both male and female listeners later emphasized God's power. When God was presented as female or gender neutral, listeners later emphasized God's mercy.[21]

Among college students, men use gender-exclusive forms like the masculine generic "he" in their writing more often than women students (even though many also regularly use gender-neutral words like "firefighter" and "chair"). Women students prefer to write "he or she," "s/he," and to use "they" as a singular. (Novelist Marge Piercy used "per" as a gender-neutral pronoun in her book *Woman on the Edge of Time*.) When women read "he," they are also more likely than men to interpret it as a generic or gender-inclusive pronoun. If they didn't do so, they would be excluding themselves.[22] In 1980, J. Silveria observed that maleness is often attributed to gender-inclusive and gender-neutral words because of a "people = male bias" in English.[23] In a recent experimental test of this hypothesis, psychologists Rebecca Merritt and Cynthia Kok found that the people = male bias does exist, and it is equally strong for men and women. They conclude that "children's early and consistent exposure to, and use of, generic masculine terms . . . may result in [their] equating the people category with the male image. We argue that once this cognitive bias is formed, it is quite resistant to change. Thus, even when people eventually acquire grammatical understanding of generic masculine pronouns, the bias results in increased male rather than female imagery for most people."[24]

What difference does using masculine generics really make? At the very least, using the generic masculine can be ambiguous. Many legal controversies have arisen in the past about whether "he" and "man" were meant in a generic sense to include all people or a specific sense to apply to men.[25] In 1908 Charlotte Stopes, one of the first women to analyze gender in the English language, examined the use of the word "man" in British charters and legal statutes. She concluded that "man" always included woman when there was a penalty to be incurred, but never included women when there was a privilege to be conferred! A survey of two hundred years of Canadian law found that, depending upon the social climate and personal biases of judges, the so-called generic masculine had been interpreted sometimes to include women and at other times to exclude them.[26] At its worst, the use of masculine generics discourages and excludes women. Psychologists Sandra Bem and Daryl Bem found that when job advertisements written in supposedly generic masculine language were rewritten in unbiased language, more high school girls were encouraged to apply for them.[27] In a recent study, college students were found to be more willing to go to counselors who used inclusive language than to those who used exclusive language, because the latter were seen as sexist. The effect was greater for women, especially feminist women, than for men.[28]

Since the 1970s many professional associations, government agencies, religious demoninations, and publishers have adopted the *American Heritage School Dictionary* guidelines for the use of nonsexist language. In 1972 this dictionary became the first dictionary to write definitions and sample sentences that were nonsexist and to include entries such as "Ms." *Roget's The-*

saurus has eliminated sexist categories and replaced masculine generics like "mankind" with actual generics like "humankind." In 1980, the Modern Language Association (MLA) formally revised its editorial policy and urged contributors to be sensitive to the social implications of language and to use wording "free of discriminatory overtones." The same year the National Council of Teachers of English passed a resolution calling for teaching gender-neutral language in school classrooms. In 1991 the new *Random House Webster's College Dictionary* became the first gender-neutral dictionary; its editor, Sol Steinmetz, explained, "We wanted to emphasize the social consequences of language more than any dictionary has before. Language is more than just a bunch of words."[29] Despite resistance from some language "purists," there has been significant change in many people's usage. The most common changes have been to gender-inclusive forms such as "he or she" and "women and men" and to gender-neutral forms like "chairperson," "firefighter," and "humanity."

Those writers who attempt to make the idea of using gender-neutral language look unnecessary or silly—suggesting that to do so would mean using terms like "personhole cover" and "efemcipated"—seem reluctant to acknowledge the power of language. Before sexual harassment was named, many women suffered alone without realizing that the things that happened to them were part of a pattern of male dominance and sexism in American society. Naming sexual harassment also led to legislation making it illegal in the workplace and schools. In the area of race, society has already acknowledged the power of words to harm people. Eliminating demeaning terms for African Americans from acceptable speech heightened people's awareness of racism and has helped create a more civil and open society.

In order to show how blind critics of gender-inclusive language were to sexism and the power of language, Douglas Hofstadter once wrote a satirical essay entitled "A Person Paper on 'Purity in Language.'" In it he switched words like "gender" and "sexism" to "race" and "racism," and "women's libber" to "black libber," in order to drive the point home:

> It's high time someone blew the whistle on all the silly prattle about revamping our language to suit the purposes of certain political fanatics. You know what I'm talking about—those who accuse speakers of English of what they call "racism." But let us grant that in our society there may be injustices here and there in the treatment of either race from time to time, and let us even grant these people their terms "racism" and "racist." How valid, however, are the claims of the self-proclaimed "black libbers," or "negrists"—those who would radically change our language in order to "liberate" us poor dupes from its supposed racist bias? . . .

There is nothing denigrating to black people in being subsumed under the rubric "white"—no more than under the rubric "person." After all, white is a mixture of all the colors of the rainbow, including black. Used inclusively, the word "white" has no connotations whatsoever of race. . . . [30]

"Social inequality is substantially created and enforced—that is, done—through words and images," states law professor Catharine MacKinnon.[31] In *Only Words*, she argues that words that victimize and target people on the basis of sex should be treated by law as discriminatory acts. Susan Sontag has referred to language as "the most intense and stubborn fortress of sexist assumptions."[32]

DID YOU KNOW?

- Languages are always changing. Before the eighteenth century, when "he" became the grammatically correct way to indicate an indefinite person or people in general, the pronoun "they" was used.

- The California State University system changed its official motto, *Vir veritas vox* (Man, truth, voice) to *Vita veritas vox* (Life, truth, voice) to avoid gender specificity.

- When the Minnesota legislature ordered the removal of gender-specific language from state statutes, the Office of the Revisor of Statutes ended up deleting or replacing twenty thousand gender-specific pronouns; of these, only 301 were feminine.

- As recently as 1989, sentence examples in the *Random House Dictionary* used male gender terms three times as often as they used female gender terms. When the female gender was used, most sentences reflected stereotypes prejudicial to women. Newer editions use gender-neutral language, provide explanatory notes next to words that are considered offensive to certain groups, and contain supplementary information on avoiding sexist language.

- In 1986, the *New York Times* finally accepted "Ms." as a correct honorific for use in news articles. Other newspapers have stopped using any honorifics and instead refer to people by their names only.

- "Herstory" was coined by feminists in the 1970s to make a political point—that history largely told "his" story, not hers. The word "history," however, comes from the Greek "histor" (meaning learned, knowing) and has no connection to the English word "his."

- By eliminating the words "man" or "men" from "woman" and "women," "womyn" is similarly used to make a political statement.

- The word "misogyny"—hatred of women—comes from the Greek "mis-

---

ogunes" (from "misos," hatred, and "gune," woman). It first appeared in English in 1620 (spelled "misogeny"). It wasn't until 1946—more than 320 years later—however, that the word "misandry" (hatred of men) arrived on the scene.

English has many more words describing women in terms of their sexuality than it does for men. It is said that there are five hundred synonyms for "female prostitute" compared to sixty-five for the male equivalent.

The word "skirt," a slang term for a woman, developed from the Old English "scyrte," meaning shirt. By 1300, it referred to the lower part of a woman's gown; by 1560 it had become the standard English name for a woman. It acquired negative, sexual overtones in the late 1800s: a "light skirt" was a loose woman; to go "skirt hunting" meant to search for women in order to have sex; a "bit or piece of skirt" referred to both a woman and her vagina. Today the term is often used on campus, but directed against men as a put-down for any display of weak or supposedly unmasculine behavior.

The Johnson O'Connor Research Foundation has reported that the vocabulary used by young adults has declined dramatically in the last half century. The average eighteen-year-old tested in 1992 could choose the correct definitions of only 30 percent of the words on a standard vocabulary list, compared to 80 percent in 1940.

_____ *WHAT YOU CAN DO* _____

Use gender-neutral language and encourage others to do so. Substitute gender-indefinite terms for gender-specific ones: "first-year student" (for freshman); "person, people, humanity, or humankind" (for man and mankind); "chairperson or chair" (for chairman); Member of Congress or Representative (for Congressman). In place of the generic "he," use "he or she" or "she or he," or alternate. In place of "his," use "his or her" or "her or his." Try pluralizing (e.g., "Writers who care about their readers' opinions . . . ") or using the second person (e.g., "if you care about your readers' opinions, you will . . . ") instead. For further ideas, consult some inclusive language guides (see Resources).

When you buy a dictionary, look for one, like the *Random House Webster's College Dictionary* (1991), that is gender neutral.

Use inclusive, nondiscriminatory language. Avoid using terms and expressions that reinforce inappropriate attitudes or assumptions about persons or groups based on age, disability, ethnicity or race, religion, or sexual orientation.

Avoid using "girl" when referring to an adult. Call women "women."

Eliminate demeaning slang terms for women, such as "chick," "skirt," and "babe," from your own speech.

☒ When someone makes sexist comments (e.g., "Bros before hos"), uses derogatory terms for women (e.g., bimbo, bitch, slut), or tells demeaning sexist jokes around you, speak up. Your lack of response only perpetuates the practice. The best way to speak up (either in public or privately afterward) will depend upon the language used, the intent of the speaker, and the setting in which it occurred. If incidents involving a professor keep recurring in the classroom, report them to the appropriate administrator.

☒ Obtain a guide to bias-free language. It will help when you are writing and are unable to come up with a more inclusive way of stating your ideas. The campus writing center, library, and women's studies program will have copies of books and guidelines on nonsexist language.

☒ Check your university's bylaws, college catalogue, admissions viewbook, and other publications for biased language. If this hasn't already been done, it might be a project a student group could undertake. Bring any examples of biased language to the attention of the proper administrators, and suggest bias-free alternatives.

☒ Find out if your university or college has a language policy. If so, help make it more widely known.

☒ Encourage campus organizations (as well as government agencies, companies, and the media) to use gender-neutral language.

☒ If one of your courses uses a textbook with biased language, bring the matter to the attention of the professor and let her or him know that you find it offensive. Depending upon the kind of course it is, it may be good to point out examples during class discussion in order to heighten other students' awareness.

—————————————— *RESOURCES* ——————————————

Books

American Psychological Association. 1994. *Guidelines to Reduce Bias in Language.* 4th ed. Washington, D.C.: American Psychological Association.

Bierce, Ambrose. 1911. *Devil's Dictionary.* Cleveland, Ohio: World.

Cameron, Deborah. 1992. *Feminism and Linguistic Theory.* 2nd ed. Boston: St. Martin's.

Coates, Jennifer. 1993. *Women, Men and Language.* 2nd ed. New York: Longman.

Crawford, Mary. 1995. *Talking Difference—On Gender and Language.* London: Sage.

Frank, Francine Wattman, and Paula Treichler. 1989. *Language, Gender, and Professional Writing: Theoretical Approaches and Guidelines for Nonsexist Language.* New York: Modern Language Association of America.

Hofstadter, Douglas. 1985. "A Person Paper on 'Purity in Language' by William

Safire, Alias Douglas Hofstadter." In *Metamagical Themas*, by Douglas Hofstadter, pp. 159–167. New York: Basic.

Key, Mary Richie. 1975. *Male/Female Language*. Metuchen, N.J.: Scarecrow.

King, R. 1991. *Talking Gender: A Guide to Nonsexist Communication*. Toronto: Longman.

Lakoff, Robin. 1976. *Language and Women's Place*. New York: Octagon House.

———. 1990. *Talking Power: The Politics of Language in Our Lives*. New York: Basic.

Maggio, Rosalie. 1991. *The Dictionary of Bias-Free Usage*. Phoenix: Oryx.

McConnell-Ginet, S., R. A. Borker, and N. Furman (eds.).1980. *Women and Language in Literature and Society*. New York: Praeger.

Miller, Casey, and Kate Swift. 1978. *Words and Women*. Garden City, N.Y.: Anchor.

———. 1988. *The Handbook of Nonsexist Writing*. 2nd ed. New York: Harper & Row.

———. 1991. *Words and Women: New Language in New Times*. New York: HarperCollins.

Mills, Jane. 1989. *Womanwords: A Dictionary of Words About Women*. New York: Holt.

Pearson, Judy, Lynn Turner, and William Todd-Mancillas. 1991. *Gender and Communication*. 2nd ed. Dubuque, Iowa: William C. Brown.

Penelope, Julia. 1990. *Speaking Freely: Unlearning the Lies of the Father's Tongues*. New York: Pergamon.

Perry, Linda, Lynn Turner, and Helen Sterk (eds.). 1992. *Constructing and Reconstructing Gender: The Links among Communication, Language and Gender*. Albany: State University of New York Press.

Piercy, Marge. 1976. *Woman on the Edge of Time*. New York: Knopf.

Roman, Camille, Suzanne Juhasz, and Cristanne Miller (eds.). 1994. *The Women & Language Debate: A Sourcebook*. New Brunswick, N.J.: Rutgers University Press.

Sorrels, Bobbye. 1983. "Tale of Two Sexes." In *The Non-Sexist Communicator: Solving the Problems of Gender and Awkwardness in Modern English*, by Bobbye Sorrels, Englewood Cliffs, N.J.: Prentice Hall.

Spender, Dale. 1990. *Man-made Language*. 2nd ed. London: Routlege.

Swartz, Marilyn, and Task Force of the Association of American University Presses. 1995. *Guidelines for Bias-Free Writing*. Bloomington: Indiana University Press.

Tannen, Deborah. 1990. *You Just Don't Understand*. New York: Morrow.

———. 1994. *Talking from 9 to 5*. New York: Morrow.

———. 1996. *Gender and Discourse*. New York: Oxford University Press.

Thorne, B., C. Kramarae, and N. Henley (eds.). 1983. *Language, Gender and Society*. Rowley, Mass.: Newbury House.

Video

Sexism in Language: Thief of Honor, Shaper of Lies. Produced by Lynn Lovdal, professor of communications and women's studies at Ohio University, this 1995 video looks at the gender bias that permeates everyday language. It is quick paced and often funny, and has been compared to Jean Kilbourne's *Still Killing Us Softly* in terms of its effectiveness. Available for rental or sale from University of California Extension, Center for Media and Independent Learning, 2000 Center Street, 4th Floor, Berkeley, CA 94704. Phone: (510) 642–0460.

Organization

Modern Language Association of America, 10 Astor Place, 5th Floor, New York, NY 10003–6981. Phone: (212) 475–9500. The MLA is the professional association of college and university teachers of English and modern foreign languages. Among its many other functions, it serves as a clearinghouse for information of interest to teachers of English literature and composition. The MLA publishes books, bibliographies, a newsletter, two journals, and pamphlets, including information on gender-neutral or bias-free language usage.

CHAPTER 4

W o m e n

a n d   S p o r t s

When I was 8, I cried as my father tried to explain to me why my brother could play Little League Baseball, while I, who had just reached the age of eligibility, was still somehow ineligible. Two years later, my best friend Linda Brauer and I joined a nearby team . . . but I hadn't learned about the grueling and sometimes humiliating struggle of the girl, Maria Pepe, two years older than me, who had sued Little League Baseball all the way to the New Jersey State Supreme Court in order to be allowed to play the game.
—Barbara Findlen, *Listen Up*, 1995[1]

No person in the United States shall, on the basis of sex, be excluded from participation in, be denied the benefits of, or be subjected to discrimination under any educational program or activity receiving federal financial assistance.
—Title IX of Public Law 92–318

SINCE TITLE IX was passed as part of the Educational Amendments Act of 1972, discriminating against women in the classroom or on the athletic field has been illegal. The effect of Title IX has been stunning.[2] More female athletes

---

are playing team sports with better equipment, better coaching, and better scholarship opportunities than ever before.[3] In 1972 only 1 in 27 high school girls played on athletic teams; today the number is 1 in 3. The percentage of college athletes who are women has doubled in the last twenty-five years and continues to grow.[4] Today 36 percent of all college athletes are women. Many of the American athletes competing in the 1996 Olympics were beneficiaries of Title IX.

A wealth of research shows that participating in sports—competitively or just for fun—is good for women. Any athletic activity, even running or working out on a StairMaster, makes women more physically fit. It also confers long-term health benefits. One recent study found that women who have exercised regularly since their teenage years have a significantly reduced risk of breast cancer later in life. Fitness and sports participation also boost confidence and self-esteem. All athletes take pride in their performance and in the hard work behind it. "Playing a sport definitely affects the way I feel about myself, physically and emotionally," explained one student athlete. "I love to play. And when I'm playing, I get in shape and am happier with myself." Athletes also benefit from others' positive views of them. According to a lacrosse player, "When I tell people I play a sport in college, they often look at me with a lot of respect. And it makes me feel good about myself."

Playing sports, particularly intercollegiate sports, also teaches discipline and responsibility. Although it may cut down on the amount of time available for socializing and studying, most players find that belonging to a team makes them use their time more efficiently. "I know when games and practices are and how much time they take up," one basketball player reported. "I have less time to study, but because it's so concentrated, I end up doing more work. I really should play a sport all year round." Research by Julie Larble with Mexican-American high school students found that participation in sports influenced young women's identity, challenging the "Maria paradox" by steering them away from passivity and submission to male authority. A National Collegiate Athletic Association (NCAA) study of basketball players on campuses with major athletic programs found that female athletes spend just as much time at their sport as male athletes do, but more time studying and attending classes.[5] Nationally, female athletes have higher graduation rates than male athletes or female students as a whole. Research on Latina high school athletes supports this finding; they were more likely than nonathletes to improve their academic standing, to graduate, and to attend college after high school.[6]

In 1988, the Civil Rights Restoration Act mandated that colleges or universities receiving any federal funding—even as indirectly as students paying their tuition with government loans—must enforce Title IX.[7] To comply a school must meet one of three "effective accommodation" requirements. First, it must provide female and male students with an opportunity to participate in inter-collegiate sports in numbers that are substantially proportional to their enroll-ments. Second, if sports for one sex are inadequate, the school must be able to show a history and ongoing practice of expanding the athletics program to meet the developing interests and abilities of that sex. And third, if the institu-tion is not expanding its athletics program for the underrepresented sex, it must be able to convincingly show that the interests and abilities of that sex are fully supported by its current program.

University athletics programs must provide women and men with equal treatment in twelve areas: the selection of sports and the level at which they are played (i.e., varsity, junior varsity, club), equipment and supplies, schedul-ing of games and practice time, travel and per diem allowances, the opportunity to receive coaching and academic tutoring, the assignment and compensation of coaches and tutors, provision of locker rooms and practice and competititve facilities, medical and training facilities and services, housing and dining fa-cilities and services, publicity, administrative and clerical support, and re-cruitment opportunites. All coeducational institutions with varsity teams that receive federal funds must provide detailed data, broken down by gender, on what is spent for recruiting, student financial aid (separated into men's and women's teams), and coaching salaries, as well as data on the full- or part-time status of all head and assistant coaches, and expenses and revenues generated by women's and men's teams. This information must be compiled annually and disclosed to students and potential students.[8] The data also make it easier for athletes, lawyers, and the Department of Education to prove cases of gen-der bias.

Women athletes and coaches are responsible for defining Title IX in the courts. In the late 1970s, coaches and women players at Washington State University filed a Title IX complaint with the U.S. Department of Education's Office for Civil Rights, charging gender bias in the funding of WSU's sports programs. Dissatisfied with the slow pace of the Department of Education's response, they filed a civil lawsuit in federal court in 1979. When the case finally came to trial in 1982—well after the women who had brought the origi-nal complaint had graduated—the judge nevertheless ruled in the players' fa-vor and directed Washington State to provide scholarships and slots for players proportional to the ratio of women and men in the undergraduate student body. (Football, however, was exempted from the ratio.) A year later, the U.S. De-partment of Education finally found Washington State to be in violation of Title IX. In 1987 the State Supreme Court overruled football's exemption, se-curing even more slots and scholarships for women at Washington State.

Another important Title IX case was brought in 1991 after the College of William and Mary dropped its women's basketball program. Although the college planned to use the money from women's basketball to fund other women's sports, team members contested the decision. The Attorney General of Virginia agreed with them, defining "equal opportunity" as the right for women to have programs in every sport in which men had programs—if they so desired—even if the overall amount of money being spent on women's programs was already proportional to that being spent on men's programs.

Women athletes have also sued Brown University for gender bias. In 1995, a U.S. District Court rejected the university's plan to balance the number of women and men athletes by creating women's junior varsity teams in basketball, lacrosse, tennis, and soccer. The judge ordered Brown to elevate the existing women's club sports of fencing, gymnastics, skiing, and water polo to varsity status, commenting that "counting new women's junior varsity positions as equivalent to men's full varsity positions flagrantly violates the spirit and letter of Title IX."[9] In 1996, a U.S. Appeals Court also supported Title IX and ruled against Brown, stating: "Interest and ability rarely develop in a vacuum; they evolve as a function of opportunity and experience."[10] In 1997, the Supreme Court rejected Brown's appeal to overturn the lower courts' decisions. Its varsity positions will now have to match the overall percentage of men and women in the student body.

Despite these cases and many others, noncompliance remains a problem more than twenty-five years after Title IX was enacted. It is estimated that fewer than 5 percent of National Collegiate Athletic Association (NCAA) colleges and universities are in full compliance. Major universities, for example, sponsor men's varsity hockey yet keep women athletes playing at the club level, despite the tremendous growth in women's hockey. The University of Wisconsin added softball and women's lacrosse rather than varsity hockey because these programs are less expensive.[11] A 1991 study by the NCAA found "disturbing inequalities" in the funding of men's and women's college athletics: men received 70 percent of the scholarship money, 77 percent of operating budgets, and 83 percent of recruiting money.[12] "Most major educational institutions are violating Title IX," claims Arthur Bryant, executive director of Trial Lawyers for Public Justice. "The only thing that will make change is for athletes to enforce their rights, through litigation."[13] As of 1996, colleges and universities are legally required to disclose funds and participation statistics to anyone who asks.[14]

Typically, when school athletic budgets are cut, the first programs to go are non-revenue-producing sports, which includes most of the sports women participate in. To give some gender "balance" to the cuts, some men's sports like tennis, wrestling, gymnastics, and swimming are also cut. Universities are usually very reluctant to cut revenue-producing sports like football, men's basketball, and men's ice hockey. When any men's program is cut, however, Title IX is usually blamed, which creates resentment toward women athletes and women's programs. National organizations like the College Football Association (CFA), the American Football Coaches Association, and the National Wrestling Coaches Association have all lobbied Congress to change Title IX. According to Donna Lopiano, executive director of the Women's Sports Foundation, however, if the NCAA cut the number of football scholarships Division I schools can legally give from eighty-five to sixty-five or sixty, every one of these schools would have enough money to comply with Title IX. When a very expensive sport like football is left alone and non-revenue-producing men's sports are cut, there end up being fewer sports opportunities for both women and men.

Negotiation is an alternative to legal action. Five women athletes and nine coaches from women's teams at the University of Pennsylvania filed a bias complaint in 1994 with the U.S. Department of Education's Office for Civil Rights. The main issue was gender equity in facilities and coaching. The locker room used by the women's track team, for example, was in dismal condition. The women's practice field was located far from campus and had no security and no telephone available in case of emergency. And so on. The case was resolved after Carol Tracy, the executive director of the Women's Law Project in Philadelphia and a former head of Penn's Women's Center, arranged for a negotiated settlement. She brought in Fred Shabel, a former athletic director and vice president at Penn, to mediate. All parties agreed beforehand that any gains for the women's programs would not be made at the expense of the men's programs. Within two months a settlement was reached. The key that made it possible was that "student-athletes and the coaches were able to identify specific problems and suggest solutions, and their demands were reasonable and specific."[15]

Some states have taken an active approach to gender equity. Massachusetts, during Governor William Weld's administration, submitted a bond bill to provide $7.4 million in capital improvements to women's athletic facilities at the four University of Massachusetts campuses. Among other things, the money was earmarked for improved lighting and turf conditions for women's field hockey and soccer, new shells and launches for women's crew teams, improved women's softball fields, and better women's locker and training rooms. According to Michael Hooker, president of the University of Massachusetts at the time, "We are well on our way toward ensuring unprecedented opportunities for our female athletes, far beyond what the law requires." Washington has also made a commitment to gender equity. In 1989, the state legislature passed three bills providing additional scholarships for women athletes, requiring four-year public institutions to develop a sex equity plan, and establishing a conference to discuss women's sports issues.

In daily practice, however, many schools continue to discriminate against women athletes and programs. Often it takes the form of—in the words of sociologists Nijole Benokraitis and Joe Feagin—"supportive discouragement."[16] Frequently, for example, women's teams must schedule their practices or use training and weight rooms at odd hours in order to fit in with the schedules of men's teams. In other cases, women's teams must practice and play in poorer facilities. At one college the women's soccer team was ranked in the top fifteen nationally, while the men's soccer was not nationally ranked and played only regional games. Nevertheless, the men's team practiced and played its games in an artificial grass stadium with a seating capacity of two thousand, while the women's team played on an auxiliary field with two small metal stands. One day after Ohio State University field hockey coach Karen Weaver informed an NCAA review team about the poor condition of the artifical turf women played on, she was fired (she later filed a sex bias suit against the university). She had been complaining to the university about the field since 1991, and many of her players had suffered injuries because of it.[17]

In many schools, men's teams routinely fly to away games and stay over-night on bus trips if a game is located several hours away, while the women's teams always travel by bus (or van) and have to return on the same day. Men's teams are also likely to receive preferential treatment at the equipment room and are more likely than women's teams to have their own trainers. "The women's basketball team took a trip to Connecticut this past season and didn't have a trainer the entire weekend," reported one female player. "When I asked why, the reasoning was that the other team could supply a trainer. But I noticed that when the men's basketball team took a trip to Alfred and Ithaca for a weekend, a trainer was appointed to go. Things like this have occurred through-out the season." At some colleges, it's common for male athletes to be given their equipment, while women must buy their own or be happy with men's team hand-me-downs. At others, male athletes regularly get substantially more meal money than female athletes. Men's teams also routinely receive more publicity than do women's teams.

Coaching and sports administration is another area of gender bias. Currently, only 21 percent of college women's athletic programs are headed by women, and women fill only 33 percent of all administrative jobs in women's programs.[18] With the passage of Title IX, many men's and women's athletic departments were merged. One result was that women lost decision-making power; over half the coaching jobs and nearly 85 percent of the administrative jobs went to men.[19] According to Linda Carpenter, a professor of Physical Education at Brooklyn College and an expert on Title IX, now that women's sports are receiving more money, women's teams are able to pay their coaches more. One consequence of the higher salaries is that men are being attracted to the jobs. (With some notable exceptions, however, salaries for coaching women's teams on average are still half of those for men's teams.)

Male athletic directors seem quick to hire male coaches. Between 1972 and 1994, the number of women coaches for women's collegiate teams decreased from over 90 percent to 49 percent.[20] Meanwhile, 98 percent of coaches for men's teams are men. In 1991, Howard University had to pay its women's basketball coach Sanya Tyler over a million dollars in damages. She claimed that she had been unfairly passed over for the post of athletic director and that as a coach she was paid less than male colleagues. This was the first judgment in which a court awarded monetary damages to a plaintiff in a sex bias case under Title IX.[21] According to Donna Lopiano, Executive Director of the Women's Sports Foundation, few male athletic directors make "paper hires" (based strictly on a candidate's written qualifications). Most use their personal networks, which tend to exclude women.

Another problem, according to some, is that not enough women are applying for coaching jobs. According to Karen Partlow, director of the American Sports Education program, women do not apply for coaching jobs unless they feel very well qualified. Donna Lopiano believes this is due to the way women are brought up. "Every male who has played basketball thinks they [sic] can coach it. Women have always believed that they need to be credentialed to be hired . . . while males have the attitude that they can do everything." Few young girls think of careers in coaching, while boys learn early that there are professional opportunities for them in athletics; if not as players, then as coaches. Sports remain recreational for most young women, who usually plan to pursue other careers.

Other forms of gender bias also play a role in steering women away from coaching and administration. Women coaches who are unmarried are often assumed to be lesbian and are sometimes discriminated against for this reason. Some male athletic directors are said to only hire men or married women to coach women's teams because they want to avoid any possibility of charges of lesbianism, which could hurt their programs; others are undoubtedly homophobic. Even woman coaches who are married may be considered unreliable because of their family commitments. "If you are a woman looking for a coaching job, your chances are best if you are divorced with no children," claims Lopiano. "That proves you are not homosexual and [you] have no children to support."[22] Male coaches are rarely judged by their marital status or sexual orientation.

Sports and Gender Roles

Traditional gender traits for American women did not include being athletic and strong. This is one reason that early media coverage of female athletes

Young Ladies Baseball Club No. 1, 1890–1891 season. Courtesy National Baseball Hall of Fame Library, Cooperstown, N.Y.

often focused on women's physical appearance rather than their talent. In 1925, for example, the *Baltimore Evening Sun* described a citywide track meet attended by five thousand young female athletes as "a girly show if ever there was one." The headline for *Life* magazine's 1940 photoessay on Iowa girls' basketball read: "Pretty Virginia Harris Leads Hansell to Iowa Basketball Championship."[23] Professional women baseball players during the 1940s had to play in short skirts and bare legs. A remnant of this was present even during 1996 Olympics coverage, with references to runner Gail Devers's long, painted fingernails and one announcer describing rhythmic gymnast Maria Petrova's "va-va-voom" figure. *Sports Illustrated* has published an annual swimsuit issue since 1964, featuring photographs of shapely female models wearing revealing swimsuits that no one could conceivably wear to swim competitively. The models are not depicted as athletes but as sexual objects for the magazine's heterosexual male readership to enjoy. Although *Sports Illustrated* launched *Women Sport* magazine in 1997, fewer than 10 percent of the parent magazine's editorial pages are devoted to women's athletic achievements.

In American society athleticism is equated with heterosexual masculinity. *Sports Illustrated*'s swimsuit issue, which appeals to a heterosexual male audience, reinforces this point each year.[24] Because women athletes (and their coaches) are performing in a traditionally male-dominated domain and are

crossing the boundaries of socially constructed definitions of appropriate female behavior, they are viewed as sexually deviant (i.e., lesbian) as well. Early women's sports organizations were aware of the stigma of athletics for women and worked to counter this image. According to historian Susan Cahn in *Coming On Strong: Gender and Sexuality in Twentieth-Century Women's Sport*, the All-American Girls Softball League, which started in 1943, was careful to have its players convey an image of "respectable femininity." The league's first spring-training sessions included a mandatory evening charm school, where players were taught makeup, posture, fashion, and table manners. Hair had to be shoulder length or longer; boyish bobs were out. Athletes had to wear makeup and nail polish, and could never appear in public wearing shorts, slacks, or jeans. Team owners had the right to reject "masculine" players and to fine players who violated the other rules.

Today, women athletes—especially in team sports like softball, basketball, and field hockey—deal with the same stereotypes and stigmas.[25] So do other women involved in sports. More than half of female administrators surveyed, according to the Feminist Majority Foundation's Task Force on Women and Girls in Sports, said that others assumed they were lesbians because of their involvement in sports: 51 percent of women coaches and 46 percent of women athletes agreed. College men often refer to female athletes as "dykes" and "lesbos." Unfortunately, many women athletes also feel compelled to distance themselves from the lesbian stigma.[26] Some do so by socializing almost exclusively with other athletes, thus avoiding anyone who might react negatively to their athletic participation. Others conceal or play down their athletic skill, seldom talking about it to anyone but close friends. Some women use what sociologist Erving Goffman labeled "disidentifiers." When off the field or court, they wear dresses, skirts, makeup, and earrings and make a point to be seen with men, supposedly things no "real" lesbian would do.

Homophobia hurts all athletes, regardless of their own sexual orientation. Some women become heterosexually promiscuous just to "prove" they are not lesbians. Others avoid hanging around with women whose company they would enjoy. Some women athletes make rude comments about teammates they suspect or know to be lesbians and form friendship cliques on the basis of sexual orientation rather than personal compatibility and shared interests. When rumors of lesbianism are directed against coaches, careers and entire sports programs can be ruined; coaches may be blackballed and potential recruits steered away from certain schools. If you engage in any of these practices or know people who do, think about the implications and harm they do and talk about it. "Homophobia in sports not only causes discrimination against lesbians; but it also hurts all women by perpetuating the stereotype that sports are not feminine, thus preventing some girls and women from enjoying athletic participation and successful careers in athletics."[27] Homophobia in women's athletics is just beginning to be discussed openly. At the annual Women's Basketball Coaches Association meetings in 1996, more than five hundred coaches, athletic directors, and other members for the first time discussed the serious negative effects homophobia has on women athletes and programs.[28]

Many male athletes and coaches, especially in contact sports, often exhort one another or their players to work harder or perform better by referring to them as "sissies," "girls," or "ladies." Mariah Burton Nelson, in *The Stronger Women Get, the More Men Love Football*, cites other examples of the use of women-denigrating language in male sports and quotes rugby songs that describe violence against women. Is this kind of language linked to behavior? In some cases, yes. A recent study of student athletes at ten Division I universities showed that while male athletes made up little more than 3 percent of the male university population, they made up 19 percent of the students reported for sexual assault.[29] "By encouraging boys to become aggressive, violent athletes, and by encouraging girls to cheer for them, we perpetuate the cycle of male aggression and violence against women."[30]

The Media

Women's sports are slighted by many campus newspapers and public relations offices, which continue to regard men's sports as more legitimate and interesting. Campus radio stations, for example, may air men's hockey and football games, but give no coverage to comparable women's games. The same pattern exists in the larger media, where female sports are underrepresented and women athletes are still marginalized. Several studies during the 1980s and early 1990s found that between 80 and 90 percent of newspaper and televised sports reporting covered men's sports.[31] The 1992 Olympic "Dream Team" in men's basketball received enormous press attention, while the U.S. women's basketball team, which had won forty-five of its last forty-seven international basketball games and two consecutive Olympic gold metals, received virtually none. Sports commentary is also gender marked. Sociologist Michael Messner and his associates found that "the language used by commentators tends to mark women's sports and women athletes as other, infantilize women athletes, and frame their accomplishments negatively or ambivalently."[32]

Times are changing, however. In the 1996 Summer Olympics, women won 38 of the U.S. athletes' 101 medals and generated enormous public interest. This time the women's Olympic basketball team received as much press attention as the men's team did, gaining new respect for the women's game. Two women's professional basketball leagues, the Women's National Basketball Assoication (WNBA) and the American Basketball League (ABL), are now playing, with games covered by network television. (There are also professional women's softball and baseball teams.)[33] As more women's professional and college sports are shown on television, women athletes everywhere will gain further public credibility and support. The commercialization of women athletes and women's sports has also begun. A number of new magazines aimed at women have sprung up, including *Sports Illustrated*'s *Women Sport*, Condé Nast's *Sports for Women*, and a range of fitness magazines. Women athletes are now on Wheaties boxes and can be seen on television leaping through the air in Nike commercials, endorsing—along with male athletes—both good and bad products and companies.[34]

_____ *DID YOU KNOW?* _____

- In 1996, swimmer Amy Van Dyken became the first U.S. woman to win four gold medals in one Olympics.

- Women from other countries also made major breakthroughs. Fatima Roba became the first African woman to win a medal in an Olympic marathon. Ghada Shouaa won a heptathlon, becoming the first Syrian athlete to win a gold medal in the Olympics. Still, twenty-seven countries do not send women to the Olympics because of Islamic beliefs and dress codes.

- Only a fifth of U.S. college women's athletics programs today are headed by women.

- Between the years of 1923 and 1938, tennis player Helen Wills Moody won the U.S. national singles title seven times, the Wimbledon singles title eight times, and took gold medals at the 1924 Paris Olympics in both women's singles and doubles. In her early years she also championed dress reform in women's sports, wearing a knee-length, white pleated skirt (and signature white visor) instead of the long skirts, petticoats, and stockings worn by most women players. This served as an important transition to tennis shorts, which became acceptable in the 1930s.

- The performance gap between male and female athletes has narrowed dramatically in the last twenty-five years. The gap in time between men and women competing in the Boston Marathon narrowed 38 minutes between 1970 and 1995. The current gap is just 16 minutes.[35] Until 1972, marathon running was for men only. In 1984, when the women's marathon was introduced in the Summer Olympics, Joan Benoit's winning time was 2:24.52—a time that would have won thirteen of the previous twenty all-male Olympic marathons.

- The longer the race, the better women perform. Top female ultra-marathon runners and marathon swimmers outperform men. New research indicates that women are better able than men to metabolize fat and to delay burning off their bodies' stores of carbohydrates, which results in severe muscle fatigue. Estrogen also seems to delay fatigue and to increase the delivery of oxygen to women's muscles.

- In 1996, American women athletes earned 61 cents for every dollar male athletes earned.

- Nationally, it is estimated that college men's teams still receive five times the money that women's teams receive; three times the operating funds; and twice the scholarships.

- The reason most frequently given for football's preferential treatment and funding is that it makes money for the school. In fact, NCAA figures indicate that of the 524 NCAA football programs, 454 lose money.

- Many Division I college football coaches claim they need 105 players (with 85 on full scholarships—the current NCAA limit) to build a winning team, while NFL professional football coaches consistently produce winning teams with a limit of 47 players.

- The money spent to fund approximately five football scholarships (depending on the college or university) could fund an entire women's soccer program.

- In 1996, Deana Lansing, a guard on the University of Portland's women's basketball team, broke an NCAA women's record by making fourteen consecutive three-point shots.

- Only 19 women served on the United States Olympic Committee's hundred-member board of directors in 1996; only 7 women served on the 106–member International Olympic Committee. There are still 63 more medal events for men than there are for women in the Olympics.

- In 1997, Dee Kantner and Violet Palmer became the first women to referee regular-season games in the men's National Basketball Association. Now women finally referee in all four major men's professional sports leagues: NBA, NFL, NHL, and major-league baseball.

- About 80 percent of women executives in Fortune 500 companies self-identify as having been "tomboys" who played sports as girls, according to Donna Lopiano, executive director of the Women's Sports Foundation.

WHAT YOU CAN DO

- Try out for and play a sport!

- Support women's athletic teams. Attend games, support fund-raisers, help with publicity, and demand equal coverage of men's and women's athletics in the campus newspaper and on radio. Consider covering a women's sport for your college's newspaper or writing a pro–women's sport editorial.

- If your school uses a gender-biased mascot, urge the adoption of a gender-neutral one. Complain in writing if your school adds "lady" to an already gender-neutral team name; for example, Lady Tigers or Lady Warriors.

☒ Don't tolerate homophobic remarks or discriminatory behavior based on sexual orientation on any team you belong to. Encourage your coaches, both male and female, to speak out against it. Organize a team showing of Dee Mosbacher's film *Out for a Change: Addressing Homophobia in Women's Sports* (see Resources). Make sure your school's antidiscrimination policy includes sexual orientation, and if necessary remind your athletic director of this.

☒ Obtain a copy of *Achieving Gender Equity: A Basic Guide to Title IX for Colleges and Universities*, published by the National Collegiate Athletic Association (see Organizations), or obtain the Title IX guidelines from your state Department of Education. If you think that your school is not in compliance, bring the matter to the attention of your athletic director, the Title IX officer of your school (if you have one), or the school's athletic counsel (if you have one). You may also want to speak to other players, your parents, trusted coaches, and professors, who can support you in your complaint. The Women's Sports Foundation (see Organizations) can also provide you with advice and assistance. If your school does not try to rectify the situation, or consistently puts the matter off, find allies and consider filing either a civil lawsuit in federal court for damages or injunctive relief (instant action) or a complaint with the U.S. Department of Education's Office for Civil Rights. The Department of Education is supposed to investigate and give the offending school a chance to comply. If the school refuses, the department will then prosecute the case and seek to cut off the school's federal funds.

☒ Be aware of your rights, and remember that Title IX is only a tool. Statutes don't make changes; people do.

RESOURCES

Books

Birrell, Susan, and Cheryl Cole (eds.). 1994. *Women, Sport, and Culture.* Champaign, Ill.: Human Kinetics.

Blais, Madeline. 1995. *In These Girls, Hope Is a Muscle.* New York: Warner.

Cahn, Susan. 1994. *Coming On Strong: Gender and Sexuality in Twentieth-Century Women's Sport.* New York: Free Press.

Cohen, Greta (ed.). 1993. *Women in Sport: Issues and Controversies.* Newbury Park, Calif.: Sage.

Costa, Margaret, and Sharon Guthrie (eds.). 1994. *Women and Sport: Interdisciplinary Perspectives.* Champaign, Ill.: Human Kinetics.

Creedon, Pamela (ed.). 1994. *Women, Media, and Sport: Challenging Gender Values.* Thousand Oaks, Calif.: Sage.

Davis, Laurel. 1996. *The Swimsuit Issue and Sport: Hegemonic Masculinity in Sports Illustrated.* Albany: State University of New York Press.

Davis, Michael. 1992. *Black American Women in Olympic Track and Field: A Complete Illustrated History.* Jefferson, N.C.: McFarland.

Guttman, Allen. 1992. *Women's Sport: A History.* New York: Columbia University Press.

Hargreaves, Jennifer. 1994. *Sporting Females: Critical Issues in the History and Sociology of Women's Sports.* New York: Routledge.

Melpomene Institute for Women's Health Research. 1993. *The Bodywise Woman: Reliable Information about Physical Activity and Health Research.* Champaign, Ill.: Human Kinetics.

Messner, Michael, and Donald Sabo (eds.). 1990. *Sport, Men and the Gender Order: Critical Feminist Perspectives.* Champaign, Ill.: Human Kinetics.

Nelson, Mariah Burton. 1991. *Are We Winning Yet? How Women Are Changing Sports and Sports Are Changing Women.* New York: Random House.

———. 1994. *The Stronger Women Get, The More Men Love Football: Sex and Sports in America.* San Diego, Calif.: Harcourt Brace.

Remley, Mary. 1991. *Women in Sport: An Annotated Bibliography and Resource Guide.* Boston: Hall.

Salter, David. 1996. *Crashing the Old Boys' Network: The Tragedies and Triumphs of Girls and Women in Sports.* New York: Praeger.

Sandgold, Mona, and Gabe Mirkin (eds.). 1992. *The Complete Sports Medicine Book for Women: Revised for the '90s.* New York: Simon & Schuster.

Sandler, Bernice Resnick. 1989. *The Restoration of Title IX: Implications for Higher Education.* Project on the Status and Education of Women. Washington, D.C.: Association of American Colleges & Universities.

Sheehan, Richard. 1996. *Keeping Score: The Economics of Big-Time Sports.* South Bend, Ind.: Diamond Communications.

Shoebridge, Michele. 1987. *Women in Sport: A Select Bibliography.* New York: Mansell.

Woodlum, Janet. 1992. *Outstanding Women Athletes: Who They Are and How They Influenced Sports in America.* Phoenix: Oryx.

Videos

Gender Equity: Not Just for Athletics Anymore . . . or Ever. Video by Dennis Black. Collegiate Conferences, 4200 University Avenue, Suite 2000, Madison, WI 53705. Phone: (800) 206–4805.

Out for a Change: Addressing Homophobia in Women's Sports. Video. This twenty-eight-minute video by Dee Mosbacher, a San Francisco psychologist and filmmaker, comes with a leader's guide that contains discussion questions and a bibliography. University of California Center for Media, 2000 Center Street, 4th Floor, Berkeley, CA 94704. Phone: (510) 642–0460.

Organizations

National Association of Intercollegiate Athletics (NAIA), 6120 South Yale, Suite 1450, Tulsa, OK 74136. Phone: (918) 494–8828. The Association publishes statistics and works to develop intercollegiate athletic programs "as an integral part of the total educational program" of colleges and universities.

National Collegiate Athletic Association (NCAA), 6201 College Boulevard, Overland Park, KS 66211. Phone: (913) 339–1906. Fax: (913) 339–0030. The Association is devoted to achieving uniformity and equity in the policies and practices of intercollegiate athletics; specialized committees include Legislation and Interpretation, Legislative Review, and Women's Athletics. It also operates a statistics service and publishes the guide *Achieving Gender Equity: A Basic Guide to Title IX for Colleges and Universities.*

National Women's Law Center (NWLC), 11 Dupont Circle, Suite 800, Washington, DC 20036. Phone: (202) 588–5180. The Center conducts research on current and proposed policies and regulations to evaluate their legality and constitutionality and impact on women's rights. It also provides legal advice on Title IX and other issues that may involve discrimination against women.

U.S. Department of Education Office for Civil Rights (OCR), 330 C Street SW, Washington, DC 20202. The Office of Civil Rights has twelve regional enforcement offices that handle illegal discrimination cases. Their addresses and telephone numbers are listed in the U.S. Department of Education Web site (www.ed.gov/offices/OCR). The address cited above is the office to contact for OCR publications; available titles are listed in the same Web site.

Women's Sports Foundation (WSF), Eisenhower Park, East Meadow, NY 11554. Phone: (800) 227–3988. The Foundation was started in 1974 by women athletes, including Billie Jean King and Donna de Varona. Its purpose is to promote healthy sports opportunities for girls and women. The Foundation sponsors an information and resource clearinghouse on women's sports and fitness. It compiles statistics; runs an internship program; develops educational guides; provides travel and training; publishes information on college scholarships, careers in sports, and Title IX compliance, including *Women's Athletic Scholarship Guide* and *Playing Fair: A Guide to Title IX in College and High School Sports.* The Foundation also publishes a bimonthly newsletter, *The Woman's Sports Experience*, and information packets on a variety of subjects, including *Eating Disorders* and *Nutrition/Weight Control.*

DEALING

WITH

DIVERSITY

CHAPTER 5

Sexual Identity

and Homophobia

When you say "homosexuals," do you mean guys? Or chicks goin' at it too?
> —Question addressed to a bisexual student after she had spent several minutes discussing the need to protect gay rights, *Listen Up*, 1995[1]

MORE THAN THIRTY years ago, research by Alfred Kinsey and associates showed that a continuum in sexual orientation exists, from exclusive heterosexuality to exclusive homosexuality. In single-sex environments, heterosexuals may engage in homosexual behavior.[2] Similarly, lesbians and gays may become involved in heterosexual relationships, including marriage, due to social expectations or initial confusion about their own sexual orientation. Exclusive heterosexuals sometimes have homoerotic fantasies, as the following excerpt from a student journal indicates:

> I don't consider myself lesbian or even bisexual, yet I've had sexual dreams (not really sexually explicit, but still sexual) and thoughts about one particular girlfriend of mine. And I was pretty surprised when one day she told me that if she'd ever be with a woman, it would only be

with me. I told her I felt exactly the same way, and we talked about it and came to the conclusion that our feelings came not from a real sexual attraction to each other but from the very deep sense of love we have for each other.

Before we talked I was a little disturbed by my thoughts—every guy I seemed to be meeting was one disappointment after another, and so I thought maybe I'm not heterosexual. . . . Now my friend and I joke and say that if either of us had a penis, we'd be perfect for each other.[3]

Homosexual behavior is found in most societies, although how it is interpreted varies from one culture to the next. Many cultures that condone same-sex sexual relationships do not categorize people engaging in them as homosexual or bisexual. The ancient Greeks, for example, tolerated, even encouraged, activities and emotional and sexual expressions which contemporary Americans would define as homosexual, yet did not distinguish between homosexuals and heterosexuals. As used in American culture, the terms "homosexual," "bisexual," and "heterosexual" refer to a person's emotional affiliation, sexual behavior, and self-identity. Psychologists classify a person as homosexual when her or his primary erotic, emotional, and social interest is in members of the same sex.[4] A person is heterosexual whose primary interest is in members of the opposite sex. People are considered bisexual if they are attracted to people of either sex.

Sexual identity develops over a period of years, especially during adolescence. By the time most people are in college, their sexual identity is established, although they may not have chosen to express it. Like everyone else, lesbians and gays learn to believe that heterosexuality is the "normal" sexual orientation, and many internalize homophobia as a result. In college, students often have their first exposure to an environment in which homosexuality can be discussed and in which they see people who are openly lesbian, gay, and bisexual. It is not surprising, therefore, that college is often the place where lesbians, bisexuals, and gay men acknowledge and come to terms with their sexual identity.

The most frequently cited figure for the percentage of the American population that is homosexual or bisexual is 10 percent. In places like San Francisco and New York, where large gay communities exist, the number probably surpasses this. Nationally, however, according to research conducted by the National Opinion Research Center at the University of Chicago, 2.8 percent of men and 1.4 percent of women identify themselves as homosexual or bisexual. But even this lower figure means that more than 10 million Americans are exclusively homosexual or are bisexual. Twice that many, however, have had a same-sex experience, and even more have felt a same-sex attraction.[5] More-

over, these figures do not include persons who do not openly identify as either homosexual or bisexual.

The word "lesbian" is derived from Lesbos, the ancient Greek island whose culture condoned same-sex sexual relations and in the sixth century was home to the bisexual woman poet Sappho. "Gay" was initially a code word used among male homosexuals that gradually became a common term for both homosexual men and women. Like the word "man," however, when "gay" is used as a generic label it tends to make women invisible. Many other words for gay men and lesbians are pejorative and are used primarily by heterosexuals; some, like "queer" and "dyke," however, are also used by lesbians in an affectionate or humorous way or to make a political statement. Queer studies in academia is an increasingly common alternative to gay and lesbian studies.

American society strongly endorses heterosexuality. The dominant Christian ethic regards procreation as the ultimate justification for sex; homosexuality, therefore, is seen as sinful and aberrant. As recently as 1994, the associate dean at Yale University's Divinity School, along with twenty other socially conservative Christian and Jewish scholars, signed a six-page document equating homosexuality with immorality.[6] Many other Americans feel this way at some level. A student describes her mother's reaction to her own emerging lesbianism:

My mom said that homosexuality is genetic and that I don't have the "disorder." She said that one can clearly tell when a woman's *really* a lesbian because she's masculine and manly and she hasn't felt "right" for most of her life, and I'm not like that at all. She thinks homosexuality and bisexuality are too common, too rampant among people of my generation. She said that people are choosing it for the wrong reasons. She thinks some people's desire to live an alternative lifestyle stems from TV, music, books, and all this other stuff.

So I took a deep breath and argued that people are just becoming more open these days about their feelings and are not so afraid to express themselves. I said that liking someone of the same sex is all about one's feelings—one's *true* feelings—not just a chance to be different or like the people who have songs written about them. My mom calmed down and got a little bit more rational. She said that every parent wants her child to have a healthy, heterosexual relationship, then she began to cry. . . . This entire conversation left me with a lot to think about and unfortunately more to worry about. One thing that struck me deeply was the huge difference in opinion about homosexuality between my parents' generation and people my age. It's such a stressing topic, I just want to SCREAM!

Homophobia Affects Everyone

Homophobia—the fear and loathing of homosexuality in others and oneself—is widespread in American society. More than twenty states still have antisodomy laws, although an equal number of states have eliminated them in recent years. Ironically, sodomy laws actually ban sexual acts that many heterosexuals engage in; yet they are used to infringe on the rights and privacy of lesbians and gays. A recent *Newsweek* poll found that 78 percent of Americans surveyed believe that lesbians and gays should have the same job opportunities as heterosexuals, but 45 percent also believe they threaten the American family and 61 percent disapprove of their having adoption rights.[7] A survey conducted by the National Gay and Lesbian Task Force Policy Institute in five cities found that violence and harassment against homosexuals has not diminished. Given such a social climate, it is easy to understand why many lesbians and gays remain "closeted," and why heterosexuals have difficulty accepting any homosexual feelings in themselves. There are signs that society is becoming more tolerant, however. When comedian Ellen DeGeneres came out on the popular television show *Ellen* in 1997, the episode drew a large national audience and a positive response.

Homophobia and harassment of lesbians and gays occur on college campuses as they do in the rest of society. On campus homophobia takes many forms: jokes, disparaging remarks (e.g., "Did you go to the Indigo Dyke concert last night?"), the casual use of denigrating terms, open discrimination or intimidation (one student told me, "All I did was walk into the campus center holding Kelly's hand, and some guy yelled at us: 'Fucking lesbians!'"), and occasionally, violence. In 1991, a fraternity at Syracuse University was suspended by its national organization after selling T-shirts with antihomosexual slogans, including one that advocated violence.[8] Fliers were posted at California State, Northridge, offering free baseball bats to participants in a fictitious "gay bashing and clubbing night" to be held at a nearby park.[9] Homophobic letters to the editor are not uncommon in student newspapers. At some schools, announcements and posters for meetings and events sponsored by gay and bisexual student organizations are routinely ripped down; some groups keep the names of members confidential out of fear. At the University of Wisconsin at Whitewater, a female student who spoke out for gay rights was assaulted and suffered a concussion. She later received a note in the mail stating, "Dyke, you got what you deserved." The student was actually heterosexual, which shows that supporters of gay rights also become symbols and targets for those who are homophobic. In one recent year, 19 percent of the more than seven thousand incidents of harassment and violence directed toward lesbians, gays, and bisexuals that were reported to the National Gay and Lesbian Task Force occurred on college campuses.[10]

Homophobia also results in institutionalized discrimination. On some campuses, lesbian and gay student groups have financial support withheld or do not have the right to use university facilities for their meetings.[11] In 1992, for example, the governor of Alabama signed legislation preventing gay students from receiving public money or using state university buildings. In 1995, the Gays and Lesbians of Notre Dame (a Catholic university) were expelled from campus facilities by the administration, sparking student protests. Yeshiva University has been criticized by Orthodox Jews for recognizing gay student groups. Lesbians and gays can also be discriminated against in other ways. A survey of physicians in a county medical association found that nearly a third of its members would not want to admit a qualified but openly lesbian or gay applicant to medical school.[12]

Many heterosexual students seem unaware that there are lesbian, gay, and bisexual students on campus. One reason is the strong heterosexual bias that exists in mainstream society; heterosexual students simply go through life assuming that everyone else is heterosexual. Because of homophobia and harassment, many lesbians and gays decide it is less painful and safer to conceal their sexual identity; many heterosexuals do not show their support for gays and lesbians because they fear they may also be victimized (or considered lesbian). Bisexuals often find themselves in a double bind. They are subject to homophobic victimization, but they also can be rejected by lesbian and gay students because of their interest in and association with heterosexuals. Lesbians who do not define themselves as either "butch" (masculine) or "femme" (feminine) may also have problems with other lesbians.

If you are heterosexual, try to imagine what it must feel like to be treated differently and rejected because of who you are rather than anything you do. It hurts to have a straight female friend or acquaintance overreact to a touch or some other expression of warmth, because they misinterpret it as a sexual advance. Try to imagine what it must feel like to hide an important part of who you are and not be able to be yourself. One student recounts the stress she experienced: "During the time when I wasn't able to admit to anyone how I felt about Cynthia, I got really sick and depressed and tired. I spent my summer sleeping in bed and going to the doctor to have tons of blood tests in order to see why I was so lethargic. Everyone else said I had a virus, but I know my sickness stemmed from the stress I had of 'living with a secret.'"

It is painful not to fully accept yourself, but just as painful to be rejected (or risk rejection) by parents, family members, or friends when you come out. Whether openly gay or closeted, all lesbians (and gay men) live with the fear of what could happen because of widespread homophobia. Some people have entertained thoughts of suicide; nationally, 30 percent of fatal youth suicides are lesbians and gay males. Some resort to drugs and pills; lesbians and gay males are 35 percent more likely than heterosexual youths to be involved with substance abuse. Fortunately, most lesbians and gays who come out feel that an enormous burden has been lifted and enjoy a new sense of confidence and pride in openly identifying as gay. The new relationships they form bring strength and satisfaction. Heterosexuals who have personal contact with lesbians and gays who are open about their sexual identity usually develop more positive attitudes toward homosexuality. According to one student, knowing openly gay people "takes the mystery [and fear] out of it." Some campuses provide open, supportive environments for homosexual and bisexual students. The University of Kansas at Lawrence has an annual Gay and Lesbian Awareness (GALA) Week that includes a parade, lectures, and dance. Graduating seniors have pinned pink triangles to their robes and mortarboards; others have worn T-shirts with slogans like "Out is in" and "We're here. We're queer. Get used to it." As a result of the high visibility of lesbians and gays on campus, the university has been nicknamed Gay U.

Homophobia

Homophobia affects us all. Whether you are lesbian, gay, bisexual, or heterosexual, you will experience in some way the negative effects of homophobia. Homophobia makes many women fear or dislike aspects of their own personalities or appearance that are not sufficiently "feminine." Homophobia also divides women. Some female students do not describe themselves as feminists, even when they share feminist views and support feminist goals, partly because the term is strongly associated with lesbianism. Straight women, particularly, do not want to risk harassment and labeling as male-bashing "dykes." How many college women fail to stand up for their rights as women and their feminist beliefs for this reason? How many avoid taking women's studies courses, joining women's groups, or participating in demonstrations having to do with women's issues?

Some lesbian and bisexual women react with anger to this situation. In the opinion of Anastasia Higginbotham, a young bisexual woman, "Any feminist who fears being called lesbian, or who fears association with a movement demanding civil rights for gays, lesbians and bisexuals, is not *worthy* [emphasis added] of being called feminist."[13]

Gay men often find it even more difficult than lesbians to be open about their sexual identity because they are more likely than women to be viewed as a threat by heterosexuals. According to a lesbian student interviewed by sociologist Ruth Sidel for *Battling Bias: The Struggle for Identity and Community on College Campuses*, when gay men run for campus offices, some fraternities wage an all-out campaign against them.[14] American men are generally more homophobic than American women and place more pressure on each other to conform to conventional gender norms. When college men regularly mock each other with homophobic insults like "fag" and "homo" or sexist taunts like "pussy," "skirt," and "woman," they are distancing themselves from gays and from women—anything not "masculine"—and thus enforcing heterosexual male behavior. In other words, they are defining for each other what it means to be "real men." Homophobia among heterosexual men is strongest when it is directed at gay men rather than lesbians. In contrast to the disgust many heterosexual men say they feel at the thought of gay sex, for example, many of these same men find the idea of two women together sexually arousing—not because they approve of lesbian relationships, but because they imagine "having" both women.

How many college men avoid certain activities or courses, such as art or dance, because they fear being ridiculed by their peers and having their heterosexuality questioned? How many heterosexual students—female and male—cut themselves off from friendships with lesbian and gay students because they fear being stigmatized by the association? How many heterosexual men avoid getting emotionally close to other men, thus limiting the depth of their friendships to competitive "buddyship"? How many men avoid speaking out against sexism and misogyny due to homophobia? The logic (illogic!), seldom explicitly stated, goes something like this: If you defend women's rights, you are interested in "feminine" things, and therefore you are not fully "masculine," which must also mean you're gay. The sexually aggressive talk about women and sex that is typical of many heterosexual men insulates them from accusations of homosexuality and neutralizes the erotic bonds that develop among close male friends, fraternity brothers, and teammates who play, shower, dress, and live together.[15]

Competitive athletics is an arena of campus life that is especially hostile to homosexuals. In American society, sports is an important definer of masculinity ("Be strong," "Play like a man"), and to be a man is to be heterosexual. (Male homosexuals, in contrast, are usually stereotyped as feminine and weak.) Homophobic and sexist comments from players and coaches are common: "If someone on the team misses a catch in practice," reports a gay football player, "other guys call them 'pussy' or 'faggot.' Boy, wouldn't they like to know [about me]." Although the "butch" stereotype of lesbians is less inconsistent with being athletic than is the "effeminate" stereotype of gay men, female athletes also suffer from homophobia.[16] "My teammates always talk about the other team after a game," reports the lesbian member of a college lacrosse team. "'What a bunch of fucking dykes those girls all were,' they'll say. I can't say, 'Hey, look at me.' I'd be completely ostracized. So instead, I put up with their comments." As discussed in the previous chapter, to avoid being harassed as "lesbians," some female athletes deliberately contradict lesbian stereotypes by avoiding being seen in public with groups of women, by accentuating their femininity (e.g., wearing their hair long), and by making a point of being seen with men.

The dorm is another arena of campus life that can be difficult for lesbians and gays. One of the most challenging relationships on campus is the one formed during the first year between roommates. If you are a lesbian or bisexual woman, the odds are that you will end up with a roommate who is heterosexual, and possibly homophobic as well. If you are heterosexual, don't automatically assume that your roommate is too. Be sensitive to the feelings, rights, and privacy needs of others and to the possibility that you do not share the same sexual orientation.

The Heterosexual Curriculum

During the past twenty years, courses about lesbian and gay history, literature, and culture have become more common on college campuses. Some are offered within the framework of women's studies courses whose faculty typically include such perspectives in most of the courses they teach. But increasingly, other departments and programs are offering courses like Homosexuality in American Culture, Reclaiming Gay and Lesbian History, Politics and Culture, and Queer Fiction. Sarah Lawrence College offers two full-year courses on lesbian literature and politics. Lesbian studies programs (lesbian and gay studies, queer studies) exist at some universities, including Rutgers, Yale, and Berkeley. Other universities and colleges are in the process of establishing them. But the reverse is also true. In 1995, the president of Texas A&M rejected a proposal for a required health course that included an open treatment of AIDS and homosexuality. He cited financial reasons, but others believed he was responding to criticism from conservative alumni and other groups.[17]

The study of human sexuality in general and homosexuality in particular has been going on for a long time, of course. In the past, the topic of homosexuality was often introduced into the college curriculum (and in some places it still is) in courses with titles like Abnormal Psychology or The Sociology of Deviance, titles that are implicitly homophobic and offensive to lesbian and gay students. In other areas of the curriculum, the issue of homosexuality was usually submerged. In English and American literature courses, for example, the homoeroticism in the work of Emily Dickinson and Walt Whitman was simply ignored. Sociology courses on the family typically focused exclusively on heterosexual relationships.

Many faculty still do not incorporate homosexuality into the curriculum because of their own ignorance. Others, however, avoid doing so because it can be such an emotionally charged subject to deal with in the classroom.

Bonnie Zimmerman, a self-identified lesbian professor of women's studies at San Diego State University, has described her own and others' difficulties in introducing lesbian studies into the curriculum.[18] Many faculty worry about student reactions: Will students automatically assume that the material is sexually suggestive, will they reject the instructor and everything she or he has to say because of it, and how will their homophobia emerge in the classroom? Faculty also worry about their own handling of the material. What is a good lesbian novel? How should such a potentially sensitive subject be taught? How can I find time to master the research literature in this area?

Despite the difficulties, the rewards of incorporating lesbian and gay scholarship into the curriculum are many, including: validating the reality and experiences of lesbian and gay students; liberating all students from the prejudices and misconceptions about homosexuality held by mainstream society; expanding the boundaries of what is knowable (a major goal of all education); and pushing the limits of social tolerance and the acceptance of diversity outward. If you are not homosexual, imagine what it must be like to be lesbian or gay in a learning environment that is heterocentric, that assumes that everyone at all times has been, is, or will be heterosexual. Your contemporary history or social movements class studies the civil rights movement, women's liberation, hippies, and environmental politics, but skips gay liberation. Your philosophy class reads *The Symposium* but ignores the different forms of love discussed by Plato. Your literature, music, and art history classes are filled with the works of lesbian and gay writers and artists, but the professor seems to treat these people as honorary heterosexuals or else as sexless spinsters and bachelors. Your women's studies class spends weeks talking about heterosexual marriage, dating, contraception and abortion, and women's relationships to men, but only one class period on homosexuality. In medical school, discussions and workshops on the challenges of being a female physician concentrate on the best timing for marriage and childbearing. "It left me, and I'm sure closeted lesbian women as well, feeling abandoned and alone," reports one former med student.[19] An inclusive curriculum, in contrast, would use the gay liberation movement as a model of social activism, would speak openly about the effect of sexuality on literary and artistic creation, would identify homosexuals in history, and would not structure course material around an assumption of heterosexuality.

_____ *DID YOU KNOW?* _____

▓ A recent survey of 250 public and college libraries found that 14 percent had no books on gay issues.

▓ A survey of eighty-two U.S. medical school directors found that less than four hours of course time is spent on homosexuality during four years of medical school, and then usually in lectures on human sexuality.

- A report by the Massachusetts Governor's Commission on Gay and Lesbian Youth documents a history of administrative discrimination by colleges and universities against lesbian, gay, and bisexual student groups as well as "out" lesbian and gay professors.
- The National Gay and Lesbian Task Force reports that 75 percent of the respondents to a national survey had "been verbally harassed because of their sexuality."
- In 1997, the University of Minnesota received the largest gift donated to a U.S. college to help gay students. Alumnus Steven Schochet announced plans to donate half a million dollars. When he was a student at Minnesota in the 1950s and the administration discovered he was gay, he was forced to seek counseling and have regular meetings with the dean. "Things are better there now," he says. "I just want to do my part."[20]
- It was not until 1973 that the American Psychiatric Association recommended unanimously to remove homosexuality from its list of mental disorders. Only in 1980 did *The Diagnostic and Statistical Manual of Mental Disorders* (3rd ed.) reflect this new awareness.

WHAT YOU CAN DO

- Support lesbian, gay, and bisexual students. Many campuses have student groups geared to gay issues, both curricular and social. Consider joining one. If a student group does not already exist, consider forming one. Encourage both heterosexuals and homosexuals to join.
- Ensure that the student union provides space for lesbian and gay students to hold meetings and that student speakers' forum invites speakers on lesbian, gay, and bisexual issues.
- If you are heterosexual, do not assume everyone else is. Pay attention to the language you use and to the assumptions it contains. Don't automatically assume, for example, that other women will want to bring their boyfriends to a social event. Instead, ask them to bring their partners or significant others.
- If you are heterosexual, do not tell homosexual jokes or use terms like "queer," "fag," "lesbo," or "dyke" as slurs. When people around you do, speak up and explain why you believe such terms are wrong. Make people aware of the climate these jokes contribute to and the harm they can cause.
- Bring issues to the surface. Problems can't be solved if we don't talk about them. Work to educate the student body on gay and lesbian issues and on the harm that homophobia does to us all. Encourage the administration to include sexual orientation in the diversity awareness programs it presents

during freshman orientation. Antihomophobia workshops help counter stereotypes and improve the campus climate for lesbians and gays.

- ☒ Bring speakers and entertainers to campus. Many of the organizations listed at the end of this chapter have speakers' bureaus. Local lesbian groups can also make recommendations.

- ☒ Enlist the assistance of top-level administrators and respected faculty members in heightening campus awareness. The 1993 report "Making Colleges and Universities Safe for Gay and Lesbian Students," issued in Massachusetts by the Governor's Commission on Gay and Lesbian Youth, offers concrete suggestions for administrative policies and procedures.

- ☒ Check to see if your college includes "sexual orientation" in its student conduct code, sexual harassment policy, and affirmative action statements. All institutions have policies stating that they do not discriminate on the basis of age, race, gender, and religion, but not all include sexual orientation. This is an important step toward reporting and stopping problems surrounding sexual orientation and homophobic violence and harassment.

- ☒ Check to see if your administration offers spousal benefits to gay or lesbian partners of employees. If it doesn't, campaign for a change in the existing rules.

- ☒ Lobby to have a coordinator appointed, if your school's administration doesn't already have one, to deal with lesbian, gay, and bisexual equity. The coordinator could be in charge of organizing workshops, seminars, and outreach programs for faculty, staff, administrators, and students.

- ☒ Encourage faculty to implement courses and incorporate homosexuality into the curriculum. Play your part in educating faculty when they make homophobic statements in class or their courses are overly heterocentric. Discuss your concerns with them after class or during office hours. Most faculty will respond to this approach.

- ☒ Encourage the administration to provide faculty workshops and other incentives to help faculty to implement this aspect of diversity in their courses.

- ☒ If you think you are considering coming out, consult the Resources section at the end of this chapter for organizations and publications that can help you. OUTRIGHT (the Portland, Maine, Alliance of Lesbian and Gay Youth) publishes a pamphlet called "I Think I Might Be a Lesbian . . . Now What Do I Do?" Write the Campaign to End Homophobia, PO Box 819, Cambridge, MA 02139 for a copy.

- ☒ If you are lesbian or bisexual, begin your fight against internalized homophobia by examining how it has affected you. Keep a journal of your feelings and experiences. (Be sure, at some point, to make a list of the positive things about being lesbian or bi.) Writing will help you clarify your thoughts.

☒ If you need people to talk to, join a student group that deals with lesbian and gay issues. Most campuses have at least one. If your campus does not, consider organizing a group with some of your friends to talk about the issues that concern you. For personal, professional guidance visit the campus counseling center or ask for a referral to a therapist who regularly counsels lesbians. You can also call a hot line (listed under Organizations).

☒ If you want help thinking of ways to respond to other students' insensitive remarks or nosy questions, get a copy of Ellen Orleans's *Who Cares If It's a Choice? Snappy Answers to 101 Nosy, Intrusive & Highly Personal Questions About Lesbians & Gays.*

RESOURCES

Books

Balka, Christie, and Andy Rose (eds.). 1989. *Twice Blessed: On Being Lesbian or Gay and Jewish.* Boston: Beacon.

Blumenfeld, Warren J. (ed.). 1992. *Homophobia: How We All Pay the Price.* Boston: Beacon.

Borhek, Mary. 1983. *Coming Out to Parents.* New York: Pilgrim.

Boykin, Keith. 1996. *One More River to Cross: Black and Gay in America.* New York: Anchor.

Duberman, Martin, et al. (eds.). 1990. *Hidden from History: Reclaiming the Gay and Lesbian Past.* New York: Penguin.

Due, Linnea. 1996. *Joining the Tribe: Growing Up Gay and Lesbian in the 1990's.* New York: Anchor.

Evans, Nancy J., and Vernon Wall (eds.). 1991. *Beyond Tolerance: Gays, Lesbians and Bisexuals on Campus.* Alexandria, Va.: American College Personnel Association.

Fahy, Una. 1995. *How to Make the World a Better Place for Gays and Lesbians.* New York: Warner.

Garber, Linda (ed.). 1993. *Lesbian Sources.* New York: Garland.

George, Susan. 1993. *Women and Bisexuality.* London: Scarlet.

Hutchins, Loraine, and Lani Kaahumanu (eds.). 1991. *Bi Any Other Name: Bisexual People Speak Out.* Boston: Alyson.

Katz, Jonathan N. 1992. *Gay American History: Lesbians and Gay Men in the USA.* New York: Meridian.

Kirk, Marshall, and Hunter Madsen. 1989. *After the Ball: How America Will Conquer Its Hatred of Gays in the '90s.* New York: Doubleday.

Lobel, Kerry (ed.). 1986. *Naming the Violence: Speaking Out About Lesbian Violence.* Seattle: Seal.

Luczak, Rayond (ed.). 1993. *Eyes of Desire: A Deaf Gay and Lesbian Reader.* Boston: Alyson.

Money, John. 1995. *Gay, Straight, and In-Between: The Sexology of Erotic Attraction.* New York: Oxford University Press.

Moraga, Cherríe and Gloria Anzaldúa (eds.). 1983. *This Bridge Called My Back: Writings by Radical Women of Color.* 2nd ed. New York: Kitchen Table/Women of Color.

Orleans, Ellen. 1994. *Who Cares If It's a Choice? Snappy Answers to 101 Nosy, Intrusive & Highly Personal Questions About Lesbians & Gays.* Bala Cynwyd, Penn.: Laugh Lines.

Pharr, Susan. 1988. *Homophobia: A Weapon of Sexism.* Little Rock, Ark.: Chardon.

Pratt, Minnie Bruce. 1995. *S/He.* Ithaca, N.Y.: Firebrand.

Ramos, Juanita (ed.). 1994. *Compañeras: Latina Lesbians, an Anthology.* New York: Routledge.

Roscoe, Will (ed.). 1988. *Living the Spirit: A Gay American Indian Anthology.* New York: St. Martin's.

Skidway, Caroline, et al. 1988. *The Lesbian in Front of the Classroom.* Herbook, PO Box 7467, Santa Cruz, CA 95061.

Smith, Barbara (ed.). 1983. *Home Girls.* Latham, N.Y.: Kitchen Table/Women of Color.

Thompson, Mark (ed.). 1994. *Long Road to Freedom: The Advocate History of the Gay and Lesbian Movement.* New York: St. Martin's.

Trujillo, Carla (ed.). 1991. *Chicana Lesbians: The Girls Our Mothers Warned Us About.* Berkeley: Third Woman.

Vaid, Urashi. 1996. *Virtual Equality: The Mainstreaming of Gay and Lesbian Liberation.* New York: Anchor.

Weinberg, Martin, et al. 1995. *Dual Attraction: Understanding Bisexuality.* New York: Oxford University Press.

Weise, Elizabeth Reba (ed.). 1992. *Closer to Home: Bisexuality and Feminism.* Seattle: Seal.

White, Mel. 1995. *Stranger at the Gate: To Be Gay & Christian in America.* New York: Simon & Schuster.

Wolfe, Susan, and Julia Penelope. 1993. *Sexual Practice, Textual Theory.* Cambridge, Mass.: Blackwell.

Young, Ian. 1995. *Stonewall Experiment: Gay Psychohistory.* New York: Cassell PLC.

Videos

Embracing Our Sexuality. This forty-five-minute video listens to nine women—ranging in age from twenty-one to seventy-one and from diverse racial backgrounds and sexual orientations—talk about sex. Made by Jennifer Campion, Bianca Cody Murphy, and Betsy Wisch, it is good for prompting discussion and creating empathy and acceptance. New Day Films, Department WM, 22–D Hollywood Avenue, Hohokus, NJ 07423. Phone: (201) 652–6570.

Forbidden Love: The Unashamed Stories of Lesbian Lives. Ten women talk about lesbian sexuality and survival in the 1950s and 1960s. Their stories are interwoven with archival photographs, tabloid headlines, film clips, and book covers from lesbian pulp fiction to bring this period of lesbian history alive in a compelling and humorous way. This eighty-five-minute video was made by Aerlyn Weissman and Lynne Fernie. Women Make Movies, 462 Broadway, Suite 500–E, New York, NY 10013. Phone: (212) 925–0606.

Honored by the Moon. In this fifteen-minute video by Mona Smith, Native American lesbians and gay men speak about their unique historical and spiritual role. Interviews with activists and personal testimony show the positive and painful experiences of being Native American and homosexual. Women Make Movies, 462 Broadway, Suite 500–E, New York, NY 10013. Phone: (212) 925–0606.

L Is for the Way You Look. This twenty-four-minute, often entertaining video by Jean Carlomusto examines lesbian history and the women who have served as role models and objects of desire for young lesbians. It also discusses how media images of lesbians affect the construction of identity, and how lesbians have been written in and out of history. Women Make Movies, 462 Broadway, Suite 500–E, New York, NY 10013. Phone: (212) 925–0606.

One Nation Under God. Filmmakers Teodoro Maniaci and Francine Rzeznik examine who is asking lesbians and gay men to change their sexual orientation and why. This film looks at the sometimes comic attempts to "cure" homosexuality through shock therapy, beauty makeovers for lesbians, and Homosexuals Anonymous. For information, contact P.O.V., PO Box 750, Old Chelsea Station, New York, NY 10113.

Out for a Change: Addressing Homophobia in Women's Sports. This twenty-eight-minute video by Dee Mosbacher, a San Francisco psychologist and filmmaker, examines homophobia in women's sports. It includes a leader's guide with discussion questions and bibliography. University of California Center for Media, 2000 Center Street, 4th Floor, Berkeley, CA 94704. Phone: (510) 642–0460.

Out: Stories of Lesbian and Gay Youth. This forty-three-minute video by David Adkin and the National Film Board of Canada tells the compelling personal stories of lesbian and gay youth from varied racial backgrounds. Faced with social isolation and the threat of violence, they are at high risk for problems like dropping out of school, living on the streets, and abusing drugs, yet they make it through and are getting on with their lives. The video also gives voice to supportive adults—parents and counselors. Winner of a Gold Apple at the National Educational Film Festival in 1996. Filmaker's Library, 124 East 40th Street, New York, NY 10016. Phone: (212) 808–4980 or (514) 283–9256.

Sex and Selfhood: New Issues for Men of Conscience. A series of four twenty-minute videos made by author John Stoltenberg (*The End of Manhood: A Book for Men of Conscience*; see Resources, chapter 1) to challenge myths of manhood; the topics include sexual objectification, male bonding, homophobia, and pornography. Aimed primarily at men, Stoltenberg's critique offers a valuable analysis of the consequences of our culture's definition of masculinity. According to Gloria Steinem, "He knows inside every male human being, there is a whole person wanting to be free." Kundschier/Manthey Video Design, 614 East Grant Street, Minneapolis, MN 55404. Phone: (612) 333–7414.

Speaking for Ourselves: Portraits of Gay and Lesbian Youths. Video by Diversity Productions. Inter-Media Inc., 1300 Dexter North, Seattle, WA 98109. Phone: (800) 553–8336.

Thank God I'm a Lesbian. This fifty-five-minute film by Laurie Colbert and Dominique Cardona is an uplifting and entertaining documentary about the diversity of lesbian identities. Women speak frankly and articulately about a wide variety of issues: coming out, racism, bisexuality, the evolution of the feminist and lesbian movements, outing, and compulsory heterosexuality. Women Make Movies, 462 Broadway, Suite 500–E, New York, NY 10013. Phone: (212) 925–0606.

Organizations

American Civil Liberties Union, Lesbian and Gay Rights Project, 132 West 43rd Street, New York, NY 10036. Phone: (212) 944–9800, ext. 545. An organization that defends lesbian and gay rights through direct litigation and as cocounsel with other organizations. It has published *The Rights of Gay People: An American Civil Liberties Union Handbook.*

Center for Lesbian and Gay Studies (CLAGS), City University of New York Graduate Center, 33 West 42nd Street, New York, NY 10036. Phone: (212) 642–2924. The Center promotes lesbian and gay studies at the university level, encouraging the development of scholarship, courses, and degree programs. It maintains a speakers' bureau and a lesbian and gay resource collection at the Mina Rees Library at The Graduate School, CUNY. The Center also awards research grants and scholarships.

Gay and Lesbian Alliance Against Defamation (GLAAD), 150 West 26th Street, Suite 503, New York, NY 10001. Phone: (212) 807–1700. It promotes accurate images of lesbians and gays in the media. It also works to identify and respond to public expressions of homophobia and see that civil rights battles fought by gays receive national media attention. It operates PhoneTree, through which members can telephone television and radio stations to protest media defamation and bigotry. It publishes brochures and a quarterly newsletter, *Images.*

International Gay and Lesbian Human Rights Commission, 520 Castro Street, San Francisco, CA 94114. Phone: (800) 462–6654. The Commission monitors, documents, and mobilizes responses to human rights violations against lesbians, gays, bisexuals, and people with HIV and AIDS worldwide. It offers educational presentations and internships and organizes speaking tours of foreign-born activists. Publishes the newsletter *Outspoken* and the monthly *Emergency Response Network* as well as human rights reports. Consult its Web site (www.ilghrc.org) for further information.

Lesbian Switchboard, 208 West 13th Street, New York, NY 10011. Phone: (212) 741–2610. This is an all-woman volunteer telephone service that provides information, referrals, and crisis counseling.

National Center for Lesbian Rights (NCLR), 870 Market Street, Suite 570, San Francisco, CA 94102. The Center is a public interest law firm specializing in sexual orientation discrimination cases, particularly those involving lesbians. It provides legal counseling and publishes the *NCLR Newsletter* (in English and Spanish) and other works such as *A Lesbian and Gay Parents' Legal Guide to Child Custody*.

National Coming Out Day (NCOD), PO Box 34640, Washington, DC 20043–4640. Phone: (800) 866–6263. The organization works to increase the lesbian and gay community's visibility and demonstrate its diversity. It coordinates National Coming Out Day on October 11—an annual event encouraging lesbians and gays to come out to friends, family, and co-workers. Also operates a speakers' bureau. It is affiliated with the Human Rights Campaign Fund.

National Gay and Lesbian Task Force (NGLTF), 2320 17th Street NW, Washington, DC 20009. Phone: (202) 332–6483. This is the oldest national lesbian and gay civil rights advocacy organization. It works for such rights through lobbying, education, and direct action. It also monitors antigay bias on campus and provides advice.

Parents, Families, and Friends of Lesbians and Gays (PFLAG), 1001 14th Street NW, Suite 1030, Washington, DC 20005. Phone: (202) 638–4200. PFLAG is a national non-profit support, education, and advocacy group for lesbians, bisexuals, and gays and their families and friends. It maintains a speakers' bureau and publishes booklets, including "Coming Out to Your Parents."

CHAPTER 6

Racism in the

Colorblind Academy

Someone will ask me where I'm from and I'll say "San Francisco."
They will say, "No, where are you really from?" People of European
descent are not asked to trace their backgrounds. Another stereotype
is that Asian Americans excel in math and science, which do not rely
on language. Many do excel in these subjects, but there are numerous
others pursuing liberal arts degrees.

—Lareina Yee, Barnard College[1]

I think white people think education is good, but Indian people often
have a different view. I know . . . that education provides jobs and skills.
It's true. That's why I'm here. But a lot of these kids [Native American
students], their parents, they see education as something that draws
students away from who they are. And then there's the obstacles.
There's no money. . . . You can't figure out the papers and you wind up
thinking you're dumb. So you leave.

—Native American student[2]

"STUDENTS OF COLOR" is a broad category, encompassing diverse backgrounds and experiences. Native Americans have many tribal affiliations. Some
have grown up on reservations, speak a tribal language, and have strong ties to

Indian traditions, while other students do not. Latinas include women from many different cultural backgrounds.[3] Asian students may be Hindu, Muslim, Buddhist, or Christian, and often don't define themselves as students of color. African-American students come from different parts of the country and different socioeconomic backgrounds, their families may trace their ancestry to the Caribbean or Africa. Sometimes students whose families come originally from India and Pakistan are also considered "students of color," as are many interracial and international students. The only thing uniting everyone is the belief that a higher education will open doors of opportunity.

Although the student population of most colleges and universities is predominantly white, there are important regional differences as well as more than a hundred historically black colleges and about thirty tribal colleges. The most ethnically diverse schools are usually found in urban areas. At New York University, for example, 16 percent of undergraduates are African Americans, Latinos, and Native Americans, and another 27 percent are Asian. At Occidental College in Los Angeles, the numbers are reversed, with 27 percent African-American, Latino, and Native American students and 17 percent Asians.

As you might expect, the college experience can vary enormously from one school to the next. If you are African-American and attend a small, historically black college in the South, you are bound to have a very different experience from someone attending a predominantly white school in the Midwest or a large, ethnically diverse university in the Northeast. Nationally, few schools have a student body that is more than 10 percent African American; the average enrollment is about 5 percent.[4] After graduating from the University of Texas–Pan American University, which was about 80 percent Latino, it was a shock for Norma Cantu—who later became head of the U.S. Department of Education's Office for Civil Rights—to go to Harvard Law School as one of only thirteen Latinos in an entering class of five hundred.[5]

If you are a student of color at a college or university with few others, you are likely to feel conspicuous and perhaps isolated, especially at first and especially if you don't easily fit into any one group. A student from the West Indies reported feeling estranged from both black and white students: "White students ignore me because all they see is my blackness. They do not care to know me as a person, as a woman. For other blacks I am isolated because I am West Indian. I am culturally different."[6] If you have parents from different racial or ethnic backgrounds, you may resist being classified by others on the basis of only one part of your heritage. Sometimes class differences also intrude. Students of color from a poor part of the inner city may find it difficult to relate to those from affluent suburbs, and vice versa. And unless you have had many white friends in the past, you may also find assimilating into the dominant white student culture on campus stressful. Many students of color, in their eagerness to fit in, end up sacrificing some of their own traditions and ways of doing things. If you are a student of color, one of the biggest challenges you may face is being true to yourself—knowing and remaining who you are.

There is much greater sensitivity to diversity on college campuses today, and generally harmonious relationships between students of different backgrounds. You may not experience any overt racism during your college years; most students arrive on campus with a positive attitude, not expecting to find racism. Colleges are meant to be colorblind, yet racism lingers in many subtle forms. A recent survey of 550 student newspaper editors found that while over half characterized race relations on their campuses as "excellent" or "good," just under half thought they were only "fair" or "poor."[7] According to research by John Bunzel, former president of San Jose State University and author of *Race Relations on Campus: Stanford Students Speak*, although nearly two-thirds of Stanford's seniors believed that "most people on campus are fair to all racial and ethnic groups," many felt racially alienated by the time they graduated.

As college campuses become more diverse, the likelihood of some inter-group conflict—at least in the beginning—increases. Howard Ehrlich, who tracked "ethnoviolence" on college campuses for many years as director of Towson State University's Center for the Applied Study of Ethno-violence, makes the following analogy: "If you have more cars, you'll have more auto theft. If you have more potential targets of hostility, they'll be used."[8] Surveys conducted by the Center indicate that between 25 and 80 percent of students of color, depending on the school they attend, are exposed to at least one racial incident each year. Women of color are also exposed to sexism. Incidents can occur at small colleges and large universities; at private, public, and church-run institutions; and in every part of the country. Although they often reflect the thoughtlessness or immature behavior of a small number of students on campus, they do reveal that a racial divide still exists in American society. Being discriminated against or belittled because of your race/ethnicity is painful and may even prompt you to ask: "Is this really *my* campus?"

Most experts agree that two underlying reasons for the persistence of racial stereotyping and antagonism are people's lack of accurate information about other groups and their lack of opportunities to work together toward positive goals. College provides a setting in which both these factors are minimized. Unless you are attending a school with very little racial diversity, you have the opportunity not only to learn about other groups' histories, cultures, and issues through your courses but also to socialize and work with students from other backgrounds toward mutual goals—winning a tournament, organizing a fund-raising event, getting out a newsletter, and, ultimately, graduating. Many students, however, fail to make the effort to know others who are different from themselves. Based on a survey of sixteen hundred first-year students, Bowling Green State University's Director of Student Affairs concluded that "most [white] students don't agree with negative stereotypes of minorities, but they don't disagree. . . . I'm not sure they intend in any way to harm anyone, but most don't do anything to break down barriers. They don't feel they've done anything for which *they* need to make up."[9] Health and Human Services Secretary Donna Shalala, former chancellor of the University of Wisconsin, agrees: "I'm not sure I'd use a negative term like 'indifference' to describe them [white students]. What I ran into here was enormous inexperience [with members of other groups]."[10]

If you are a student of color or an international student attending a school where there are few others, you may feel emotionally drained at times. Some black students feel that they are automatically presumed wrong, guilty, or dishonest because of their skin color. African-American students have told me that they always feel on guard or that they have to explain themselves to white students, faculty, and administrators. One student said he sometimes feels his sole purpose for being on campus is to "educate the white folks." Other issues also create stress. Some students who come from families with modest incomes feel guilty for not being able to contribute to family income while they are in school and this places added pressure on them to do well. If life on campus differs dramatically from life at home, the adjustment can be stressful, no matter how stimulating or exciting college is. Some students are pressured by their parents to choose courses and career paths they have little interest in. Many Indian students, for example, become premeds due to parental pressure.

Students of Indian background and other Asian cultures may feel shut off from some aspects of campus social life. Many have parents who do not approve of dating, especially with students from other ethnic backgrounds. If they do date, they usually hide the fact and then must live with the stress of their deception. Some Indian and Chinese women students marry partners their parents have chosen for them while they are still attending college. (Similarly, Latinas may face the prospect of giving up their independence and returning to their parents' home after graduation to await marriage.) Other students' own cultural and religious beliefs may make blending in difficult. An Iranian student, a popular and vocal feminist during her first two years on campus, adopted modest Muslim dress and withdrew from many of her previous activities and friendships as she learned more about her background and religion.

Having friends from your own background and a place on campus where you can feel completely comfortable is important for everyone. This is why students of color, biracial students, and foreign students often organize their own student groups, join special-interest or theme houses, and lobby the administration for multicultural centers and group housing. For African-American students, historically black colleges have provided residential and social environments that are free from racism—"but not necessarily from sexism."[11] Within some universities—whether historically black colleges or predominantly white schools—black sororities are an important social outlet for African-American women.

Stereotyping and Exclusion

Dealing with stereotypes is a fact of life for many people: all Asians are good at science and math; all African Americans excel at sports; all women are bad drivers. Separate stereotypes exist for some women of color. Asian women are "passive." Latinas are "sexpots." African-American women are domineering "bitches." If you speak with an accent, you have probably run into people who assume that you don't fully understand English or that you are not very bright. Many students of color report receiving looks of disbelief when they make an intelligent comment in class. Older faculty—especially in the sciences and engineering—may doubt your academic ability both because of your gender and because of assumptions they make about your background (e.g., no books in the home) based on your ethnicity. "My professor in biology did not know how to treat me," claimed one African-American student. "He seemed surprised when I told him I wanted to be a doctor." Some faculty may also misinterpret behavior which reflects cultural differences, such as the respectful silence or lack of eye contact of some Latinas and Asian women as a lack of interest or independent thought.

Stereotyping also occurs when an individual is treated as a spokesperson for an entire ethnic group. If you are asked for the African-American, Asian, Latino, or Native American point of view or are called on in class to comment only when a "minority" issue is being discussed, the message is sent—whether intended or not—that you are seen not as an individual but as a member of a group. White students, in contrast, are seldom asked to speak for anything or anyone other than themselves. When race or ethnicity are only mentioned during classroom discussions of poverty, crime, and family disorganization, it is natural to feel annoyed. If you visit a faculty member for help and end up being quizzed about your life back home instead, you may begin to feel like a minority specimen rather than an individual seeking help, even though this may be a sincere attempt to get to know you.

Today, students are much more enlightened about racial, ethnic, and other differences than they were a generation ago. Many students have friends from other backgrounds, and few students question any student's right to be on campus. Whether you are a white student or a student of color, however, you are bound to meet a few students, especially at elite schools, who assume that all students of color are only on campus because of their skin color or Spanish surname.[12] The reality is that elite private colleges and public universities take many criteria besides racial or ethnic background into consideration when making admissions decisions. These include an individual student's high school grades, class standing, and test scores, as well as muscial or artistic talent, athletic ability, and personality, as revealed in her admission essay and interview. Linda Wightman studied thousands of law school applicants, comparing those who were admitted solely on the basis of grades and Law School Admission Test (LSAT) scores with those who were admitted partially because of their ethnic background. She found that a high percentage of the latter went on to successfully pass the bar, indicating that they were equally capable of doing graduate work.[13] One of the largest affirmative action programs on many campuses is seldom acknowledged. The children of alumni and alumnae, known as "legacies," often receive preference even when they have lower average SAT scores than the rest of the applicant pool.[14]

Another misconception held by some white students is that students of color receive an unfair amount of financial aid. In fact, students from wealthy homes—regardless of race—are still ten times as likely to graduate from college as students from families with modest incomes.[15] One recent study found that African-American graduate students had received significantly less financial support from universities and the federal government than had white students and international students doing graduate work.[16] Nationally, 85 percent of all college students need some kind of financial aid, which comes in the form of loans, grants, work study, or a combination of the three. A third of all first-year students list financial assistance as having been a top factor in their selection of a college.[17]

Women's studies classes are generally open classrooms where students are encouraged to speak and different voices are heard. But even here students of color may sometimes feel excluded. If most students in the class are white, if the course content contains little discussion of how racism combines with sexism to affect men's and women's lives, if there are only one or two assigned readings by women of color, if some groups are excluded completely, it would be difficult for students of color not to feel slighted. One Asian student described her feelings this way:

> I knew "women of color" was supposed to include Asian American women, but I could not find any in the class readings. Were there no Asian American feminists? Were there none who could write English? . . . Were we Asian American students in the class the first to think about feminism? A class about women, I thought, was a class about me, so I looked for myself everywhere and found nothing. . . . My emerging

identification as a woman of color was displaced through the writings of black and Chicana women, and I had to read myself, create my politics, through theirs; even now, to a certain extent, I feel more familiar with their issues than those of Asian American women.[18]

Another issue that sometimes emerges both in women's studies classes and on campus in general is the skepticism with which some women of color regard feminism. As discussed in chapter 1, many African-American women feel uncomfortable with feminism because they believe the women's movement has, until recently, slighted their input and ignored their concerns. Many student feel torn: Should they regard gender or race/ethnicity as the most important factor in their lives? This is one reason historically black colleges have been slow to develop women's studies courses; in 1990 only 5 of 116 black colleges offered them.[19] Sometimes white students who are feminists react negatively when black women place race before gender and treat racism as a more serious issue than sexism. It is unreasonable, of course, for anyone to expect someone else to "prioritize their pain," in the words of Mary O'Neal, director of Affirmative Action at Southern Connecticut State University.

Outside the classroom, stereotypes and the issue of group loyalty often lead to the misinterpretation of each other's behavior and motives. This happens both between groups and within them. If few students of color attend a particular college event, and if they always sit together in the dining hall, other students may label them "separatists," even though these white students usually sit together, and few attend minority-sponsored events. If white students question the wisdom of an event being planned by students of color, they risk being treated as outsiders who have no right to speak, or worse, being labeled as "racists."

Students of color are not immune to stereotypes and misunderstandings caused by cultural differences. Latino students sometimes resent African-American students for assertively making their agenda known on campus while their own issues seem submerged. African-American students, on the other hand, are likely to feel frustrated when Latinos do not communicate or articulate their issues forcefully. Among Latinos, cultural differences separate Puerto Ricans from Dominicans from Mexican Americans, making consensus difficult.

Relationships between college roommates are often easily strained; living in close quarters with someone who has different sleep and study patterns, who likes music you hate, who has different ideas about neatness or nudity, or who constantly seems to have her boyfriend over can cause even old friends to part company. When students come from very different backgrounds, there is even more potential for annoyance, hurt feelings, and miscommunication. Some white students, for example, may avoid talking openly about subjects they think are racially or culturally sensitive, which can be interpreted as disinterest or aloofness by students of color. Other students err in the opposite direction, bringing up the topic of race or ethnicity so often in a misguided attempt to show that they are open-minded that it is irritating, if not insulting, to the student of color.

Robert Blauner believes that African Americans and whites basically talk past each other because they define the term "racism" differently.[20] Racism in the United States, he points out, once meant a belief in the superiority of whites based on the assumed inferiority of blacks. In the 1960s, however, academics, civil rights leaders, and most African Americans began to embrace a broader definition of the word, one that included the concept of "institutional racism"—the idea that social structures, not just the actions of individuals, create and maintain racial segregation, disadvantage, and a social atmosphere that makes people of color feel uncomfortable and unwanted. This expanded definition of racism makes sense to students of color who live the experience, yet most white students cling to a narrower definition that limits racism to a belief in racial superiority—a belief very few hold—and to overt, individual acts.

According to research by psychologist Charles Judd and his associates, most white students "have been socialized to believe that it is *wrong* to make distinctions on the basis of skin color and that members of ethnic minorities as a whole are no different from the majority white population [emphasis added]."[21] Most white students also grew up in fairly segregated environments in which this belief was rarely challenged. In contrast, students of color have been socialized to respect and value their ethnic heritage and to realize that race and ethnicity do make a difference. Many have had extensive contact with whites and have learned from personal experience that interethnic relations are still far from smooth in American society. To them, race and ethnicity are important group distinctions.

These differences in socialization experiences and ideas about racism and group distinctions help explain why an African-American student was offended when her white friend told her, "It's easy for me to be friends with you because I can forget you're black and just remember you're you." Meant as a compliment, this remark rankled. "At the time I couldn't figure out exactly why that bothered me, but it sure did! Later I realized it bothered me because I couldn't see why she had to 'forget' I was black because I *am.* . . . I see no reason to transcend my African-American identity. It is a key part of who I am and something I am *proud* of—not something I wish to be diminished."[22]

This also explains why many white students are either confused or annoyed by African-American fraternities, Latino cultural houses, and the like, which separate students on the basis of color and ethnicity. They have been taught that it is wrong to make distinctions on the basis of skin color, and that segregation is wrong. (Some majority students also regard such organizations and their budgets and facilities as unfair privileges.)

Most students of color, in contrast, take pride in their ethnicity and may see white students' failure to acknowledge and respect ethnic differences as a form of racial prejudice. White students are unlikely to see the situation this way, although fully 84 percent of all entering college students acknowledge racial discrimination to be a problem in America.[23] Many white students find the idea or knowledge that racism still exists threatening because they "find it difficult to differentiate between the charge that a social structure or institution is racist and the accusation that they, as participants in that structure, are *personally* racist [emphasis added]."[24]

To address racism and diversity on campus, most colleges and universities have introduced changes to their curricula. Paula Rothenberg identifies three types of diversity study programs that have been instituted on American campuses.[25] The first—"race, class and gender studies"—sets out to examine how racism, sexism, class privilege, and heterosexism have affected different groups in society, both historically and at present. Such programs are interested in analyzing different systems of oppression and in contrasting them to discrimination and prejudice. The second—"multicultural studies"—examines cultural diversity, celebrates the cultures of previously marginalized people, and adopts a critical perspective on the social construction of knowledge. A third type of diversity study is usually referred to as "global studies," or as "internationalizing the curriculum." Such programs seek to educate students about the history and culture of groups around the world, without necessarily adopting the kind of critical and analytical perspectives found in the race, class, and gender studies or multicultural studies (or anthropology, for that matter).

As Rothenberg points out, multiculturalism has frequently been attacked as "political" or "ideological," been trivialized as "fluff," or so diluted in order to fend off criticism, that on some campuses it is little more than a "tacos and egg-rolls" or "diversity as variety" program. Most critics of multiculturalism seem unfamiliar with what its goals really are, namely, "exposing students to critical perspectives on the past and present and teaching them to rethink basic categories of perception and analysis, to operate within multiple frameworks of analysis and metaphor, to examine alternative paradigms and models. . . ."[26]

"This can be a fascinating journey for students," note Connie Chan and Mary Jane Treacy. "However, it also leads to a painful examination of American history as conquest, exposes the legal disenfranchisement of non-European groups, and addresses the structural inequalities maintained in current public policies. . . . [It challenges] some of the fundamental beliefs of our society: the existence of a meritocracy, the expectation that social justice applies to all citizens equally, and the emphasis on the individual as somehow separate from, and uninfluenced by society, among others."[27] Anything so challenging to the prevailing ideology and our past understanding of history is bound to be resisted by many students and to come under fire in society at large.

Since the mid-1980s, multiculturalism on campus has acquired many detractors on the political right, who dismiss it as mere "political correctness" or as pandering to special interests. Nancy Baker Jones has referred to the many editorials, articles, and books attacking multiculturalism as the "assault literature," pointing out that the so-called political correctness "debate" is not a debate at all, since there is no exchange of views going on.[28] Academic programs like Africana studies, Latin American studies, and women's studies, which have broadened the curriculum to include the history, achievements, and perspectives of women and people of color, have made people in academic life critically rethink the past and have generated important new research questions. According to Edward Said, professor of English and comparative literature at Columbia University, this new information and questioning has resulted in major intellectual advances in the humanities amounting to "a Copernican revolution in all traditional fields of inquiry."[29]

On campus, facilities like theme housing and multicultural centers provide students of color with places to meet and share ideas and experiences; special deans and administrative offices provide institutional support. To expect students of color not to want to group together on the basis of common background and interests would be to hold colleges up to an unrealistically high standard of racial and ethnic integration—"an idealistic vision where everyone is singing 'Kumbaya,'" as a woman of color at Occidental College humorously observed.[30]

Nevertheless, such intiatives often bring controversy. When nine white students were assigned rooms through Wesleyan University's random housing lottery in Malcolm X House, an African-American theme house, many black students protested, until the administration arranged a room swap for the white students with other black students living elsewhere on campus.[31] At the University of North Carolina, Chapel Hill, a proposal to build a privately funded African-American cultural center was initially opposed by UNC's chancellor, who believed it would further separate black and white students on campus. Most students of color disagreed with his decision, and nearly three hundred students staged a demonstration in front of his home. After a special committee appointed by the chancellor ended up approving the idea of a separate cultural center, a new controversy erupted over how centrally located it should be on campus.[32]

Speech codes aimed at eliminating hate speech are favored by most students.[33] They have nevertheless been challenged. In California, conservative legislators passed the Leonard Law, explicitly forbidding high schools and universities to restrict students' rights to free speech. Soon after its adoption in 1993, the T-shirt Incident at the University of California, Riverside, put the law to the test. It began when the Phi Kappa Sigma fraternity threw a "South of the Border Fiesta" during rush week and advertised the event with T-shirts depicting a sombrero-wearing Mexican and bare-chested Indian carrying a six-pack of beer and bottles of liquor. The campus chapter of Movimiento Estudiantil Chicano de Aztlan (MECdA) objected to the stereotyping. The university agreed. Its judiciary committee ordered the T-shirts destroyed, and the interfraternity council decreed that each member of the fraternity must attend multicultural awareness seminars and perform sixteen hours of community service in a Chicano or other Latino neighborhood. The fraternity also formally apologized to MECdA, whose members, nevertheless, requested even stronger university action. The university dissolved the fraternity's chapter for three years, prompting it to threaten to sue under the Leonard Law. The fraternity argued that its members' rights to free speech had been curtailed and pointed out that the T-shirt had been designed by two of its Hispanic members and that its chapter was one-third Hispanic and more ethnically diverse than the UC Riverside campus as a whole. Forced to look at its disciplinary actions in the context of "free speech" (and faced with the prospect of legal fees and publicity), the university settled out of court. These examples show how complicated interethnic and race relations on campus can be.

There are encouraging signs too. Colleges and universities are working hard to eliminate racism on campus, and at some schools, students of color report experiencing little or no racism. But as one black administrator told me, "We are so busy making nice, that we hide the issues [surrounding racism]. Then when something happens, students are not well equipped to handle it. It's an environment issue—students of color are not being well prepared." In another positive note, a recent survey of first-year students found that 62 percent said they "frequently" socialized with someone from another racial or ethnic group.[34] Researchers at the Universities of Michigan and Arizona found that students of color are more likely than white students to dine with, date, and study with students from other racial and ethnic backgrounds. About half the African-American students, for example, reported "frequently" dining with and studying with someone from a different ethnic background, while only 20 percent of white students did. If you are a student of color, you probably do things and go places with white friends more often than they express interest in or attend minority-sponsored events. Typically there are more majority-sponsored activities to attend, but differences in preferred activities also exist.

Despite the many friendships and activities that crosscut different groups of students, pressures also exist among students of color to demonstrate loyalty and solidarity with students from their own racial or ethnic backgrounds. Some African-American students report feeling pressured by others to "represent" or "act black" if they spend too much time with white friends. They may be called "oreos"—black on the outside but white on the inside. Latinos sometimes accuse each other of being "coconuts." A small number of students of color can make white students who attend their events feel unwelcome. Several white women who went to a black fraternity dance at Union College, for example, described during a class discussion the next day being stared and laughed at and told to "Get off the floor, honkies." When speakers and entertainers like Louis Farrakhan, Afrocentrist Leonard Jeffries, and rapper Sister Souljah are invited to campus by student organizations, segments of the white student body who consider them anti-Semitic or antiwhite will be outraged in the same way that many African-American students are outraged when former Ku Klux Klansman David Duke or conservative scholars like Dinesh D'Souza and Charles Murray are invited to speak.

Issues for Women of Color

Interracial dating is one of the most sensitive issues facing women of color on campus. It is particularly sensitive for African-American women, because it usually involves black men dating white women. Within the African-American community, what is often called a color complex—a historical preference for light skin and other white physical attributes—is seldom openly discussed; even filmmaker Spike Lee has encountered criticism when he has dealt with the issue in films like *Jungle Fever.*

Feelings about interracial dating are complex. It is not just an issue of a black student not demonstrating group loyalty or racial pride. Many black women believe that interracial dating shows that black men have accepted Eurocentric standards of beauty—light skin, straight hair, fine features—and rejected those of their own race.[35] The situation is especially sensitive on campuses where women of color outnumber men. When male students of color date white women, many young African-American women experience this as a personal rejection, which strikes at the very core of their identity and sense of self-worth and pride. When male students of color say that white women accept them for who they are and put less pressure on them than do black women, they are seen as buying in to the stereotype of African-American women as "castrating bitches." Interracial dating also results in damaged relations between women students, with some African-American women viewing white women who date black students as predatory competitors.

Most black students simply avoid discussing the issue because it is painful, and they do not want to risk hurting or alienating members of their support group. At some schools, however, some African-American women have taken a public stand. At Brown University, for example, several women created a Wall of Shame in one of their rooms on which they wrote the names of famous black men who date or have married white women. A second list naming students who were dating whites was posted on a door. While creating the list undoubtedly released some of their frustration, it also hurt some of the students whose names were on it as well as other students on campus who are the children of mixed marriages.[36]

Creating a supportive environment for all students is far from problem free. Race and gender create complex dynamics. On my campus a fashion show organized by the student activities committee to generate money for charity became embroiled in controversy. Models for the show were chosen from an ethnically diverse pool of male and female students who had been nominated on the basis of their contributions to the college community, not looks. (Despite the event's being a fashion show, the organizers thought they were making a positive statement by not choosing models on the basis of physical appearance.) For reasons that were never fully explained, however, the final selection of models did not include any African-American women or Latinas, although some had been nominated (the models did include black and Latino men as well as Asian and Indian women).

Members of a black sorority took issue and wrote to the student newspaper that they "were deeply saddened by the continued neglect of issues dealing with women of color."[37] In a less dispassionate letter distributed on campus, some women demanded an apology. Besides being excluded from what turned out to be a popular and successful fund-raising event, the women were undoubtedly also influenced by the emotional baggage of the color complex. Even if the oversight was completely unintentional, however, they were justifiably upset that no one on the selection committee had noticed that no African-American women or Latinas had been selected.

In a letter to the editor, a white student trivialized their concerns by writing that she had been excluded from the fashion show too even though she is a Californian and from "a slightly different culture, as different as most of the minority students come from"; furthermore, she was "tired of hearing about minority students waiting to have things handed to them on a platter."[38] As a black dean of students at another college once told me, "African-American women's assertiveness is often misunderstood on white campuses. Their directness and verbal strength are interpreted in terms of stereotypes; they're seen as quick to anger, hostile, hard, bitchy, rather than just assertive. Black women on campus face a double whammy—they're both a minority and women. Consequently, many African-American women see themselves as never winning."

During your years in college you may be faced with some difficult decisions. Whether you are a student of color or not, what you do makes a difference. After an incident in which a few fraternity members at Eastern Illinois University shouted obscenities and threw food at Native American and gay and lesbian students taking part in the homecoming parade, more than a thousand students, professors, and staff members rallied to decry racism on campus. Sixty student groups, including other fraternities, reaffirmed their commitment to multiculturalism by assembling a Unity Quilt made up of three-foot cloth squares decorated by each group and hanging it from the roof of the student union.[39] At Indiana University, at least four hundred students representing a coalition of interests rallied on Martin Luther King Day, seeking new cultural and academic programs for minority groups. After meeting with students, the chancellor agreed to create a Latino studies department and an Asian cultural center and to make the King remembrance day an official campus holiday.[40]

DID YOU KNOW?

- The public tends to overestimate the size of minority groups. According to a 1990 Gallup poll, when people were asked how large the African-American population was, they guessed 32 percent (real size today, 12 percent). They guessed that Latinos comprised 21 percent of the population (real size today, 10 percent), and that Jews comprised 18 percent (real size, 3 percent). They believed that 71 percent of the U.S. population was comprised of just these three groups!

- People of color make up nearly 30 percent of the U.S. population (and 85 percent of the world's population). By the year 2080, however, more than half of all Americans will be people of color, and this change will continue to be reflected on college campuses.

- Since the 1970s, *The Journal of Blacks in Higher Education* (JBHE) has been tracking the progress of African-American students compared to that of white students, using a variety of indices. Its Higher Education Equality Index now stands at 71 (100 points would represent parity between blacks and whites).

- The top ten college choices of African-American women are: Howard University, Spelman College, Clark Atlanta University, Hampton University, Morgan State University, Florida A & M University, North Carolina A & T University, Temple University, Florida State University, and Virginia State. Eight are historically black colleges and universities.

- There are over one hundred historically black colleges and universities in the United States, with more than a quarter million students. Approximately 17 percent of African-American undergraduates attend them; 27 percent of those who receive bachelor's degrees receive them from HBCUs.

◈ Spelman College, for African-American women, is one of about eighty women's colleges in the United States and Canada.

◈ Since 1968, twenty-nine tribal colleges have opened. Most are located on reservations, with students coming from 250 federally recognized tribes. Seventy percent of the more than 25,000 students attending them are women.

◈ In the nineteenth century, Oberlin College was a center of abolitionist activity and a major stop for runaway slaves on the Underground Railroad. It was then one of the few predominantly white institutions to regularly enroll black students. It still has one of the largest black enrollments of any leading liberal arts college.

◈ Dartmouth College, William and Mary, and Princeton University, among others, began as institutions with explicit mission statements to educate Indian people and "civilize" them.

◈ The "model minority" myth, that all Asian Americans are hardworking, highly educated, and financially successful, is not true. Seventy percent of Asian-American workers have incomes that place them below the middle class.

◈ The ethnic composition of entering college students in the 1990s is roughly 8 percent African American, 2 percent Native American, 4 percent Asian, 4 percent Latino, and 82 percent white.

_____ *WHAT YOU CAN DO* _____

◼ College opens up new worlds. Attend events sponsored by Latino, Asian, Indian, African-American, Native American, and international students and enjoy new foods, new music and dance, new ideas, and new friends.

◼ Become better informed. Whether you are a minority or a majority student, you would benefit from taking courses that relate to the history, cultural background, and current status of minority groups in the United States. If your campus does not offer many such courses, join with other students to ask specific departments or the administration for more.

◼ In the classroom, respect the viewpoints and opinions of others. This means really listening to what they are trying to say, even if you are not inclined to agree with them or if what they say makes you feel uncomfortable. Play your part in positive discussions and debates. Articulate your own point of view, but also acknowledge those of others.

◼ Students are the most important players in creating a positive campus climate. Don't make remarks that stereotype others' behavior, abilities, or achievements. Even racist remarks embedded in jokes demean people, both listeners and tellers. Remember, your own ethnic identity does not give you immunity.

◪ Pockets of racism exist on most campuses. Some incidents are annoying; some can be painful or scary. Some recent examples: Racist jokes were handed out by a teaching assistant to students in an English class at Arizona State University. Graffiti, including the letters "KKK" and the message "NIGGERS GO HOME," was written on elevator doors and walls in two Harvard University dormitories. Asian students at the University of California, Irvine, were sent e-mail messages containing racial slurs and death threats. During a campus debate on political correctness at the University of Pennsylvania, the mostly black residents of Du Bois College House received telephone bomb threats. If an incident like this occurs on your campus, make sure that it is openly discussed and not swept under the carpet. All students need to confront racism on campus. Organize a forum for students to discuss the issue and think of ways combat it.

◪ Your living group, club, or organization can plan programs, speakers, and film series that deal with race, cultural difference, and the like. (Check the Resources section of this chapter for some ideas.) Don't forget comedians; humor heightens awareness in an enjoyable way.

◪ When you invite speakers and performers to your campus, don't forget people of color. It sends a strong positive message when people of color are associated with a range of issues—politics, journalism, literature, sports, and entertainment—as they are in real life, not just supposedly minority issues.

◪ Think about the symbolism and implications of the events you help plan and how they are implemented. Look critically at the advertising for your events; remember the T-shirt Incident.

◪ Inappropriate racial or ethnic remarks made in class alienate students of color and can reinforce majority students' prejudices. If a professor says something that disturbs you, speak to him or her. Explain how you interpreted the remark or example that was used. Prejudicial attitudes and expressions are so ingrained in American culture that even the most supportive faculty member can blunder. Alert him or her to subtle classroom behaviors you have noticed, such as dissimilar eye contact or different patterns of responding to questions and comments from minority students. If they are approached in a nonaccusatory way, most faculty members will be grateful for the feedback. And you can know that you did the right thing. Should you be rebuffed, speak to the departmental chairperson.

◪ If you need advice or help, remember that there are many people on campus you can turn to. The quality of student life is monitored by the student affairs, dean of students, and student activities offices. The residence life office handles issues relating to your living situation. The counseling center can help you with issues of a personal nature. Various religious groups also exist, such as the Newman Association, Hillel, Christian Fellowship, Muslim

Students' Group, Ecumenical Campus Ministries, and more. Your campus may also have a multicultural center and a special dean of minority or multicultural affairs, an international center, as well as a women's center. You will also find the names of many organizations and referral centers related to specific topics at the end of each of the chapters of this book.

 Join or volunteer your time to a campus group or off-campus organization that is working for racial and gender equality and understanding.

 If you are a majority student, try to increase the participation of students of color in the clubs or service groups you belong to. Make sure all students feel welcome to join and that publicity for your events reaches all segments of the campus community.

 If you are a majority student, make an effort to get to know students of color and international students. Don't be complacent and expect them to make all the overtures. International students often form their strongest friendships with students of color, partially because both often feel marginalized on campus.

 If you are a student of color, join a campus organization or club that will make it easier for you to meet and do things with students from backgrounds different from your own. Make any ethnic organization you belong to open to all students.

 Demand fair and comprehensive coverage of all campus groups and issues in your student newspaper. Support the appointment of students of color as reporters and editors, and voice your disapproval when articles and cartoons contain racist and sexist overtones. Help educate other students.

 If your campus needs but does not have a multicultural center, join with other students to approach the administration. Contact students on other campuses for information and ideas about how it could be organized. On smaller campuses, a combination resource room–lounge in the college center that provides a place to talk, to read magazines and newspapers like *Emerge, Asia Week,* and *The Minaret,* and to find information on diversity issues might provide the support students need.

 Look around you. Does artwork on campus—painting, photographs, sculptures, museum displays—reflect the diversity of your student body? Do the faculty and administration include a fair representation of people of color, especially in nontraditional positions (e.g., not only in minority affairs)? If not, join with other students to approach the administration about changing the situation.

Books and Other Publications

Anzaldúa, Gloria (ed.). 1990. *Making Face, Making Soul/Hacienda Caras: Creative and Critical Perspectives by Women of Color.* San Francisco: Aunt Lute.

Asian Women United of California (ed.). 1989. *Making Waves: An Anthology of Writings by and about Asian American Women.* Boston: Beacon.

Bordewich, Fergus. 1996. *Killing the White Man's Indian: Reinventing Native Americans at the End of the Twentieth Century.* New York: Doubleday.

Bunzel, John. 1992. *Race Relations on Campus: Stanford Students Speak.* Stanford, Calif.: Stanford Alumni Association.

Chideya, Farai. 1995. *Don't Believe the Hype: Fighting Cultural Misinformation about African-Americans.* New York: Plume.

Corova, Teresa, et al. (eds.). 1986. *Chicana Voices: Intersections of Class, Race, and Gender.* Austin, Texas: Center for Mexican American Studies.

Dubois, Ellen Carol, and Vickie Ruiz (eds.). 1994. *Unequal Sisters: A Multicultural Reader in U.S. Women's History.* 2nd ed. New York: Routledge.

duCille, Ann. 1996. *Skin Trade.* Cambridge, Mass.: Harvard University Press.

Featherston, Elena (ed.). 1997. *Skin Deep: Women Writing on Color, Culture and Identity.* San Francisco: Featherston & Associates.

Fiol-Matta, Liza, and Marian Chamberlain (eds.). 1994. *Women of Color and the Multicultural Curriculum.* New York: Feminist Press.

Flemming, Jacqueline. 1984. *Blacks in College: A Comparative Study of Students' Success in Black and in White Institutions.* San Francisco: Jossey-Bass.

Garrett, Hongo (ed.). 1995. *Under Western Eyes: Personal Essays from Asian America.* New York: Anchor.

Garza, Hedda. 1994. *Latinas: Hispanic Women in the United States.* New York: Franklin Watts.

Gates, Henry Louis, Jr., et al. 1995. *Speaking of Race, Speaking of Sex.* New York: New York University Press.

Giddings, Paula. 1984. *When and Where I Enter: The Impact of Black Women on Race and Sex.* New York: Morrow.

Golden, Marita, and Susan Richards Shreve (eds.). 1996. *Skin Deep: Black Women and White Women Write about Race.* New York: Anchor.

Hernton, Calvin. 1992. *Sex and Racism in America.* New York: Anchor.

Holland, Dorothy, and Margaret Eisenhart. 1990. *Educated in Romance: Women, Achievement, and College Culture.* Chicago: University of Chicago Press.

hooks, bell. 1990. *Yearning: Race, Gender and Cultural Politics.* Boston: South End.

HUES: Hear Us Emerging Sisters. HUES magazine was developed by three former University of Michigan students who wanted to create a truly multicultural women's magazine. It is published twice a year, in April and October. HUES, PO Box 7778, Ann Arbor, MI 48107–8226. Phone: (800) HUES-4U2.

Jacob, Evelyn, and Cathie Jordan (eds.). 1993. *Minority Education: Anthropological Perspectives.* Norwood, N.J.: Ablex.

Kim, Elaine, Lilia Villanuera, and Asian Women United of California. 1997. *Making More Waves: New Writing by Asian-American Women.* Boston: Beacon.

Lomotey, Kofi (ed.). 1997. *Sailing Against the Wind: African Americans and Women in U.S. Education.* Albany: State University of New York Press.

Long, Courtney. 1996. *Love Awaits: African-American Women Talk about Sex, Love and Life.* New York: Bantam.

Mayberry, Katherine (ed.). 1996. *Teaching What You're Not: Identity Politics in Higher Education.* New York: New York University Press.

Miller, L. Scott. 1995. *An American Imperative: Accelerating Minority Educational Advancement.* New Haven, Conn.: Yale University Press.

Moraga, Cherríe, and Anzaldúa, Gloria (eds.). 1981. *This Bridge Called My Back: Writings by Radical Women of Color.* 2nd ed. New York: Kitchen Table/Women of Color.

Moses, Yolanda. 1989. "Black Women in Academe: Issues and Strategies" (pamphlet). Washington, D.C.: Association of American Colleges.

Nelson, Jill. 1997. *Straight, No Chaser: How I Became a Grown-up Black Woman.* New York: Putnam.

Nieves-Squires, Sarah. 1991. "Hispanic Women: Making Their Presence on Campus Less Tenuous" (pamphlet). Washington, D.C.: Association of American Colleges.

Polakow, Valerie. 1993. *Lives on the Edge.* Chicago: University of Chicago Press.

Rooks, Noliwe. 1996. *Hair Raising: Beauty, Culture and African American Women.* New Brunswick, N.J.: Rutgers University Press.

Schuman, David, and Dick Olufs. 1995. *Diversity on Campus.* Boston: Allyn & Bacon.

Sleeter, Christine. 1996. *Multicultural Education as Social Activism.* Albany: State University of New York Press.

Smith, Robert C. 1995. *Racism in the Post–Civil Rights Era: Now You See It, Now You Don't.* Albany: State University of New York Press.

Taylor, Jill McLean, et al. 1996. *Between Voice and Silence: Women and Girls, Race and Relationships.* Cambridge, Mass.: Harvard University Press.

Terkel, Studs. 1993. *Race: How Blacks and Whites Think and Feel about the American Obsession.* New York: Anchor.

Trent, William. 1991. *College in Black and White.* Albany: State University of New York Press.

von Lowe, Kreuter. 1996. *Forgotten Promise: Race and Gender Wars on a Small College Campus.* New York: Knopf.

Weis, Lois, and Michelle Fine (eds.). 1993. *Beyond Silenced Voices.* Albany: State University of New York Press.

Williams, Patricia J. 1991. *The Alchemy of Race and Rights*. Cambridge, Mass.: Harvard University Press.

Wilson, Kathy, and Midge Russell. 1996. *Divided Sisters: Bridging the Gap Between Black Women and White Women*. New York: Anchor.

Yen-Mei Wong, Diane (ed.). 1988. *Making Waves: An Anthology of Writings By and About Asian American Women*. Boston: Beacon.

Videos

Blue Eyes. This ninety-three-minute video shows what happens to a diverse group of people who are subjected to racist treatment in an experiment run by Jane Elliot, an experienced and dynamic diversity trainer. It shows just how much hate speech, lowered expectations, and dismissive behavior can affect people's behavior and beliefs about themselves. The film also points out that sexism, homophobia, and ageism work the same way. Excellent for heightening awareness and provoking discussion. Produced by Claus Strigel and Bertram Verhagg. California Newsreel, 149 9th Street, San Francisco, CA 94103. Phone: (415) 621–6196.

Domino: Interracial People and the Search for Identity. This forty-four-minute video tells the personal stories of four women and two men of mixed parentage. Each one's identity has been shaped by the experiences of the parents, family politics, and the hierarchies of race, gender roles, and class. They demonstrate how having two cultures can be a source of strength. Films for the Humanities, PO Box 2053, Princeton, NJ 08543–2053. Phone: (800) 257–5126 or (609) 275–1400.

Frontline: Racism 101. This fifty-eight-minute video reports on racially motivated violence and harassment on several campuses. Interviews are conducted with students and faculty. It is no longer available from PBS, but may be available through your library or audiovisual service.

In Search of the Dream: A Story of the African American Experience. This six-part video series looks at the cultural, economic, and political life of African Americans from 1619 to the present, combining historical photographs and film footage with contemporary interviews. In part 2, "Stirrings," Haskell Ward recalls his college years and discusses trends in the 1990s with college students at Morehouse, Spelman, Morris Brown, and Clark Atlanta University. He evaluates African-American progress with student activists, educators, politicians, and civil rights leaders. Films for the Humanities, PO Box 2053, Princeton, NJ 08543–2053. Phone: (800) 257–5126.

Korean Americans. This fifty-minute video gives an overview of Koreans in America and their attempts to retain traditional cultural values while participating in U.S. life. Films for the Humanities, PO Box 2053, Princeton, NJ 08543–2053. Phone: (800) 257–5126.

The Politics of Love—In Black and White. This thirty-three-minute video, produced by Ed Burley and Chris Weck, explores romance between the races on college campuses. Interracial couples discuss their pains and joys, while other students discuss the political implications of their relationships. The filmmakers—one black, one white—discuss survival tips for students. Excellent for generating discussion. Available from California Newsreel, 149 9th Street, San Francisco, CA 94103. Phone: (415) 621–6196.

A Question of Color. This fifty-six-minute documentary by African-American filmmaker Kathe Sandler examines black identity and "color consciousness," the feelings many African Americans have about themselves and their appearance and about the degree to which skin color, hair, and facial features conform to a European ideal. California Newsreel, 149 9th Street, San Francisco, CA 94103. Phone: (415) 621–6196.

Race, the Floating Signifier. In this video, sociologist Stuart Hall goes beyond discussing the effects of race to look at how and why "differences of hair, skin, and bone" form the basis on which so much social classification takes place. He examines how race is represented. Because the meaning of race depends upon cultural context, he describes is as a "floating signifier." Available in two lengths, the forty-five-minute classroom edition, and an eighty-five-minute version that includes the full lecture he gave at Goldsmiths College in London, as well as a twenty-minute question and answer session. Media Education Foundation, 26 Center Street, Northampton, MA 01060. Phone: (800) 897–0089 and (413) 584–8500.

Skin Deep. This fifty-three-minute video follows students from the University of Massachusetts, Texas A & M, Chico State, and UC Berkeley to a challenging racial awareness workshop. The filmmaker, Frances Reid, than accompanies them back to their homes and campuses to discover why they think the way they do. Excellent for promoting discussion. Available from California Newsreel, 149 9th Street, San Francisco, CA 94103. Phone: (415) 621–6196.

The Status of Latina Women. This twenty-six-minute video compares the experiences of U.S. Latinas with women in Latin American countries. It examines how successful Latinos regard professional women, as well as at the myths and mystique of machismo. It also profiles a Latina feminist. Films for the Humanities, PO Box 2053, Princeton, NJ 08543–2053. Phone: (800) 257–5126.

Women of Hope: Latinas Abriendo Camino. This twenty-eight-minute documentary, produced by the Bread and Roses Project, profiles twelve women who have broken new ground in their lives and achievements, in politics, writing, theater, and other areas. It includes important archival footage and features a soundtrack of diverse and important Latin music. A study guide and posters are also available. Films for the Humanities, PO Box 2053, Princeton, NJ 08543–2053. Phone: (800) 257–5126.

Organizations

American-Arab Anti-Discrimination Committee, 4201 Connecticut Avenue NW, No. 300, Washington, DC 20008. Phone: (202) 244–2990. This is a nonsectarian organization that seeks to protect the rights of Americans of Arab descent. It fights discrimination in education, employment, and political life and works to prevent stereotyping of Arabs in the media.

Anti-Defamation League of B'nai B'rith, 1100 Connecticut Avenue NW, No. 1020, Washington, DC 20036. Phone: (202) 452–8320. Jewish organization that combats anti-Semitism and discrimination in education, employment, and politics. It also conducts programs and provides school curricula on reducing prejudice toward all groups.

Latino Civil Rights Task Force, 2701 Ontario Road NW, 2nd Floor, Washington, DC 20009. Phone: (202) 332–1053. The Task Force's mission is to empower the Latino community by advocating on its behalf, providing leadership, and increasing awareness of public policies that affect Latinos, including in the area of education.

MANA: A National Latina Organization, 1725 K Street NW, Suite 501, Washington, DC 20006. Phone: (202) 833–0060. MANA helps campus groups organize and offers scholarships to Latinas. It runs mentoring programs to develop the educational, professional, and leadership abilities of Latinas and is also involved in advocacy work on civil rights and health issues. Web site: http//www.Hermana.org/.

Minority and Disabilities Alumni Project, Council on International Educational Exchange (CIEE), 205 East 42nd Street, New York, NY 10017–5706. Phone: (888) 268–6245. CIEE operates a program for students of color and students with disabilities who are interested in participating in work, study, or volunteer programs abroad. A list of advisors will provide you with information and the names of students who have participated in study abroad.

NAACP (National Association for the Advancement of Colored People), 4805 Mount Hope Drive, Baltimore, MD 21215–3297. Phone: (410) 358–8900. The NAACP works to reduce racism and promote the advancement of African Americans. It maintains a college division which runs national programs to promote student leadership and to help students organize. Its educational wing makes a wide range of information and publications on racism, civil rights, minority issues, and African-American culture available. There are local chapters in many areas.

National Conference of Puerto Rican Women, 5 Thomas Circle, Washington, DC 20005. Phone: (202) 387–4716. The Conference is involved in political advocacy work for Latinas. It offers workshops and seminars on various topics and can refer you to other local and national organizations for Latina/os. It offers scholarships to Latinas and assistance to students who are trying to organize.

National Council of La Raza, 111 19th Street NW, Suite 1000, Washington, DC 20036. Phone: (202) 785–1670. The Council conducts research on education, employment, health, and civil rights and organizes political action aimed at the advancement of Latinos. It operates the College Leadership Forum, which trains and provides information and technical assistance to student groups and groups serving their interests. The Forum is developing an information network of organizations and services for Latino students.

National Institute for Women of Color (NIWC), 624 9th Street NW, Washington, DC 20001–5303. Phone: (202) 298–1118. NIWC's goal is to promote educational and economic equity for women of color (African-American, Hispanic, Asian-American, Pacific Islander, Native American, and Alaskan Native women). It serves as a networking vehicle, promotes cooperation between general women's organizations and women of color, sponsors seminars and workshops, conducts internship and leadership development programs, and compiles statistics.

National People of Color Student Coalition (NPCSC), 1413 K Street NW, 10th Floor, Washington, DC 20006. Phone: (202) 347–5442. The NPCSC is comprised of seven caucuses representing Native Americans, African Americans, Latinos/as, Arab Americans, Asians and Pacific Islanders, Lesbian, Gay, and Bisexual Students of Color, and International Students of Color. The organization seeks to expand federal support for higher education and fights for greater access for students of color. It monitors legislation, organizes conferences, and serves as a support network for student activists throughout the country. The Students of Color Strategy and Policy Department Resource Center provides information on curriculum reform, affirmative action, hate crimes, campus violence, retention programs, and statistics on the status of students of color in higher education. GrassRoots Organizing Weekends (GROW) teach students the skills to make change on their campuses. *NAMALIA* is a quarterly journal that publishes articles, poems, artwork, and photographs by students of color.

Organization of Chinese Americans (OCA), 1001 Connecticut Avenue NW, Suite 707, Washington, DC 20026. Phone: (202) 223–5500. The organization promotes the advancement of all Asian Americans. Its work includes political advocacy and organizing local and national cultural, educational, health, and professional programs. Its college outreach service helps Asian students with programming and communication and will refer you to other local and national Asian groups.

Organization of Pan Asian American Women (OPAAW), PO Box 39218, Washington, DC 20016. Phone: (202) 682–9100. The organization focuses on public policy issues affecting Asian Pacific women. It is interested in the global status of women but also monitors affirmative action and educational equity in the United States. Its main emphasis is on leadership and professional development and coalition building. It offers some internships to college students.

Women of Color Resource Center, 2288 Fulton Street, Suite 103, Berkeley, CA 94704. Phone: (510) 848–9272. The Center is an information clearinghouse that publishes a national directory of organizations and resources for women of color. It can direct you to local and national groups working on issues of importance to you.

CHAPTER 7

B e y o n d

t h e   C o e d

One understanding that I discovered once I made the decision to return
to college was that I was entitled to do this. I did not have to be
superwoman (continue the traditional woman's role in my home) and
that I had the right to expect my family to support me. Many women
feel they are infringing on their family's lives, not realizing their own
worth. No attempt at guilt-tripping me could pass through my armor of
determination to fulfill the dream I'd had since high school.
                                    —Kathy Blackburn, Mount Holyoke College, 1997

HIGHER EDUCATION was once seen as the four-year period between high
school and the beginning of a profession. The traditional college students were
male undergraduates between the ages of eighteen and twenty-four who were
attending school full-time.[1] Our stereotyped image shows them in heavy college-
letter sweaters and beanies; the few "coeds" on campus wear full skirts, sweater
sets, white ankle socks, and saddle shoes. Today, the picture has changed. A
majority of college students are women, and over 40 percent are twenty-five
years old and older. You may be one of them. If not, you may share the classroom with someone who is.

"My Mom wonders if I can stay at your place for a few hours until she finishes her grant proposal."

The first "nontraditional" (older) students to arrive on college campuses were veterans—including a few women—taking advantage of the G.I. Bill following World War II. Since then, business and government's growing need for a highly educated workforce has swelled the numbers of older adults going to college. The women's movement, which opened new horizons for women and new opportunities in the workplace, as well as a high divorce rate, have contributed to the number of women seeking higher education. To serve their needs, universities began training specialists in so-called adult education in the 1960s and 1970s, and many new community colleges were built. In 1976, Congress passed the Lifelong Learning Act, which states that "American society should have as its goal the availability of appropriate opportunities for lifelong learning for all its citizens."

Depending on the size and type of school you attend, there may be many or very few nontraditional students on campus. If you are a younger under-graduate, you may seldom think about the issues facing the older women students you see or about the ways in which they enrich the college environment. If you are a nontraditional student, you may feel well provided for, or marginalized and alone.

NO SINGLE PROFILE fits the nearly 5 million older students now attending college. Most are women between the ages of thirty-five and forty-four, although many are still in their twenties and some are much older. They come from many ethnic backgrounds; approximately 12 percent are African-American women, and 6 percent are Latinas.[2] According to one national survey, most older women students are married, but others are single, either by choice or because of separation, divorce, or the death of their partner. Many women students are parents. Mary Jo Wilson returned to college and graduated with a business degree while she was raising six children, including quintuplets.[3] Most nontraditional students work full-time and go to classes part-time, but about 30 percent study full-time. What all these women share is a wealth of life experiences and a perspective on education that differs from that of most younger undergraduates.

Many women are "returning" or "reentry" students who interrupted their college education for a variety of reasons. "I wasn't able to keep up with the tuition and living expenses of college once my financial aid package was cut," explained one thirty-five-year-old attending Union College. "I was paying for school on my own. My plan was to take off one term and return to school, but I ended up getting a good job. . . . I'm returning now for my own personal satisfaction and perhaps to move on to graduate school." Another woman originally dropped out of Pennsylvania State University because she felt "too young to figure out what to do with my life."[4] Other nontraditional students are going to college for the first time. A woman who married right after high school and started a family finally enrolled in college at age forty-seven: "I've always had an overwhelming desire to attend college, but until now personal circumstances prevented me from doing so."

Most women return to college to acquire the training or credentials that will enable them to get a more fulfilling job or advance in their careers. Research has shown that women and African Americans are the two groups that benefit the most financially from having earned a college degree; they have the largest earnings advantage over people with similar backgrounds who have only a high school diploma.[5] One risk older women face, however, is being channeled into stereotypically female fields such as social work, teaching, and nursing rather than business, engineering, or computer science. Some older students are in college to update their professional training. Nurses and engineers, for example, are often required to take courses on a regular basis in order to maintain their licenses to practice. Others return to school to pursue their intellectual interests. "I want to increase my critical thinking ability," explained one thirty-five-year-old. "I don't want to be one of those older people who floats through life without thinking. And I don't want to be bored when I'm older." What all these women share is the desire for "more"—more fulfilling work, more intellectual stimulation, more financial security, more independence.

Because nontraditional students are by definition older than undergraduates who enter college straight from high school, one of the first sensations many experience is the feeling of being "odd woman out." For most younger undergraduates, college is as much about personal growth and experimentation as it is about acquiring knowledge and skills. More older students have a clear educational or professional goal. "The younger students don't know why they're in college, but I do," claims one fifty-year-old who works as a secretary while attending school part-time. Still, many older women students are also searching and, like younger undergraduates, end up changing their majors to fields they knew little about before.

If you are a nontraditional student, you have several potential advantages over younger undergraduates. To begin with, you are likely to be more knowledgeable: You have experienced more, heard more, talked more, and probably read more than they have about matters that relate to your courses, especially in the social sciences and humanities. In contrast to younger students who are too young to remember or who had not yet been born, you may have marched in protests against the war in Vietnam or watched the Apollo moon landing on television. You most likely have had personal and work experiences—parenting, starting your own business, living abroad, being an emergency-room nurse— that few younger undergraduates have. Many work and domestic skills, such as writing memos and reports, wiring new lights, caring for an ill parent, interpreting your children's test scores, and filling out income tax forms will help you make sense of course material in the social sciences and humanities as well as the sciences and engineering.

Occasionally, you may run into a patronizing faculty member who treats you as if you are only in school because you were bored at home. Some younger faculty may seem uncomfortable or wary of you, especially if you are older than they are. Both factors could cause them to ignore you in class and exclude you from informal interactions. But most faculty typically enjoy having older students in class because they are usually serious students whose life and career experiences enrich class discussions. If you are a younger student and share a classroom with older students, you may be surprised to hear their perspectives on different issues. One young women's studies major, for example, told me she was "shocked" when she participated in a small group discussion with several older women who expressed the view that the "ideal marriage" would be one in which husband and wife lived apart and just visited on the weekends. "I just couldn't believe they were saying this," she remembers. "I had this romantic notion that two people who loved each other would always want to be together." Another student liked having an older woman in her Issues in Feminism class: "It was great having her in class because we were discussing a lot of issues and social situations that as young students we hadn't experienced. We were talking about sexual harassment one day and saying things like, 'I'd just quit,' 'I'd complain.' Then she told us it had happened to her but that she couldn't quit because she had kids and needed her job. It's easy for us to think, 'Well, I'd do something,' but she'd actually been in these situations. It made me see that a lot is much easier said than done." In some cases, the experiences women relate—such as domestic violence—may make younger undergraduates acutely uncomfortable, but they still learn from them.

Older students are more likely than younger students to question an instructor's assumptions, pushing the class to examine the subject matter in more depth. They often become discussion and team leaders. According to an older student at Mount Holyoke College, "We tend to help female traditionals retrieve their voices. We set up a balance in how discussions take place. For example, personal experiences count as legitimate ways of making a point." Most faculty believe that nontraditional students have a positive influence on teaching and the classroom environment.[6] They report that younger students sometimes turn to older students for advice and that during class they subtly solicit their approval through eye contact and deferential body language.

If you are an older student, you may find yourself treated as a parental figure by some younger undergraduates, which is something you may or may not appreciate. You are also likely to see faculty members as equals whose expertise simply differs from your own. You expect good teaching; your time is precious. For both reasons, you may be more critical of and less deferential to faculty than younger undergraduates. Some older students report having difficulty finding the right demeanor and discussion style to use in class, that is, in adopting an appropriate student role. Sometimes their assertiveness upsets faculty. Younger undergraduates may also resent the appearance that an older student is "taking over" the class. One thirty-one-year-old woman who returned to college after a fifteen-year absence explained it this way: "I forgot the unwritten rules of class and came across as too assertive and as taking up others' time. But this [education] is *real* to me. It's important for me to grasp the information and really understand."

Personality, however, also plays a role, as it does for younger undergraduates. Some older students lack confidence and are excessively quiet. "I have a problem entering class discussions," said one. "Taking one course a term is difficult. I don't seem to have that thought connection. When you're in school full-time for four years, your thoughts are building. As a part-time student, my thoughts seem disconnected." A student in the Frances Perkins program at Mount Holyoke told me that she and many of the other women she knows initially repeated behaviors that were common during her high school years: "I had to work at being vocal in a class. Once I became vocal, I had to learn to temper my enthusiasm. By my junior year, I had learned the art of listening, speaking, and feeling, and I participated as an *active* member of the class. These were unreachable skills for me in high school, which I think related to subliminal and overt [gender] discrimination in the educational system."

Faculty today teach a wide range of students, some of whom treat them as unapproachable authority figures. Others look to them as mentors; still other students treat them informally as peers. Just as returning students may have difficulty adapting to the classroom, some faculty are confused about how to relate to them. Confusion may be partially to blame for what appears to be a higher incidence of sexual harassment between male faculty (and staff) and returning women students. Some faculty may see mature students as contemporaries rather than as students, making some men mistakenly believe that it is all right to approach them sexually. A woman who dropped a class because she felt uncomfortable with the faculty member's sexual advances explained the consequences: "I am a single parent paying my own way through school, and I was so upset about this man coming on to me that I just dropped the class in the middle of the quarter. I will now have to pay again to take it over."

Nontraditional students tend to be highly motivated students who feel the pressure of time to absorb all that they can. Because they are usually making a personal as well as financial sacrifice to return to school, they do not want to waste the experience. Comparing herself to younger students, one woman said, "I appear to be more efficient about my studying. I guess it's because I have to be. I only have so much time to get the job done." Another woman believes that "anyone who raises kids learns how to be a *great* organizer." Unlike younger undergraduates, returning students are also less likely to be distracted by newfound freedom or to view college as a place to explore relationships and discover who they are. "I think college is easier for me," commented one thirty-two-year-old. "I don't feel the pressures to 'fit in,' decide sorority or not, find 'my group' or my boyfriend or girlfriend. I've made lots of friends here, but the pressure to do so wasn't there. Being older, my friends and 'who I am' are already pretty defined. I often think about how hard it must be for the young women coming in. It's no surprise that so many of them have eating disorders."

Because older students have had more experience juggling personal, family, and work responsibilities and prioritizing tasks, they also are less likely to be tempted to abandon their studies by offers of pizza and beer or a late-night party. They are also likely to be more aware of the financial costs of an education.

Nontraditional students do face difficulties, however. Like other students, many feel especially anxious when they first arrive on campus. Will I be able to handle the course material? How can I find time to read everything? Do I deserve to be here? Can I compete with these sharp young kids? One woman who returned to college after an absence of thirty-one years recalled, "The fear of not being capable was overwhelming. . . . I'm still a bit terrified, but I've discovered that the younger students are too." According to a director of admissions who has worked with many returning students, "They experience a lot of anxiety. They think they'll be unique, the only one, although this is changing now that more people are going back to school. When they first come back, they worry: 'Can I do my homework? Can I be as disciplined as I once was?'" Older women who grew up learning that girls do poorly at math and science may experience real anxiety in some courses. Even more importantly, returning students often have high expectations and are very hard on themselves if they do not live up to them. Those in special programs for older students like the Frances Perkins program at Mount Holyoke or the Ada Comstock Scholars program at Smith College are in constant contact with people who have experienced or are empathetic to their problems.

Like younger undergraduates who must study amid the chaos of dorm life and the demands of an active social life, the mature student often struggles to find time and an undisturbed place where she can spread out her books and work. One student described her home situation: "I study in the basement—like Virginia Woolf's 'room of one's own'—except I don't really have a room of my own. I study late at night, but even then I have the interruption of thoughts, everything I should be taking care of. I don't really think it's a female thing, but at my age I have so many responsibilities."

Another student goes to bed at six P.M. with the alarm set at two A.M. so that she can wake up and work for several hours without interruption: "Otherwise, I'm on call and the phone does not stop ringing." While most young undergraduates are encouraged by their families to stay in school, some returning women students receive subtle and overt pressure to leave. Their children may not understand why they have gone back to school and may resent the time they spend studying. Some partners think that the financial sacrifice is not worth it or complain about being neglected. "Younger students are encouraged and prodded to get an education," observed one woman who works full-time in a hospital radiology lab while attending a nearby liberal arts college. "My motivation is all internal. There aren't many people offering encouraging words to me. Quite frankly, I think my family would prefer that I was not attending college at my age. My siblings appear to feel intimidated by me, and at times are downright negative. Very few people are able to comprehend that working full-time and going to school full-time, or even half-time, is not an easy accomplishment. I spend countless hours studying, which minimizes the amount of time I have for socializing." Employers and colleagues, too, may fail to understand why a woman really needs to return to school, and suspect that she is doing so at their expense.

Other women receive full support from family and friends despite the change in everyone's routine. Many women in the Frances Perkins program at Mount Holyoke, for example, live on campus and see their partners or families on weekends at most. "The interesting thing is," noted one participant, "after a few weeks of settling in at school, the guilt disappears. I think this has everything to do with a supportive environment and a lack of contact with those who stimulate negative feelings. One women told me she no longer felt guilty once she discovered that her family's suffering was based on the fact that they had to take care of themselves. She thought it was a good experience for everyone."

Despite most older students' greater maturity and management skills, by reentering school they are taking on the equivalent of a second job, with all the extra time and effort it demands. As one woman told me,

> When I see the younger students in groups for study sessions, I know the reality for me is to work forty hours a week and then spend my weekends, not only doing domestic chores, but studying as well, which doesn't give me much leisure time. Younger students are able to go full-time and graduate after four years. An evening student who works days takes at least two years longer. After attending school for five years, I'm becoming weary. I'm still quite enthusiastic about my major, but I'm finding school much more laborious and tedious than I did two years ago.

It is not surprising that returning women report that the most important factor in their success at college is having the support of their family or partner or being involved in a specialized program.

Single women may have fewer competing roles to play than do women with partners, but if they have young children, their burden is magnified. They must fulfill their children's needs, pay the extra cost of their education themselves, and manage their job and household alone. Child care is one of the most important issues facing returning female students. Some colleges and universities provide child care.[7] This may be a small cooperative run by parents who pay a nominal fee and volunteer their time and services. Other schools have child development centers run by the psychology department or school of education, which sometimes give priority to children of single parents. They usually offer high-quality care while functioning as a training site for students. But often university child care services provide too few spaces. When on-campus services are not available, which is true at many schools, women must make their own arrangements, usually with family or friends, since alternatives like private day care centers, nursery schools, and in-home care are expensive. When courses are unexpectedly canceled or an emergency arises, child care arrangements are upset, placing an added burden on the student.

One of the most frequent recommendations nontraditional students and the education professionals who work with them make is for colleges and universities to provide better support services, especially child care. Even something as rudimentary as a list of names and telephone numbers of students who can sit with your children while you attend class is valuable. At Pennsylvania's Cedar Crest, a kid-sitting program was started that matches younger undergraduates with students who have children. In exchange for providing child care on the evenings a woman has to attend classes, younger students get a change of scene: children, a house and yard, pets, and perhaps a chance to do their laundry.

Nontraditional students also need institutional flexibility. Even women with partners are likely to have major household and child care responsibilities in addition to their jobs. Many need classes offered outside the normal school day, and most would appreciate conveniences such as an effective mail-in registration service. They also need access to the bookstore and offices like the bursar and registrar after five P.M. as well as a properly staffed library open in the evenings and on weekends. Yet many colleges do not provide this kind of after-hours support. Advisors, too, usually set their office hours to accommodate the traditional undergraduate who can easily come during the day. As a result, many nontraditional students receive little or no advising. At some schools, older students are not even assigned campus mailboxes. If you are a younger student, it isn't difficult to imagine how complicated going to school can be for older women and to understand the feelings of isolation many experience. If you are a nontraditional student, this may sound all too familiar.

Some women return to school after dealing with domestic violence, an acrimonious separation, the death of a partner, or an addiction. Some attend school while suffering nightmares and living in fear. For them, college provides a safe haven as well as an opportunity to learn. A faculty member at Schenectady Community College remembered her distress when a student showed up at her office with a black eye and explained, "I'm sorry my paper's late. My husband beat me up." Other women, she noted, might never admit such a thing, for fear of losing the faculty member's respect. Many victims of domestic violence are ashamed about what has happened and often blame themselves, believing that the abuse is an example of their failure. According to one nontraditional student, "Women's studies courses help women come out of the closet—get rid of the shame and stop being the victim. My Psychology of Women and Psychology of Oppression courses were filled with women who owned their 'disorders.' By exploring the roots of women's willingness to help subjugate themselves and by learning that women had lacked a vocabulary that allowed them to formulate and verbalize their thoughts and feelings, many women's lives were changed. Women got mad, sad, and ACTIVE."

Even when they are not dealing with serious issues, nontraditional students still need support and encouragement. Some women arrive on campus knowing the college catalogue inside and out, but others feel totally lost. All would benefit from a special orientation program, open house, or workshop that gives them an opportunity to ask questions, meet students like themselves, and get advice on how to adjust to college life, including topics like time and stress management, career development, and financial aid. When such services are not provided, the only opportunity they have to share their concerns is when they happen to find themselves clustered in the same class or program with other older students. As one student explained, "You need something more than a statement in the catalogue that just tells you to overcome your 'hesitancy' about reentering the classroom."

A growing number of universities and colleges do offer special services and programs for nontraditional students: orientation, basic math classes, writing tutoring, workshops in computer and study skills, personal and career counseling, peer support groups, and child care. According to a College Board survey of 3,100 colleges, 35 percent had special admissions counselors, 40 percent offered financial aid for returning students, and 15 percent had on-campus housing for them. Mills College in California reserves some campus apartments for single mothers and provides returning students with the Resuming Lounge, a place where they can meet to talk and socialize. Since 1971, the University of Maine has run the Onward Bound program for nontraditional students who need special help making the transition to college; most are single mothers. The program offers financial aid, counseling, and peer support as well as non-credit courses in reading, writing, and math. Graduates then go on to the four-year program at the university. Vermont's Trinity College added weekend courses in 1979, in addition to its day and evening classes, in order to provide maximum flexibility for nontraditional students. The weekend courses are held on alternating weeks and combine three-hour classes with independent study. Participating faculty, advisors, and the bookstore are also available during weekend hours. In 1989 Trinity also instituted a program for single mothers on welfare, providing full child care and help with transportation, books, supplies, and living expenses.[8] In return, students perform community work in addition to their course work.

Despite the difficulties, the rewards of higher education are high. College gives most women new confidence in their intellectual abilities as well as increased job opportunities and greater financial security. Some women with children report that going to school brought them closer together. According to one mother, it's "a feeling of camaraderie. When your child sees you doing homework, you have more credibility in her eyes; it's a shared experience. And, by the same token, you can relate to your child's work."[9]

Another woman believes that in order to get the most out of college, it is important to develop the right attitude: "Older students want college to fit into *their* schedule. They are constantly stressed over fitting college into their lives. I think they should be told that they have it backward. The whole experience becomes a lot more pleasant for everyone once that's understood. . . . You become more relaxed, you enjoy making friends, you become more involved instead of just putting in the hour for class and taking the tests. This is where it's easier for the younger students. College *is* their life, so they approach it from that point of view."

_____ *DID YOU KNOW?* _____

- More than half the students attending tribal colleges are single parents with an average of three dependents.

- During the 1990s, the number of nontraditional students entering college increased at a higher rate than that of younger students. In 1996, 40 percent of undergraduates were twenty-five and older. By 2000, nearly half will be.

- You are never too old. Several women over sixty have enrolled in the Ada Comstock Program at Smith College and lived in campus dormitories with students forty years younger than themselves. Women in their seventies have graduated from several colleges.

- Marilyn Charell, a forty-eight-year-old mother, was once elected student body president of San Jose State.

- Women between the ages of twenty-five and thirty-four with college degrees earn 88 percent more than do women of the same age with high school diplomas.

- Several women's colleges offer programs designed specifically for nontraditional students. These include the McBride Scholars Program at Bryn Mawr College, the Frances Perkins Program at Mount Holyoke College, the Ada Comstock Scholars Program at Smith College, and the Elisabeth Kaiser Davis Program at Wellesley College.

- The University of Michigan runs the Center for the Education of Women, which helps women identify their career goals, and provides scholarships to returning students.

- Undergraduates at the University of Michigan voted to tax themselves one dollar per student per year to fund scholarships for students who need help paying for child care. The money raised is matched by the Regents. The University of Wisconsin, Madison, has had a similar program for over a decade.
- According to a large-scale study of nontraditional and traditional students at four-year public and private colleges and universities, 74 percent of reentry women had at least a 3.0 GPA, in comparison to 62 percent of reentry men, 52 percent of younger female students, and 42 percent of younger men.[10]

_____ *WHAT YOU CAN DO* _____

If You Are a Younger Woman Student

- Seek out some of the nontraditional women students on campus. Offer your friendship and see if there is any way you can help. If you know they have young children and live near campus, you might offer to baby-sit. Or you might simply give them your phone number, so that they can contact you in the future about assignments or class notes. Inform them of events you think they would be interested in. Even if they do not need help, you will probably enjoy and benefit from knowing someone who has had different life experiences than your own.
- A student group you belong to could organize a child care and support service for nontraditional students.
- If you belong to a campus women's group, extend an invitation to join to the returning female students on campus.

If You Are a Nontraditional Student

- Take the time to really explore the campus. Learn where buildings are located. Make it feel like your own campus.
- Take advantage of the services and opportunities offered by the university. Study the academic register and student handbook to learn what is available. Get a list of campus organizations. Many clubs are available that will allow you to pursue a special interest such as acting, hiking, skiing, singing, pottery, or taking photographs. Some sponsor activities that your partner or children can also participate in. Read the student newspaper and the bulletins posted in the student union and women's center to learn about upcoming meetings, guest speakers, and films. Call the gym about aerobics classes, use of the weight room, and recreational swimming. Find out its hours and policy on bringing guests. Remind yourself to enjoy college and incorporate all that it offers, not just the course work, into your life.
- A recent report by the College and University Work/Family Association has identified twenty-nine especially family-friendly campuses that have a variety

of innovative programs to help employees (and, in certain areas, students) handle the conflicting demands of work and family.

■ Don't try to do more work than you reasonably can. Don't enroll in three or four classes, for example, if you are working full-time. Start out by taking one class, or else work part-time if you can afford to do so. Set manageable goals, and don't think about all the credits you need to graduate at once.

■ Get organized. Write down all your weekly and daily commitments (college, work, and family) in a planner. Keep phone numbers in it too, including the library, bookstore, registrar's office, your instructors, and one or two class-mates in each of your courses. Just knowing you are organized will make college less stressful.

■ Schedule a few hours each day strictly for study, and create a work space that is just for your use.

■ If you feel insecure about study skills or writing papers, visit the campus writing center to see what services it offers. Buy a guide to better study skills and paper writing, and develop good habits early. Discuss paper ideas as well as note-taking, reading, and exam-preparation techniques with other students. And don't browbeat yourself if you don't get an A on every exam, every paper, every course.

■ Go to the library and ask for an orientation tour. Every university and college library has written self-guided tours, or librarians willing to show you how to use the library and computers efficiently. Don't hesitate to ask reference librarians for help with your research; they are trained professionals. Many specialized bibliographies and computer search programs are available.

■ Call the computer center to find out about training sessions. Find out what computer resources on campus are available to you.

■ Talk to other returning students, and see if there is a possibility of sharing child care, transportation, or shopping. Just getting to know a few other people in the same position as yourself will make college easier. The registrar or what may be called the Office of Continuing Education (Lifelong Learning, Adult Education) should be willing to provide you with some names.

■ Visit your assigned advisor. If your advisor's office hours are inconvenient, explain your need and set up a new time. If you need help beyond this person's scope or you are not satisfied with the academic advice you get, contact another familiar faculty member. Colleges and universities provide a broad range of other counseling services through their Academic Advising Office, Counseling Center, Placement or Career Development Office, Health Service, Dean of Students, Student Affairs Office, Financial Aid Office, or Office of Continuing Education.

- Get to know your professors. They probably enjoy having you in class, and most faculty are happy to discuss course material outside of class. Some may even turn to you for feedback about the course. In the future, you may also need a recommendation; the more your professors know you, the better the letter they will be able to write.

- Get to know other students, even if they are significantly younger than you are. You may want to organize a study group; pass around a sign-up sheet to a few people in one of your courses. Arrange your first meeting in the college center or library, and go from there. Having a study group will help make you feel a part of campus life.

- If you have time, join a student organization (call the Student Activities Office for information). If enough nontraditional students attend your institution or it runs a continuing education program, it may have a returning student association. (If it does not, perhaps you should start one.) Your institution is also likely to have a women's center and one or more women's groups. Not only will you derive support and enjoyment from such groups, you may also be able to make valuable contributions to them.

- Communicate. Let family members, partners, friends, employer, and co-workers know what your goals are and enlist their support. Don't forget to explain your child care plans to your children. You may be surprised at how flexible people are once you explain your goals. Don't forget to speak to your supervisor or personnel officer at work to find out what support your workplace offers. Some employers release employees for part or full days so they can attend school; others provide financial help to attend college.

- Delegate tasks and responsibilities. If you have children, they can probably do more for themselves than you or they think they can. If you have a partner, he or she should be willing to help more. Co-workers may be able to take over a special project for you if you ask. If you can afford to do so, hire people to assist you. Your town may have an affordable youth employment service. Consider advertising for help in the student newspaper.

- Develop flexible standards. For the period that you are in school, you may have to be satisfied with doing less at home and not taking on extra projects at work. This doesn't mean not doing your job in either place, just being realistic.

- Schedule time for yourself and for those who are important to you. Consider developing ritualized activities that you can share with others and some just for yourself. Read to your children a half hour each night; spend one evening each week with your partner—go to dinner, watch a video, share a bottle of wine. Make exercise a priority: walk, cycle, swim, play tennis, join an aerobics class, use the exercise bike, treadmill, or StairMaster in the gym (you can read while you do it). Write these activities into your weekly schedule along with class time and other responsibilities. You will feel better.

■ Explore financial aid opportunities fully. Older students can qualify for the same low-interest federal loans as do younger students. When applying for financial aid, include all your expenses. Many colleges will consider commuting expenses, day care costs, rent, and other costs if you must pay them in order to attend college. If you have children in college, you may be able to save money by enrolling at the same time, since the total expense may qualify you for financial aid. You may also be able to get full or partial tuition reimbursement from your employer. According to one report, 72 percent of full-time employees at midsize to large companies are eligible for financial assistance to cover the costs of job-related classes; 22 percent get help even if their studies are unrelated to their work.[11] Check *The Foundation Directory* at the library or career development center. (Professional associations and private foundations like the Jeanette Rankin Foundation give educational grants to older women.) In addition, you can save money by starting at a two-year college, then transferring into a four-year school.

RESOURCES

Books

Apps, Jerold. 1988. *The Adult Learner on Campus.* New York: Cambridge University Press.

Aslanian, Carol, and Henry Brickell. 1980. *Americans in Transition: Changing Reasons for Adult Learning.* New York: College Board.

Astin, H. S. (ed.). 1976. *Some Action of Her Own: The Adult Woman and Higher Education.* Lexington, Mass: Heath.

Bianchi, Anne. 1990. *Smart Choices.* Princeton, N.J.: Peterson's Guides.

CUPA Foundation. 1997. *College and University Reference Guide to Work-Family Programs.* Washington, D.C.: College and University Personnel Association Foundation.

Haponski, William, and Charles McCabe. 1986. *New Horizons: The Education and Career Planning Guide for Adults.* Princeton, N.J.: Peterson's Guides.

Hawes, Gene. 1985. *The College Board Guide to Going to College While Working: Strategies for Success.* New York: College Board.

Knowles, Malcolm. 1990. *The Adult Learner: A Neglected Species.* 4th ed. Houston, Texas: Gulf.

Lennox, Joan H., and Judith H. Shapiro. 1990. *Life Changes: How Women Can Make Courageous Choices.* New York: Crown.

Riley, Julia. 1991. *Living the Possible Dream: The Single Parent's Guide to College Success.* Boulder, Colo.: Johnson.

Schlossberg, Nancy. 1991. *Overwhelmed: Coping with Life's Ups and Downs.* New York: Dell.

Scott, Nancy. 1980. *Returning Women Students: A Review of Research and Descriptive Studies.* Washington, D.C.: National Association for Women Deans, Administrators, and Counselors.

Shields, Charles. 1994. *Back in School: A Guide to Adult Learners.* Hawthorne, N.J.: Career.

Siebert, Al, and Bernardine Gilpin. 1989. *Time for College: When You Work, Have a Family, and Want More from Life.* Portland, Ore.: Practical Psychology.

Organizations

College and University Work/Family Association (CUWFA), c/o Director, Child and Family Services, Stanford University, 845 Escondido Road, Mail Code 7140, Stanford, CA 94305–7140. Phone: (415) 723–2660. CUWFA is a national organization that provides information on work/family issues in higher education and works to facilitate the integration of work and study with family and personal life. It works primarily with higher education professionals such as student services administrators and child care program directors. It maintains a database of campus work/study programs. Web site: http://www.virtua.com/cuwfa/

National Coalition for Campus Children's Centers (NCCCC), 515 King Street, Suite 410, Alexandria, VA 22314. Phone: (703) 836–3326. Founded in 1980, this nonprofit coalition promotes child care centers on campus. It organizes an annual conference, conducts research, and provides information through its publications and videotapes on planning and organizing child care centers and other child care issues. A list of campus child care centers is also available.

CHAPTER 8

Women and

Disability

I have been told many times how "lucky" I am to be only moderately disabled. "It could have been much worse," they say, an attitude which perplexes me. . . . In my view I am not lucky or unlucky, I'm just disabled.

—Marsha Saxton, "Born and Unborn," 1984[1]

I'm a member of three minorities: I'm a woman, Asian, and disabled. Which do I identify with most strongly? It's like a triangle. It depends on the circumstances which point of the triangle is on top.

—Quoted in *With Wings*, 1987[2]

APPROXIMATELY 12 PERCENT of college students have some kind of disability.[3] Although most able-bodied people visualize someone using a wheelchair when they hear the word "disabled," the term covers not only physical disabilities that prevent a person from getting around without aid but also hearing and visual impairments, as well as a host of hidden conditions. The latter include attention deficit/hyperactivity disorder (AD/HD) and learning disabilities (LD), which can involve difficulty in communicating, writing, reading, listening comprehension and reasoning, or mathematical ability.[4] Other forms of disability include psychological impairments, such as anxiety disorders and rare conditions like Tourette's Syndrome.

The earliest attempt to integrate people with disabilities into the educational system began in the early nineteenth century with the founding of special schools such as Gallaudet University for the deaf and hearing impaired. After World Wars I and II, federal rehabilitation programs provided education and training for veterans with disabilities (most of whom were men). Real awareness and support for the disabled, however, did not begin until late in the civil rights era. The first disability legislation was the Architectural Barrier Act of 1968, which required physical accessibility to all federal buildings. This was followed by the Rehabilitation Act of 1973, which, among other things, made it illegal for any institution or program receiving federal assistance, including most colleges and universities, to discriminate on the basis of disability.[5] The Education for All Handicapped Children Act (1975) guaranteed all children with disabilities the right to public education in the most integrated setting possible.

With the passage of this law, a large pool of students wanting to go on to higher education was created. By the 1980s, colleges and universities across the country were receiving growing numbers of qualified applicants. The Americans with Disabilities Act (ADA), passed in 1990, is considered the disabled Bill of Rights. It ensures that no program, service, or activity offered by a public institution can be denied to someone with a disability. This includes all aspects of campus life.[6]

Despite legislation like the ADA, however, students with disabilities are still the last group on campus to be recognized as having special needs. If you have a physical disability, you may have discovered that you do not have access to all buildings on campus—doorways are too narrow for your wheelchair, ramps are too steep—or that you can only sit in the very back or front of your classrooms. A University of Wisconsin law student named Bridget McGuire, who had been a carpenter for twelve years before becoming disabled, took matters into her own hands. She brought a power saw to class one day and calmly cut off the end of a desk to make room for her wheelchair after failing to get the accommodation she needed from school officials.[7]

Deaf students can run into difficulties if their professors do not know how to meet their communication needs. Blind or visually impaired students may discover that the technology and services they need to do their best, even something simple like being provided with a reader or someone who can tape books for them, are not available. Faculty and administrators may not be as flexible as they should be when they are faced with a student with a learning disability. They may not understand the need for extra time or a different test format so that the students can read and fully understand test questions and be able to demonstrate their true knowledge of the subject. Some students with learning disabilities may need to take fewer courses than usual per term.

Your university's attitude toward students with disabilities can be judged by the degree to which it accommodates them. Do the physically disabled have easy and safe access to all campus buildings: classrooms, the student center, library, dorms, computer lab, gym? Is a transportation service provided for those who need it? Are library stacks wide enough and at least some classroom desks and lab benches high enough for wheelchairs? Does the library provide a large print, braille, and audiotape book service? What about equipment like amplified telephones, computers with synthesized voice and large print output, and optical character recognition (OCR) scanners that read English-language books aloud? Are all programs as well as facilities accessible? Are college policies flexible? For example, can a course substitution be made (e.g., for a hearing-impaired student who cannot learn to speak a foreign language) and extended time taken to earn a degree when necessary? Has the your school made an attempt to train faculty and staff and inform and sensitize the student body?[8]

Colleges and universities are not required to offer "special education" programs, but they are required, under both the Rehabilitation Act and the ADA, to examine the accessibility of their programs, services, and facilities and make "reasonable" changes to accommodate students with disabilities.[9] More and more students are going to court when their reasonable needs are not met. At the University of Miami, for example, four students filed a class-action lawsuit in federal court against the university for not providing them with services to take down notes, which they could not do for themselves. A class-action suit was brought against Boston University for reducing its program of services to students with learning disabilities.[10] Disabled students are also fighting for the opportunity to compete with other students in sports, and more are expressing interest in going abroad on study programs.[11]

The biggest hurdle for many students with disabilities is social, however. Most able-bodied students lack information and are uninterested. They may feel awkward around people with disabilities, not know how to relate to them, or reject them as friends. Some disabilities can create real communication difficulties. Blind students, for example, do not see expressions, gestures, or posture, and therefore cannot read other people's body language or use the same body language and gestures themselves. As a result, their communication styles and demeanor sometimes can discourage able-bodied students who want to interact with them. A student with a learning disability may not be able to tell the difference between a sincere and a sarcastic remark, in the same way that someone with a visual impairment cannot easily distinguish between "b" and "d," even with normal or above normal intelligence.

Studies have found that able-bodied students' attitudes toward people with disabilities vary, depending upon the type of disability and on the situation in which they are interacting. In academic settings, the able-bodied feel more comfortable around people who use wheelchairs than they do around blind students. In social settings, however, they feel just the opposite.[12] Research also indicates that professors prefer to deal with students who have certain disabilities. They regard hearing impairments and most physical disabilities, for example, as being less handicapping for academic work than visual impairments and cerebral palsy.

Being disabled means experiencing a lot of frustration, discouragement, and tension. If you have a learning disability, you may have a short attention span, difficulty understanding and remembering certain information, and problems with identifying main ideas, taking notes, and managing your time.[13] You may lack confidence and experience more stress and interpersonal difficulties than nondisabled students.[14] Because American culture places such high value on independence and self-reliance, it is difficult for someone who needs help to have to depend on others. This is a problem many elderly people face too. You may find it a struggle to keep your dignity and self-respect, while having to ask for help. "Wanting both to be assisted and to be left alone, to be accommodated and to live normally," explains mental health counselor Wendy Lustbader, "dependent people may push [others] away at the same time that they hope others will find ways to make life easier for them."[15] If you have a disability, you may keep your able-bodied friends at a distance because you believe that you've already burdened them enough with requests for help. You may also hold back information about yourself and your disability, because you are unsure how much you should tell them. You may ask yourself if the support you might get is worth the embarrassment of disclosing your problems.

Like most people who are in some way different from the majority, students with disabilities also have to deal with stereotypes. One pervasive stereotype is the belief that anyone with a visible physical disability is also mentally impaired. If you have such a disability, you have probably been spoken to as if you were a child or had questions about you addressed to the able-bodied person you were with. The same thing used to happen quite commonly to all women. (I remember my own outrage many years ago at having two male acquaintances in Ireland address questions about me to my husband, while we were riding together in the same car!) Researchers have found that most able-bodied students believe that disabled people are submissive, introverted, and dependent. Students with psychological disabilities may also suffer from the media stereotype of the psychologically impaired as being potentially violent.

All people with disabilities suffer the stigma of presumed incompetency. Cheryl Ann Fischer took Case Western Reserve University to court after its medical school rejected her application because she is blind. She wrote:

> I just know I would be a good doctor. I can learn anything a [sighted] medical student does, only in different ways. . . . Sure I'd need an assistant to read the patient's chart to me and do the ear, nose, and throat exam. But I would be the one asking the relevant questions. I could do the physical part of the exam by touch. So many clues to what's wrong with a person manifest themselves in ways they aren't dependent on sight. . . . I think anyone who's been through something like going blind can better understand what sick people go through. Who knows? Maybe that would be my reputation—that I was a doctor who understood.[16]

After initially winning a lower court ruling, she lost in the Ohio Supreme Court in a 4–3 decision characterized by one of the dissenting justices as "prejudice, pure and simple."[17]

Dealing with stereotypes and deflecting negative reactions and inappropriate remarks takes emotional stamina, both to find ways to be appropriately assertive and to resist internalizing feelings of inferiority. Many students with disabilities struggle with the problem of not being acknowledged by others. You may find that you have little opportunity to share your everyday feelings and observations about the world with other students, which is likely to make you feel isolated, depressed, or angry. When researcher Nancy Weinberg asked people with physical disabilities if they would choose to become able-bodied if they had the opportunity, however, most did not wish to change.[18] They were happy with who they were; to change would mean becoming someone else. Even many of the people who had been disabled by injury later in life said they would not wish to change or else felt ambivalent about the idea.

Nancy Weinberg also conducted in-depth interviews and analyzed nearly 250 published autobiographies, essays, and interviews with the disabled. What she found was a range of attitudes. Some people were very bitter; others saw their disability mainly as an inconvenience. Still others embraced being disabled, regarding it as a gift, opportunity, or challenge. This group included Kitty O'Neal, a deaf stuntwoman: "Being deaf is not a handicap. Rather, it is a challenge to conquer, like being called on to do a difficult stunt."[19]

Having a disability is in some ways more of a challenge for women than it is for men. Women with disabilities are less likely to be employed, to have life partners, or to receive high-quality rehabilitation services than are men. Most medical research and rehabilitation efforts have focused on men. According to

Michelle Fine and Adrienne Asch, this is because disabilities by definition imply dependency, which is the opposite of autonomy, which is perceived as masculine. Because women are already regarded as passive and dependent in comparison to men, disabled woman are viewed as less "wounded."[20] Most studies of how people cope with physical disability also have been conducted with men.[21]

Women with disabilities share with able-bodied women the burden of living in a youth- and beauty-obsessed culture. According to a woman with NTD (neural tube defect), "We are beset with messages to buy products which hide or disguise our differences and body functions, and strive to achieve rigid standards of appearance. Such standards are particularly harsh on disabled women whose appearance or body function may be further from 'acceptable.'"[22]

Some women with disabilities feel unattractive because it is often difficult to find even reasonably stylish clothing to wear. Researchers have found that able-bodied college students consider women with disabilities to be less feminine than other women and disabled men to be less masculine.[23] If you have a physical disability, you have probably been treated by the able-bodied as if you are asexual.

Yet students with disabilities are not exempt from the problems faced by able-bodied women, including the risk of sexual assault. In some cases, they are more vulnerable. According to a deaf student at Gallaudet University who was raped in her dorm room by a fellow student, "When he got on top of me, I said [signed and mouthed the word] no. I cried. He did it anyway. When it was over, I kicked him in the groin. He told me if I told anyone, he would make me suffer."[24] Another deaf student who was raped was not provided with a trained interpreter when she went to the police station to report the incident. She typed out her own statement but was unable to communicate her case effectively enough to the officer in charge for the police to pursue the investigation: "I felt like I was raped twice."[25] Deaf and hearing-impaired students who have been victimized by sexual assaults at Gallaudet reportedly hesitate to tell the administration, partly out of a sense of loyalty to the institution. According to a faculty member, "Part of the difficulty for deaf women in dealing with women's issues like rape involves a fear of trashing the deaf community." Denise Snyder, executive director of the D.C. Rape Crisis Center, concurs: "The deaf community is small and close-knit. If you make a fuss at Gallaudet, you've closed a big door."[26]

IN THE EARLY 1980s, the interdisciplinary field of disability studies emerged. Now courses like the Social and Psychological Aspects of Disability and (Dis)Abling Images in Literature, Film, and the Media are taught on some campuses, and a curriculum development project in disability studies has been developed at Hunter College. There is clearly a need for scholarship and courses examining disability. According to psychologist Carol Gill, president of the Chicago Institute of Disability Research and herself disabled, "Disability is a socio-political phenomenon as much as it is medical. Our issues are not caused by biology, any more than the issues of women's oppression are caused by sex."[27]

As with women's studies, disability studies bring to light omitted histories, ideas, and literature. Focusing on disability, like focusing on gender, also deepens our understanding of difference and helps us better understand the social construction of knowledge and categories. Feminist scholars have grappled with a variety of issues that are faced by women with disabilities; increasingly, feminist perspectives are being brought into the disability rights movement. In recent years, for example, feminist thinkers have raised radical questions about cultural attitudes about the body. "Some of the same attitudes about the body which contribute to women's oppression generally," says Susan Wendell, "also contribute to the social and psychological disablement of people who have physical disabilities."[28] Likewise, women with disabilities have challenged feminist assertions such as the belief that women should have an inalienable right to reproductive choice, including the right to abort "defective" fetuses. Women with disabilities have not only also brought their knowledge and experiences to feminism and the women's movement, but at a personal level, they can teach other women about accepting their bodies and dealing with limitations. According to Barbara Hillyer, "The disability rights movement taught me to struggle with the experience of human limitation, to hear each person's story in distinctive detail, as I tried to understand where the boundary may lie between ability and disability, between physical and social, between the personal and the political. Here I learned anew the other movement's [women's liberation movement] first lesson, that the personal is political."[29]

_____ **DID YOU KNOW?** _____

▓ An estimated 50 million people in the United States have disabilities: more than half are women. Approximately 16 percent of American women are disabled.

▓ When people in one survey were asked if they considered their disability to be: 1) a "fact of life," 2) an "inconvenience," 3) a "cause of frustration," 4) a "terrible thing that happened," or 5) the "worst thing that ever happened," 60 percent viewed their disability as just a fact of life.

▓ All colleges receiving federal funds must designate at least one person to serve as a contact for students who identify themselves as having disabilities. This person (or office) is responsible for ensuring that appropriate accommodations are made to help them perform on an equal level with other students and to guarantee that they do not encounter discrimination in any area of college life.

- Some universities have specialized committees to implement policies affecting disabled students. The University of Rhode Island, for example, has six committees composed of staff, faculty, and students, focusing on: facilities, adaptive technologies, communication technologies, library access, recreation access, and housing and dining.

- Four percent of women with disabilities have college degrees, compared to 20 percent of nondisabled women.

- Approximately 40 percent of students with disabilities have a visual impairment, 25 percent are deaf or hard of hearing, and 20 percent have learning disabilities. The rest have other conditions.[30]

- Medical researchers still do not know why some disabling illnesses occur more frequently in women than in men. Spina bifida, for example, is twice as common in women as in men.

- The first National Conference on Disabled Women and Girls was held in 1982.

- Heather Whitestone, who is profoundly deaf, was the first person with a disability to be named Miss America.

- In 1997, the National Organization on Disability organized a protest in Washington, D.C., to object to the new Franklin D. Roosevelt Memorial's failure to depict FDR—who had been paralyzed by polio—in a wheelchair. They felt an important opportunity to diminish stereotypes of people with disabilities as incapable and to provide a positive role model to children with disabilities was missed.

_____ *WHAT YOU CAN DO* _____

- Seek out women's studies courses in feminist theory and those dealing with cultural constructions of the body. Other programs and departments at your school may offer courses specifically on disability.

If You Do Not Have a Disability

- Learn more about the issues that students with disabilities face. Talk to them and assist them when you can. Contact the office of the dean of students to ask if there are any students on campus you could help by taping or reading texts aloud or taking class notes.

- Before extending help to someone, ask if the person would like your help. If the answer is yes, then give it in a matter-of-fact way so that the need for help recedes into the background.

◩ Research indicates that to increase understanding and mutual comfort, reduce prejudice, and make interaction easier between able-bodied students and those with disabilities, it is necessary to create opportunities for extended contact and to find ways for students to work together toward common goals.

◩ Make sure that when an organization you belong to is planning and publicizing events, especially off-campus ones, that an invitation is extended to people with "special transportation or accommodation needs." Include the name and phone number of the person they should contact on all your publicity for the events.

◩ When planning to attend a conference or rally on a women's issue, extend the invitation to women with disabilities. Consider the idea of teaming those who express interest with able-bodied students who will accompany them, share the experience, and be available to render assistance if necessary.

◩ Everyone relies on signs to find places. Students whose mobility is impaired need signs that clearly indicate where accessible entrances are located. High-contrast or braille signs should be provided for students with vision impairments. Likewise, students who are deaf or hearing impaired need signs posted near public telephones indicating which phones have special telecommunications devices. If you are an able-bodied student, you could work with disabled students to conduct a campus audit to determine problem areas and jointly present your findings to the administration. You might also develop a campus guide and map to resources and facilities for students with disabilities. If you have a disability and your needs are not being met, speak to the administration about it.

◩ While few colleges or universities can afford to provide all of the estimated twenty thousand technological services and adaptive solutions available to the disabled, there are many things they can do. Textbooks on tape or student readers can help blind and many learning disabled students. Adaptive computer software and hardware, including voice output via synthesized speech, alternative forms of keyboard access, and enlarged print, are also available. The computer lab itself should be physically accessible, with wide aisles, tables high enough for a wheelchair, keyboards at adjustable heights, and a dedicated work station located near the staff area to make getting assistance easy. Text telephones (TT) or telecommunications devices (TDD) for deaf students should be available on campus, and in offices like admissions and financial aid that regularly communicate with the public. The library could be equipped with a Kurzweil Reading Machine (KRM), which converts printed material into synthesized audio text using an optical scanner.

If You Have a Disability

 Do not hesitate to speak to your professors about your needs. You may, for example, need to borrow their notes, use a tape recorder or laptop computer in class, have more time on exams, or use a different exam format.

 If you have a visible disability and feel cut off from other students, try talking to them about typical college events such as sports, buying tickets to a performance, a recent party, or studying for exams. Show that you share common interests.

 Social-psychological research indicates that disabled people who are open about their disability are better liked than those who are not. By acknowledging your disability, you show that you are comfortable with yourself. You also make able-bodied students feel more comfortable and legitimize their natural curiosity.

 Teach students how to relate to people with disabilities appropriately. Let them know, for example, that using words related to a disability such as "walk," "see," and "hear" is all right. When they offend you or stereotype you, correct them in a nonhostile way.

 Be sure to find out what services are available to you. Some campuses have an office for students with disabilities or else a designated person in the office of the dean of students who can help you resolve problems. Check with the university's financial aid office to see if state-supported grants provided under federal vocational rehabilitation programs are available.

 If you are interested in going abroad, check the Council on International Education Exchange's (CIEE) Web site for minority and disabled students. It provides information on work, study, and volunteer programs abroad, placing you in contact with other students with disabilities who have participated (see Organizations).

_____ *RESOURCES* _____

Books and Other Publications

Beisser, Arnold. 1989. *Flying Without Wings: Personal Reflections on Being Disabled*. New York: Doubleday.

Bolles, R. N. 1991. *Job-Hunting Tips for the So-Called Handicapped or People with Disabilities*. Berkeley: Ten Speed.

Cordoni, Barbara. 1990. *Living with a Learning Disability*. Rev. ed. Carbondale: Southern Illinois University Press.

Dalke, C. L. 1991. *Support Programs in Higher Education for Students with Disabilities: Access to All*. Gaithersburg, Md.: Aspen.

Deegan, M. J., and N. A. Brooks. 1985. *Women and Disability: The Double Handicap.* New Brunswick, N.J.: Transaction.

Department of Justice. 1997. *A Guide to Disability Rights Laws.* Washington, D.C.: U.S. Department of Justice. Available free from Consumer Information Center, Department 68, Pueblo, CO 81009.

DisAbility News Online. This is an online magazine sponsored by Access by Design. It provides news updates and information on new products and technologies that promote more efficient daily living. Web site: http: // www.access-by-design/ablenews.

Disability Rag. This monthly journal regularly includes articles of interest to women with disabilities. It is an action-oriented publication aimed at people committed to disability rights. *Disability Rag*, PO Box 6453, Syracuse, NY 13127.

Driedger, D. 1989. *The Last Civil Rights Movement: Disabled Peoples' International.* London: Hurst.

Ferguson, L. M., D. L. Ferguson, and S. J. Taylor (eds.). 1992. *Interpreting Disability: Qualitative Reader.* New York: Teachers College Press.

Fielding, P. M. (ed.). 1994. *A National Directory of Four Year Colleges, Two Year Colleges and Post High School Training Programs for Young People with LD.* 7th ed. Tulsa, Okla.: Partners in Publishing.

Fine, Michelle, and Adrienne Asch. 1988. *Women with Disabilities: Essays in Psychology, Culture and Politics.* Philadelphia: Temple University Press.

Garnett, Katherine, and Sandra LaPorta. 1991. *Dispelling the Myths: College Students and Learning Disabilities.* New York: Hunter College and National Center for Learning Disabilities.

Gerber, P. J. 1991. *Speaking for Themselves: Ethnographic Interviews with Adults with Learning Disabilities.* Ann Arbor: University of Michigan Press.

Hillyer, Barbara. 1993. *Feminism and Disability.* Norman: University of Oklahoma Press.

Jepson, Jill (ed.). 1992. *No Walls of Stone: An Anthology of Literature by Deaf and Hard of Hearing Writers.* Washington, D.C.: Gallaudet University Press.

Jezer, Marty. 1997. *Stuttering: A Life Bound Up in Words.* New York: Basic.

Karp, Rashelle S. 1991. *Library Services for Disabled Individuals.* Boston: Hall.

Keith, Lois. 1996. *"What Happened to You?": Writing by Disabled Women.* New York: New Press.

Kelly, Kate. 1995. *You Mean I'm Not Lazy, Stupid or Crazy!* New York: Scribner's.

Kravets, Marybeth, and Imy Wax (eds.). 1995. *The K & W Guide to Colleges for the Learning Disabled.* 3rd ed. Cambridge, Mass.: Educators Publishing Service.

Kriegsman, Kay Harris, et al. 1992. *Taking Charge: Teenagers Talk About Life and Physical Disabilities.* Rockville, Md.: Woodbine House.

Lakoff, Robin Tolmach. 1989. "Women and Disability: Review Essay," *Feminist Studies* 15 (Summer): 365–375.

Lewis, Erica-Lee. 1996. *Help Yourself: Advice for College Bound Students with Learning Disabilities.* New York: Random House.

Light, Danielle. 1993. *Thinking Right Among Left Brainers: One Woman's Experience of Attention Deficit Disorder and Dyslexia.* Mt. Shasta, Calif.: Mt. Shasta.

Lipkin, Midge. 1993. *Colleges with Programs or Services for Students with Learning Disabilities.* Belmont, Mass.: Schoolsearch.

Lonsdale, Susan. 1990. *Women and Disability: The Experience of Physical Disability among Women.* New York: St. Martin's.

Luczak, Rayond (ed.). 1993. *Eyes of Desire: A Deaf Gay and Lesbian Reader.* Boston: Alyson.

Mairs, Nancy. 1997. *Waist-High in the World: A Life among the Nondisabled.* Boston: Beacon.

Milota, Cathy. 1993. *Count Me In: Resource Manual on Disabilities.* Rev. ed. Minneapolis, Minn.: PACER Center.

Nadeau, Kathleen. 1994. *Survival Guide for College Students with ADD or LD.* New York: Magination.

National Clearinghouse on Women and Girls with Disabilities. 1990. *Bridging the Gap: A National Directory of Services for Women and Girls with Disabilities.* New York: Educational Equity Concepts.

Padden, Carol, and Tom Humphries. 1988. *Deaf in America: Voices from a Culture.* Cambridge, Mass.: Harvard University Press.

Panzarino, Connie. 1994. *The Me in the Mirror.* Seattle: Seal.

Quinn, Patricia (ed.). 1994. *ADD and the College Student.* New York: Magination.

Saxton, Marsha, and Florence Howe. 1987. *With Wings: An Anthology of Literature By and About Women with Disabilities.* New York: Feminist Press.

Sclafani, Annette, and Michael J. Lynch. 1995. *College Guide for Students with Learning Disabilities.* 11th ed. Miller Place, N.Y.: Laurel. (Includes section on scholarships.)

Shapiro, Joseph. 1993. *No Pity: People with Disabilities Forging a New Civil Rights Movement.* New York: Times.

Van Cleve, John Vickery (ed.). 1993. *Deaf History Unveiled: Interpretations from the New Scholarship.* Washington, D.C.: Gallaudet University Press.

Wendell, Susan. 1989. "Toward a Feminist Theory of Disability," *Hypatia* 4 (Summer): 104–124.

Women and Disability Awareness Project. 1984. *Building Community: A Manual Exploring Issues of Women and Disability.* New York: Educational Equity Concepts.

Woods, James. 1989. *How to Succeed in College with Dyslexia.* Dallas, Texas: Sem-Co.

Zola, Irving (ed.). 1982. *Ordinary Lives: Voices of Disability and Disease.* Cambridge, Mass.: Applewood.

Videos

American Culture: The Deaf Perspective. This is a four-part series exploring the culture and heritage of deaf Americans. Program 1, "Deaf Heritage," looks at the emergence of Deaf identity, including the development of American Sign Language. "Deaf Folklore" shows how traditions and values are passed on through humor, stories, and games. "Deaf Literature" samples the poetry and drama of the deaf on stage and screen. The final program, "Deaf Minorities," examines seven individuals' search for cultural identity, including an African-American woman and a lesbian. Produced by the San Francisco Public Library. Media Production, San Francisco Library, Civic Center, San Francisco, CA 94102. Phone: (415) 557–4400.

The Disabled Women's Theatre Project. This sixty-minute video performance was written, performed, and produced by women with physical disabilities. It uses dance, comedy, and drama to convey the painful and absurd moments in the lives of women with disabilities. Women Make Movies, 462 Broadway, Suite 500–E, New York, NY 10013. Phone: (212) 925–0606.

Gifts of Greatness. This inspirational sixty-minute musical/drama highlights the lives of famous people who have overcome dyslexia, including Patty Duke and Julie Harris. Produced by Joyce Bulifant in 1991. Media Production, San Francisco Public Library, Civic Center, San Francisco, CA 94102. Phone: (415) 557–4400.

Language Landscape: A Presentation of Deaf Performance Art. This video is a compilation of short performances by deaf artists: entertainer Mary Beth Miller, the dance troupe Misign, filmmaker Sam Supalla, storyteller Ben Behan, and poet Ella Mae Lentz. Media Production, San Francisco Public Library, Civic Center, San Francisco, CA 94102. Phone: (415) 557–4400.

A Picture of Success. This video, featuring Pat Buckley Moss and Dr. Larry Silver, tells the story of a successful dyslexic. Media Production, San Francisco Public Library, Civic Center, San Francisco, CA 94102. Phone: (415) 557–4400.

Positive Images: Portraits of Women with Disabilities. This fifty-eight-minute video, focusing on the lives of three strong and articulate women, was produced by Julie Harrison and Harilyn Rousso. It locates disability as a women's issue and examines the social, economic, and political issues women with disabilities face. Women Make Movies, 462 Broadway, Suite 500–E, New York, NY 10013. Phone: (212) 925–0606.

Toward Intimacy: Women with Disabilities. Made by Debbie McGee and the National Film Board of Canada, this hour-long documentary shows that women with disabilities are not asexual beings. It looks at the lives and challenges of four women with physical disabilities who have found meaningful love relationships. Filmakers Library, 124 East 40th Street, New York, NY 10016. Phone: (212) 808–4980.

Organizations

ABLEDATA, 8455 Colesville Road, Suite 935, Silver Spring, MD 20910–3319. Phone: (800) 227–0216. A national database of information on assistive technology.

Association on Higher Education and Disability (AHEAD), PO Box 21192, Columbus, OH 43221–0192. Phone: (614) 488–4972 (Voice/TDD). AHEAD promotes the equal rights and opportunities of disabled students, staff, faculty, and graduates. It conducts surveys on issues of importance to college students with disabilities, offers a resource referral system, and provides information on the law and accommodations on campus. Barnard College's *From Access to Equality: A Resource Manual for College Women with Disabilities* (1987) and many other publications are available from AHEAD.

Disability Studies Project, Hunter College, 1016 West, 695 Park Avenue, New York, NY 10021. Phone: (212) 772–4723. The Project produces and updates the "Disability Studies Bibliography." The first version was also published in vol. 47 (April 1995) of *Radical Teacher*, along with several articles on disability studies.

Disabled Womyn's Educational Project, PO Box 8773, Madison, WI 53708–8773. Phone: (608) 256–8883. Founded in 1988, this group supports legislation sensitive to the needs of lesbians with disabilities. It maintains a small reference library and a speaker's bureau and publishes a newsletter, *Dykes, Disability & Stuff Quarterly*.

Gallaudet University, 800 Florida Avenue NE, Washington, DC 20002–3695. Phone: (202) 651–5000 (Voice/TTY). This is the only liberal arts university in the world for people who are deaf. Its library produces lists of available captioned videotapes.

HEATH Resource Center, One Dupont Circle NW, Suite 800, Washington, DC 20036–1193. Phone: (800) 544–3284 or (202) 939–9320. HEATH is a program of the American Council on Education. It is a national clearinghouse for information on postsecondary education for individuals with disabilities, including educational support services, policies, campus opportunities, vocational technical schools, adult education programs, and independent living centers. HEATH also publishes fact sheets, a semiannual *Resource Directory*, and guides like *How to Choose a College* and *Resources for Adults with Learning Disabilities*.

International Dyslexia Association (IDA), 8600 LaSalle Road, Chester Building, Suite 382, Baltimore, MD 21286–2044. Phone: (800) 222–3123. The IDA (formerly the Orton Dyslexia Society) is an international, nonprofit research and educational organization. It will send a packet of free information on dyslexia and provide referrals to diagnosticians, educational therapists, and tutors. It has more than forty branch offices, which sponsor information meetings and support groups.

Learning Disabilities Association of America (LDA), 4156 Library Road, Pittsburgh, PA 15234. Phone: (412) 341–1515. The LDA is a national nonprofit organization. It provides free information on learning disabilities and can refer you to one of seven hundred local chapters. It publishes a quarterly newsletter, *Newsbriefs*, maintains a resource center with over five hundred publications for sale, and operates a film rental service.

National Alliance for the Mentally Ill (NAMI), 2102 Wilson Boulevard, Suite 302, Arlington, VA 22201. Phone: (800) 959–6264. NAMI provides information about and resources for people with psychiatric disabilities. It also works to end discrimination against people with brain disorders.

National Center for Learning Disabilities (NCLD), 381 Park Avenue South, Suite 1401, New York, NY 10016. Phone: (212) 545–7510. NCLD is a nonprofit organization dedicated to improving the lives of individuals with learning disabilities. It raises public awareness, produces education tools like the five-part video series *We Can Learn*. It also runs a referral service. Members receive a special packet of information on LD and regular updates.

National Library Service for the Blind and Physically Handicapped, Library of Congress, 1291 Taylor Street NW, Washington, DC 20542. Phone: (202) 707–5100. The Service provides lists of recorded and braille books and magazines available through a national network of cooperating libraries that provide free loan of these materials and playback equipment. The bimonthly publication *Talking Book Topics* is available in large print, cassette, and disc formats. The Service also publishes the pamphlet "Braille Literacy: Resources for Instruction, Writing Equipment, and Supplies" in large print and braille.

National Mental Health Association (NMHA), 1021 Prince Street, Alexandria, VA 22314–2971. Phone: (703) 684–7722 or (800) 969–NMHA. NMHA provides information and resources for people with psychiatric disorders.

National Network of Learning Disabled Adults (NNLDA), PO Box 32611, Phoenix, AZ 85064. Phone: (602) 941–5112. NNLDA is run by and for people with learning disabilities. It provides a free newsletter and list of self-help groups.

Networking Project for Disabled Women and Girls, YWCA, 610 Lexington Avenue, New York, NY 10022. Phone: (212) 735–9766. This is a project of the Young Women's Christian Association of New York City aimed at increasing the educational, social, and career aspirations of adolescent girls with disabilities by linking them to successful role models. It also operates an advocacy training program and preemployment training.

Recordings for the Blind (RFB), 20 Roszel Road, Princeton, NJ 08540. Phone: (800) 221–4792. This is a national, nonprofit organization through which blind or visually impaired students and those with learning disabilities can register to obtain taped texts. RFB also offers resources for taping any text-book not available through its own extensive holdings.

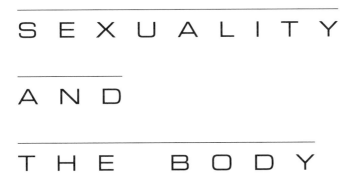

SEXUALITY

AND

THE BODY

CHAPTER 9

Eating and Body Image

Why are women nowadays so concerned with fat grams in this and that, and nutrition, and obsessive exercise, and how they look? Don't we understand yet that we should feel and look good for ourselves, not for others?

—Student at a small liberal arts college

MORE DIETING AND EATING DISORDERS are found on campus than anywhere else in America. The signs are everywhere. At a small liberal arts college, women in one residence hall spend so much time examining themselves in front of a full-length mirror that it has become the best place to post event and speaker announcements. Campus gyms are crowded with women working out on StairMasters, treadmills, and exercise bikes. In dining halls, women students eye each other's plates. "I feel like whenever I sit down to have a well-balanced meal," complained one person, "that I'm doing something wrong." Another student reported in class that many of her sorority sisters disappear into the bathrooms immediately after meals to vomit, while others compulsively avoid eating fat. "Some never eat any fat," she claimed. "They eat a plain bagel and corn, peas, or broccoli covered in ketchup and a diet coke. They avoid dessert and are paranoid about any oil that might have been put in the vegetables or pasta."

"It's almost a competition on who's eating, who's exercising," remarked a student during a discussion of anorexia in a women's studies class, "[but] these women need more than a bowl of Special K and a three-mile daily run to stay healthy. Their bodies need *some* fat." While working out clearly promotes fitness, and eating healthy, low-fat foods is something we should all try to do, some people cross the line between good exercise and watching their diet to compulsive and harmful behavior. What's the difference between being concerned about your weight and having an eating disorder? It's important to know the facts.

Bulimia (from the Greek meaning "ox hunger") is an eating disorder that involves compulsive eating or "bingeing" and then purging. The bulimic eats large amounts of food in a short period of time, and then tries to rid her body of the excess calories by vomiting, using laxatives or diuretics, or fasting and overexercising. As a result, her weight fluctuates dramatically; a bulimic can lose ten or more pounds in a single binge-purge cycle. A clinical diagnosis of bulimia includes binge eating twice a week for at least three months with associated vomiting, depression, and feeling out of control. Anorexia nervosa (originally meaning "loss of appetite from nervous causes") is a separate but related disorder. It involves severely limiting caloric intake—in other words, starving the body to be thin. A person is clinically diagnosed as an anorectic who loses between 15 and 25 percent of her (or his) expected body weight, misses three menstrual cycles, and is depressed and preoccupied with food. Although anorexia nervosa was known to physicians and named as early as the 1870s, it wasn't until the 1970s that the American public became aware of it.

Both diseases are relatively uncommon in the general population. Historian Joan Jacobs Brumberg, in *Fasting Girls: The Emergence of Anorexia Nervosa as a Modern Disease*, places the overall incidence of the disease in the United States at no more than 1.6 cases per 100,000 population. Among young women, however, the number is dramatically higher. Approximately 2 million women between the ages of nineteen and thirty-nine and 1 million teenage girls in the United States are affected by either anorexia nervosa or bulimia. Some experts place the total figure at nearly 5 million. Between 90 and 95 percent of all anorectics are young and female, and an estimated 10 to 20 percent of college women have an eating disorder. The diseases are also associated with professions in which weight and thinness are critical such as modeling, ballet, gymnastics, and figure skating for women and wrestling for men. The average height and weight of female gymnasts participating in the 1992 Olympics was four feet nine inches and 83 pounds. According to the Women's Sports Founda-

FASHION

Life, 1913

tion, as many as 60 percent of female athletes participating in "appearance" sports like gymnastics and figure skating suffer from eating disorders.

Many factors contribute to the occurrence of bulimia and anorexia nervosa. Culture plays a very important role. Both diseases are found primarily in countries with advanced economies that are heavily influenced by Western media and advertising: the United States, Canada, Western Europe, Japan, and Brazil. It is ironic that in India, even the poorest women eat 1,400 calories a day, while American women on a Hilton Head diet, to cite one example, eat as few as 800.[1] In a comparison of American and Austrian college students with bulimia nervosa, researchers found that the disease affected women in both cultures the same way, but that the American students were much more dissatisfied with their bodies.[2] Other research comparing American high school girls with those in Spain also found that Americans wanted much thinner bodies.[3] As Mary Pipher has pointed out in *Reviving Ophelia: Saving the Selves of Adolescent Girls*, "Girls are not irrational to worry about their bodies. Looks do matter. Girls who are chubby or plain miss much of the American dream. The social desirability research in psychology documents our prejudices against the unattractive, particularly the obese, who are the social lepers of our culture. Girls are terrified of being fat, as well they should be. Being fat means being left out, scorned, and vilified."

The fact that young African-American women are much less likely to suffer from either anorexia nervosa or bulimia than are middle- and upper-class white women, however, indicates that race/ethnicity and social class also play a role in determining who falls victim to eating disorders. For most African-American women, looking good encompasses a wider range of body types, not just the superthin model. Their attitude toward aging is also better than that of most young white women, who tend to regard it as deterioration from the young and thin ideal.

Clearly, American society as a whole places far too much emphasis on women's appearance. Popular culture and advertising—despite the advances women have made in recent years—continue to depict women primarily as ornamental sex objects and show models and film stars with incredibly thin bodies. Even some top film actresses are not perfect enough and use body doubles for revealing scenes. After attending the 1996 Academy Awards ceremony, nineteen-year-old actress Alicia Silverstone was lambasted in the tabloid media for having gained a modest amount of weight. Celebrities such as Jane Fonda, Paula Abdul, Sally Field, and the late Princess Diana acknowledged suffering from eating disorders. Magazines aimed at young African-American women, such as *BE* and *Sisters in Style*, carry the same messages and advertisements as other women's fashion magazines. According to some observers, they are contributing to a change in attitudes about appearance and body size among African-American women.

Today's standards of attractiveness emphasize the body (not the face) and glorify thinness. Since the 1950s the average weights of fashion models, *Playboy* centerfolds, and Miss America contestants have all dropped steadily. If Barbie—the most popular doll among young girls—were a real woman, her measurements would be 36–18–33.[4] Few women can meet the new beauty ideal. In the midst of plenty, we have become a fat-phobic society, with the heaviest burden borne by women. In a study of gender differences in body image, psychologists Laurie Mintz and Nancy Betz found that 30 percent of college women of normal weight regarded themselves as overweight. Other research has found that 50 percent of college women are unhappy with their body and weight. According to researchers at the University of California, 80 percent of fourth-grade girls in San Francisco are already dieting.

Some observers speculate that our greater exposure to nude bodies on cable television and in movies has raised the standards of perfection for everyone. In the last ten years, eating disorders have increased among men and boys. The

National Association of Anorexia Nervosa and Associated Disorders estimates that 1 million males now suffer from bulimia or anorexia. More men are also resorting to cosmetic surgery in order to look younger (motivated partly by job insecurity).

Other developments in American society have contributed to the problem. Many more foods are available to us at the same time that eating has become desocialized. Many Americans no longer eat together at the family table, instead "grazing" throughout the day. These patterns are exaggerated on college campuses, where food is available at any time, where meals can easily be skipped, and where there is incessant talk among women about food, weight, and exercise. The college environment is particularly conducive to eating disorders for other reasons as well. It is comprised of young women and men— the most vulnerable age group—living in an academically and socially stressful environment. It is also a largely unstructured and unsupervised environment. A bulimic student, for example, may study until two or three in the morning, have coffee for breakfast, nonfat yogurt for lunch, and then be ravenously hungry by evening. When she's that hungry, it's hard for her to be rational about food, and she is likely to binge and purge.

Alcohol and drug use can exaggerate the pressures and insecurities many young women experience as the following student's personal account and observations show:

> When I smoked marijuana, I'd get the "munchies" and consume a tremendous amount of food. Then I'd be repulsed by myself. It was at this point that my purging began. It continued after my drug experimentation. Whenever I was stressed out, feeling overwhelmed, or "gross," I remembered how much better purging made me feel. Body image is often magnified when drugs and alcohol are used. At a formal, a friend of mine was intoxicated and began to cry because she was afraid her dress would burst. Her insecurity about her body was magnified by the alcohol. Girls who suffer from various problems often use alcohol and drugs to let out their insecurities. But once they're drunk or high, their image of themselves drops even further.

In addition to culture, personal factors also play a part in determining who falls victim to bulimia and anorexia. Psychologists have found that many anorectics are perfectionists, yet they often have low self-esteem. An estimated seven out of ten women with eating disorders are also clinically depressed or are depression-prone.[5] One reason for feelings of inadequacy may be that they are unable to live up to their own unrealistic standards of beauty and body size. Many researchers believe that women turn to anorexia when they are unable to cope with the demands and pressures of their lives. According to

Vivian Meeham, president of the National Association for Anorexia Nervosa and Associated Disorders, "Any major life change can precipitate an eating disorder. It's a way of coping, however badly, with life's problems." Research by University of Toronto psychiatrist David Garner seems to confirm this. He found that anorectics scored much higher on measures of perceived "ineffectiveness" on an Eating Disorders Inventory (EDI) test than did other women. By taking control of their body weight and eating behavior, anorectics attempt to gain a sense of control over their lives. Some may also have a genetic predisposition to depression and, therefore, a predisposition to anorexia and bulimia.

Still other young women wish to stave off sexual maturity. By starving their bodies they remain childlike; they do not even menstruate. In some cases this rejection of sexual maturity includes a rejection of society's definition of women as inferior to men, as this student's analysis in a journal entry reveals:

> When I was fifteen years old, and I had just developed hips, I wanted to cut them off. This was obviously the product of my still wishing I was a male in a world that favored males. If I had hips and breasts, how was I going to deny my female sexuality? So I set about to get rid of them. I tried all different methods. I would go a few days with no food and then have some soup or something. Then I found that all you have to do is vomit afterward and you could eat all you want. So I did this for awhile. . . . It is the unhealthy and life-threatening reaction of women to the bogus beauty ideals created by men. . . . [Women] learn to hate their female bodies so much that they will go to any pains to make them disappear. . . . I felt there was power in the boyish figure and weakness in girlish curves.[6]

Many young women with eating disorders become sexually inhibited. In the words of one of my students who is a recovering anorectic,

> I completely shut myself off to boys. I became what is known as a "tease" because of how I flirted with boys at parties and other social settings, then when I was alone with them wouldn't display any sexual interest at all. I went from being a "normal adolescent" who was curious about sex to a junior in high school who could stand nothing but brief goodnight kisses. Even that sometimes disgusted me. Having spoken with several anorexics and bulimics (as well as my therapist) about this change in my sexual behavior and desire, I have come to the conclusion that it is quite common. Whether it's due to low self-esteem, distorted body image, insecurity, or a feeling that sexual behavior has somehow become "dirty," many girls will not allow themselves to be sexually active while suffering from an eating disorder.

Family dynamics can also contribute to eating disorders. Many anorectics belong to "overly enmeshed" families, that is, families in which parents and children are too tightly bonded to each other and in which parents exert excessive control over their daughters' lives. More recently, eating disorders have been linked to sexual and physical abuse. In such cases, a young woman uses her body to say—and to signal to others—what is unspeakable. For some abuse victims, anorexia also may produce a feeling of safety ("I cannot be hurt because I am almost invisible").[7] Women have long used the body and food to express themselves: the appetite as "voice."[8] Numerous feminist writers, such as Susie Orbach in *Hunger Strike: The Anorectic's Struggle as a Metaphor for Our Age*, have interpreted modern anorexia as a type of unconscious protest against patriarchal society and male definitions of femininity: the anorectic's behavior as "political discourse."

Once either anorexia nervosa or bulimia becomes advanced, biological processes also become a factor. British psychologists George I. Szmukler and Digby Tantam believe that anorexia nervosa is best understood as a dependence disorder in which sufferers become addicted to the physiological and psychological effects of starvation. Most medical research to date points to a malfunction in the hypothalamus, the organ that controls—among other things—digestion, metabolism, and body temperature. Other research suggests that a decrease in the amount of serotonin, a neurotransmitter that some experts believe is associated with mood and eating functions, contributes to the compulsive eating behavior seen in bulimics. Bulimia has been successfully treated in some patients with imiprimine, an antidepressant. Many researchers now regard eating disorders as chronic illnesses characterized by periods of remission and relapse.

The interplay of all these factors—cultural, psychological, and biological—can be seen by looking at a single hypothetical case of anorexia nervosa: A young woman may begin to eat less because of the many societal images of thinness that surround her and because her friends are doing the same thing. Being thin is important to her sense of self-worth. From her friends and from media articles on the topic, she learns how to go about restricting her diet and how to purge and exercise to lose weight. Her dieting and exercising become obsessional, however, because of personality or family issues. She may refuse food as a way to deal with stress and gain control of her life, as a bid for attention, to hurt her parents, or even to delay the onset of her own adult sexuality. If her diet control and exercising bring results, they will bring her emotional satisfaction and prompt her to continue dieting and overexercising, until finally it becomes difficult to stop. After months of semistarvation, her body and mind adjust to the feeling of hunger and nutritional deprivation, and eventually, biochemical processes come into play.[9]

Among the physiological problems caused by eating disorders are dry skin, lowered body temperature and basal metabolic rate, retarded bone growth, slowed heart rate, the cessation of menstruation, lethargy, lowered resistance to disease, and gastrointestinal disturbances. The more extreme the case, and the longer a bulimic or anorectic fails to receive treatment, the more damaging and less reversible the injury to her body becomes. The repeated vomiting of bulimia damages the stomach and esophagus, causes the salivary glands to swell, gums to recede, and tooth enamel to erode. "Do you know what finally made me give in and get help for myself?" wrote one student. "I went to the dentist, and I had nine cavities. He told me that the enamel on my teeth had been worn off. The same week . . . one of my teeth shattered from biting into a sandwich. . . . Like a lead brick it hit me: this was just one sign of how I was destroying my body."[10]

Treatment for eating disorders is usually conducted on an outpatient basis and consists of individual psychotherapy, family counseling, and nutritional therapy. But according to Joan Jacobs Brumberg, "The profusion of therapeutic treatments and the multiplicity of services available to anorectic women ultimately suggests confusion rather than confidence in the struggle with eating disorders."[11] Treating bulimics and anorectics is difficult. They usually deny they have a problem and resort to various strategies to conceal it such as wearing bulky clothing to hide their emaciation, skipping meals or being absent at mealtimes, secretly bingeing and purging in their room or car, and quickly changing the topic when eating behavior is discussed.

_____ *DID YOU KNOW?* _____

- A recent study at one university showed that 77 percent of the 1,200 women surveyed were on a diet; 16 percent acknowledged vomiting to avoid gaining weight.

- The average height and weight of an American woman is five feet four inches and 142 lbs. The average height and weight for a fashion model is five feet nine inches and 110 lbs., 23 percent less. A generation ago models weighed only 8 percent less than the average woman. Today, only one woman in forty thousand matches a model's size and shape.

- At any one time, 50 percent of American woman are on a diet. The diet industry produces revenues of $33 billion a year.

- Ninety-five percent of the people enrolled in weight loss programs are women, even though men and women are overweight in equal proportions.

- At least 2 million Americans use diet pills; thirty thousand bulimics abuse syrup of ipecac, an over-the-counter drug to induce vomiting in case of poisoning.

❖ Between 40 and 50 percent of anorectics also show symptoms of bulimia.

❖ A bulimic's binge can last from one to eight hours, during which she can consume from 3,400 calories (about one pecan pie) to 20,000 calories (equivalent to 210 brownies, five and a half layer cakes, or eighteen dozen macaroons) in a single binge.

❖ An estimated one hundred fifty thousand American women die from anorexia nervosa each year.

_____ *WHAT YOU CAN DO* _____

⊠ If you think that you (or a friend) have a serious problem with food, answer yes or no to the following questions:

1. I constantly think (and talk) about eating, weight, and body size. I spend a lot of time daydreaming about food.
2. I become anxious before eating.
3. I'm terrified about being overweight.
4. I don't know when I am physically hungry.
5. I go on eating binges and can't stop eating until I feel sick.
6. I often feel bloated or uncomfortable after meals.
7. I skip meals and try to keep the calories I eat under 1,000 a day.
8. I weigh myself frequently.
9. I exercise a lot and am rigid about my exercise plan.
10. I sometimes avoid social situations so I can maintain my eating or exercise schedule.
11. I believe that being in control of food lets others know that I can control myself.
12. I have taken laxatives or forced myself to vomit after eating.
13. I believe food controls my life.
14. I feel extremely guilty after eating.
15. I eat when I am nervous, anxious, lonely, or depressed.
16. I don't think I look good in my clothes.
17. Because of my weight and appearance, I'm more uptight than I'd like to be around people whom I find sexually attractive.
18. I don't drink any beverage (except water) that is not a diet drink.

If you answered yes to any of these questions you may have a problem with food and body image. If you answered yes to several, seek help. It is very difficult, if not impossible, to deal with these issues on your own. Virtually all college and university counseling and health services have someone trained in this area or can provide you with a referral. Ask for information and help. Your community probably has an eating disorders clinic; consult the telephone book or a local hospital.

 To help a friend with an eating disorder, talk to her confidentially and informally. Focus on her health, not on her weight or appearance. Strongly encourage her to get professional help. One of the central tasks of treatment is to make a bulimic or anorectic understand that it is not herself or her weight, but her behavior, that is the problem. Remember, people who suffer from eating disorders often deny their problem. Let the conversation end in a way that allows you to return to the subject later. Don't take a rejection personally, and in the meantime, seek advice from a counselor on how to help your friend.

 Obtain information about eating disorders from your college or university counseling center or health service or from the books and organizations listed in this chapter's Resources.

 Do not become a friend's food monitor or counselor. She needs your uncritical friendship as well as professional help in order to recover.

 Heighten campus awareness by inviting a speaker on eating disorders, showing a video such as *The Famine Within* or *Slim Hopes*, and arranging for a nutrition and eating disorders workshop. Contact the student health service or counseling center for the names of local experts. Most cities have clinics and organizations devoted to eating disorders; check the Yellow Pages or a local hospital, or consult one of the organizations listed at the end of this chapter. The Massachusetts Eating Disorder Association, based in Brookline, for example, provides educational seminars and workshops that are designed for a variety of audiences, including athletes, coaches, and students.

 Start a student eating awareness discussion group. Your group could also invite speakers, show videos, and sponsor workshops on nutrition, body image, and eating disorders.

 Encourage the campus health service or counseling center to sponsor a National Eating Disorders Screening Program (NEDSP). The program is an educational and screening service especially designed for college students. It is run by the sponsoring facility using materials (lecture, slides, video, informational brochures, screening questionnaires and interview guidelines, posters, referral resource lists) provided by the national NEDSP office (see Organizations).

 Start a BAM (Boycott Anorexic Marketing) chapter and help promote a healthier image of girls and women in the media (see Organizations).

 Encourage the office of residence life or the dean of students to train resident advisors about eating disorders and have them talk to incoming first-year students about the risks and how to detect a possible problem.

☒ If your campus does not have a nutritionist, ask the administration to get one. A nutritionist can work with dining services to help create healthy, low-fat meals. Sometimes the poor selection of food in dining halls forces students who are health conscious to end up eating salads (and half starving themselves) as their only healthy option. A nutritionist could also run a campus wellness program, providing students with information on good nutrition and working with those who have problems with food and body image.

☒ To maintain a healthy diet and weight and avoid fat-cell storage, experts advise the following: Eat only when you are hungry; stop eating when you are comfortable, not full; eat five mini-meals instead of two or three large meals; eat lightly at night when your metabolism is slowest; get 20 to 30 percent of your calories from fat (this will provide you with the fatty acids and fat soluble vitamins your body needs while still outsmarting your fat cells); and get regular aerobic exercise (at least forty-five minutes three times a week).

_____ *RESOURCES* _____

Books

Atwood, Margaret. 1991 (1969). *Edible Woman.* New York: Bantam.

Bordo, Susan. 1993. *Unbearable Weight: Feminism, Western Culture, and the Body.* Berkeley: University of California Press.

Brown, Catrina, and Karin Jasper (eds.). 1993. *Consuming Passions: Feminist Approaches to Weight Preoccupation and Eating Disorders.* Toronto: Second Story.

Bruch, Hilde. 1988. *Conversations with Anorexics.* New York: Basic.

Brumberg, Joan Jacobs. 1988. *Fasting Girls: The Emergence of Anorexia Nervosa as a Modern Disease.* Cambridge, Mass.: Harvard University Press.

———. 1997. *The Body Project: An Intimate History of American Girls.* New York: Random House.

Fallon, Patricia, Melanie Katzman, and Susan Wooley (eds.). 1994. *Feminist Perspectives on Eating Disorders.* New York: Guildford.

Hutchinson, Marcia G. 1993. *Transforming Body Image: Learning to Love the Body You Have.* Freedom, Calif.: Crossing.

Kano, Susan. 1989. *Making Peace with Food: Freeing Yourself from the Diet/Weight Obsession.* New York: Perennial Library.

Lark, Susan. 1995. *Women's Health Companion: Self Help Nutrition Guide and Cookbook.* Berkeley, Calif.: Celestial Arts.

Newman, Lesea. 1994. *Eating Our Hearts Out: Personal Accounts of Women's Relationship to Food.* Freedom, Calif.: Crossing.

O'Neill, Cherry Boone. 1985. *Dear Cherry: Questions and Answers on Eating Disorders*. New York: Continuum.

Orbach, Susie. 1985. *Hunger Strike: The Anorectic's Struggle as a Metaphor for Our Age*. New York: Norton.

Pipher, Mary. 1995. *Reviving Ophelia: Saving the Selves of Adolescent Girls*. New York: Ballantine.

Rooks, Noliwe. 1996. *Hair Raising: Beauty, Culture and African-American Women*. New Brunswick, N.J.: Rutgers University Press.

Ryan, Joan. 1995. *Little Girls in Pretty Boxes: The Making and Breaking of Elite Gymnasts and Figure Skaters*. New York: Doubleday.

Seid, Roberta Pollack. 1989. *Never Too Thin: Why Women are at War with Their Bodies*. New York: Prentice Hall.

Siegal, Michele. 1988. *Surviving an Eating Disorder: New Perspectives and Strategies for Family and Friends*. New York: Harper & Row.

Thompson, Becky. 1994. *A Hunger So Wide and So Deep: American Women Speak Out on Eating Problems*. Minneapolis: University of Minnesota Press.

Way, Karen. 1992. *Anorexia Nervosa and Recovery: A Hunger for Meaning*. Binghamton, N.Y.: Haworth.

Whitaker, Leighton, and William Davis (eds.). 1989. *The Bulimic College Student: Evaluation, Treatment and Prevention*. Binghamton, N.Y.: Haworth.

Wolf, Naomi. 1991. *The Beauty Myth*. New York: Morrow.

Videos

Betty Tells Her Story. In this classic twenty-minute documentary by Liane Brandon, Betty tells the story of her search for "the perfect dress," and why she never got to wear it twice. The first time, it is funny; the second time, very painful. Excellent for prompting discussion of beauty, identity, and the media. New Day Films, Department WM, 22–D, Hollywood Avenue, Hohokus, NJ 07423. Phone: (201) 652–6590.

The Famine Within. A powerful ninety-minute documentary by Katherine Gilday that examines how young women become obsessive about weight and body image. It examines the power of consumerism and the mass media, showing that the ultralean body of the fashion model has become the generalized standard for women. Also available in 118– and 55–minute lengths from Direct Cinema, PO Box 10003, Santa Monica, CA 90410. Phone: (800) 525–0000.

Recovering Bodies: Overcoming Eating Disorders. In this thirty-four-minute video seven college students (five women and two men) recount their experiences with eating disorders. Both professionals and students discuss the variety of psychological and physical symptoms involved and give advice on how to help sufferers. Media Education Foundation, 26 Center Street, Northampton, MA 01060. Phone: (800) 897–0089.

A Season in Hell. This fifty-nine-minute video by Walter Brock examines one young woman's four-year struggle with anorexia and bulimia. Beginning with her decision at age fourteen to diet after a boy had rejected her as overweight, it follows her through high school, college, hospitalization, and an engagement. Winner of several film prizes. New Day Films, Department WM 22–D. Hollywood Avenue, Hohokus, NJ 07423. Phone: (201) 652–6590.

Slim Hopes: Advertising and the Obsession with Thinness. Produced by Jean Kilbourne. This compelling thirty-minute video examines the influence of advertising images of thinness on women. Media Education Foundation, 26 Center Street, Northampton, MA 01060. Phone: (800) 897–0089.

Organizations

About-Face, PO Box 77665, San Francisco, CA 94107. Phone: (415) 436–0212. About-Face is a grassroots, volunteer effort to combat negative and distorted images of women and to promote healthy alternatives through education and activism. It is especially concerned with body image and eating disorders. Its Web site provides sample letters to use as models for writing to magazines and advertisers to protest negative images of women. You can also submit articles, news clippings, and ads. Web site: http://www.about-face.org/.

American Anorexia/Bulimia Association (AABA), 293 Central Park West, Suite 1K, New York, NY 10024. Phone: (212) 501–8351. The Association acts as a referral service, provides links between new and recovered members, organizes self-help groups, publishes fact sheets and a newsletter, and maintains a speakers' bureau.

American College Health Association (ACHA), PO Box 28937, Baltimore, MD 21240–8937. Phone: (410) 559–1500. A national, nonprofit organization for institutions of higher education that promotes health in its broadest aspect for students and other members of the college community. The ACHA produces many useful brochures on health and safety issues for college students. Website: http://www.acha.org/.

Boycott Anorexic Marketing (BAM), 56 Lothrop Street, Beverly, MA 01915. Phone: (617) 738–6332. BAM has targeted advertisers like Calvin Klein, Image hair products, and Capri cigarettes, which feature anorecticlike models. It also collects advertisements which promote healthy images and presents them with awards. Both activities draw media attention to the issue. BAM's goal is to create a healthier ideal for young girls, based on realistic images of physical beauty and strength.

National Association of Anorexia Nervosa and Associated Disorders, Box 7, Highland Park, IL 60035. Phone: (847) 831–3438. The Association seeks to educate the public about eating disorders and related illnesses and methods of treatment. It provides information and referrals, publishes fact sheets and a newsletter, and operates a hot line, generally staffed by recovered anorectics or their family members. It also fights the production, marketing, and distribution of dangerous diet aids and the use of misleading advertising.

National Eating Disorders Screening Program (NEDSP), One Washington Street, Suite 304, Wellesley Hills, MA 02181–1706. Phone: (617) 239–0071. The screenings are designed for college students and must be sponsored by a college or university health or counseling center.

CHAPTER 10

Women,   Drinking,
and   Drugs

People complain about drinking all the time, but it never changes. We talk about it in the Outing Club a lot because no one will give up drinking to get up early to go on a trip. Yet these same people complain that there is nothing to do. Even my friends talk about how the fraternity thing is so old, but they won't give drinking up to come hiking. It's really surprising because most of them are pretty outdoorsy.
                    —Women student at a small liberal arts college

DRINKING IS THE CENTRAL ACTIVITY of many campus parties and is virtually synonymous with college spring breaks. A recent survey conducted in Panama City Beach, Florida, during spring break found that three-quarters of the male students and 40 percent of the women students got drunk every day.[1] Depending upon the location and characteristics of your school, between 60 and 90 percent of students drink.[2] A study at one university discovered that within two months of arriving on campus, 81 percent of the first-year students had begun drinking.[3] Nationally, a fifth of students drink to intoxication several times a week, and nearly a half have also tried or used at least one drug besides alcohol.[4] Nearly a third of college students have smoked pot in the last year; 14 percent use it regularly. According to a Yale student, "Weed isn't even *trying* anymore. That's like, standard, the base line. It's the modern beer: you can't even get *away* from it."[5]

Many students regard drinking to get drunk as the normal way to have a good time. This approach to drinking usually comes as a shock to foreign students, most of whom drink in moderation or with meals and don't see the "fun" in getting sick. Students of color, too, are less likely to binge drink, preferring other ways to socialize and relax. According to one African-American student, "It's a white thing." One study found that white students are also five times more likely than Asian students to be heavy drinkers (within the Asian group, Japanese students drank the most, followed by Filipinos, Koreans, and Chinese).[6]

When researchers with the Alcohol Studies Program at the Harvard School of Public Health conducted a national survey of nearly eighteen thousand students at 140 colleges, they found that 44 percent of students had binged—defined as men drinking five drinks at one sitting and women drinking four—at least once in the past two weeks, and a fifth had done so three or more times.[7] According to Henry Wechsler, director of Harvard's Alcohol Studies Program and one of the study's authors, "binge drinking is arguably the No. 1 public health hazard and the primary source of preventable morbidity [disease] and mortality for the more than 6 million full-time college students in America."[8] The study also revealed what you already know, that some schools are "party schools." At a third of the schools studied, binge drinkers made up more than half the student body.

Women are drinking more today than they used to, although they still drink less than men. Nationally, over a third of college women binge drink (compared to half of the men), and 17 percent are frequent binge drinkers (compared to 23 percent of the men).[9] Researchers from the Addictive Behaviors Research Center at the University of Washington found that once women students start to drink, they continue throughout their college years.[10] Most women drink because it is part of college culture. Some, however, may also feel extra pressure. According to a College of William and Mary student, "I feel like I have to try twice as hard [in academics] because I'm a woman. Alcohol reduces the stress."[11] Women are frequently targeted by male students at parties and encouraged to drink. They sometimes pressure each other to drink. Although Greeks are banned from hazing, it still occurs and is not restricted to fraternities. In 1996, for example, a sorority at Union College was suspended after several pledges reported that they had been forced to participate in drinking games that left one student unconscious.

Drinking is hard to escape. Alcohol is easily available, and drinking, for many students, is associated with some of the most pleasant social aspects of undergraduate life: parties, dormitory living, watching athletic events, and informal socializing. Researchers have found that students who belong to social groups like sororities and fraternities drink more frequently and heavily than do other students.[12] Although few students see anything wrong with their own or their friends' drinking, alcohol abuse on campus does create other problems. Drinking often results in fights, accidental injuries, vandalism, interpersonal problems, car accidents, and sometimes, death. In 1996, Bowdoin College closed two fraternities after a visiting University of Maine student died after falling from the roof of one of the houses. His blood-alcohol content was twice the legal limit for driving. In 1997, an MIT student died from alcohol poisoning during fraternity rush. A recent national report also found that alcohol is involved in 90 percent of all violent crimes on campus and 40 percent of students' academic problems.[13]

Binge drinkers are much more likely than light drinkers or abstainers to have unplanned and unsafe sexual activity. Drinking has long been viewed in our culture as an element of courtship, as a way of breaking down the barriers between people who are potential sex partners. Alcohol has become a cue for sexual activity, especially in the early stages of a relationship. One study found that 50 to 60 percent of sexual encounters with new partners occur in conjunction with drinking.[14] Many students (including some women) interpret women's drinking as a sign of sexual interest and availability.[15] Women who drink and are around heavy drinkers are also at much higher risk of being sexually assaulted than are women who do not drink. Unfortunately, few women consider drinking to be a risk factor. It is. Alcohol is involved in fully 90 percent of campus rapes.[16]

Students who abuse alcohol also abuse the rights and safety of others. An alcohol abuser can turn into a date rapist, a drunken driver, or the vandal who sets fire to the dormitory bulletin board accidentally or for fun. At schools where more than half the student body drinks heavily, other students are twice as likely to be insulted or humiliated; to be pushed, hit or assaulted; and to experience unwanted sexual advances than are students who attend schools with fewer binge drinkers. Nondrinking students are also more than twice as likely to have their property damaged, to end up having to take care of a drunken friend, and to have their study and sleep disrupted because of other students' drinking.[17] The indirect effects of alcohol abuse can also be significant, including the costs added to tuition and fees to cover vandalism to college property and the difficult to calculate costs of damaged community relations and school image. How much does a "party school" reputation diminish the value of everyone's degree after graduation? Henry Wechsler advises sober students to speak up and not to tolerate this impairment to the quality of their colleges.

Drinking in small amounts helps most people unwind and socialize more easily. After several drinks, however, drinkers actually interrupt their companions more and listen less to what they have to say—hardly a recipe for good communication or relationships. Within minutes of someone's taking a drink, alcohol reaches the brain and starts to distort speech, cloud judgment (thought and cognition), slow reflexes, and impair coordination and vision. It lowers inhibitions and usually increases the desire for sexual activity in both men and women, which often leads to unsafe and questionable consensual sex and contributes to sexual assault. True consent and the fullest enjoyment of sexuality require a person to be clear-thinking and in control. How many women on campus now wake up unable to clearly remember what happened to them the night before, or realizing that they had unsafe sex with someone they wouldn't normally choose as a partner—or worse yet, having been raped?

How Much Do You Know About Alcohol?

Gender influences how people react to alcohol. Because women are on average smaller than men, it takes fewer drinks for most to reach the same blood alcohol concentration as a man and longer for their bodies to metabolize the alcohol. Even if a woman weighs the same as a man, she is likely to become more intoxicated on the same amount of liquor. This happens because alcohol does not diffuse as rapidly into body fat as it does into body fluid, and women's bodies contain more body fat and less body fluid then men's. The same number of drinks, therefore, will result in a higher concentration of alcohol in a woman's blood. To put it another way, two or three drinks for a woman equals four drinks for a man. Women also have less of the protective enzyme alcohol dehydrogenase (ADH), which breaks down alcohol in the stomach and reduces the amount of pure alcohol that enters the bloodstream. Because of this, women absorb about 30 percent more alcohol into their bloodstream than do men.

Other gender differences also exist. Alcohol affects women more just before they menstruate than at other times of the month. Women who take birth control pills or medications containing estrogen remain drunk longer and have higher blood alcohol concentrations than those who do not, because their livers must metabolize both the estrogen and the alcohol. Drinking large amounts of alcohol also can reduce the effectiveness of oral contraceptives. Female alcoholics suffer more liver damage than do alcoholic men, most likely because of the lower level of the enzyme alcohol dehydrogenase in their stomachs.

Because the liver can only metabolize about half an ounce of alcohol an hour, the faster people drink, the higher their peak blood alcohol concentration. Intoxication or being drunk is really a sign of alcohol poisoning, indicating that you have drunk more alcohol (and at a faster rate) than your body can process it. Having a high tolerance for alcohol is nothing to be proud of. It only

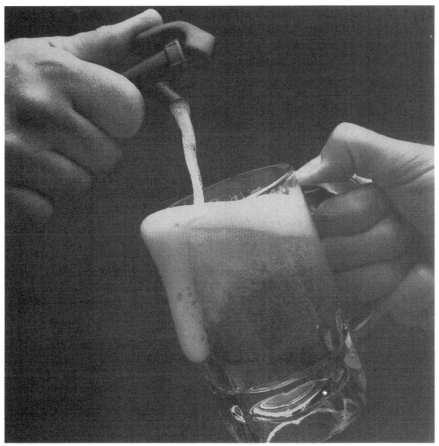

A lot of campus rapes start here.

Whenever there's drinking or drugs, things can get out of hand.
So it's no surprise that many campus rapes involve alcohol.

But you should know that under any circumstances, sex without
the other person's consent is considered rape. A felony, punishable
by prison. And drinking is no excuse.

That's why, when you party, it's good to know what your limits are.
You see, a little sobering thought now can save you from a big
problem later.

© 1990 Rape Treatment Center, Santa Monica Hospital

means that you need to drink more to feel the effects; it also indicates that you have a problem with alcohol. What a person drink matters. Straight alcohol like vodka is absorbed into the bloodstream faster than beer or wine, which contain some nonalcoholic chemicals. Mixing alcohol with a carbonated beverage dilutes a drink, but, surprisingly, it also speeds up the absorption of alcohol into a person's bloodstream.

Drinking different kinds of drinks does not influence how a person feels; what produces a bad reaction is drinking too much. The amount of food people eat before they drink does, however, make a difference. A person who drinks on an empty stomach will get drunk faster because the stomach will "empty" the alcohol more quickly into the small intestine, which is where most alcohol is absorbed into the bloodstream. Drinking on a full stomach gives stomach enzymes more time to digest the alcohol. (Milk, however, does not stay in a person's stomach long enough to do any good.) Unfortunately, a survey of two thousand first-year women students found that those on diets, who were likely to have little food in their stomachs, were more likely to drink than women who were not on diets.

Although drinking is stimulating at first, alcohol is actually a depressant drug that is quickly carried by the blood to every part of the body, numbing brain cells and slowing down the central nervous system. When a person is very tired, has been ill, or is under emotional stress—not uncommon states for college students—alcohol will only exaggerate the mood she is in. HALT is an acronym that can help you remember times when it's especially smart to avoid drinking: Hungry, Angry, Lonely, Tired. Few people realize that alcohol also depresses the body's immune system, making a person more susceptible to sore throats, colds, and other illnesses.

If you think it's safe to drink if you're only taking nonprescription medications, think again. Even common medications can produce side effects. When painkillers containing aspirin, like Bufferin, Anacin, and Alka-Seltzer, are mixed with alcohol, for example, there is an increase in the likelihood of irritation and bleeding in the stomach and intestines, as well as liver damage. Alcohol dissolves the coating on time-release capsules and coated pills so that a full dose is felt immediately instead of being properly delayed. Many prescription drugs also become less effective or can cause serious side effects when combined with alcohol. If you drink while taking antibiotics for an urinary tract infection, for example, you can experience nausea and vomiting. When painkillers like Demerol and codeine are combined with alcohol, they reduce central nervous system functioning and can cause difficulty in breathing, and even death. One of the main reasons fraternity and sorority hazing was outlawed on college campuses is that drinking games sometimes kill.

Alcohol is so commonly used, both on campus and off, that it's easy to forget that it is a regulated drug. Laws in all fifty states control its manufacture and use; state and local governments regulate when and where people may purchase and consume it. It's illegal to give or sell alcohol to anyone under the age of twenty-one. People who violate these laws—whether it's a parent giving a drink to one of their son's or daughter's friends or a student's use of a fake ID—may be fined or arrested. If you are underage, drink, and are caught, you could have your driver's license revoked or have to do court-mandated community service. Most colleges and universities have rules about underage drinking and other drug use as well. Amendments to the Drug-Free Schools and Communities Act in 1989 took away the flexibility schools had to deal with illegal alcohol and drug use on campus. Before, colleges and universities could design their own combination of enforcement and education programs. Today, they are under much more pressure to prevent drug usage and to punish student possession, use, and distribution of drugs. The sanctions imposed on students vary from school to school, but they can include suspension or expulsion. Any university found in violation of federal guidelines risks losing its federal aid; not surprisingly, alcohol and drug arrests on college campuses have been increasing. In 1995, there were over fifteen thousand liquor-law violations and nearly seven thousand drug-law violations reported on campus.[18]

To deal with excessive drinking and drug use, administrations are taking action. Utah State has banned alcohol at parties since 1995. The University of Rhode Island banned drinking at all campus events, including football games. Other colleges have introduced stricter student conduct codes and have toughened their sanctions. In 1991, the Drug Enforcement Agency (DEA) and police investigated the Greek system at the University of Virginia for six months before raiding three fraternities. One student spent four months under house arrest, and another student went to a minimum-security prison for eleven months. The men's soccer team at the University of North Carolina was placed on probation and forfeited two games after a first-year student was hospitalized for alcohol poisoning after a team party.[19]

Most schools run educational programs on alcohol and drug use. At larger universities, like the University of Pennsylvania, special offices of Alcohol and Drug Education serve as resource and referral centers for students. On other campuses, peer education programs, in which trained student volunteers run workshops for other students, are popular and effective. More students are realizing that they can have a good time without getting drunk or high and that they don't have to tolerate students who abuse alcohol or drugs. In 1995, the University of Colorado's twenty-six fraternities and sororities voted to ban alcohol from all gatherings held in chapter houses. According to the president of one house, "We haven't lost a single member because of the new rules, and as far as losing potential members because they can't party here, we're probably better off without them."[20]

Tobacco and Other Drugs

Many Americans have stopped smoking, and even more are trying to quit. To replace lost profits, tobacco companies began aggressively targeting new smokers—teenagers and young adults, especially women. Proportionately more cigarette ads are placed in women's magazines than in publications targeted at men or a general audience. At the time of writing there were at least fifty Web sites promoting the smoking lifestyle.[21] Cigarette companies have turned to even more creative ways to advertise, such as financially backing the careers of young female singers. Philip Morris, for example, gives away one performer's CDs to anyone attending her concerts who buys two packs of Virginia Slims. Such advertising ploys apparently are successful; women under twenty-three years of age are the fastest-growing group of new smokers. Today, 20 percent of young women graduating from high school smoke, compared to 10 percent of young men. Each day an estimated sixteen hundred teenage girls start smoking. Since the 1920s, the tobacco industry has portrayed cigarettes as a form of rebellion, romance, and emancipation for women. The long-running Virginia Slims campaign—"You've come a long way, baby"—took this a step further, equating women's liberation with the freedom to become addicted to nicotine. Today, advertisements still feature attractive—and *healthy*—young women and men smoking in beautiful or romantic settings. As suggested in the previous chapter, many young women also smoke as a way to avoid eating and gaining weight.

Because nicotine in cigarettes does not produce dramatic intoxicating or mind-altering effects, it's easy to underestimate its power. It is, however, a physically and psychologically addictive drug. When inhaled, it travels almost immediately to the brain, producing a mild euphoria, especially when a person is smoking the first cigarette of the day. Whenever smokers take more frequent and deeper puffs, they are unconsciously trying to reproduce this sensation again. Nicotine is also a nervous system stimulant that affects blood pressure, heart rate, hormone production, muscle tension, and more. The smoke in cigarettes contains carbon monoxide, which when inhaled passes into the bloodstream and interferes with the ability of red blood cells to transport oxygen throughout the body. Smokers also inhale tars, microscopic particles that form a sticky substance in the lungs, which impairs the respiratory system. Lung cancer is a bigger killer of women than is breast cancer. Research also has shown that women who smoke have a greater risk of developing osteoporosis—or brittle bones—in their later years. The most serious health risks from smoking, in addition to cancer, is heart disease. Women who take birth control pills

© 1995 Mary Lawton

and smoke significantly increase their risk of hardening of the arteries, stroke, and heart disease.

In 1997, the Liggett Group, manufacturers of Lark, L&M, and Chesterfields, became the first major tobacco company to admit that smoking causes cancer and other diseases (e.g., emphysema, heart disease, stroke), that nicotine is addictive, and that the industry targets underage smokers. The same year, the Food and Drug Administration banned tobacco sales to people under eighteen years old (and required proof of age for anyone under twenty-six). The effect of cigarette smoking on women's health is startling. Nationally, smoking kills more women than alcohol, illicit drugs, car accidents, suicide, and homicide—combined! It is the number one cause of premature death in women, and accounts for approximately 20 percent of all deaths.[22]

Most students tune out drug messages. "They tell you all your life not to do any drugs at all," one Yale student explains. "Then you try pot, and because you find out they lied to you about that, you feel free to try all the other things. You think that what they were saying wasn't true about any drug so none of them are going to be a big deal."[23] Not all drugs are the same, however. Some are physically addictive and very dangerous, while others can be psychologically addictive but are far less damaging to your health, especially in the short run. Most students who try drugs do so out of a combination of availability, curiosity, and peer pressure. "Once you know two or three people who've done it," explained a woman student, "then soon you're doing it, too. It's not peer *pressure*, exactly—it's peer *presence*."[24]

Marijuana is the drug of choice on most campuses. Ironically, when the legal drinking age was raised to twenty-one, it became easier on some campuses to use marijuana than to drink. "It's not regulated," explained a Berkeley student. "It's less expensive than going out and drinking. And you don't get a hangover when you're high."[25] So many University of Michigan students use cannabis that they organize an annual Hash Bash, which draws thousands of students as both participants and observers. Although marijuana is far less potent a drug than many others and is even prescribed for patients with some illnesses, high doses result in sensory distortion and impair your ability to perceive and react to your environment. A recent study among college students found that heavy marijuana use adversely affected their mental flexibility and ability to concentrate and learn.[26] Cannabis also suppresses the immune system and contributes to irregular ovulation in women. Hashish (a concentrated form of marijuana) sometimes produces hallucinations and, occasionally, panic attacks. Heavy users of either—like cigarette smokers—also increase their risk of chronic lung disease.

There are many other kinds of drugs: depressants (i.e., barbiturates, tranquilizers, and methaqualone); psychedelics like psilocybin mushrooms and hallucinogens (e.g., LSD, PCP, mescaline, ecstasy); stimulants (e.g., cocaine and amphetamines); antianxiety drugs (e.g., Librium, Valium, Serax, Equanil); narcotics (i.e., opiates like opium, morphine, codeine, heroin); and inhalants. All are found on college campuses. Each drug has its signature effect and carries risks that vary with the way it is consumed and the amount that is taken. Many illegal drugs also contain impurities that can have unpredictable effects.

Nationally, LSD is one of the fastest-growing drugs on campus. Psilocybin mushrooms and mescaline from the peyote cactus are common at some schools. "Twenty years ago, it was alcohol, sometimes pot," says Susan Robbins, a professor of graduate social work at the University of Houston who also teaches pharmacology. "Now it's pot and LSD and mushrooms."[27] Phencyclidine (also called PCP, angel dust, or peacee pill) is also found on some campuses. Hallucinogenic drugs and psychedelics change perception, thought, and mood. Emotions, colors, and sounds are intensified; hallucinations and delusions can occur, sometimes producing anxiety, confusion, and panic attacks—a "bad trip." The effects of PCP are unpredictable. In rare cases it has caused psychotic attacks that make the user temporarily insane, and, occasionally, violent. An overdose can lead to convulsions, ruptured blood cells in the brain, and death.

Stimulants or "uppers" (e.g., nicotine, caffeine, amphetamines, and cocaine) speed up the central nervous system, increasing heart rate and blood pressure, muscle tension, and the strength of your heart's contractions. Students on some campuses abuse Ritalin, or methylphenidate, a stimulant often prescribed for children who have attention deficit/hyperactive disorder. "It makes you really hyperactive," says one female student. "Anything you want to read, you want to read it right then. Anything you want to do, you want to do it right then . . . [but] you get a bad headache afterwards."[28] Ritalin is physically addictive and can have serious side effects, including seizures and strokes, especially when inhaled through the nose. Rohypnol, known as roofie, is another prescription drug (used in some countries for insomnia) that has been abused by a few students in border states like Florida, California, and Texas. It has also been slipped into women's drinks at campus parties, causing blackouts and memory loss.[29]

Amphetamines (variously known as speed, bennies, pep pills, crystal meth, and ice) cause increased activity and an initial feeling of alertness and self-confidence. Users sometimes feel depressed, and heavy doses can cause hallucinations and paranoia. Prolonged use can result in psychological changes including psychosis (irrational fears and hallucinations). Continued heavy use usually leads to heart problems and can result in heart failure. Cocaine (also called coke, snow, and flake) is another stimulant that is extracted from coca leaves and often diluted with substances like bleach, talc, and Ajax cleanser. Crack (or rock) is cocaine that has been processed into a potent form. The immediate effects of cocaine and crack are feelings of alertness, restlessness, and confidence. Once the high is over and the crash sets in, however, the user feels exhausted and depressed. Cocaine raises blood pressure and heartbeat and constricts the blood vessels. When inhaled over a long period, it destroys the nasal passages; when smoked, it causes lesions in the lungs. Crack produces a short, intense high, followed by an intense crash. Large doses often produce delusions, and as the high wears off, paranoia, anxiety, and nervous exhaustion. It is extremely addictive. Both cocaine and crack are unpredictable and dangerous drugs that can cause convulsions, respiratory paralysis, and death. Len Bias, a University of Maryland basketball player, was in peak physical condition when he died suddenly from a cocaine overdose in 1986.

Narcotics include opiates (including opium, morphine, codeine, and heroin) and synthetic drugs such as methadone. Opiates cause drowsiness and apathy, reduce hunger, make limbs feel heavy, make it difficult to concentrate, and result in impaired judgment and self-control. The health risks from long-term use include malnutrition and hepatitis. Overdoses can cause coma, respiratory arrest, and death. All narcotics are highly physically addictive. Most drugs create psychological dependency. Each time a user experiences a pleasurable feeling or feels less anxious or stressed, she or he is encouraged to use the drug again. A woman student who slipped into addiction says, "I lost three years . . . If I could have given myself any advice, it would have been to be cautious: you can do irreparable harm to your mind and body and cut years off your life that you might care about later. . . . I wish I'd really been more *sure* about what I was doing."[30]

_____ *DID YOU KNOW?* _____

- Smoking has become so socially unacceptable in the wider society that it has entered the realm of taboo and fetish. "Smoxploitation" films with titles like *Smoky Kisses* and *Sorority Girls Smoke* now exist that show nothing but conventionally attractive (what else?) women smoking.

- American college students spend an estimated $5.5 billion annually on alcohol. This exceeds the operating costs for running all college and university libraries ($1.7 billion) and all scholarship and fellowship programs ($1.6 billion).

- Approximately 55 percent of all college newspaper advertising revenue comes from alcohol ads.

- Although most of the 10 million problem drinkers in America are men, women are catching up. The National Council on Alcoholism and Drug Dependence (NCADD) estimates that 4.1 million American women are alcoholics or problem drinkers whose drinking has caused family or job difficulties or run-ins with the law. Alcoholics Anonymous, which used to be virtually all-male, now has a membership that is 35 percent women.

- One recent survey of college students found that smokers reported consuming almost twice as many alcoholic drinks per week as did nonsmokers. They also had eight times the frequency of marijuana use and were four times as likely to use other illegal drugs.

- Fewer young African Americans than whites smoke, due partly to family and community reactions against cigarette manufacturers, who are widely believed to target black youths. African-American women have the lowest smoking rate compared to black and white men and white women.
- Alcohol-related highway deaths are the number one killer of college-age students.
- Nearly half of all Americans who have ever smoked have quit, and 70 percent of adults who now smoke want to quit.
- A recent report from Columbia University's Center on Addiction and Substance Abuse revealed that two out of three students who commited suicide were legally intoxicated at the time of death.
- Women make up nearly half (48 percent) of all smokers in the United States.
- The percentage of women who smoke varies from one ethnic group to the next: 41 percent of Native American women smoke, 24 percent of white women, 21 percent of African-American women, 13 percent of Latinas, and 10 percent of Asian-American women.
- Ten percent of all women between the ages of eighteen and twenty-five have used an illegal drug in the past month.

_____ *WHAT YOU CAN DO* _____

 Think before you overdrink or use drugs. Ask yourself: What will I gain? What could I lose? Take an honest look at who you are and think about your values and beliefs. Treat yourself and your body with respect.

Ⓧ As an experiment, go to a fraternity or other party where there is heavy drinking and remain completely sober. Watch what everyone does as the night wears on, and imagine yourself in the place of the drunk women you see. Decide if this is how you want to act or to be treated. This experience may cure you of the desire to overindulge.

Ⓧ If you think someone you know has a problem with alcohol or other drugs or suspect that you might, here are some warning signs:

1. She (or he) gets drunk or high often, and now needs to drink or take more drugs to achieve the same effect as before.

2. She has trouble remembering what happened while she was using drugs or drinking.

3. She has problems keeping up with course work and meeting other obligations. She sometimes skips important social or sports events because of a hangover or in order to get high.

4. She has dropped old friends and now hangs out mainly with students who drink or use drugs a lot.

5. She seems unable to have a good time unless alcohol or drugs are available.

6. She seems to think and talk about getting high a lot and sometimes says she needs a drink or drug.

7. She has gone to class intoxicated or high.

8. She is moody and gets irritated or angry easily and without apparent cause. She gets angry if someone suggests something is wrong.

If any of these warning signs apply to a friend or to you, seek help. Let your friend know how much you care and how her (or his) drinking or drug use is affecting your friendship. Be honest and specific, saying exactly what behavior makes you unhappy and explaining how it relates to her drinking or drug use. Don't get discouraged if she gets angry, refuses to listen, and denies the problem. All you can do is say how you feel and suggest places to get help. If a friend ever approaches you with similar concerns about you, listen to what she has to say, even if it hurts and you don't believe it.

☒ Plan ways to avoid or resist pressure to overdrink or use drugs. Avoid places where people drink just to get drunk or always use drugs. Make friends with students who drink moderately or don't drink or use drugs at all. Go to dances, plays, films, concerts, and sporting events where drinking and drug use are not the focus. Join a club or student organization that will keep you busy with interesting activities.

☒ When you drink, decide on a limit beforehand and stick to it. Once your limit has been reached, refuse more. You can give a reason—"No thanks, I'm in training" or "No thanks, I'm the designated driver"—but remember, you don't owe anyone an excuse.

☒ If you take any medication, check the labels carefully or ask a doctor whether alcohol will change the medication's effect.

☒ Never exert pressure on other students to drink or use drugs. If they choose not to, respect their decision and encourage other students to do the same.

☒ When going off campus to drink, choose a designated driver who will remain sober. Try to prevent friends who have been drinking from driving, even though you may fear that you will cause an argument or not be able to convince them. Call a taxi or a sober friend.

☒ If you are going to drink, eat beforehand and then drink slowly, alternating drinks with food or nonalcoholic drinks. This will help reduce the effects of alcohol on your system. If you eat a substantial meal while you drink, you can reduce your peak blood alcohol.

☒ Keep stress under control. Set realistic goals for yourself, and get organized so you can avoid getting stressed out about course work and other obligations. Keep a positive attitude; most problems are short-term. Exercise regularly, eat healthy foods, and get enough sleep. If you feel good, you will be less inclined to overdrink or to escape through drugs.

☒ Remember HALT—Hungry, Angry, Lonely, Tired. Avoid drinking and drug use, especially at these times. Your emotional state affects your reactions. Drinking (and many drugs) will only intensify these feelings; it won't allow you to escape them.

☒ Help heighten campus awareness of the link between alcohol abuse and sexual assault, vandalism, fighting, poor grades, and accidental injuries as well as related issues such as the targeting of college students by alcohol-industry advertising. Bring in speakers; show films; organize panel discussions of drinking on campus. Make people aware of the effects of bingeing on the quality of campus life for all students. If you believe that alcohol abuse on campus is compromising the quality of your college experience, make your views known (see Organizations).

☒ Consider starting a BACCHUS chapter on campus to promote responsible decision-making about drinking and other health issues (see Organizations).

☒ When your college or university reports campus crime statistics, make sure it includes information on whether or not alcohol or drugs played a role. It often takes startling school statistics to make people aware of the effects of alcohol and drugs, and too often these numbers are left out of reports.

☒ Encourage student government and other student organizations as well as the administration to sponsor alcohol-free social events—dances, concerts, comedians—for everyone on campus to enjoy.

☒ Consider canceling subscriptions to magazines that carry ads promoting smoking for women, or organize a boycott. When you stop subscribing, send a postcard to the publisher explaining why. (The publisher's name and address can be found on or near the contents page.)

☒ Encourage the campus newspaper not to accept liquor ads.

☒ If you think you have a problem with alcohol or drugs, or your friends have suggested you might, don't ignore their warnings. You could damage your health, your education, and your relationships. Go to the counseling center and speak to a trained professional who can help you break your dependency, change your habits, and help you evaluate your goals. The student health service has information about drugs and alcohol and treatment programs for substance abuse. Both the counseling center and health service can also help you find professional treatment off campus. Almost every university and college also has a student support group that meets regularly to talk about issues surrounding alcohol and drug use (see Organizations).

☒ If you or a friend have a problem with drugs, try these referral hot lines for information:

Alcohol and Drug Helpline (800) 821–4357

Cocaine Abuse Hotline (800) 262–2463 [COCAINE]

National Drug Abuse Hotline (800) 662–4357 [HELP]

CDCP: Smoking, Tobacco, and Health hot line (800) 232–1311

⊠ If you smoke, your choice of the best way to stop will depend on why you smoke.[31] If you smoke for a lift (to keep from slowing down), find a healthy substitute such as running, walking, or other exercise. If you smoke to relax (it's enjoyable) or relieve tension (it helps you deal with anger or takes your mind off your troubles), try substituting exercise or a new social activity or hobby. If you smoke because you are physically addicted (you find it unbearable not to smoke or feel uncomfortable without a cigarette in your hand), you may need to quit "cold turkey." A nicotine patch works for many people.

⊠ If you are psychologically addicted (you smoke out of habit or automatically, without thinking), change your daily pattern and eliminate a few cigarettes each day. Ask yourself each time you are about to light up if you really want that cigarette. If you enjoy handling cigarettes, try doodling instead or playing with some object in your hand to give yourself tactile stimulation. Keep healthy snack foods like carrots and celery around to chew or suck on. Visit the campus health center for help and information. There may be a stop-smoking program on your campus. You can order publications like "Quick Tips for Smoking Cessation" and the "African-American Quitting Guide" through the CDCP hot line mentioned above.

—————————————— *RESOURCES* ——————————————

Books and Other Publications

Alexander, Linda Lewis, and Judith LaRosa. 1994. *New Dimensions in Women's Health.* Boston: Jones & Bartlett.

Boston Women's Health Book Collective. 1992. *The New Our Bodies, Ourselves: A Book By and For Women.* New York: Simon & Schuster.

Commission on Substance Abuse at Colleges and Universities. 1994. *Rethinking Rites of Passage: Substance Abuse on America's Campuses.* New York: The National Center on Addiction and Substance Abuse at Columbia University. (See also Organizations.)

Delaney, Sue. 1989. *Women Smokers Can Quit: A Different Approach.* Evanston, Ill.: Women's Healthcare.

Ettore, Elizabeth. 1992. *Women and Substance Use.* New Brunswick, N.J.: Rutgers University Press.

Glantz, Sharon. 1996. *The Cigarette Papers.* Berkeley: University of California Press.

Jacobson, Bobbie. 1982. *The Ladykillers: Why Smoking Is a Feminist Issue.* New York: Continuum.

Lader, Malcolm, et al. (eds.). 1992. *The Nature of Alcohol and Drug-Related Problems.* New York: Oxford University Press.

Nichlaides-Bouman, Ans (ed.). 1993. *International Smoking Statistics: A Collection of Historical Data from 22 Economically Developed Countries.* New York: Oxford University Press.

Of Wine and Women. This is an education and prevention curriculum for women. South Carolina Commission on Alcohol and Drug Abuse, 3700 Forest Drive, Columbia, SC 29204.

Rabin, Robert. 1993. *Smoking Policy: Law, Politics, and Culture.* New York: Oxford University Press.

Sandmaier, Marian. 1992. *The Invisible Alcoholics: Women and Alcohol Abuse in America.* 2nd ed. Blue Ridge Summit, Penn.: TAB.

Van Den Bergh, Nan (ed.). 1991. *Feminist Perspectives on Addictions.* New York: Springer.

Videos

Advertising Alcohol: Calling the Shots. This effective thirty-minute documentary video is based on a slide presentation by Jean Kilbourne. Cambridge Documentary Films, Box 385, Cambridge, MA 02139. Phone: (617) 354–3677.

The Inner Struggle. A series of student-produced video vignettes about women using drugs, alcohol, and food to deal with stress, anxiety, and feelings of inadequacy. Discusses resources available on campus to develop healthier coping strategies. The Stone Center, Wellesley College, 106 Central Street, Wellesley, MA 02181. Phone: (617) 283–2838.

The Last to Know. This is a film by Bonnie Friedman about women alcoholics. New Day Films, 79 Riverview Drive, Wayne, NJ 07470. Phone: (973) 633–0212.

To Your Good Health: Women and Drinking. A series of student-produced video vignettes that deal with problem drinking, helping a friend, and assessing risk factors. The Stone Center, Wellesley College, 106 Central Street, Wellesley, MA 02181. Phone: (617) 283–2838.

Organizations

Alcoholics Anonymous (AA), World Services Headquarters, 475 Riverside Drive, New York, NY 10115. Phone: (212) 870–3400. AA is a worldwide self-help organization for recovering alcoholics, with local chapters in most communities and on many campuses. It offers pamphlets geared to women, and to lesbians and gay men. In some cities, it sponsors special meetings for women and gays. To find local meetings, contact your school's counseling center or your local phone directory.

American College Health Association (ACHA), PO Box 28937, Baltimore, MD 21240–8937. Phone: (410) 559–1500. ACHA works with colleges and universities to promote health in the broadest sense for students and other members of the college community. It compiles statistics and publishes reports on student health and related issues.

BACCHUS and GAMMA Peer Education Network, PO Box 100430, Denver, CO 80250–0430. Phone: (303) 871–3068. BACCHUS is a student alcohol awareness and health education program with chapters on many college campuses.

Center for Science in the Public Interest, 1875 Connecticut Avenue NW, Suite 300, Washington, DC 20009–5728. Phone: (202) 332–9110. The Center produces publications and videos on the marketing of alcohol and other addictive products to minorities.

Center of Alcohol Studies, Rutgers University, 607 Allison Road, Smithers Hall–Busch Campus, Piscataway, NJ 08854–8001. Phone: (732) 445–4442. The Center publishes the *Journal of Studies on Alcohol* as well as bibliographies on alcohol-related issues including alcohol advertising.

Institute on Black Chemical Abuse Resource Center, 2616 Nicollet Avenue South, Minneapolis, MN 55408. Phone: (612) 871–7878. The Institute makes referrals to local organizations that deal with drug abuse among African Americans.

The National Center on Addiction and Substance Abuse at Columbia University, 152 West 57th Street, 12th Floor, New York, NY 10019. Phone: (212) 841–5200. The Center conducts research and regularly publishes reports.

National Clearinghouse for Alcohol and Drug Information (NCADI), PO Box 2345, Rockville, MD 20847–2345. Phone: (800) 729–6686 or (301) 468–2600. NCADI is a federal information service that offers free publications on women and alcohol, bibliographies, free computer searches, treatment referrals, and prevention and education resources.

National Council on Alcoholism and Drug Dependence (NCADD), 12 West 21st Street, New York, NY 10010. Phone: (212) 206–6770. NCADD provides information and fact sheets.

Office of Smoking and Health, Centers for Disease Control and Prevention, 4470 Buford Highway NE, Atlanta, GA 30341. Phone: (770) 488–5705. The Centers for Disease Control and Prevention can provide you with facts about smoking.

SALIS (Substance Abuse Librarians and Information Specialists), Alcohol Research Group, 2000 Hearst Avenue, Berkeley, CA 94709. Phone: (510) 642–5208. SALIS publishes an annual directory giving a complete list of resources.

Women for Sobriety, Box 618, Quakertown, PA 18951. Phone: (215) 536–8026 for referral to a local group. This is a national self-help organization for women dealing with all types of substance abuse.

Women's Alcohol and Drug Education Project, Women's Action Alliance, 370 Lexington Avenue, Suite 603, New York, NY 10017. Phone: (212) 532–8330.

CHAPTER 11

Sexuality and

Reproductive Issues

NOT THAT LONG AGO, universities treated students as parents might, especially when it came to monitoring their drinking and sexual behavior. In the 1960s, many university dormitories had curfews, guest sign-ins, and resident adults known as "house parents," and men were not allowed to go to women's rooms. At Columbia University, an "open-door" policy required men to keep their doors propped open the width of a book during a woman's visit. Harvard men could only have a woman in their rooms from four to seven P.M. on weekdays and Sundays and from noon to midnight on Saturdays. The University of Iowa simplified things by housing male and female students on opposite sides of the Iowa River. In 1972, when Oberlin became the first college to allow women and men to share the same dorms, the story made the cover of *Life* magazine.

Today, women at coed schools not only share dorms with men, but also floors, suites, bathrooms, and, in some cases, rooms. One result is that the "opposite sex" has been demystified, and many platonic friendships have developed between male and female students. Despite this more open atmosphere, however, sexual relationships on campus can be often problematic. With the virtual disappearance of moral restrictions against premarital sex among many—but not all—today, new tensions have been created for college women and men over appropriate sexual behavior. Few women today, for example, feel that they can avoid sex simply by saying it's wrong; instead they must communicate their real feelings to a potential partner. Many men on campus are confused about what degree of intimate behavior signals a woman's sexual consent. Despite much more liberal attitudes, a double standard of sexual behavior also remains. Many male students still believe that it's their job to convince a woman that she wants to have sex. Added to these communication and value issues is the health risk of sexually transmitted disease.

Most college students today are sexually active. Researcher Betsy Foxman, at the University of Michigan, found that 79 percent of the more than five hundred undergraduates she surveyed were sexually active. The National Center for Health Statistics reports that half of young women between the ages of fifteen and nineteen have had sex at least once, although this figure is down from a high of 55 percent in 1990.[1] On many campuses, casual sexual encounters ("hooking up") have largely replaced dating. This term, however, has somewhat different meanings for men and women. For many men, it refers to a one-night stand with a woman they may hardly know and may not particularly care about, during which they try to obtain as much physical pleasure as they can. Most women students I've talked to say they only hook up with men they care about and do not necessarily consider sexual intercourse to be part of the bargain. Students who are "seeing each other," on the other hand, have an ongoing relationship, care about each other, and are sexually involved, although they are usually free to see other people. Calling someone a boyfriend or girlfriend usually implies a greater commitment as well as exclusivity. How students on your campus feel about sexual relationships and the terms they use to describe different kinds of relationships will depend upon the particular characteristics and location of your school.

Nationally, casual sex has been losing some of its social legitimacy and appeal in recent years. A 1996 survey found that the number of first-year students who agreed with the statement "If two people like each other, it's all right for them to have sex even if they've known each other for only a very short time" had dropped to 42 percent, from a high of 52 percent in 1987.[2]

Although universities no longer try to control students' sexual behavior as they once did, administrators do worry about it. Some have addressed the issue in student conduct codes. Antioch College, for example, adopted a controversial written policy that requires students to inform their sex partners if they have any communicable diseases and to obtain their verbal approval before moving to a new level of sexual intimacy. Other schools rely on informing students of the need to practice safer, responsible sex through voluntary workshops and programs for incoming students, often held during orientation. At the University of Wisconsin at Madison, a sex educator known as Tim the Condom has broken the ice during orientation activities by wearing a full-body condom or pulling a regular one over his head. UCLA tried offering "sex and cookies," showings of an erotic video demonstrating safer sex practices, followed by dessert. But even such entertaining or otherwise enticing educational programs do not reach all students. And even when students do attend, messages about the need for responsible sex practices and the health risks of sexually transmitted diseases do not always sink in.

More than thirty sexually transmitted diseases pose serious health risks to women. The infection rate is especially high among the young.[3] The growing use of alcohol on campus is partly to blame for the rising rate of sexually transmitted diseases, including chlamydia, gonorrhea, syphilis, genital warts, genital herpes, hepatitis B, cervical cancer, and human immunodeficiency virus (HIV) and for unplanned pregnancies among college women. Hepatitis B has increased 77 percent among young adults in the last decade. This is a highly contagious disease—a hundred times more contagious than HIV—that is easily spread through sexual activity and contact with blood or other body fluid; more than half the people who have it show no symptoms. The American College Health Association (ACHA) recommends vaccination against hepatitis B for all college students. Chlamydia is also common on campus; it is also the most prevalent STD in the United States. Studies at some schools have found the human papilloma virus (genital warts) in as many as half of sexually active women. Genital herpes, for which there is no cure, is also common. Mercifully, the incidence of HIV on college campuses is low—about half what it is in the general population—but this is of course a lethal STD.

Unfortunately, many people who are infected with a sexually transmitted disease develop no outward symptoms and don't seek treatment. Women can easily be infected because the vagina provides a warm, protected environment where bacteria and viruses can flourish. Women who are sexually active, especially if they have more than one partner, are at risk. Even women in committed, monogamous relationships may be, because either partner may have been infected in the past without knowing it. Even lesbians can be at risk if they or their partners have ever had sex with a man. Current infection rates in the United States indicate that by the age of twenty-one, one in four women can expect to contract an STD.

Although most college health services provide free condoms, most students do not regularly use them. A survey by the University of Iowa's student health service found that only 9 percent of male students said they used a condom every time they had sex; fewer than 20 percent had used them for more than half their sexual encounters. What this means is that most sexually active heterosexual women at the University of Iowa are having unprotected sex. A survey of four hundred Boston University undergraduates found that only 28 percent of the men and women who are sexually active use condoms. The main reason students gave for not using them was their unavailability, yet most of these same students know where to find beer, even though alcohol is banned on campus and underage drinking is illegal.

The real issue with condom use is not availability or even information about the risks of STDs and the responsibility of parenthood. A study at Queens College, CUNY, for example, found that 60 percent of the students—from diverse ethnic backgrounds—considered themselves "knowledgeable" or "very knowledgeable" about HIV/AIDS. (White, African-American, and Latino students rated themselves as significantly more knowledgeable, however, than did Asian students.)[4] For most students, the topic of STDs and condoms is simply embarrassing and awkward. Many women fear that they will insult their partner, stifle his or her sexual interest, or jeopardize the relationship by bringing up the subject. Researchers at UCLA found that even when women students do attempt to convince a reluctant partner to use a condom, they usually avoid talking about the issue of safer sex practices; instead, they simply threaten to withhold sex or else cite their fear of getting pregnant as the reason.[5] According to Lisa Kaeser of the Alan Guttmacher Institute of New York, many young women are more worried about pregnancy than about STDs. "They don't want pregnancy to interfere with their lives," she says. "But STDs, not to mention HIV, can do a pretty good number on interfering with your life."[6]

A lot of campus sex occurs when people are drunk and their thinking is blurred. Many people in their twenties also feel invulnerable: "It can't happen to me." University of Michigan researchers found that the more sexual experience college women had, the less likely they were to make sure their partners use condoms. "As these girls gain experience and confidence, they seem to feel more invulnerable," explains researcher Betsy Foxman.[7]

Television public service announcements on HIV/AIDS usually emphasize the risks that men face: They feature twice as many male as female authorities, three times as many male as female celebrities, and ten times as many male as female narrators. According to Deborah Johnson, who has studied these ads cross-culturally, this gender bias in advertising has the effect of minimizing the risks women face. It also undercuts "the rights of women in relationships by positioning men as the sole sexual decision-makers."[8] Many women already find asking a male partner to use a condom awkward because of entrenched gender-based power differences. To ask a male partner in a committed, long-term relationship to use one is even more difficult for many women because it is often interpreted as a lack of trust, rather than just a wise decision about a means of health protection. "Studies on every continent demonstrate that both men and women perceive them [condoms] to be for use when having sex with 'others,' not stable partners," explains Johnson.[9]

What are the implications for sexually active women of not using condoms? According to physician Bernadine Healy, author of *A New Prescription for Women's Health*, "There may be no better example of gender bias in the annals of medicine than the neglect of STDs in women."[10] Untreated chlamydia and some other STDs can cause pelvic inflammatory disease (PID) and internal scarring, which can prevent many women from ever having children. I once had a student to whom this happened, and I will never forget her anguish; her life was changed forever. Untreated hepatitis B can cause cirrhosis and liver cancer, and may eventually kill. Although the AIDS virus is still spread primarily among gay and bisexual men and between drug users who share needles, it can be transmitted to women through sexual intercourse. And now that researchers have discovered that the monkey AIDS virus can cause infection when it is dabbed on the back of a monkey's mouth, oral sex must be considered risky. Until 1993, the Centers for Disease Control's clinical definition of AIDS did not include symptoms and experiences that are unique to women— gynecological problems such as recurring yeast infections and cervical cancer. This omission delayed testing for HIV in women. Women have not been included in most clinical trials of AIDS drugs. As a result, treatments that prolong men's lives may harm women. The widely used drug azidothymidine (AZT), for example, has been found to cause vaginal cancer in mice. Nationally, AIDS is now the sixth leading cause of death among women between the ages of eighteen and forty-four. (It is the second leading cause of death among men between these ages.) Women who have had an STD before, use oral contraceptives (although these decrease their risk of cervical cancer as well as prevent pregnancy), or who are pregnant are at an increased risk of becoming infected with an STD.

MOST COLLEGE STUDENTS were exposed to sex and contraception education in high school and know how to go about getting more information. Many campus health services not only provide information but also dispense free condoms. Other forms of birth control are available from Planned Parenthood clinics and private doctors. Nevertheless, pregnancies do occur on campus. In a culture in which sex is romanticized (and motherhood is to a large extent idealized even though mothers' work is not valued), women and men do not always think clearly about the long-term effect of their actions. The heat of passion, diminished decision-making due to drinking, carelessness, and a host of other factors are also responsible.

Americans tend to have polar attitudes toward abortion. Most people who oppose it usually do so on moral or religious grounds. Many consider questions such as: Do abortions cause pain to fetuses; are fetuses living human beings; are pregnant women psychologically scarred by abortion; does legal abortion devalue human life? Prochoice advocates, in contrast, view women's moral and legal right to make decisions about their own bodies as paramount, and ask questions such as: Who will raise and care for unwanted children; what harm is done to a teenage girl by bearing a baby; how many women will end up getting back-alley abortions if it is made illegal? Before *Roe v. Wade*, an estimated ten thousand women died each year in the United States from the aftereffects of illegal abortions; half were women of color. Thousands of unwanted children were also born each year. According to anthropologist Faye Ginsburg, however, both antiabortion ("prolife") and prochoice activists "envision their work as a full-scale social crusade to enhance rather than diminish women's position in American culture. While their solutions differ, both sides share a critique of a society that increasingly stresses materialism and self-enhancement while denying the value of dependents and those who care for them."[11]

Many factors shape women's attitudes and behavior toward abortion—education, urban vs. rural residence, race/ethnicity, marital status, income, and support networks. College women are more likely to terminate an unwanted pregnancy than are women with less education.[12] Women who live in cities are twice as likely to seek an abortion—largely because of availability—than women in rural areas.[13] Unmarried white women are more likely than unmarried black women to obtain an abortion.[14] In the general public, opponents of legalized abortion are more likely than advocates to hold traditional gender-role attitudes and also to oppose premarital sex, homosexuality, sex education, contraception, and liberal divorce laws. Among students, opponents tend to be older students, more religious students, and those who know least about abortion.[15]

Women who choose abortion do not do so casually. A national survey by the Alan Guttmacher Institute of nearly ten thousand women who had abortions in 1994 and 1995 found that they came from all racial, religious, and socioeconomic groups and that most had an abortion only after their birth control method had failed. Most also planned to have a child in the future.[16]

The Supreme Court ruled in 1973 in *Roe v. Wade* that the Constitution protects a woman's right to choose an abortion. This right has been under attack ever since, even though a large majority of Americans support it. In 1996, when Republican members of Congress held a news conference in front of the Supreme Court to urge party leaders to abandon their antiabortion position, they argued not only that a Constitutional amendment to outlaw abortion would never be approved by Congress but also that their antiabortion position did not reflect the views of most Americans. Nevertheless, the fight continues. Federal funding for abortions was banned in 1976, and private funding is fast disappearing as a result of the lobbying efforts by conservative "Right to Life" groups. Many charities and companies that once supported Planned Parenthood have stopped because of the pressure. In 1988, the United Way eliminated its automatic funding for Planned Parenthood. In 1990, AT&T dropped its support after twenty-five years, even though the money it had given was used exclusively for teen pregnancy prevention programs. The withdrawal of financial support and harassment by antiabortion groups—including picketing; harassment and assaults on doctors, staff, and clients; vandalism, burglary, arson, and bombings—has resulted in the closing of many clinics. In many cities, some of the clinics listed in the Yellow Pages are run by antiabortionists, who use scare tactics to dissuade the women who come in from having abortions.

The Supreme Court has indicated its willingness to restrict women's right to control their own reproduction. In 1989, in *Webster v. Reproductive Health Services*, it upheld various restrictions on abortion, including a prohibition on using public facilities to perform them. In 1992, however, the Court upheld women's basic right to an abortion in *Planned Parenthood of Southeastern Pennsylvania v. Casey*, while at the same time allowing significant restrictions, such as a twenty-four-hour waiting period and parental notification in the case of minors. Today, abortion services are available in only 16 percent of the 3,135 counties in the United States.[17] The states of North Dakota and Nebraska have only one provider each. A 1991 study found that only 12 percent of American teaching hospitals with programs in obstetrics/gynecology now require their medical residents to learn how to perform abortions, down from 23 percent five years earlier. Today, nearly one-third of medical schools offer no training whatsoever in performing abortions.

_____ **DID YOU KNOW?** _____

▧ About 12 million Americans become infected with an STD every year; one in five Americans has a sexually transmitted disease right now. STDs are more common than measles, chicken pox, mumps, and TB combined.

▧ Very little health research has included lesbians. Two long-range studies of 160,000 women recently undertaken by the Women's Health Initiative should help correct this; both will address sexual orientation.

▧ The World Health Organization predicts that by the year 2000, as many as 80 percent of AIDS cases worldwide will be transmitted heterosexually. Today, teenage girls in the United States have the same infection rates for HIV as do teenage boys.

- The number of HIV-infected people in the United States is still growing. According to the Centers for Disease Control, one in every one hundred men and one in every eight hundred women in the United States are infected.
- Although African-American women and Latinas comprise 19 percent of the total population of women in the United States, they make up 72 percent of all AIDS cases diagnosed among women. AIDS is now one of the leading causes of death among Latinas. In some states, it is the leading cause of death for African-American women.
- Mothers infected with HIV can pass the virus to their infants through the placenta before birth, through the birth canal at the time of delivery, and later, through their breast milk.
- According to a study reported in the *New England Journal of Medicine*, 20 percent of men (compared to 4 percent of women) said they would lie to a date about having had a negative HIV-antibody test in order to have sex.
- The majority of condom purchasers are women.
- Public money spent for contraceptive services fell by one-third in the decade between 1980 and 1990.
- In 1990, 28 percent of births in the United States were to unmarried women.
- The risk of death from childbirth is eleven times higher than from an abortion. Less than 1 percent of all abortion patients experience a major complication.
- In 1991 alone, arsonists caused over one million dollars in damage to abortion clinics.
- If you are under eighteen and live in a mandatory-parental-consent state, you may have to obtain a parent's consent to obtain an abortion or else get permission from a judge. Thirty-eight states have enacted parental consent or notice requirements for minors seeking abortions.

_____ *WHAT YOU CAN DO* _____

- If you are sexually active, protect yourself from an unplanned pregnancy by using an effective contraceptive. There are many forms available, including condoms, birth control pills, hormonal implants (Norplant), hormone injections (Dep-Provera), intrauterine devices (IUDs), diaphragms, cervical caps, condoms, sponges, and spermicides (gel, foam, cream).
- If you are sexually active, reduce you risk of contracting an STD by following the Planned Parenthood Association's "Seven Steps to a Healthier and Safer Sex Life":
  1. Be selective when you choose a partner. Avoid anyone with signs of infection, and only have sex with someone who takes your health concerns seriously and cares about you.

2. Limit your partners. It is safest to have sex with only one person who is only having sex with you.
3. Use latex condoms every time you have sex.
4. Talk to your partner about sex and your health concerns, before the heat of passion. Make conversation a part of your sexual relationship.
5. Keep medically fit. Have regular checkups (including STD tests), eat well, get plenty of rest, and limit your use of alcohol and drugs.
6. If you think you have been exposed to an STD, be responsible. Get tested, urge your partner to get tested, follow your medication instructions carefully, and do not have sex until you and your partner have been tested and are considered cured.
7. Stay in charge. Don't let alcohol or drugs jeopardize your self-control or your ability to think or communicate clearly.

▣ Order a "Protection Pack Sampler and Education Booklet" from Women's Health America (see Organizations). It includes a sixteen-page safe sex education booklet that tells you "everything you ever wanted to know about safe sex, but didn't know who to ask." It includes information on STDs and HIV testing. The sampler pack contains an assortment of latex condoms, personal lubricants, dental dams, and gloves and finger cots.

▣ Learn to communicate comfortably about sex and condom use. It doesn't do any good to be prepared if you don't end up using protection. Choose the right moment to ask your partner what he or she knows about STDs, including HIV. For lesbian and bisexual women, a conversation about bisexuality can lead to the topic. Anticipate a partner's possible objections beforehand, and think about what you might say. Sample dialogue is available in an educational booklet produced by Women's Health America (see Organizations). Try humor and playfulness. If your partner says he won't feel as much wearing a condom, tell him he won't feel anything unless he does. A Swedish public service announcement on AIDS shows a woman who wants to start using condoms snapping one on her partner's bare behind. They laugh and then begin to talk about it. A guide for college women suggests saying something like, "OK, we need to have the mandatory condom discussion. You're going to wear one. End of discussion. Let's move on to more exciting things."[18]

▣ To help protect other women on campus, organize a peer-led discussion of safer sex techniques and the health risks of unprotected sex. It should focus on increasing knowledge of STDs, encouraging women to carry condoms, attacking the double standard of sexuality that labels a woman who is prepared for responsible sex as "promiscuous," and helping women improve their communication skills with sex partners. To avoid embarrassment and get a discussion going, women could pass written questions to a facilitator. The program could include role-playing to show how couples can discuss condom use. If your university has a school of nursing or a medical school, nursing or medical students might be good facilitators (see the Comstock article in Resources). Other resources include your campus's peer facilitators, student health service, residence hall advisors, women's center, residence life office, counseling center, and local Planned Parenthood office.

- Have a student group you belong to set up a table in the campus center with samples of contraceptives and safer sex literature. Condoms come in more than a hundred different shapes and sizes, including some designed for women's bodies. One type is a polyurethane sheath with two diaphragmlike rings that fit over the cervix and rim the vagina. This does not provide the same level of protection against all types of STDs, however, as condoms designed for men or another type of female condom.[19] This is the bikini condom or female pouch, a latex panty that has a built-in pouch that fits inside the vagina. Latex dental dams are also available for use during oral sex. Help teach other students how to protect themselves. Ask a gynecologist or nurse from the student health service or Planned Parenthood to join you to answer questions.

- Familiarize yourself with STD symptoms and those of pelvic inflammatory disease (PID). The student health service and women's center will have pamphlets. You can also call the national *STD hot line*: (800) 227–8922, between eight A.M. and eleven P.M. EST.

- Have a Pap smear every year.

- Learn about HIV. For information, visit the student health center or call the twenty-four-hour *CDC national hot line* (800) 342–2437 (AIDS); for information in Spanish, call *Linea Nacional de SIDA* (800) 344–7432 (SIDA) between eight A.M. and two P.M. EST. The *Project Inform* national hot line also provides information on HIV/AIDS: (800) 822–7422. Most states also have hot line numbers. For testing, try the student health service (although not every university or college provides it), a Planned Parenthood office, or the American Red Cross.

- Support pregnant women on campus. Organize a network of women to help with rides to doctors' appointments, act as Lamaze partners (if necessary), provide emotional support during an on-campus pregnancy, and help with child care after the birth. Try to include women who already have been pregnant in your group.

- If you think you (or a friend) might be pregnant, get a test as soon as possible. You can buy a home test at the drugstore or go to a clinic to get a blood or urine test and a physical exam. It is important to find out as soon as you can. If you are not pregnant, you will be able to relax and know that your late period was due to stress, overexercise, a recent illness, or a change in your diet. The scare you received may also make you think more seriously about birth control and about using safer sex methods.

- ⊠ If you are pregnant, you have an important decision to make and not a lot of time to make it in. Should you decide to have a baby, the sooner you start receiving prenatal care the better. If you decide to terminate your pregnancy, you should explore your options immediately. Having an early procedure is safest. Your decision will be influenced by many things, including the circumstances under which you became pregnant, who the father is, how religious you are, the implications for your financial situation, the kind of support networks you have, how much you know about abortion, and your own feelings about the "right" thing to do. Discuss your situation with an experienced counselor, trusted friends, and your partner and family members (if you feel comfortable doing so). Visit the student health service, counseling center, or your local Planned Parenthood clinic.

- ⊠ Contact the Pregnancy Helpline: (800) 228–0332. The hot line provides over-the-phone counseling and can refer you to local organizations that provide adoption, abortion, and prenatal care services.

- ⊠ Campus health services vary in what they offer pregnant students. At some universities, including Harvard and the Massachusetts Institute of Technology, the student health plan covers both pregnancy counseling and abortion services. Only some schools offer prenatal care. If you are considering having a baby and you receive financial aid, find out how taking time off from school or taking a reduced course load would affect you. If you do not want to alert the financial aid office before finding out, enlist the help of your partner or a friend to get the information for you.

- ⊠ If you support women's right to choose and the work of Planned Parent-hood, use Working Assets Long Distance, MCI, or Sprint as your telephone service rather than AT&T, which dropped its support for Planned Parent-hood.[20] Write to the chairman of the board of AT&T to explain why you are changing telephone companies: AT&T, 32 Avenue of the Americas, New York, NY 10013. *Working Assets Long Distance* (800–788–8588) places 1 percent of the cost of every call you make into an action fund, which goes to a variety of environmental, peace, and human rights groups. Among the women's organizations it funds are Planned Parenthood, the National Abortion Rights Action League (NARAL), and the National Black Women's Health Project. Encourage your friends to do the same.

- ⊠ To support abortion rights, call the national office of the *National Abortion Rights Action League* at (202) 973–3000 to get the number of your local

NARAL office. Ask if they have a "Use Your Voice for Choice" program. In Maryland, for example, when you sign up for the "Affinity Fund," 8 percent of the cost of your long-distance U.S. telephone calls go to the Maryland NARAL chapter.[21]

------------------------------- *RESOURCES* -------------------------------

Books and Other Publications

Ammer, Christine. 1989. *The New A-to-Z of Women's Health: A Concise Encyclopedia*. Alameda, Calif.: Hunter House.

Baird, Robert, and Stuart Rosenbaum (eds.). 1993. *The Ethics of Abortion: Pro-Life vs. Pro-Choice*. New York: Prometheus.

Berer, Marge, and Ray Sunandra. 1993. *Women and HIV/AIDS: An International Resource Book*. San Francisco: HarperCollins.

Blake, Jean. 1990. *Risky Times: How to Be AIDS-Smart and Stay Healthy*. New York: Workman.

Boston Women's Health Book Collective. 1992. *The New Our Bodies, Ourselves: A Book By and For Women*. New York: Simon & Schuster.

Chalker, Rebecca, and Carol Downer. 1992. *A Woman's Book of Choices: Abortion, Menstrual Extraction, and RU-486*. New York: Four Walls, Eight Windows.

Comstock, Karen Glover. 1994. "A Peer Educator STD Prevention Program for Women Students," *Public Health Reports* 109 (2): 181–182.

Corea, Gena. 1992. *The Invisible Epidemic: The Story of Women and AIDS*. New York: HarperCollins.

Dobkin, Rachel, and Shana Sippy. 1995. *Educating Ourselves: The College Woman's Handbook*. New York: Workman.

Eisenberg, Arlene, et al. 1991. *What to Expect When You're Expecting*. New York: Workman.

Healy, Bernadine. 1996. *A New Prescription for Women's Health*. New York: Viking.

Jackson, Donna. 1992. *How to Make the World a Better Place for Women in Five Minutes a Day*. New York: Hyperion.

Kitzinger, Sheila. 1985. *Women's Experience of Sex: The Facts & Feelings of Female Sexuality at Every Stage of Life*. New York: Viking Penguin.

Kloser, Patricia, and Jane Craig. 1994. *The Woman's HIV Sourcebook: A Guide to Better Health and Well-Being*. Dallas: Taylor.

Korte, D., and R. Scaer. 1992. *A Good Birth, a Safe Birth: Choosing and Having the Childbirth Experience That You Want*. Boston: Harvard Common.

Legato, Marianne. 1997. *What Women Need to Know*. New York: Simon & Schuster.

Lunneborg, Patricia. 1992. *Abortion: A Positive Decision*. Westport, Conn.: Bergin & Garvey.

Mosse, Julia, and Josephine Heation. 1991. *The Fertility and Contraception Book*. London: Faber & Faber.

O'Leary, Ann, and Loretta Sweet Jemmott (eds.). 1995. *Women at Risk: Issues in the Primary Prevention of AIDS*. New York: Plenum.

Rogers, Judith, and Molleen Matsumura. 1992. *Mother to Be: A Guide to Pregnancy and Birth for Women with Disabilities*. New York: Demos.

Rubin, Eva (ed.). 1996. *The Abortion Controversy: A Documentary History*. Westport, Conn.: Greenwood.

Sexual Etiquette 101. A guidebook for college students on sexual health and responsibility. Emory University Family Planning Program, 69 Butler Street SE, Atlanta, GA 30303.

Stern, Phyllis (ed.). 1993. *Lesbian Health: What Are the Issues?* Bristol, Penn.: Hemisphere.

Stewart, Felicia, et al. 1987. *Understanding Your Body: Every Woman's Guide to Understanding Gynecology and Health*. 3rd ed. New York: Bantam.

Villarosa, Linda (ed.). 1994. *Body & Soul: The Black Women's Guide to Physical Health and Emotional Well Being*. New York: HarperCollins.

White, Evelyn (ed.). 1994. *The Black Women's Health Book: Speaking for Ourselves*. 2nd ed. Seattle: Seal/Feminist Press.

Winikoff, Beverly, and Suzanne Wymelemberg. 1992. *The Contraceptive Handbook: A Guide to Safe and Effective Choices*. Yonkers, N.Y.: Consumer Reports.

Videos

The Heart of the Matter. This sixty-minute documentary film by Gini Reticker and Amber Hollibaugh explores the mixed messages young women receive about sex and sexually transmitted diseases. If focuses on one HIV-positive African-American woman and "opens a window on understanding women's sexuality in the age of AIDS." P.O.V., PO Box 750, Old Chelsea Station, New York, NY 10113. Phone: (212) 645–8527.

Women and AIDS: A Survival. This twenty-two-minute video is designed to raise awareness and provide information about the risk of AIDS to heterosexual women. It furnishes essential medical information from female health professionals and prevention guidelines, including well-acted vignettes that illustrate effective communication regarding safer sex and the use of condoms. Includes commentary by women with AIDS. Produced by Terry Looper. University of California Extension, Center for Media and Independent Learning, 2000 Center Street, 4th Floor, Berkeley, CA 94704. Phone: (510) 642–0460.

Women, HIV and AIDS. This hard-hitting, fifty-two-minute documentary examines the special problems of women in the AIDS epidemic. It encourages frank discussion of many topics including safer sex for both straight and lesbian women, health care, and advocacy. Contact Filmakers Library, 124 East 40th Street, New York, NY 10016. Phone: (212) 808–4980.

Organizations

Advocates for Youth, 1025 Vermont Avenue NW, Suite 200, Washington, DC 20005. Phone: (202) 347–5700. Advocates is a political action and educational organization which publishes literature on STDs, safer sex, and birth control in Spanish and English.

Alan Guttmacher Institute, 120 Wall Street, 21st Floor, New York, NY 10005. Phone: (212) 248–1111. The Institute conducts research and advances programs and policies that promote women's reproductive health and choice. It provides information and educational materials such as "Contraception Counts: State-by-State Information" (1997).

American Social Health Association (ASHA), PO Box 13827, Research Triangle Park, NC 27709. Phone: (919) 361–8400. ASHA is a nonprofit organization that organizes education programs on STDs, runs support programs for people with STDs, and produces many information pamphlets on all types of STDs. It also operates the Centers for Disease Control and Prevention's national hot lines on STDs and AIDS (see What You Can Do).

Center for Women Policy Studies, 2000 P Street NW, Suite 508, Washington, DC 20036. Phone: (202) 872–1770. The Center is home to the National Resource Center on Women and AIDS, which can answer questions you may have on legislation dealing with women and AIDS.

Gay Men's Health Crisis (GMHC), 129 West 20th Street, New York, NY 10011. Phone: (212) 337–3532. This was one of the first organizations to work on HIV/AIDS issues. It provides information on HIV/AIDS (including Peg Byron's *Women Need to Know about AIDS*), safer sex practices, and gay/lesbian issues. It is home to the Lesbian AIDS Project, which is involved in political action, counseling, and referrals.

National Abortion Federation, 1436 U Street NW, Suite 103, Washington, DC 20009. Phone: (202) 667–5881. The Federation can provide you with information on abortion policy and answer questions about services that are available in your state. The Federation also makes referrals to local abortion providers and to places that help with funding. It publishes numerous fact sheets and pamphlets, such as "Having an Abortion: Your Guide to Good Care."

National Abortion and Reproductive Rights Action League (NARAL), 1101 14th Street NW, Washington DC 20005. Phone: (202) 973–3000. The League provides up-to-date information on reproductive rights and sexuality education laws around the country. It works to educate Americans on reproductive issues, to elect prochoice candidates, and to advocate for prochoice legislation. NARAL fact sheets provide current information on reproductive issues. The NARAL Campus Organizing Project (COP) is a joint effort with the United States Student Association designed to preserve women's right to choose by helping campus activists organize and join the grassroots political work of other community activists.

National AIDS Information and Education Program, Centers for Disease Control and Prevention (CDCP), 1600 Clifton Road, Mail Stop E-25, Atlanta, GA 30333. Phone: (404) 639–0956. The program provides the latest information about HIV/AIDS prevention and will send it to you confidentially if you ask.

National Women's Health Network, 1325 G Street NW, Washington, DC 20005. Phone: (202) 347–1140. The Network produces a $5 AIDS packet with valuable information. It also has compiled a national listing of reputable women-owned and women-run clinics, and can provide you with referrals.

Planned Parenthood Federation of America, 810 7th Avenue, New York, NY 10019. Planned Parenthood is involved in a wide range of women's health issues, including political action for reproductive rights, family planning counseling, gynecological care, STD testing, and abortion services. It has local offices and clinics in most cities and towns that often provide a speakers' bureau. If you can't find an office listed in your local telephone book, call (800) 230–7526 or the national office (212) 541–7800.

Students Organizing Students (SOS), 1600 Broadway, Suite 404, New York, NY 10019. Phone: (212) 977–6710. This is an organization of high school and college-age women who advocate for women's health.

Women's Health America (WHA), 429 South Gammon Place, Madison, WI 53719. Phone: (800) 858–3980 for information or (608) 833–9102 for customer service. WHA is a national organization devoted to providing current health information to women. In addition to the Protection Pack Sampler and Education Booklet mentioned earlier (What You Can Do), it offers educational videos, books, cassettes, and a bimonthly newsletter with the latest health news on prevention, diagnosis, treatment, and self-help tips for women. A portion of WHA's revenues supports women's health research and education.

Rape and

Sexual Assault

Please don't call me a survivor. I really don't feel like one. I still live my life as if I were raped yesterday. Essentially I was; it happens again every night in my dreams. I am not a victim either. I am just a woman— and a statistic.

—Emilie Morgan, "Don't Call Me a Survivor," 1995[1]

A STUDY BY the Senate Judiciary Committee in 1990 concluded that rape in the United States was occurring in "epidemic proportions." In that year alone, over a hundred thousand rapes were reported, with ten times the number said to go unreported.[2] An estimated 80 percent of rapes are acquaintance rapes, in which the victim and rapist know each other. (Rape is legally defined as sexual penetration by force or threat of force, without consent, whether perpetrated by a stranger or by an acquaintance.) Although most college students—female and male—reject the use of any kind of force to obtain sex, acquaintance rape is nevertheless a problem on campus, and it could happen to you. A national survey of nearly seven thousand students at thirty-two colleges and universities conducted by Mary Koss, a professor at Kent State University, found that

15 percent of women students had been raped (not all the rapes had occurred on the college campus while they were attending school, however), and another 12 percent had been the victims of attempted rape.[3]

Rape does not always involve a man forcing himself on a woman. Rapes occur among homosexuals, and there are cases of women raping men.[4] Ninety-nine percent of the persons arrested for forcible rape in the United States are men (89 percent of all violent crimes are also committed by men), and most of the rapes are committed against women.[5] Why do some men rape? A study by Eugene Kanin is revealing. He compared the behavior and attitudes of date rapists to other college men and found that the rapists were very heterosexually active men who had been socialized into a "hyper erotic male culture" that views sexual success as the main way to establish manhood and to maintain self-esteem.[6] Such men regularly try to seduce women, using a variety of strategies: intoxicating them, threatening to abandon them or terminate the relationship, and lying about being in love or wanting a permanent relationship. They also belong to a subculture (which includes fraternities and sports teams) that treats women as sexual targets. Their close friends share their exploitative attitudes toward women and often pressure them to be sexually active. For example, 93 percent of the rapists (compared to 37 percent of other college men) said that their best friends would "definitely approve" if they used the strategies described above with certain women: "teasers," "economic exploiters," "bar pick-ups," and "loose" women. When such women refuse to have sex, rape-prone men find it easy to justify using threats and force against them.

On campus, "fraternities have been in the forefront of bias-related incidents," including rape.[7] Not all fraternities are alike, nor are all fraternity brothers. Nevertheless, fraternity members account for 63 percent of all student sexual assaults nationally even though they make up only one-quarter of the student body.[8] Fraternities also have a history of other violence—hazing, fighting, and property damage—which has given them trouble with insurance companies. They have described as the third riskiest property to insure, just behind toxic waste dumps and amusement parks.[9] Some schools have responded by banning all single-sex fraternities or abolishing fraternities altogether.

When sociologists A. Aryes Boswell and Joan Spade examined eight fraternities at Lehigh University, they found that some were "low-risk" houses for women and others were "high-risk." Low-risk houses tended to be somewhat smaller, had few members who were varsity athletes, had fewer serious disciplinary incidents reported against them, and held positive attitudes toward women. Many members had regular girlfriends, and parties were characterized by equal numbers of women and men, a friendly atmosphere, dancing, and conversation between couples. According to the researchers, "Respect for women extended to the women's bathrooms, which were clean and well supplied."

High-risk houses, in contrast, were larger, had more varsity athletes, more serious disciplinary reports against them, and negative attitudes toward women. Few brothers had regular girlfriends, and parties were characterized by skewed gender ratios, extremely loud music, heavy drinking, and gender segregation, with men drinking on another side of the room from women. The men also

> treated women less respectfully, engaging in jokes, conversations, and behaviors that degraded women . . . [and they] behaved more crudely . . . a brother dropped his pants . . . another brother slid across the dance floor completely naked. . . . Men were openly hostile, which made the high-risk parties seem almost threatening at times. For example, there was a lot of touching, pushing, profanity, and name calling, some done by women. . . . [Students] seemed self-conscious and aware of the presence of members of the opposite sex, an awareness that was sexually charged.[10]

Bathrooms also differed; in high-risk houses they were "filthy." The researchers conclude that fraternity behavior as typified by high-risk houses contributes to a rape culture on campus.

If your campus has fraternities, they may well dominate the social scene, especially if they are the only place where alcohol is permitted. The nature of many parties, however, fosters unhealthy gender relations. Real interaction between men and women is made difficult: There is usually no place to sit, loud music makes conversation almost impossible, and nonalcoholic drinks are often unavailable, virtually forcing students to drink. In high-risk houses, heavy drinking and "hooking up," not relationships, are the order of the day. Yet women who are sexually active are criticized by men (and often, by other women), while their male counterparts are regarded as "studs." You are probably familiar—at least by reputation—with the "walk of shame," when fraternity brothers gather on a balcony or outside to heckle women returning home in the early morning hours with remarks like "Fuck that bitch" and "Who is that slut?"[11]

According to anthropologist Peggy Reeves Sanday, in *Fraternity Gang Rape: Sex, Brotherhood and Privilege on Campus*, fraternity members' emphasis on "toughness, withstanding pain and humiliation, obedience to superiors and physical force" fosters trust and loyalty among themselves during pledging activities, but it also creates "an interpersonal style that de-emphasizes caring and sensitivity." The fact that more sensitive and critical college men drop out of the pledging process means that the remaining "brothers" are more likely to be receptive to "masculinist values and practices that encourage the use of force in sexual relations with women and the covering up of such behavior."[12] At the University of Rhode Island, an eighteen-year-old first-year student was raped at a fraternity party while at least five other men watched. Similar gang rapes—"gang bangs" or "pulling train"—have occurred on other campuses, usually associated with heavy drinking and/or drugs. The perceived "rewards" of gang rape, as reported by male rapists, include recreation and adventure, competition and camaraderie, friendship, and cooperation.[13] Sanday describes in graphic detail the drinking, coercive sexual behavior, and degrading of women—even the fraternity's own "Little Sisters"—that is a central part of many fraternities' social life. Watching pornography is another popular activity. Although the research findings on the effects of viewing pornography are mixed, researchers like Edward Donnerstein and Neil Malamuth have found that men's exposure to violent pornography increases their sexual arousal, their negative attitudes toward women, and their favorable attitudes toward sexual assault.

Male athletes are also disproportionately involved in rape and sexual assault, especially athletes involved in contact sports like football, basketball, lacrosse, and ice hockey. A 1991 study of more than ten thousand students, conducted by Towson State University's Campus Violence Prevention Center, found that 55 percent of all admitted acquaintance rapes were committed by athletes, even though they made up only 16 percent of the male student body. Athletes have also been found to be more involved than other students in fights and in risky behavior like riding with a drunk driver, not wearing a seat belt, having many sex partners, and not using contraception.

Ultimately, rape is caused by a complex set of circumstances and attitudes, both individual and societal. Acquaintance rape is dismissed by some as a "spontaneous" act driven by a natural sexual urge and therefore unavoidable, especially when the rapist has been drinking—the implication being that it is not really rape. We know, however, that acquaintance rape often involves planning. When men conspire to get women drunk or spike their drinks to lessen their ability to resist; when they intentionally lie to a woman in order to get her alone; when they force intercourse despite protests or after a woman has passed out, then sex can hardly be characterized as spontaneous or consensual.

Researchers and others who argue that men rape simply to obtain sex, and that acquaintance rapes occur because men need to satisfy themselves, especially after a certain amount of sexual stimulation and arousal has taken place, ignore the larger social picture. Although many acquaintance rapes do take place after some sex play has occurred, this explanation is too simple and paints a very negative picture of male sexuality and self-control. American society has mythologized the power of men's natural sexual urges (e.g., the myth of "blue balls"), which removes responsibility from men to exert self-control.

We also live in a violent and sexist society, one in which people often resort to force to get their way and in which women, as a group, are routinely depicted as sexual objects available for men's use. In addition, most girls are still socialized to be more compliant, solicitous of the needs of others, and passive than are boys. In such an environment, it is understandable that some men believe they have the right to act on their natural sexual impulses, despite what women say, and that some women have difficulty being as assertive as they might.[14] Depending on the psychology and past experiences of the individual rapist, rape can also represent an effort to conquer personal insecurities about masculinity or be a release of anger which is directed toward women as convenient and socially defined legitimate targets.

In many other societies, rape is nonexistent or much less common. In a cross-cultural study of rape in ninety-five societies, anthropologist Peggy Reeves Sanday found that 47 percent are "rape-free," 36 percent are "rape-present," and 17 percent—including our own—are "rape-prone."[15] The incidence or absence of rape is shaped by many factors including the status of women in society, the values that govern relations between the sexes, the attitudes taught to boys, and a society's overall tolerance for violence. If rape were motivated just by sex or the result of men acting on "natural" urges, then we wouldn't find this cross-cultural difference. Even countries very like our own in terms of economy, the mass media, political structure, and popular culture have very different rape rates. The U.S. rape rate is four times higher than that of Germany, thirteen times higher than of England, and twenty times higher than of Japan. A double standard about sex also remains in American society. On more conservative campuses especially, women risk being labeled "easy" or "sluts" if they are too sexually active; this labeling makes it easier for some men to regard them as legitimate sexual targets.

Most campus rapes happen when one or both people have been drinking heavily. As discussed in chapter 10, drinking (and drug use) diminishes everyone's ability to exercise good judgment and to communicate clearly. It also exacerbates some men's aggressive tendencies and makes it difficult for women to physically defend themselves. Many college women are aware of the risk that drinking poses and are trying to do something about it. Duke University's Women's Coalition, for example, once put up flyers warning women about the relationship between heavy drinking and date rape, and members sat outside certain fraternity houses to help drunken first-year women who had attended their fall "Cattle Roundup" parties to get home.[16] For your own safety, do not overdrink or go off with someone who has and watch your friends to help ensure that they do not fall into this trap either.

Other risk factors researchers have identified are linked to miscommunication and false expectations. When a woman says yes to sexual intercourse and then changes her mind and says no, some men feel justified in forcing her. When a man and woman have had sex before, some men believe that she has no right to refuse in the future and feel justified in using force. Many male students—especially those who hold more traditional views of appropriate gender roles—have mistaken ideas about what a woman has in mind when she initiates getting together or agrees to go to his apartment; these beliefs create additional risk factors.[17] Largely because of this, Antioch College introduced a sexual code of conduct in 1992 which requires students to obtain "verbal consent . . . with each new level of physical and/or sexual contact/conduct in any given interaction" with another student. Although the policy has been ridiculed in the media as "sexual correctness" gone berserk and an unrealistic restriction on romance, Antioch's Dean of Students replies that students demanded the policy: "It gives them some boundaries, which is what students said they needed. . . . I've got male students who say, 'Suddenly I don't feel like I have to perform.' I've got female students saying, 'I have something behind me that allows me to say no.' "[18]

Not all rapes can be avoided by exercising caution or communicating clearly. Even if you are explicit about your feelings and physically resist, someone may still try to rape you. It is important to understand that if a person has sex with you against your will, that is rape. Try not to feel guilty or ashamed; the other person has committed the crime. Even if you did something foolish like drink, you did not deserve to be raped. Does a person who walks down a street alone at night deserve to be murdered? Is the murderer any less guilty because of the victim's behavior? For every rape that is reported, many go unreported because of the woman's fear of not being believed, embarrassment, shame, guilt, social stigma, or peer pressure.

One study found that Asian students are more likely than whites to see rape victims as partially to blame for their sexual assault, due to cultural traditions in Asia that endorse low status for women. Asian women students may also be less likely to label sexual assaults as rape and less likely to report them because of self-blame or fear of repercussions.[19] Another study found that white women students hold more conservative attitudes about women's rights and roles in society and that they experienced more sexual victimization than do African-American women students.[20] Sometimes women students place pressure on other women not to report a rape, if the perpetrator is someone they know and like. Many homosexual rapes are not reported due to the fear of encountering nonaccepting attitudes. Police and counselors, however, are now receiving training on how to deal with rape in all its forms.

All sexual assault victims need help and should be encouraged to report the incident. The incident should be reported to campus officials and the police. One of the main reasons to do so is to prevent it from happening again; rapists usually strike more than once. You or the friend it happened to also need emotional support. Your local rape crisis center can provide emotional, medical, and legal advice. Many schools have rape support services and publish guidelines outlining where to seek help and what your reporting options are. Some campuses have twenty-four-hour telephone hot lines run by students who provide information and immediate emotional support. Familiarize yourself with these services and guidelines before something happens. But don't become paranoid; the odds are in your favor that you will not be victimized, and they increase greatly the more informed you are.

Most colleges and universities have disciplinary procedures covering sexual misconduct and assault and encourage students to seek justice there. But only the police can press official charges that will result in more than suspension from school. Even a rapist who gets expelled from school can transfer somewhere else and rape again. Using campus disciplinary hearings can be problematic in other ways. When a woman at Virginia Polytechnic Institute and State University accused two football players of raping her, one was found not guilty. The other player was initially found guilty and suspended for two semesters, but after a second hearing—at which he was represented by a lawyer—he was found guilty only of using "demeaning language" and reinstated and allowed to resume his old position on the football team. She then filed a federal lawsuit against both players and the university under the federal Violence Against Women Act (1994).[21] Three years earlier, four women at Carleton College who claimed they were raped by the same two male students sued the college for not protecting them by having adequately disciplined the men. Their case was settled out of court. According to Leslie Wolfe, of the Center for Women Policy Studies, college hearings are unfair to both the accused and the plaintiff since "students are stripped of due process and their rights as citizens."[22] In academic hearings, the accused is placed at risk because rape charges do not have to be proven beyond a reasonable doubt. The plaintiff is placed at risk for the reasons outlined above, and because colleges and universities have a vested interest in keeping rape charges involving students under wraps. In the United Kingdom, most colleges and universities do not adjudicate criminal offenses like rape.[23]

U.S. courts have recognized a special legal relationship between colleges, as landowners, and their students. Legally, colleges must protect students—as "invitees" onto campus premises—from foreseeable dangers. In *Mullins v. Pine Manor College* (1983), for example, the court found the college liable for the on-campus rape of a woman student. The federal Student Right-to-Know and

Campus Security Act (1990) requires universities to inform students about potential dangers by disclosing statistics and information on campus crime. New federal requirements also stipulate that colleges must have a written policy on date rape and sexual assault, including a definition, a disciplinary policy, and educational prevention programs.[24] At Cornell University, parents of new students now receive a letter informing them that sexual assault is a serious issue at the school. Once on campus, students are exposed to a week of activities and speakers devoted to the topic.[25] Many schools have counseling programs for date rape victims, mandatory classes dealing with sexual assault, and special orientation sessions focused on the issue. Students on some campuses like Bowdoin College and Union College have also formed Safe Space groups of trained students to whom students who have been sexually assaulted can turn for support and advice.

Sometimes, disciplinary or misconduct committees are made up of students and faculty who have not been properly trained to handle rape cases. The presence of too many students on a committee may also compromise the confidentiality and civil rights of both victims and alleged attackers. And as discussed earlier, the punishment for individuals found guilty of rape is often inappropriately light—probation or suspension, after which the rapist is allowed to return to school. Some schools resist involving the police because public knowledge can adversely affect admissions. Check your school's investigative and disciplinary procedures to see if they encourage reporting and protect the rights of both victim and accused.

_____ **DID YOU KNOW?** _____

- Sixteen- to nineteen-year-old women are the most likely age group to be sexually assaulted in the United States, followed by twenty- to twenty-four-year-olds.
- A large-scale study of women students at Canadian universities and colleges found that 9 percent had been victims of acquaintance rape.[26]
- One study showed that one in twelve college men admitted to acts that meet the legal definition of rape, yet few of these men identified themselves as rapists.
- Fifty-one percent of college men in one survey said they would rape if they were certain they could get away with it.
- It is estimated that 85 percent of rapes are never reported to the police and that less than 5 percent of rapists go to jail.
- One out of eight Hollywood movies depicts a rape scene. By the age of eighteen, the average American youth has watched 250,000 acts of violence and 40,000 attempted murders on TV.

☒ Protect yourself! Alcohol and drugs impair your judgment and play a role in most acquaintance rapes. Control your drinking. Don't place yourself in unnecessary jeopardy.

☒ Communicate clearly to the men you are with. On dates, pay your own way and help break down beliefs that a woman owes a man something on a date. Sexual intercourse is never a payback for an expensive meal or an evening on the town. At parties or bars, communicate honestly and unambiguously. If you do not want to engage in sexual intercourse, make your feelings absolutely clear. Don't contribute to the "No means maybe" stereotype. If you have decided to have sex with someone, say so. If you are unsure, take the time to think it through carefully until you have made a confident decision.

☒ If you are pressured to have sex against your will, escalate the forcefulness of your refusals—direct refusal, vehement verbal refusal, physical force, and screams to attract attention.

☒ Avoid vulnerable situations when possible. Always meet a man you don't know very well in a crowded setting, or go out with a group. Don't leave a party with someone you don't know very well. If you find yourself in a room with just men and begin to feel uncomfortable, leave. Don't invite a man to walk you home or to come up to your room or go to his room if you don't know him very well. If you do, be clear about his and your intent. There is no way to ensure total safety, but remember AWARE: Alert Women Avoid Rape Encounters.

☒ Heighten campus awareness, too. Obtain a video on acquaintance rape (see Resources) and arrange for showings to your women's group, sports team, or other organization. Contact male friends and officers of campus fraternities, coaches of athletic teams, and other appropriate campus groups to arrange showings that target men. Mens' attitudes and behavior need to be changed.

☒ Michael Scarce, as coordinator of Ohio State University's rape education and prevention program, targeted male students by placing the following slogan on two hundred campus urinals: "You hold the power to stop rape in your hand."

☒ If your campus is small and offers few social outlets other than the fraternity party, lobby the administration for more choices such as a campus coffeehouse and more concerts, dances, and comedians.

☒ Contact the office of the dean of students or residence life to ask what educational programs they provide on rape and sexual assault. If these seem inadequate, suggest a course of action and get support from other students, both male and female.

▣ Read your campus's sexual misconduct policy and guidelines, which can be obtained from the office of the dean of students or residence life, the counseling center, or the women's center. Check to see if your school has a clear policy and a user-friendly reporting and adjudication procedure that will encourage women to report sexual assaults.

▣ Never voice or support the idea that a woman "wanted it" or "deserved it" (e.g., because she was drinking). No one wants or desires to be raped, and nothing justifies it. Speak up when male students joke or talk in a demeaning way about their sexual conquests and use a double standard in talking about men and women.

▣ If you or a friend are assaulted or raped, report the attack to the campus authorities and the police immediately. Remember, rapists rarely attack only one woman. If they are not stopped, this tragedy is likely to occur again. Follow these guidelines:[27]

If You Are Raped

1. Do not shower, wash, douche, or change your clothes, even though your immediate reaction is to do so. Do not use any medication. If you choose to press charges, the evidence will be there.

2. Go to a friend's house and call a rape crisis line or go to the university's counseling center for immediate trained support. Your campus may also have designated advocates to contact. This is very difficult to deal with on your own.

3. Go to a hospital. They will check to see if you have internal injuries, and they will test for diseases such as AIDS and STDs and will give you a pregnancy test. They will also gather the information and evidence you will need should you desire to prosecute.

4. Report the rape to the university and the police. Most campuses have designated people for you to contact and guidelines for reporting a rape or assault. They will explain your options and guide you through the process, but the decisions will be yours.

5. Seek counseling. A trained counselor will help you deal with the trauma associated with being raped.

If a Friend Is Raped

1. Listen. Do not judge.

2. Give comfort and believe her. Let her know she's not to blame. Realize that she may be dealing with fear, embarrassment, humiliation, and guilt.

3. Encourage action. Encourage her to call the police, report the rape to university officials, contact a hot line or on-campus counselor for

support, and go to the hospital for an examination. (Tell her not to shower or douche if she has not yet done so, and tell her to save her clothes.)

4. Do not be overprotective. Encourage her to make her own decisions and to take control as soon as she feels able. (Remind her that getting help and reporting what has happened does not obligate her to press charges.)

5. Don't let your own feelings get in the way of helping her. Do not discourage action, even if you know the assailant.

6. Support her in her decisions, even if you disagree with them.

7. Get help for yourself. You may need to talk to someone about your feelings.

RESOURCES

Books and Other Publications

Bart, Patricia, and Patricia O'Brien. 1985. *Stopping Rape: Successful Survival Strategies*. Elmsford, N.Y.: Pergamon.

Beneke, Timothy. 1982. *Men on Rape: What They Have to Say About Sexual Violence*. New York: St. Martin's.

Booher, Dianne. 1991. *Rape: What Would You Do If?* Rev. ed. New York: Simon & Schuster.

Brownmiller, Susan. 1986. *Against Our Will: Men, Women and Rape*. Rev. ed. New York: Bantam.

Caignon, Denise, and Gail Groves (eds.). 1987. *Her Wits About Her: Self-Defense Success Stories by Women*. New York: HarperCollins.

Campus Gang Rape: Party Games? Part of a packet of information on rape prepared by Julie K. Ehrhart and Bernice Sandler. Project on the Status and Education of Women, Association of American Colleges, 1818 R Street NW, Washington, DC 20009.

Estrich, Susan. 1988. *Real Rape*. Cambridge, Mass.: Harvard University Press.

Friends Raping Friends: Could It Happen to You? To obtain a copy of this helpful, concise guide by Jean O'Gorman Hughes and Bernice Sandler, contact the Center for Women Policy Studies, 2000 P Street NW, Suite 508, Washington, DC 20036 or call (202) 872–1770.

Gordon, Margaret T., and Stephanie Riger. 1991. *The Female Fear: The Social Cost of Rape*. Champaign: University of Illinois Press.

Holmstrom, Lynda Lytle, and Ann Wolbert Burgess. 1991. *The Victim of Rape*. New Brunswick, N.J.: Transaction.

Johnson, Kathryn. 1992. *If You Are Raped*. 2nd abridged ed. Holmes Beach, Fla.: Learning.

Ledray, Linda. 1986. *Recovering from Rape*. New York: Holt.

Lindquist, Scott. 1989. *Before He Takes You Out: Safe Dating Guide for the 90's.* Marietta, Ga.: Vigal.

Nelson, Mariah Burton. 1994. *The Stronger Women Get, the More Men Love Football.* New York: Harcourt Brace.

Parrot, Andrea, and Laurie Bechhofer (eds.). 1991. *Acquaintance Rape: The Hidden Crime.* New York: Wiley.

Parrot, Andrea. 1992. *Acquaintance Rape and Sexual Assault: A Prevention Manual.* Holmes Beach, Fla.: Learning.

Peer Educator Training and Presentation Manual. Written by Paul Bramlett, Linda Hellmich, Charles Martin, and Wendy Perkins, the manual is designed for students who work with other students on date rape. Graduate Coordinator, Sexual Assault Recovery Service Peer Education Program, Student Health Care Center, University of Florida, Gainesville, FL 32611.

Pritchard, Carol. 1988. *Avoiding Rape On and Off Campus.* 2nd ed. Millburn, N.J.: American Focus.

Sanday, Peggy Reeves. 1990. *Fraternity Gang Rape: Sex, Brotherhood, and Privilege on Campus.* New York: New York University Press.

———. 1996. *A Woman Scorned: Acquaintance Rape on Trial.* New York: Doubleday.

Shuker-Haines, Frances. 1992. *Everything You Need to Know About Date Rape.* Rev. ed. Baltimore, Md.: Rosen.

Stan, Adele (ed.). 1995. *Debating Sexual Correctness: Pornography, Sexual Harassment, Date Rape, and the Politics of Sexual Equality.* New York: Dell.

Taking Charge. This guide, written by Rochelle Boomhower, Jackie Gale, and Andrea Kelley, is designed to help you develop acquaintance rape prevention programs. It is intended for use in residence halls but can be adapted for other settings. Johnson State College, Counseling Services, Mart. 214, Johnson, VT 05656.

Warshaw, Robin. 1988. *I Never Called It Rape: The Ms. Report on Recognizing, Fighting, and Surviving Date and Acquaintance Rape.* New York: Harper & Row.

Videos

Acquaintance Rape: The Broken Trust. This twenty-two-minute video, made in 1990, provides a straightforward discussion of sexual assault, focusing on acquaintance rape. It deals with myths and facts, types of assailants, prevention strategies, and options for victims. KDN Crime Check Video Library, PO Box 71402, Madison Heights, MI 48071. Phone: (313) 546–3385.

Against Her Will: Rape on Campus. This forty-six-minute film, narrated by survivor Kelly McGillis, explores the problems of date rape with testimonies from college women and men. It is thought-provoking and intense, and is divided into segments that cover the scope of the problem, the impact on victims, a profile of offenders, underlying causes, and institutional responses. Coronet/MTI Film and Video, 108 Wilmot Road, Deerfield, IL 60015. Phone: (800) 621–2131.

Campus Rape. This is a twenty-one-minute video featuring Corbin Bernson and Susan Dey. It includes testimonies from two stranger rape and two acquaintance rape survivors. It also gives advice on how to avoid and prevent sexual assaults. Rape Treatment Center, Santa Monica Hospital Medical Center, 1250 16th Street, Santa Monica, CA 90404.

Cry Pain, Cry Anger. This documentary by Caroline Gartner weaves together the stories of three women college students who have suffered through and dealt with the pain of date rape. Excellent for stimulating discussion. University of California Extension, Center for Media and Independent Learning, 2000 Center Street, 4th Floor, Berkeley, CA 94704. Phone: (510) 642–0460.

The Date Rape Backlash: Media and the Denial of Rape. This sixty-minute video examines the origins of the 1990s media backlash to rape. Authors and researchers like Susan Faludi, bell hooks, Mary Koss, Katha Pollitt, and Neil Malamuth are interviewed. The important issue of how and why the media use antifeminist women to dismiss and marginalize feminism is explored. Media Education Foundation, 26 Center Street, Northampton, MA 01060. Phone: (800) 897–0089.

Dating Rites: Gang Rape on Campus. This 1991 PBS documentary, filmed in part at Bucknell, was produced by Alison Stone. It includes a dramatized assault; survivor, offender, and expert interviews; and footage of a Take Back the Night march. WVIA-TV and Stonescape Productions, Public Broadcasting Center, Pittston, PA 18640.

Dreamworlds: Desire/Sex/Power in Rock Video. This powerful video was made by Sut Jhally, Professor of Communications at the University of Massachusetts at Amherst. It documents the misogyny and violence against women (including rape simulation scenes) depicted in rock videos. Media Education Foundation, 26 Center Street, Northampton, MA 01060. Phone: (413) 586–4170.

Rape: The Boundaries of Fear. This video examines how the fear of rape and assault affects women's lives. Survivors and victims talk about the precautions they must take. Men Stopping Rape, self-defense classes, and prevention workshops are discussed as ways to end the crime. Barr Films, 12801 Schabarum, PO Box 7878, Irwindale, CA 91706–7878. Phone: (818) 338–7878.

Sounds Dangerous. This is a short but effective video on campus rape produced by the Women's Center of Duke University. Women's Center, Duke University, 101–5 Bryan Center, Durham, NC 27706. Phone: (919) 684–3897.

Organizations

National Coalition Against Sexual Assault (NCASA), PO Box 21378, Washington, DC 20009. This feminist organization seeks to end sexual violence against women through education and advocacy. NCASA's membership is comprised of sexual assault programs, counseling services, women's shelters, professionals, and individuals, and includes Women of Color, Lesbian, and Victim Survivors caucuses. NCASA hosts national conferences and runs a Women of Color Institute for African-American, Asian, Latina, and Native American women, providing forums to discuss issues related to sexual assault.

NOW Legal Defense and Education Fund (NOW LDEF). Phone: (212) 925–6635. NOW LDEF publishes a Legal Resource Kit, *Violence Against Women*, and guides to legal resources: *State Index of Women's Legal Rights* and *Attorney Referral Services List*.

Planned Parenthood Federation of America, 810 7th Avenue, New York, NY 10019. Phone: (212) 541–7800. Most local Planned Parenthood offices offer a rape crisis service with counselors to help victims deal with the emotional, medical, and legal consequences of sexual assault. The service is free and confidential. Most offices also staff a twenty-four-hour rape crisis hot line. Check the Yellow Pages of your phone book, or contact the national Planned Parenthood office.

Rape Crisis Centers. Check local telephone listings for a center near you. Your local center will have published information on rape and should be able to arrange for a speaker to come to campus. It also counsels rape victims.

COLLEGE

AND

BEYOND

CHAPTER 13

Women   in

the   Media

She is passive, a spectacle to be assessed for her value to men. She is
defined in male terms. She poses, primps, reclines, and stares. She
admires herself or others. She receives advice. Her ultimate goal is
male approval, and she competes with other women for it. She is
powerless. Like a vase of flowers, she enhances the environment, but
has no influence on it.

—Samantha Sanderson, "'You've Come a Long Way, Baby'—
Or Have You?" 1990[1]

WE ARE EXPOSED to tens of thousands of advertisements each year. By the
time you enter college, it is estimated that you have seen 350,000 television
commercials alone.[2] Advertisements send two messages: one about the product or brand being sold, the other about who we are. Many ads feature women—
not real women, but a distorted image of womanhood. Although advertisers
have given some attention to feminism and the "new woman," especially at
the height of the women's movement in the 1970s, most use traditional images.
Women in ads are shown far more often in the home than in the workplace,
and their bodies are still used to sell everything from cereal to chain saws.

Most women in ads are young, thin, and white (and presumably, middle class and heterosexual). Older women are seldom seen unless they are advertising age-linked products like Geritol or Depends. When they are used to advertise other products, they are often depicted in a demeaning fashion. A print ad for a computer device that emits a programmable sound so that telephone callers can be identified shows an unflattering close-up of an older woman's face. The copy reads: "Decisions. Decisions. Will you make your mother-in-law sound like a pig or a cow?" Even the elderly woman who appeared in a popular Wendy's television ad campaign asking gruffly, "Where's the beef?" didn't paint a positive picture of older women. Underweight models far outnumber normal and overweight women in ads. The standard of beauty they portray is narrowly defined; the vast majority are also tall, young, and white, with narrow hips and full breasts. Their facial features are so remarkably alike as to be interchangeable, a fact that is sometimes used in ad imagery. Although women of color appear in ads, they are used primarily in fashion spreads and when advertisers want to target black and Latino consumers. Women with physical disabilities are almost never shown.

Women's bodies are used to advertise virtually everything. A Special K cereal commercial features a svelte young woman in a leotard preening provocatively in front of her full-length mirror. Frequently, women's buttocks, breasts, torsos, or legs are used to draw attention to an ad and to its product. Most of us are so used to seeing our bodies displayed, disrobed, and dissected that we do not question this. Educator Jean Kilbourne described a hair-product advertisement that ran in several women's magazines. Its copy read: "Your breasts may be too big, too saggy, too pert, too flat, too full, too far apart, too close together, too A-cup, too lopsided, too jiggly, too pale, too padded, too pointy, too pendulous, or just two mosquito bites. But with Dep styling products, at least you can have your hair the way you want it. Make the most of what you've got."

"This ad was not considered newsworthy," she says, and she asks us to think about the public's reaction if a jeans company ran a comparable ad aimed at men: "Your penis may be too small, too droopy, too limp, too lopsided, too hairy, too pale, too red, too pointy, too blunt, or just two inches. But at least you have a great pair of jeans. Make the most of what you've got."[3] Needless to say, no company would consider it; no ad agency would propose it.

Liquor advertisements contain some of the most sexist images of women. In a Bud Dry beer television commercial, the camera pans the body of a seductively dressed young woman while the announcer asks, "Why do gentlemen prefer blondes?" Answer flashed on the screen: "Dumb question." A print ad for Kremlyovskaya vodka shows a beautiful woman sitting on the edge of a pool wearing a skintight mermaid dress with a zipper down the front. The copy asks, "Wouldn't you just love to open *it*?" Some advertisements refer to sex explicitly. An ad for a telephone service shows three nude women leaning out from behind the blowup of a bill. The copy asks, "When was the last time you got screwed?" Next time you're browsing through a magazine or watching television, pay attention. You may be surprised by what you see.

Most fashion and beauty product ads are also demeaning to women. Social psychologist Erving Goffman has analyzed the many ways in which body position and gesture are used in advertising to indicate women's vulnerability and status inferiority to men.[4] Women in ads are often shown snuggling like children in a protective man's arms, leaning against him, or clinging to his elbow. They are typically posed in awkward positions: their bodies are off-balance or twisted, their knees bent, and their heads canted to the side or thrown back, exposing their throats. They are meant to look playful and sexy, but the image clearly depicts them as dependent and vulnerable. Women are usually positioned lower than the men in ads: seated, reclining, or lying at their feet. Many female models are shown caressing their own bodies with their hands and staring vacantly into the distance. They seem self-absorbed and detached, like objects, and the viewer is invited to regard them this way. Men, of course, are also stereotyped in ads: the distant, unemotional cowboy; the competitive, power-hungry executive; the Mr. Universe physical specimen.

A surprising number of ads link sex with violence by depicting women in danger or as victims of physical abuse. An ad for perfume—a product linked to romance—shows a woman on a city street at night with a man's shadow looming ominously in the background. Apparently she wears perfume to attract any man, even a threatening stranger. In an ad for men's shoes, a man is shown standing over the sprawled body of an elegantly dressed woman, his foot on her neck. A car polish ad shows the legs and arms of a woman's airborne body falling behind the shiny car that has just struck her. The copy reads, "Knock 'em dead on the street or the strip. . . ." In a jeans ad, a man carries off a screaming woman; she appears on the next page in the backseat of a car, apparently raped.[5]

Such images are duplicated on CD covers, posters, and rock videos, which are really extended advertisements. According to media analyst Sut Jhally, the "dreamworld" created in rock videos is a male adolescent fantasy world where all women are ready and eager for sex. Music video producers use many of the same techniques used in advertising. Women are presented as interchangeable objects to be sexually explored and used by men. The camera pans their bodies, focuses on their breasts, looks up their skirts. Story lines frequently show them as sex-starved and incapable of living without a man, as enjoying being pursued by strangers, as meaning yes when they say no, enjoying being leered at, and competing with other women for the attention of men. Men are depicted as manipulative and unfeeling sexual predators. Only by removing the music and replacing it with a neutral soundtrack and narration is Sut Jhally able to show us, in the video *Dreamworlds: Desire/Sex/Power in Rock Video,* what the images really portray.

Media representations of women have a socializing effect on their viewers and contribute to the devaluation of women. In the words of sociologists Nijole Benokraitis and Joe Feagin, "The attitudes of husbands and boyfriends are significantly shaped and reinforced by cultural pressures outside the home . . . [including] television programs, movies, mass media advertising, and the cosmetics industry [which] frequently present women as sex objects, to be manipulated for the pleasure of men."[6] Not only does advertising distort how others see us, it also makes us dissatisfied with ourselves. Everything about us can be improved with a product. Ads promise: Buy me; you'll be happier, prettier, thinner, more successful, more desirable, more. . . . It is important to remember that the models in beauty and fashion ads are highly paid professionals whose work depends upon their being thin and beautiful. Their appearance is further enhanced by skillful camera angles, lighting, wind machines, makeup, and airbrushing. The end result is an idealized perfection that is impossible for real women to achieve.

We begin receiving advertising messages early in childhood. Ads targeted specifically at children often promote gender stereotypes. A recent PlaySkool ad, for example, showed photographs of five happy children. Under each was a brief emphatic message relating to a Playskool toy. "Be a Mom!" and "Decorate Your Dreamhouse!" girls are told, while boys are encouraged to "Ride a 2 Wheeler!"; "Run Your Own Business!"; "Hit a Home Run!" When Janese Swanson and her young daughter, Jackie, saw the first ad for a voice-recording toy they had invented together, they were dismayed. The ad showed a boy holding the toy while ignoring the younger girl who was asking repeatedly for a chance to play with it. In response, Janese Swanson began Girl Tech, a company devoted to developing girl-friendly high-tech toys.[7] Barbie remains the most popular doll designed for young girls. She appeals to them because she represents the exciting fantasy world of adult femininity and sexuality, but her exaggeratedly thin body contributes to a distorted body image among young girls and, for some, to later problems with dieting, anorexia, and bulimia.

Most of the advertisements and articles in magazines like *Seventeen* that are aimed at teens and young women deal with traditionally feminine subjects: beauty, fashion, cooking, decorating, and crafts.[8] Although some articles discuss self-development and encourage feminist themes like self-reliance and "taking charge," these are overwhelmed by advertisements and editorial copy that tell young women how to become prettier and thinner so they can catch a man: "Mega Makeovers: go from so-so to supersexy." Has feminism made a difference? Some evidence suggests that the women's movement had a fairly significant impact upon the media and advertisers during the late 1960s and 1970s. The amount of editorial copy on self-development in *Seventeen* magazine, for example, increased from 7 percent in 1961 to 17 percent in 1972, before dropping back to 7 percent in 1985.[9] Today, however, the media messages young women receive can best be described as contradictory. Advice columns, editorials, and articles urge them to be strong and assertive feminists; fashion and beauty layouts show them as passive and anorectic. Anastasia Higginbotham has summarized the mixed messages this way: "Be pretty, but not so pretty that you intimidate boys, threaten other girls, or attract inappropriate suitors, such as teachers, bosses, fathers, and rapists; be smart, but not so smart that you intimidate boys or that, god forbid, you miss the prom to study for finals; be athletic, but not so athletic that you intimidate boys or lead people to believe that you are aggressive, asexual, or (gasp!) a lesbian or bisexual; be happy with yourself, but not if you're fat, ugly, poor, gay, disabled, antisocial, or can't at least pass as white."[10]

Advertisers have co-opted feminism when they thought it would help sell products. Maidenform bras celebrated the new professional woman by showing her flashing her underwear in the elevator on her way to the office. The young woman in Braemor ads, we are told, only took a job so she would have a place to wear her sweaters. The long-running Virginia Slims cigarette campaign has been telling women for years, "You've come a long way, baby." But what does this really say? "Baby" infantilizes women, and equating liberation with the freedom to smoke—a dangerous addiction—trivializes feminism and the goals of the women's movement.[11]

Gloria Steinem has described *Ms.* magazine's early struggle to find nonsexist ads and to convince advertisers to place ads in a feminist magazine. In her article "Sex, Lies, and Advertising" she describes how stereotypes of women influence advertisers and how the demands they place on the magazines that carry their ads influence the articles we read.[12] Food companies, for example, usually insist that ads for their products be accompanied by "complementary copy" in the form of recipes. Beauty product companies want their ads next to fashion spreads or articles that mention their product, something *Ms.* was not prepared to do. Many companies that offer services or products used by both women and men, such as airlines, cars, credit cards, insurance, and sound equipment, refused to believe that it was worth their while to advertise to women. Other advertisers refused to run ads in any *Ms.* issue that contained articles on subjects they considered distasteful or controversial, such as abortion or lesbianism. In the end, *Ms.* became the magazine it is today—ad-free and reader-supported. Other magazines, like *OUT* for gays, have had similar difficulty finding advertisers.[13]

Memorable Television Role Models

I am the girlfriend of either Starsky or Hutch. I will die of Leukemia in the last ten minutes of the show, or, alternatively, my past life as a hooker will be revealed and I will disappear for the good of Starsky and/or Hutch.

I am a psychotic/mute/Indian/Chicana who is restored to normalcy and neatness by a young, attractive, white, middle class doctor from the east. (Lots of flashbacks showing me whipped, raped, and force-fed)

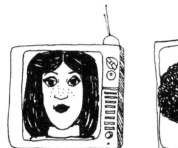

I am the sister/daughter of an unjustly imprisoned man or else the witness to a mafia crime. I am also the client of a blind freelance insurance investigator. I scream often and inopportunely. I always fall and twist my ankle when the investigator and I are fleeing the bad guys.

I am a black/white cop. I have a short snappy name. I am tough but feminine. I like to follow my own instincts about a case. This frequently gets me into trouble; I am inevitably rescued by my male, fellow officers, who are devoted to me . . . I never rescue them.

I am the woman behind the man. I spend a lot of time keeping dinner warm for my crusading policeman/coroner, lover/husband. Sometimes I nag about being left alone so much. Sometimes I am kidnapped by mafia thugs. This makes a welcome break in my routine.

© 1993 by Nicole Hollander

Women are the primary purchasers in 85 percent of American households. Most want to be treated with respect in the media and to be portrayed as adults in their full humanity and variety. If current ads are evidence, however, companies still do not understand this. According to one recent survey, 72 percent of women feel that advertising insults their intelligence, 79 percent find it boring and repetitive, and 80 percent think it misrepresents home life.[14] Perhaps this is one reason Cotton Incorporated's "The Fabric of Our Lives" ads were popular with women; they showed simple, slice-of-life scenes (although sentimentalized). Advertisers for technology are belatedly realizing how much purchasing power women have. In 1996, General Motors joined with Macy's and Condé Nast Publications to produce a common ad campaign. Ads featuring Chevrolet Cavaliers and clothing sold at Macy's appeared simultaneously in *Vogue*, *Glamour*, and *Mademoiselle* magazines. This joint approach may have been innovative, but the focus of the ads was still stereotypical and based on the advertiser's assumption that women are primarily interested in "colors and accessories" for both clothing and cars.

Advertising for computer hardware and software is still largely designed for men despite the findings of a recent advertising survey of two thousand women, which found that 65 percent had purchased a personal computer in the last two years.[15] The survey also found that most women find computer advertising unappealing and sexist. This helps explain why an Apple computer ad that broke the mold was popular with women. It showed a mother, juggling several children and a ringing telephone, preparing a report on her Apple computer. When her boss later asks her whom she hired to do it, she wryly explains that it was produced "in house."

Women in Television and Film

During the 1980s and 1990s, television and film roles for women broadened considerably. Programs revolving around the lives of smart, self-reliant working women, from single professionals to working-class moms, appeared. Today strong, complicated women play the parts of detectives, journalists, lawyers, and surgeons. Even mature women are cast as central characters: *Murphy Brown*, *Cybill*, *Grace under Fire*, and Jessica Fletcher in *Murder, She Wrote*, to cite a few. The number of African-American women as central characters has also increased. And more program plots deal with issues of special interest to women, such as gender discrimination in the workplace. Lesbians are also becoming visible on TV, in such programs as *Friends* and *Ellen*. As part of the trend to target increasingly specific and narrow markets, television is also beginning to think about attracting young women. The Lifetime cable network, for example, developed *The Place*, programming aimed just at young women.

There is still plenty of room for improvement, however. Nancy Signorelli's assessment of the situation in the late 1980s still pertains today. Women are seen less often on television than are men, and in many respects they may be considered less important. When women do appear, they are usually younger than the men; more attractive and nurturing; portrayed in the context of romantic interests, home, and family; and more likely to be victimized.[16] Television dramas still also contain mostly white casts, despite their urban settings. Most African-American female characters appear in situation comedies, and minority women other than African Americans are seldom seen. Women are still too frequently depicted as victims of kidnapping and violence.[17]

Most children's programming promotes gender stereotyping. Katha Pollitt, in a critical essay, has referred to the "Smurfette principle," a situation in which children's programs feature a group of male buddies "accented by a lone female, stereotypically defined."[18] On television, girls are invisible or tag along after boys. Most of the Muppets on *Sesame Street* are male, and April of Teenage Mutant Ninja Turtles is mainly a companion to the male superheros. The message is clear, says Pollitt: "Boys are the norm, girls the variation; boys are central, girls peripheral; boys are individuals, girls types. Boys define the group, its story, and its code of values. Girls exist only in relation to boys."[19] Saturday morning television largely ignores girls because, according to producers, more boys than girls watch television on Saturday, and boys will not watch programs with girls in the leading roles. Part of becoming "masculine" in America, it appears, involves rejecting all things female, even in cartoons and children's TV.

In film, early stars like Katharine Hepburn, Bette Davis, and Greta Garbo were cast in strong roles and earned as much as men. Then came the era of domesticity, when women withdrew to supporting roles as housewives, secretaries, and maids or else played prostitutes and victims. *Thelma and Louise*, a movie written and produced by women about two women outlaw heroes, is credited with turning the tide on domesticity and victimhood in 1991. Today, strong and interesting women's roles are reappearing. Part of the reason for this is the growing number of women who are directing and producing films. In the forty years between 1940 and 1980, women directed only fourteen feature films; in the single year 1990, they directed twenty-three (but out of a total of 405).[20] Today, women make up an estimated 9 percent of film directors. Filmmakers as diverse as Amy Holden Jones, Jane Campion, and Penny Marshall are creating films, from serious introspective works like *The Piano* to mass-appeal comedies like *Beethoven* and *Big*. Actors and entertainers like Barbra Streisand, Jodie Foster, Diane Keaton, Sally Fields, Goldie Hawn, Emma Thompson, Bette Midler, Alicia Silverstone, and Oprah Winfrey are also directing and producing. Female documentary filmmakers are also hard at work. Many of their films attack feminine stereotypes and explore women's inner conflicts.

Women also have become major consumers of film. According to recent surveys, they are the fastest growing category of frequent movie ticket buyers; they also make up a majority of the video market.[21] The "personal" films that appeal to many women and that female directors and producers often choose to make are cheaper than technology-laden action films, making them increasingly popular with cost-conscious studios, most of which now have at least some women executives. Consequently, the number of films by women and on topics of interest to women is growing.

Women are a long way from parity with men in the industry, however. According to the Writers and Directors Guilds of America, women make up an estimated 25 to 30 percent of employees in the film and television industries, and most work in low- and midlevel jobs. The belief that a production should not have too many women in executive positions is still widespread. Explains Kool Marder, a feature-production executive at Universal Pictures, "They say things like, 'Well, there's already a female assistant director, we don't want to have too many women.' You'd never hear them say that about a man; they'd never say, 'There's already a male producer. . . . '"[22] Top female stars still earn half as much as comparable male actors. Although more films like *Little Women*, *First Wives Club*, *Antonia's Line* (a Dutch film), and *A League of Their Own* are appearing with feminist themes or strong and resourceful women characters, they are still vastly outnumbered by movies in which the female characters are superficially developed or else exist merely to provide the victim or sex interest for a man.

The media portrayal of violence is troubling. The sheer number of violent images we are exposed to on television and in films creates the perception that violence is everywhere. It also desensitizes us to its horror. Men are usually depicted as aggressors and women as victims. These images are so commonplace that they seem normal, and even socially acceptable.[23] Research has found that after college men are shown sexually violent films with women as victims they feel less sympathy for women and more aggressive toward them.[24] Penny Reid and Gillian Finchilescu found that when college women watch films showing violence against women, they identify with the victims and feel more disempowered—vulnerable, intimidated, and powerless—than do students who watch films depicting violence against men.[25] The kind of violence sustained by women in films is qualitatively different from the physical violence aimed at men. Women are usually raped as well as being beaten, making media depictions of violence toward women all the more frightening to them. By making women fearful and by reinforcing the aggressor role for men, the media limits women's freedom and becomes an agent of social control.

When the film *The People vs. Larry Flynt*, about the life of *Hustler* magazine publisher Larry Flynt, was released in 1997, many feminists were appalled. The film depicted him as a somewhat sleazy free-speech crusader fighting for the right to show nudity, omitting any reference to *Hustler*'s misogynist images of women being beaten, tortured, stalked, and degraded. According to Gloria Steinem, the film would never have been made if *Hustler* published images of animals being treated with the same cruelty.[26] Nor would any mainstream producer or director have considered glamorizing the First Amendment court victories of Klansmen and American Nazis in the same way.[27]

Society's sensitivity to misogyny and mistreatment of women still lags far behind its awareness and intolerance of racism and cruelty to animals.

Women and the News

Nan Robertson, a Pulitzer Prize–winning reporter, has described what it was like during the 1970s when she worked at the *New York Times*. At that time, none of the paper's management, national correspondents, photographers, or reviewers were women. Only three out of thirty-three foreign correspondents were women, and two of the three women in top editorial positions worked in the family/style department, a traditional woman's assignment. In contrast, almost all the lower-paying, lower-ranking jobs at the paper were filled by women. And every woman at the paper, regardless of job, was paid less than men with comparable education, ability, and years of service.[28] The situation was much the same in broadcast journalism.

Today, conditions have markedly improved. Nevertheless, women still play a minority role in the news. On nightly network news programs, women report a fifth of the stories and make up a quarter of the sources who are interviewed on these broadcasts, even when a subject concerns women more than it does men.[29] A 1996 survey of twenty national newspapers found that only 15 percent of front-page references that year were to women.[30] Some papers, including *USA Today*, the *Washington Post*, and the *New York Times*, had substantially fewer.[31] Why? Only certain subjects get front-page treatment—typically politics, government, the economy, war, and major disasters. Except in the latter case, most of these articles are about men. The people who decide what goes on the front page are also still predominantly men.

When it comes to writing the news, the situation is not much better. Only a third of front-page stories and 27 percent of opinion pieces are written by women, and a disproportionate number of the latter are written by antifeminists, many of whom are supported by the conservative Independent Women's Forum.[32] Although we hear complaints all the time about the influence of feminists in society, their voices are heard infrequently in the national media. At the same time, feminism is often distorted (as discussed in chapter 1).

Just as minority students in the classroom are seldom called when a discussion topic is not a minority issue, so women's opinions are seldom solicited when a news topic is not considered a women's issue. Essayist Katha Pollitt asks: "How many women, after all, does the *National Review*, *The New Republic* or *The Atlantic Monthly*—or for that matter *The Nation*—publish on topics unrelated to gender? How often do women appear on *Nightline* or *Crossfire* when the subject isn't 'Hillary Clinton: Does Whitewater Stigmatize All Women?' or 'Is the Wonderbra Sexist?' How often, even, does a woman review a book that isn't either by a woman or about a woman's issue?"[33]

Why is this the case? To begin with, fewer women than men produce the news and make editorial assignments. Most editors and news producers also fall victim to stereotypes, assigning male reporters and writers to stories on politics, the economy, crime, foreign policy, and science, and female reporters to "women's issues" or "soft" issues like health and education. Because these are the areas in which opportunities for women in the news profession exist, many female journalists and commentators specialize in them, which helps to perpetuate the situation. Notable exceptions include correspondents like Christiane Amanpour and Cokie Roberts and syndicated columnists like Ellen Goodman, Molly Ivins, and Barbara Ehrenreich, who report and write on a broad range of topics.

Western media reaches even the smallest village in the most remote corner of the world, influencing what people desire and how they think about themselves. According to a survey conducted by the International Women's Media Foundation, most women journalists think the world's media portrays women inaccurately; it ignores women as leaders and perpetuates narrow and negative stereotypes.[34] In many parts of the world, women and their accomplishments are virtually invisible. Like American women, for example, African women are depicted narrowly either as victims of violence or sex objects.[35] While having more women design ads, produce films and television programs, and manage and report the news cannot guarantee more accurate portrayals of women, it does make them more likely. Having more women involved will broaden the scope of what we read and see. Many women journalists, for example, think that the increased numbers of women now covering U.S. presidential campaigns has changed the nature of election coverage, with fewer "horse-race" stories and more behind-the-issues stories.[36] Women will also help change occur by making their voices heard as consumers, viewers, and readers.

_____ *DID YOU KNOW?* _____

- The average American is exposed to between three hundred and five hundred advertisements a day.

- Although conventional wisdom says "sex sells," one study found that having ads with female nudes in them did not enhance people's ability to remember brand names as much as did advertisements showing forests and mountains.[37]

- Even advertisements aimed at menopausal women use sex to sell. Most ads for hormone replacement therapy, for example, play on women's fear of losing their looks and sexual desirability and suggest that the reason they should take estrogen is to stop the aging process.

❖ The National Advertising Review Board has not issued guidelines on the depiction of women in ads in the last twenty years. Advertising agencies have few rules or procedures for spotting sexist ads.[38]

❖ Women consumers make 72 percent of household purchasing decisions and make half the purchases of big-ticket items like automobiles.

❖ Women also represent more than 60 percent of the video market, and this is where Hollywood makes most of its money. Video sales bring in two and a half times as much money as box office receipts.

❖ Silent film star Mary Pickford was the first actress to produce her own flims. She also cofounded the United Artists studio.

❖ The number of women working as journalists has grown considerably in the last twenty years. In 1992, women made up 46 percent of journalists working on news magazines, 44 percent on weekly newspapers, 34 percent on daily newspapers, 26 percent for wire services, 25 percent on television, and 29 percent on radio.

❖ According to the media watchdog group Women, Men and Media, however, the number of women commentators declined in the mid 1990s. And in 1996, 28 percent of all newspaper opinion pages featured no women commentators at all.

❖ A study by Fairness and Accuracy in Reporting in New York in 1989 found that only 10 percent of the guests on *Nightline*, one of the more intellectual news talk shows, were women. Its twenty most frequent guests were male.

❖ In 1979, minority women accounted for only 8 percent of women on television. Ten years later, they made up nearly a quarter of women on television.[39]

_____ *WHAT YOU CAN DO* _____

✖ When you see an offensive ad, write to the manufacturer. *The World Almanac and Book of Facts* lists the addresses and names of the chief executive officers (CEOs) of most top companies. You can also check the *Standard & Poor's Register*, *Ward's Business Directory*, *Hoover's Handbook of American Business*, or ask a reference librarian for help. Send your complaint to the company's CEO by name. Tell him or her that you will refuse to buy the company's products until the ad is replaced and that you will encourage others to do the same. A women's group you belong to could sponsor a letter/postcard-writing campaign.

✖ Send offensive ads to Challenging Media Images of Women for use in their "Media Watch" column and to *Ms.* magazine for inclusion on its "No Comment" page (see Organizations).

⬔ Consider placing a THIS INSULTS WOMEN or THIS PROMOTES WOMEN HATING sticker on posters on public property that advertise films, videos, albums, and other products that demean women or show them being harmed. By doing so, you may make the next person who looks at them stop and think.

⬔ Call television networks to object to sexist ads and commentary. Call the main network number and ask for the office of broadcast standards and practices: ABC (212) 456–7777, CBS (212) 975–3247, NBC (212) 664–2333, Fox (310) 277–2211, MTV (212) 258–8000. If you are objecting to an ad, be sure to mention the name of the product being advertised. If you are commenting on a program, you may want to fax the producer directly by name.

⬔ Talk to your friends about what images in ads, films, and rock videos really communicate about women and men. Invite speakers to campus or arrange a film showing (see Resources for ideas) in order to heighten awareness of sexism and gender stereotyping in the media.

⬔ Invite speakers to campus to talk about the news and the way it is reported. How are women presented? How are feminist issues dealt with? What voices are heard in op-ed columns and letters in national newspapers? Choose to write a paper on one of these subjects.

⬔ Write to magazines and newspapers to express your opinion about their coverage. *Sports Illustrated for Kids* developed a supplement called "Girls and Sports Extra," which now appears six times a year, as a result of letters it received from its young female readers, who wanted to read more about female athletes and girls who excel at sports. You *can* make a difference.

_____ *RESOURCES* _____

Books and Publications

Acker, Ally. 1991. *Reel Women: Pioneers of the Cinema, 1896 to the Present*. New York: Continuum.

Baehr, Helen, and Gillian Dyer. 1987. *Boxed In: Women and Television*. New York: Pandora.

Barthel, Diane. 1988. *Putting On Appearances: Gender and Advertising*. Philadelphia: Temple University Press.

Challenging Media Images of Women is a publication dedicated to changing sexist, racist, and abusive images of women in the mass media. It invites readers to send in original ads, album covers, and descriptions of billboards, radio, or TV ads for use in its "Media Watch" column. Challenging Media Images of Women, PO Box 902, Framingham, MA 01701.

Cowie, Elizabeth. 1996. *Representing the Woman: Cinema and Psychoanalysis*. Minneapolis: University of Minnesota Press.

Davis, Laurel. 1997. *The Swimsuit Issue and Sport: Hegemonic Masculinity in Sports Illustrated.* Albany: State University of New York Press.

Dines, Gail, and Jean Humez (eds.). 1994. *Gender, Race and Class in the Media.* Newbury Park, Calif.: Sage.

Doane, Mary Ann, et al. 1984. *Re-Vision: Essays in Feminist Film Criticism.* Frederick, Md.: University Publications of America.

Douglas, Susan. 1994. *Where the Girls Are: Growing Up Female with the Mass Media.* New York: Random House.

Faludi, Susan. 1991. *Backlash: The Undeclared War Against American Women.* New York: Crown.

Gallagher, Marget, with My von Euler. 1997. *An Unfinished Story: Gender Patterns in Media Employment.* New York: UNESCO.

Garvey, Ellen Gruber. 1996. *The Adman in the Parlor: Magazines and the Gendering of Consumer Culture, 1880s to 1910s.* New York: Oxford University Press.

Goffman, Erving. 1978. *Gender Advertisements.* Cambridge, Mass.: Harvard University Press.

Haskell, Molly. 1987. *From Reverence to Rape.* Chicago: University of Chicago Press.

Hecker, Sidney, and David Stewart (eds.). 1988. *Nonverbal Communication in Advertising.* Lexington, Mass.: Heath.

Heide, Margaret. 1995. *Television Culture and Women's Lives: Thirtysomething and the Contradictions of Gender.* Philadelphia: University of Pennsylvania Press.

hooks, bell. 1996. *Reel to Real.* New York: Routledge.

Jhally, Sut. 1990. *The Codes of Advertising.* New York: Routledge.

Jhally, Sut, and Justin Lewis. 1992. *Enlightened Racism: The Cosby Show, Audiences, and the Myth of the American Dream.* Boulder, Colo.: Westview.

Kaplan, E. Ann. 1983. *Women and Film: Both Sides of the Camera.* New York: Methuen.

Key, Wilson Bryan. 1974. *Subliminal Seduction: Ad Media's Manipulation of a Not So Innocent America.* New York: New American Library.

Kirkham, Pat, and Janet Thumin (eds.). 1995. *Me Jane: Masculinities, Movies, and Women.* New York: St. Martin's.

Kuhn, Annette. 1982. *Women's Pictures: Feminism and Cinema.* London: Routledge & Kegan Paul.

———. 1985. *The Power of the Image: Essays on Representation and Sexuality.* London: Routledge & Kegan Paul.

Mills, Kay. 1990. *A Place in the News: From the Women's Page to the Front Page.* New York: Columbia University Press.

Moseley, Eva Steiner (ed.). 1995. *Women, Information and the Future: Collecting and Sharing Resources Worldwide.* Ft. Atkinson, Wisc.: Highsmith.

Norris, Pippa (ed.). 1997. *Women, Media and Politics.* New York: Oxford University Press.

Pribram, E. Deirdre (ed.). 1988. *Female Spectators: Looking at Film and Television*. London: Verso.

Roberts, Robin. 1996. *Ladies First: Women in Music Videos*. Jackson: University Press of Mississippi.

Robertson, Nan. 1992. *The Girls in the Balcony: Women, Men and the New York Times*. New York: Random House.

Rooks, Noliwe. 1996. *Hair Raising: Beauty, Culture and African American Women*. New Brunswick, N.J.: Rutgers University Press.

Rossman, Marlene. 1994. *Multicultural Marketing: Selling to a Diverse America*. New York: American Management Association.

Steinem, Gloria. 1990. "Sex, Lies, and Advertising," *Ms.* 1 (July/August): 18–28.

Straayer, Chris. 1996. *Deviant Eyes, Deviant Bodies: Sexual Re-Orientations in Film and Video*. New York: Columbia University Press.

Williamson, Judith. 1978. *Decoding Advertisements*. London: Camelot.

Videos

The Ad and the Id: Sex, Death and Subliminal Advertising. This twenty-eight-minute documentary shows how advertisers use subliminal images to motivate consumers to buy. It analyzes the images of sex and death that are camouflaged in seemingly ordinary advertisements and presents the view that advertising is sophisticated applied psychology. Written by sociologist Bernard McGrane; produced by Harold Boihem. University of California Extension, Center for Media and Independent Learning, 2000 Center Street, 4th Floor, Berkeley, CA 94704. Phone: (510) 642–0460.

Dreamworlds: Desire/Sex/Power in Rock Video. A powerful exposé of MTV made by Sut Jhally, a professor of communications at the University of Massachusetts at Amherst. Because Jhally uses a neutral soundtrack of synthesizer music and commentary, the misogynistic images and messages of music videos become all too apparent. Media Education Foundation, 26 Center Street, Northampton, MA 01060. Phone: (413) 586–4170.

The Good, the Bad, and the Beautiful. Originally a TNT special, this two-hour documentary examines women in film, and features commentary by film scholars and media critics Molly Haskell and Jeanine Basinger. It covers eight archetypes: femme fatale, romantic, bombshell, independent, fury, wisecracking dame, heroine, and goddess.

The Killing Screens: Media and the Culture of Violence. Video on media violence, with Jean Kilbourne and George Gerbner. Media Education Foundation, 26 Center Street, Northampton, MA 01060. Phone: (413) 586–4170.

Passing. This short (six-minute) film by Cydney Court is a good discussion starter. It examines the role of television images in contributing to racial and gender tension. It explores our different reflexive reactions to seeing a lone person of a race or gender different from our own walking down an urban street at night. University of California Extension, Center for Media and Independent Learning, 2000 Center Street, 4th Floor, Berkeley, CA 94704. Phone: (510) 642–0460.

Still Killing Us Softly: Advertising's Image of Women. This powerful examination of advertising images of women is the updated version of educator Jean Kilbourne's original slide/talk presentation, *Killing Us Softly.* It is fast-paced and entertaining as well as enlightening. Cambridge Documentary Films, PO Box 385, Cambridge, MA 02139. Phone: (617) 354–3677.

Warning: The Media May be Hazardous to Your Health. Warning shows how women are objectified in films and advertisements. Media Watch, PO Box 618, Santa Cruz, CA 95061–0618. Phone: (408) 423–6355.

Women Who Made the Movies. This fifty-five-minute video documents the largely forgotten careers and films of pioneer women filmmakers such as Ida Lupino and Ann Baldwin. Made in 1992 by Gwendolyn Foster and Wheeler Dixon. Women Make Movies, 462 Broadway, Suite 500-E, New York, NY 10013. Phone: (212) 925–0606.

Organizations

Center for Media Literacy, 4727 Wilshire Boulevard, Suite 403, Los Angeles, CA 90010. Phone: (213) 931–4177. The Center produces an excellent curriculum package called *Break the Lies That Bind* on sexism in the media. It also publishes the magazines *Media & Values* and *Parenting in a TV Age.*

FAIR (Fairness and Accuracy in Reporting), 130 West 25th Street, New York, NY 10001. Phone: (212) 633–6700. FAIR is a national media group that promotes free speech and a free press and encourages pluralism in the U.S. media. It compiles statistics, monitors the portrayal of women and minorities, runs a speakers' bureau, and produces the bimonthly publication *Extra!*

Filmakers Library, 124 East 40th Street, New York, NY 10016. Phone: (212) 808–4980. Filmakers Library has a large collection of documentary videos on women's studies topics, including women in other cultures, aging, health and reproductive issues, lesbian life, women in sport, and more. A catalogue of videos for rent or purchase is available.

Gay and Lesbian Media Coalition, 8228 Sunset Boulevard, Suite 308, West Hollywood, CA 90049. Phone: (213) 650–5133.

Gay Media Task Force, 71–426 Estellita Drive, Rancho Mirage, CA 92270. Phone: (619) 568–6711. The Task Force provides resources to the media, and it works with authors to promote accuracy in nonfiction works concerning gays and lesbians. It also monitors the media and acts as an advocacy group, representing gay men and women before Congress and other decision-making bodies.

Media Network, 232 East 12th Street, Suite 4B, New York, NY 10003. Phone:

(212) 253–6987. The Network is a national clearinghouse for information on social issue films, including those on multiculturalism and women's issues.

Media Watch, PO Box 618, Santa Cruz, CA 95061–0618. Phone: (408) 423–6355. Media Watch is a national organization concerned with the image of women in the media. It produces a quarterly newsletter. If you subscribe, you will receive preaddressed, prewritten postcards to send to executives, advertisers, and marketers who engage in sexist advertising.

Ms., 135 West 50th Street, 16th Floor, New York, NY 10020. (Subscription address: PO Box 57132, Boulder, CO 80322–7132.) A bimonthly, national feminist magazine that contains no advertisements. *Ms.* publishes articles dealing with a wide range of issues, including women and the media. Each issue also has a "No Comment" page that reproduces examples of sexist ads sent in by readers. When you send in a submission, include the entire page it appeared on, date, and name of publication, and your name and address.

National Black Media Coalition, 38 New York Avenue NE, Washington, DC 20002. Phone: (202) 387–8155.

National Women and Media Collection, School of Journalism, University of Missouri, PO Box 7165, Columbia, MO 65205–7165. Phone: (573) 882–1110. The collection documents women's roles in the media industry and explores the ways attitudes of women and about women have changed.

New Day Films, 22–D Hollywood Avenue, Hohokus, NJ 07423. Phone: (201) 652–6590. New Day is a filmmakers' cooperative through which independent filmmakers and producers publicize and distribute their films. It has a catalogue listing many films about women's lives and feminist issues.

OASIS (Men Organized Against Sexism and Institutional Stereotypes), 15 Willoughby Street, Brighton, MA 02135. Phone: (617) 782–7769.

Women in Communications, 10605 Judicial Drive, Suite A4, Fairfax, VA 22030–5167. Phone: (703) 359–9000. Founded in 1909, Women in Communications is a professional organization for women and men in journalism, advertising, public relations, graphic design, publishing, photography, and computer communications.

Women Make Movies, 462 Broadway, Suite 500–E, New York, NY 10013. Phone: (212) 925–0606. It produces and distributes films (listed in its catalogue) made by women on a wide range of topics, including violence against women, the women's movement, and the experience of minorities and lesbians.

Women, Men and Media, School of Journalism, GFS-315, University of Southern California, Los Angeles, CA 90089–1695. Phone: (213) 740–3920. This organization was cofounded by Betty Friedan and Nancy Woodhull, founding editor of *USA Today*. It is a research and outreach project that examines gender issues in the media.

CHAPTER 14

Women

and Work

I feel like I'm pretending at work that I don't have a family and
pretending at home that I don't have a job.
—Mureille Soria, quoted in *Work Matters*, 1996[1]

THIS CONFLICT is just one of the gender issues facing women in the workplace; there are many others. How you regard the situation of working women
today depends on your point of view. To use a familiar analogy, the workplace
glass can be seen as half full or half empty. Here are some of the facts: Today,
59 percent of women work for wages, and nearly half the labor force is female.[2]
Women are also closing the wage gap. In some fields, they earn nearly
the same as men for the same or comparable work.[3] Among all full-time sala-
ried workers, however, women still earn only 71 percent of what men earn
annually—a full 29 percent less.[4]

Much of the wage gap between men and women is rooted in history. Before mass industrialization, most women and men worked at home, their joint
labor sustaining the household. With industrialization, however, "work" became separated from home and was redefined as labor that had a paid market

value. Because domestic labor—food preparation, cleaning, craft work, emotional and nurturant care for family members—was unpaid (and largely invisible inside the home), it was no longer classified as work. The idea that domestic labor is not "real" work explains why many full-time homemakers and mothers still answer "nothing" when asked what they do for a living.

The historical connection between the domestic sphere and women also helps explain other aspects of the workplace. It is one reason secretaries and female office workers are often called upon to perform tasks unrelated to their jobs, such as running errands for their boss or serving coffee and tea. It also helps explain why much of the other work secretaries do, such as impression management and networking, is taken for granted (as part of the female role) and is therefore not recognized as real work or financially rewarded.[5] The connection between women and domestic labor also explains why certain jobs are regarded as appropriate for women, the so-called caring or helping professions of nursing, teaching, social work, and child care.

Although increasing numbers of women are moving into traditionally male fields, the American labor force is still largely segregated by sex, with women vastly overrepresented in certain lower-paying job categories.[6] Over 90 percent of all registered nurses, elementary schoolteachers, maids, secretaries, and machine operators are women; over 80 percent of all food servers and bookkeepers are. In contrast, over 90 percent of engineers, dentists, and precision production, craft, and repair workers are men; nearly 80 percent of physicians and lawyers are. The majority of American women are still channeled into low-paying clerical and service jobs with few chances of advancement or substantial raises; fully two-thirds of all Americans who work for the minimum wage are women.[7]

Sex discrimination also plays an important part in perpetuating the wage gap. Women often receive lower starting salaries than men, an earnings gap that influences their future job promotions and opportunities.[8] Although the Equal Pay Act, passed in 1963, requires employers to pay all employees the same salary for the same work, the Act has not been aggressively enforced. And the law says nothing about paying people who do different but comparable jobs the same.[9] When the salaries of more than a thousand managers working at twenty Fortune 500 companies were compared, women lagged behind men even when they had the same education credentials, agreed to be transferred, and followed other rules for advancement.[10] In a survey of nearly two hundred mid- and upper-level managers at major companies, Peter Hammerschmidt found that men earned an average of $15,000 more in annual salary than did women. After controlling for age, race, education, type of organization, and management level, he concluded that only $3,740 of this difference was *not* due to sex discrimination.[11]

© 1991 by Nicole Hollander

Some women workers are more exploited than others, of course. Immigrant women who work as maids and cleaners often work twice the hours of other workers (typically, fifteen-hour days and six-day weeks) at a fraction of the pay and without health and other benefits. The United Nations' International Labor Office estimates that there are at least 1.5 million female migrant workers from Asia alone working in the United States as domestic servants, often under terrible conditions. Working women of color face racial stereotyping and prejudice on top of gender discrimination. Women with disabilities deal with many more artificial barriers to full participation in the labor force than do able-bodied women. There is no federal law protecting lesbians from blatant exclusion.

Prepare yourself for the workplace while you are still in college. Many departments and programs on campus offer internships for course credit. These will expose you to the work of different organizations and professions and will give you valuable experience. If a department does not offer a formal internship, an individual professor may know of opportunities or may be able to arrange an internship (for independent study credit) for you. If you can afford to, find a summer internship. Members of the Senate and House of Representatives, for example, hire between three thousand and four thousand summer congressional interns. Contact them early, the November or December before the summer you want to work; each member has her or his own deadlines and application procedures. Think of businesspeople, professionals, and organizations in your hometown that might have opportunities. You can also consult a guide to internships, such as the Princeton Review's *America's Top 100 Internships* or the *Encyclopedia of Associations,* for information and addresses of organizations that work in an area of interest to you. Develop mentoring relationships with faculty members in your major. The better one of your professors knows you, the better able she or he will be to write a strong letter of recommendation. If your academic work is solid, your enthusiasm for your chosen field apparent, and you show evidence of commitment and leadership outside the classroom, you should be able to obtain the kind of supportive and thoughtful letter of recommendation that will help you enter graduate or professional school or obtain a job after leaving school.

The term "glass ceiling" refers to the invisible barriers that limit how high women can climb on the career ladder. It covers everything from exclusive partnership rules to male recreational/business activities that exclude women. Although the growing numbers of professional women and executives may make you believe otherwise, the glass ceiling has yet to be shattered. According to a study by Catalyst, a New York–based women's research and advocacy group, women make up only 10 percent of the officers at the largest U.S. companies and occupy an average of only 2 percent of senior executive positions. They hold one of the five top jobs at only one-tenth of the five hundred largest publicly traded companies.[12] Women are also underrepresented in top state and local management as government officials and administrators. In recognition of the many barriers still facing women in the workplace, Congress formed the Glass Ceiling Commission—as part of the Civil Rights Act of 1991—to develop policies to break through it.

There are many barriers to advancement. Women are usually not mentored or groomed for higher positions as actively as are men. They are often excluded from the informal networks at work that would increase their knowledge of the workplace and enhance their mobility. Their applications for promotion or training programs are often "misplaced" or ignored. Undesirable projects are dumped on them, and then the credit is taken by others, often men. "Whenever my supervisor gets a boring, tedious job he doesn't want to do," explained one woman engineer, "he assigns it to me. He praises my work and promises it will pay off in his next evaluation. Then he writes the cover letter and takes full credit. . . . I've never been given any credit for any of the projects—and some were praised very highly by our executives."[13] Women are often tracked into low-profile jobs (often on the basis of gender stereotypes) that are unlikely to advance their careers or lead to the top levels of management. A woman attorney, for example, may be assigned a specialty like domestic and family law, regardless of her training. African-American women report receiving less support for career advancement from their bosses and less acceptance by colleagues than do their white counterparts. They also perceive greater gender discrimination than do white women.[14]

Gender bias results in many women not being taken seriously in the workplace, even women business owners and executives. Women frequently complain that they are interrupted in meetings and that their ideas seem not to be heard. This may sound familiar. You have probably said something—perhaps in class—and not received much of a response, only to hear a male student say basically the same thing a few minutes later and have everyone pick up on the idea. Ironically, given that women are so often not heard, sociolinguist Deborah Tannen found that when men and women speak the same amount during workplace meetings, people think that the women talk too much!

Many women report being treated as women, rather than as professional colleagues, in their workplace. Some men seem unable not to focus on their female colleagues', employees', or bosses' gender when interacting with them. This is most true of strongly sex-typed men, those who think in terms of gender stereotypes and for whom sex is highly salient.[15] They seem unable to resist commenting on a woman's appearance, even during meetings, or telling jokes with sexual content. When challenged, they are likely to put a woman down with a sexist remark (e.g., "Look here, little girl . . ."). Even acts meant to be friendly can detract from a woman's professional credibility. Performance evaluations, for example, that describe how congenial and pleasant a person a woman is, rather than discussing her professional accomplishments, do her no favor. Calling a woman "hon" or winking at her in the workplace is demeaning and treats her as a sex object or child rather than as a valuable employee or professional colleague.

Gender differences in language use and interpersonal styles are believed by some researchers to contribute to the problem many women have with being taken seriously. According to Tannen, many women use indirect, self-deprecating language in order to state things in ways that allow others to save face. Unfortunately, their intentions are often misunderstood. A woman manager running a meeting, for example, might say to a male subordinate who arrives unprepared, "I'm sorry I didn't remind you that this issue was being discussed today." She expects him to say something like, "I really should have known. You told me about the meeting." Instead, he remains silent, probably thinking, "If she wants to take the blame, let her." When she tells employees, "Let me know what you think about this," in order to give everyone an opportunity to be heard, some men may think, "She doesn't know what to do, so she's trying to get us to decide." Her consideration and self-effacing leadership style—no matter how effective it is in getting the job done—undercut her authority.[16]

Another form of gender discrimination takes place when women are judged on the basis of their appearance rather than on their performance or qualifications. Heavy women, for example, may not be hired and are often passed over for promotion. Both women and minority professionals claim that they have to dress more formally at work than do other employees in order not to lose their authority and credibility. All women face the "double standard of aging," a phrase coined by Susan Sontag to describe the different ramifications of aging for men and women. In American society, a woman's social value is defined largely in terms of her appearance, and female beauty is predicated on youth. Consequently, women not only become "old" sooner than men, they

© 1993 by Nicole Hollander

also lose social status (which is one reason many mature women work so hard to remain youthful). Men, in contrast, become "distinguished" with age, and their social status is enhanced by experience and the wealth and career success that often come with it.[17]

Consequently, women in the workplace are more likely than men to suffer age as well as gender discrimination. In 1990, Adela Izquerdo Prieto, a nightly news anchor in Puerto Rico, was replaced at age forty-two by a younger woman. Referring to federal age discrimination laws, which apply to all workers over the age of forty, she filed an age discrimination lawsuit against her employer and won, only to lose later on appeal. More than a decade earlier, Christine

Craft, a newscaster in her thirties, was fired from a Kansas City television station after its researchers said viewers found her too old, unattractive, and "not deferential enough to men" when she was on the air. When her case was finally settled in the mid 1980s, it received considerable national attention, but the media never analyzed the underlying issue—the sex and age discrimination women face. According to Helen Norton, who studied 335 sex and age discrimination suits filed in federal and state courts between 1975 and 1995, fewer women today are winning age discrimination cases (41 percent in the 1990s, compared to 69 percent in the 1970s). She attributes this to the number of conservative judges who were appointed during the Reagan and Bush administrations.[18]

Unfortunately, women's economic importance is barely recognized. Did you know, for example, that women own one-third of American businesses—over 8 million? That they employ 18.5 million workers? That they generate 2.3 trillion dollars in revenue?[19] Or that 60 percent of new investors on Wall Street are women?[20] Much of the blame for our ignorance lies with the media, which seldom cover women in business. A report by the media watchdog group Women, Men and Media found that only 14 percent of newspaper references on the key business pages are to women. When women in business are covered by the press, their stories usually appear on the inside pages of the business section or else in the "soft news" features section.

Sexual Harassment

Sexual harassment in the workplace is a serious form of gender discrimination, as it is on campus. The term first entered the lexicon in the late 1970s with the publication of Lin Farley's *Sexual Shakedown: The Sexual Harassment of Women on the Job* and Catharine MacKinnon's *Sexual Harassment of Working Women*. The first case is believed to have been *Barnes v. Train* in 1974, in which a woman working at the Environmental Protection Agency alleged that her job was abolished after she refused to have sex with her boss. Today sexual harassment is against federal law; about fifteen thousand charges are filed each year with the Equal Employment Opportunity Commission.

What exactly is sexual harassment in the workplace? It is defined as any "unwelcome sexual conduct" that threatens a person's job or creates a hostile working environment. As on campus, it can be verbal (threats, insults, offensive or suggestive comments, messages with sexual content, pressure for dates), nonverbal (suggestive gestures or looks, displaying posters or photos of a sexual nature), or physical (cornering, trapping, pinching, rubbing, touching, kissing, sexual assault). For example, a supervisor might imply that a woman should share a room on a business trip if she wants to keep her job or promise her a promotion as soon as the two of them "get to know each other better." Co-workers can create a hostile work environment if they pressure a woman for dates, regularly leer at her or tell sexual jokes in her presence, touch her in a way that makes her feel uncomfortable or threatened, or make repeated inappropriate remarks (good or bad) about her looks.

One recent development are online sex sites on the World Wide Web. These are popping up on computer screens in even otherwise comfortable workplaces. Nielsen Media Research found that the online edition of *Penthouse* magazine is called up thousands of times a month by employees at companies like IBM, Apple Computer, AT&T, NASA, and Hewlett-Packard.[21] Women workers and experts on sexual harassment say that men who surf such sites, who use *Playboy* screen savers, or post lewd jokes on company bulletin boards and e-mail create an uncomfortable and humiliating atmosphere for their female colleagues. The climate exists whether women in the workplace glimpse the images while passing a co-worker's cubicle, the images are explicitly pointed out, or the women have to listen to the guffaws of male workers who are gathered around a nearby computer screen.[22] At the very least, office morale and teamwork between male and female employees are affected. A woman artist and Web designer reported that a male colleague's frequent jokes about the sexual material he had downloaded became a basis for male bonding in the office that left her out.[23] Many companies have now updated their sexual harassment polices to prohibit viewing sexually explicit Web sites at the office.

Although most companies have been slow to recognize it, domestic abuse also affects the workplace. It results in injury and absenteeism as well as stress that hampers an employee's job performance. It is also a major factor in workplace violence. In 1995, more than a dozen companies formed the National Workplace Resource Center on Domestic Violence to develop a model program of policies and benefits to help employees—mainly women—who have been subjected to domestic abuse. Policies include providing counseling programs, printing brochures on domestic violence and company assistance, placing signs with the names and telephone numbers of local shelters and counseling services in women's bathrooms, and sometimes enforcing protective orders at work, providing security to women employees who are being stalked by abusive partners, and even secretly moving employees to jobs in new locations.[24]

Finding a Balance

Americans are becoming increasingly interested in the overall quality of their lives. Juliet Schor, the author of *The Overworked American: The Unexpected Decline of Leisure,* reports that eight out of ten Americans would sacrifice career advancement in order to spend more time with their families.[25] They were willing to turn down a promotion, refuse relocation, move to a less stressful job, or cut back on their hours in order to help solve the work-family dilemma.

"Thank goodness you're here. His dish is empty."

Drawing by Cotham; © 1996 The New Yorker Magazine, Inc.

The most important issue for the quarter million women who answered the Department of Labor's survey "Working Women Count!" was the difficulty of balancing work and family obligations.[26] This is especially difficult for women who have young children. Most women who have children, including those with infants, now work for pay outside the home. Yet time-allocation studies show that these women do twice as much domestic work as fathers who work for pay—twenty hours a week, compared to ten hours for men.

Domestic tasks also remain segregated by sex. Most men do minor repairs, yard work, and other jobs that have traditionally been associated with men. Women continue to do about 80 percent of traditionally female tasks such as child care, cooking, cleaning, and laundry, as well as 37 percent of male-linked jobs. Although American women today spend less time doing housework than they did in the 1960s, men's participation in female tasks has increased by only two hours a week in more than thirty years. And when men do "women's work," women are likely to organize it: making the children's dentist appointments, writing their excuse notes for school, and reminding their husbands or partners of the appointments. As sociologists Nijole Benokraitis and Joe Feagin point out, "The woman is seen as 'liberated' because she works outside the home. In reality, her work has freed her spouse from having total economic responsibility for the household while only modestly increased [his] sharing of housework and child-care tasks."[27]

Of necessity, working parents develop adaptive strategies. Many combine errands like grocery shopping and delivering their children to day care with commuting between home and work. This usually means driving their own cars instead of carpooling or using public transportation, which, not surprisingly, has urban transportation authorities worried. They are now busy thinking of ways to make it more convenient for working women and men to use public transportation, do their errands, and care for their children. Some encourage day care centers to open near train stations; others let children under seven years old ride free. Washington DC Metro and the Virginia Railway Express offer a "guaranteed-ride-home program," which pays to get parents home quickly when there is a family emergency.[28]

When Secretary of Labor Robert Reich announced that he would not seek reappointment to a second term in 1996, he explained that he wanted to spend more time with his family. "There's no room for better 'balance,' " he claimed. "The metaphor is all wrong. You have to make a painful choice."[29] By the time you graduate, let's hope that you don't have to make a painful choice and that balancing work and family is no longer considered just a women's issue. There are some encouraging signs. One is the emergence of published ratings that evaluate companies on the basis of family-friendly policies, training programs, and advancement opportunities for women, and the overall quality of the work atmosphere. *Working Mother* magazine published its first list of one hundred top employers in the 1980s. In 1996, it was joined by *Business Week*'s "Work-Family Champions" list and the U.S. Department of Labor's "Honor Roll." A growing number of local community groups and agencies also publish ratings of small employers. These will provide you with important information when it's time to find a job.

Since a good rating can be used by employers to recruit workers, such lists also give companies an incentive to change. The quality of the workplace is becoming an important issue for employees. As companies downsize, those employees who remain are forced to wrestle with an increased workload. Many companies are having difficulty recruiting skilled workers. Being known as a supportive, family-friendly employer can help. Patagonia, an outdoor clothing retailer with seven hundred employees, is one example of a women- and family-friendly workplace. Fifty-three percent of its workforce are women. More than half of its top-paying jobs, including five of its eight directors, and nearly 60 percent of managerial jobs, are held by women. Its family-friendly policies include a subsidized child care center and paid leave for new fathers as well as mothers. Moreover, workers are encouraged to use their benefits. One thing you can do while you are still in school is to take one or more courses dealing with women and work; look at the offerings of the women's studies program as well as the sociology, economics, history, political science, and anthropology departments.

New legislation has also been passed. The Family Medical Leave Act, passed in 1996, requires businesses with more than fifty employees to grant up to twelve weeks of unpaid, job-protected leave to workers who need to care for a sick child, partner, or parent; for newborn or adopted children; or to deal with their own serious health condition.

If Americans are serious about giving women the chance to earn a good living and fulfill themselves through paid work, then accessible, affordable, high-quality child care must become a national priority. We currently do far less than many countries. A recent study by the Women's Bureau, a U.S. Department of Labor agency, concluded that nearly half (48 percent) of existing child care centers in the United States are "poor" quality, 35 percent are "fair," a meager 16 percent are "good," and only 1 percent are "superior." Child care workers, most of whom are women, are also some of the lowest-paid adult wage earners in the country. Most earn less than minimum wage and have virtually no opportunity for advancement, little prestige, and few benefits.

The child care problem is permitted to exist because child care has been considered a woman's issue rather than a family or societal issue. Some Americans believe that women should stay at home with their children and that those who "choose" to go to work should not receive any help. This attitude ignores the fact that most working women today do not choose to work; they need to work. They are single parents or divorced or simply need a second wage-earner's income. In any case, why should women's lives be restricted to the home? Why should women be denied the fulfillment of paid work or a professional career if they choose it? Evidence clearly indicates that women who interrupt their careers for several years to stay at home with young children never catch up in terms of income or advancement with men or with women who remained in the workforce. Although no one would deny a woman the opportunity to stay home with young children if she desires and can afford to do so, some studies have shown that mothers who work for pay are actually more satisfied with their lives—despite the added stress—than full-time stay-at-home moms.

Fortunately, some employers are responsive to the needs of their workers.

They provide referrals to community services in child care and elder care or on-site child care, and allow their employees to job share, work at home (via computer and modem), schedule flexible work hours, or work a compressed work week. A recent CIGNA survey found that 53 percent of working women and 41 percent of working men use at least one of these options. The top reasons they did so were "personal business" and "child care."[30] Other progressive policies include providing paid parental leave for birth or adoption, subsidized tutoring and help with college counseling for employees' children, and tuition reimbursement programs for employees. The National Foundation for Women Business Owners found that women-owned businesses are more likely than the average U.S. firm to offer their employees such options. Forty percent of women-owned businesses offer flextime options and 21 percent offer tuition reimbursement programs, compared to 30 and 8 percent, respectively, for all U.S. firms.

More women than men have joined labor unions during the past ten years; they now make up about 40 percent of the AFL-CIO's membership. Women are generally more supportive than men of the underlying premise of the labor movement that people need to work together to achieve their goals instead of going it alone. According to Kate Brongenbrenner, director of Labor and Education Research at Cornell University, "Women and people of color have for a long time found a greater interest in organizing than white men. And I don't think we should be surprised. They are the ones in the jobs that are most vulnerable to employer abuse and have the most to gain from unionization."[31]

_____ **_DID YOU KNOW?_** _____

- Approximately 65 million women are in the labor force.
- Women-owned businesses in the United States employ one out of every four company workers, or nearly 20 million people—a third more than Fortune 500 firms employ worldwide.[32]
- The growth rate in women-owned businesses since the late 1980s has been highest among minority women. According to the U.S. Census Bureau, the number of firms owned by women of color grew by 85 percent between 1987 and 1992. More than a third of minority-owned firms are owned by women.
- The fastest growing areas for women-owned businesses are in nontraditional industries, including construction, wholesale trade, manufacturing, and agribusiness.
- As women's earning power increases, more married women are earning more than their husbands. Today, approximately 29 percent of women in two-salary households earn more than their husbands do.

- According to *Working Woman* magazine, the highest-paid male executive in 1995 earned an incredible $65.5 million in salary and bonuses. The highest-paid female CEO earned $11.6 million.
- After United Way fired its male CEO amid scandal, much of it involving financial abuse, the charity replaced him with a woman who was paid less than half his salary.
- Only 2 percent of all secretaries, stenographers, and typists are men, but their average weekly earnings are higher than those of women in these jobs.
- The Equal Employment Opportunity Commission can afford to legally pursue only a small number of the complaints it receives.
- When 645 male and 270 female executives were evaluated by their co-workers, women outscored the men in 28 of 31 categories, including the ability to meet deadlines, boost productively, and generate ideas. Male executives scored higher in handling pressure and coping with frustration.[33]
- Nonpoor families spend about 6 percent of family income on child care. The poor spend 22 percent—almost a quarter of their income.
- The number of people with severe disabilities who have jobs increased by 27 percent between 1991 and 1994. Experts attribute this to passage of the Americans with Disabilities Act in 1990.
- The Ms. Foundation for Women started Take Our Daughters to Work Day in 1993, to bolster self-confidence for adolescent girls. Since then, it has been expanded by some businesses to include boys (a source of controversy for many feminists) and has gone online in an effort to show girls that there is a place for them in the world of paid work.
- One study of 116 recent minority graduates from several elite colleges found that they received 23 percent more job offers and slightly higher starting salaries than their white counterparts. They had stronger résumés, had started their job search earlier, and had held more internships while in college.[34]

_____ **WHAT YOU CAN DO** _____

- Do your homework! A lot of information is available on careers and job opportunities. Begin with the databases at your campus's career development or placement office.
- Obtain internships while you are still in college. The Feminist Majority Foundation posts an online internship directory listing organizations with opportunities for women. Web site: http://www.feminist.org/911/internship/internship.html. The Public Leadership Education Network (PLEN) also produces a guide for college women to internships and other resources in Washington, D.C. Write: PLEN, 1001 Connecticut Avenue NW, Suite 900, Washington, DC 20036. Phone: (202) 872–1585.

☒ Get *Working Mother* magazine's annual survey of "The Best Companies for Working Mothers," published each October. Also look at *Business Week*'s "Work-Family Champions" and the U.S. Department of Labor's "Honor Roll." These ratings will help you learn about what policies and programs to look for when you are seeking a job, as well as give you information about specific companies.

☒ If you are interested in starting a business or acquiring training with a view to someday starting your own business, contact the National Foundation for Women Business Owners (see Organizations) for information. It regularly publishes research reports on all aspects of women in business and business ownership.

☒ When you need a product or service, think about supporting women-owned businesses. To find out what businesses in your area are owned by women, consult the Women's Yellow Pages. A growing number of cities (e.g., Los Angeles, Atlanta, Boston, Cleveland, Albuquerque) and regions around the country (e.g., upper New York State, Puget Sound area) publish these directories. To find out if your area has one, call the Women in Business Yellow Pages, 819 South Wabash Avenue, Suite 606, Chicago, IL 60605. Phone: (312) 294–6300.

☒ Before beginning your job search, learn what the pay is for the jobs you are interested in. The National Association of Colleges and Employers conducts an annual survey of starting salary offers, broken down by occupation and gender. Most college placement or career development offices have a copy. Your school may also survey its own graduates about the offers they received. Ask the industry sources you meet at association meetings and job fairs what someone with ten years' experience in a particular job should make. Another source of information is professional magazines in the fields you are interested in. Many online want ads from newspapers around the country list salary ranges. Remember, salaries are negotiable. Know what the kind of job you want usually pays, but hold your cards until it is clear that the employer you are interviewing with wants you.

☒ Once you have a position, stay tuned in to what your job is worth by talking to other people in your field, to the staff of professional organizations, and to headhunters. If you are not earning what you should, ask for more, or consider looking for another position if the job market makes it realistic to do so.

☒ When you take a job, familiarize yourself with your employer's sexual harassment policy. Then set a positive example at work by being professional at all times and by treating fellow employees with respect and letting them know you expect the same. And if you are ever harassed, don't quietly accept the behavior. Make your feelings known and follow these recommended steps:

1. Confront your harasser, clearly telling him or her what behavior offends you and that you want it to stop. If you prefer, write a letter and have a co-worker deliver it or send it registered mail. Keep a copy.
2. Keep a record of all incidents, where and when they occurred, and who witnessed them.
3. If the behavior doesn't stop, speak to your supervisor. Bring your record, so you can provide details. Afterward, write down what your supervisor said, and what the supervisor does later. If your supervisor is the harasser, talk to his or her boss or to your personnel or human resources director.
4. If the harassment continues, contact a union representative, a grievance committee, an affirmative action officer, an employee support or advocacy group, or a lawyer.
5. Consider filing a formal complaint with the federal Equal Employment Opportunity Commission, state attorney general's office, district attorney, or state or city department of human or civil rights.
6. Seek counseling and emotional support for yourself, and be supportive of anyone else who is being sexually harassed. Encourage her or him to take action, and offer to be a witness.

☒ Balancing work and family is an important workplace issue for women and men. Consider volunteering your time at an established and reputable child care center near campus. You will learn firsthand about some of the issues involved in balancing work and home, and also enjoy yourself. Encourage a male friend to volunteer with you; men need to take an active role in child care, too.

☒ After you graduate, support child care in the workplace and early childhood education in public schools by writing your representatives in Congress. If you are considering ever becoming a parent, consider child care criteria in the jobs you seek and accept.

☒ Put your money where your values are. Support companies that have family-friendly policies by buying their products and avoiding products made by companies that do not. Author Donna Jackson recommends purchasing the *Shopping for a Better World* guide ([800] 729–4237) published by the Council on Economic Priorities.[35] It rates companies on ten key issues, including family-friendly policies, minority hiring, and environmental policy.

☒ If you have a disability, don't let stereotypes limit your choice. Your parents, teachers, and past advisors may not have been aware of all that is available to you; you may not have been exposed to many role models of successfully employed professionals with disabilities. Take courses in many subjects in order to find out what you like. Try to get the same kind of work experience—part-time work, summer jobs, internships—many able-bodied students have by the time they leave college. Check on what programs are available at your school. Northeastern University, for example, runs a large cooperative education program in which students alternate study with paid work experience. It is open to students with disabilities. The Career Planning and Placement Center at UC Berkeley has the Disabled Student and Alumni Program, which works with employers to help recruit, select, and employ students and alumni with disabilities in internships, summer jobs, and careers.

⊠ If you have a disability, begin now to find out about life after college. Contact the HEATH Resource Center and the ERIC Clearinghouse for information on career opportunities for people with disabilities (see Organizations). The magazine *Careers & the disABLED* also provides valuable information, including job announcements and success stories (Equal Opportunity Publications, PO Box 202, Centerport, NY 11721). Richard Bolles's *Job Hunting Tips for the So-Called Handicapped or People Who Have Disabilities* gives encouragement and sound advice as well as references to many other publications and government resources.

──────────────────── *RESOURCES* ────────────────────

Books and Other Publications

Albelda, Randy, Robert Drago, and Steven Shullman. 1997. *Unlevel Playing Fields: Understanding Wage Inequality.* Burr Ridge, Ill.: Irwin/McGraw-Hill.

Amott, Teresa, and Julie Matthaei. 1996. *Race, Gender, and Work: A Multi-cultural Economic History of Women in the United States.* Boston: South End.

Barber, Elizabeth. 1994. *Women's Work: The First 20,000 Years.* New York: Norton.

Blau, Francine, and Ronald Ehrenberg (eds.). 1997. *Gender and Family Issues in the Workplace.* New York: Russell Sage.

Bolles, Richard N. 1991. *Job Hunting Tips for the So-Called Handicapped or People Who Have Disabilities.* Berkeley, Calif.: Ten Speed.

Braddock, David, and Lynn Bachelder. 1994. *The Glass Ceiling and Persons with Disabilities.* Public Policy Monograph Series No. 56. Chicago: Institute on Disability and Human Development.

Briles, Judith. 1996. *Gendertraps: Conquering Confrontophobia, Toxic Bosses, and Other Land Mines at Work.* New York: McGraw-Hill.

Coltrane, Scott. 1996. *Family Man: Fatherhood, Housework, and Gender Equity.* New York: Oxford University Press.

Conrad, Pamela. 1995. *Balancing Home and Career: Skills for Successful Life Management.* 3rd ed. Menlo Park, Calif.: Crisp.

Dunn, Dana (ed.). 1996. *Workplace/Women's Place: An Anthology*. Los Angeles: Roxbury.

Edminston, Alexandra. 1996. *Confessions from the Cubicle: Women Talk about Surviving in Today's Work Force*. Toronto: Publishing Prose.

Farlay, Lin. 1978. *Sexual Shakedown: The Sexual Harassment of Women on the Job*. New York: McGraw-Hill.

Friedman, Sara Ann. 1996. *Work Matters: Women Talk About Their Jobs and Their Lives*. New York: Viking.

Gaskell, Jane. 1991. *Gender Matters from School to Work*. London: Taylor and Francis.

Goldman, Anne. 1996. *Take My Word: Autobiographical Innovations of Ethnic American Working Women*. Berkeley: University of California Press.

Hays, Sharon. 1996. *The Cultural Contradictions of Motherhood*. New Haven, Conn.: Yale University Press.

Hochschild, Arlie, with Anne Machung. 1989. *The Second Shift: Working Parents and the Revolution at Home*. New York: Viking.

Kaser, Joyce, with Bette George and Arleen LaBella. 1995. *Honoring Boundaries: Preventing Sexual Harassment in the Workplace*. Amherst, Mass.: Human Resource Development.

Kearney, Katherine, and Thomas White. 1995. *Men and Women at Work*. Franklin Lakes, N.J.: Career.

Kessler-Harris, Alice. 1982. *Out to Work: A History of Wage-Earning Women in the United States*. New York: Oxford University Press.

King, Julie Adair. 1995. *The Smart Woman's Guide to Interviewing and Salary Negotiation*. Franklin Lakes, N.J.: Career.

Lynch, Frances. 1995. *Draw the Line: A Sexual Harassment Free Workplace*. Grants Pass, Oreg.: Oasis/PSI Research.

MacKinnon, Catharine. 1979. *Sexual Harassment of Working Women*. New Haven, Conn.: Yale University Press.

MacLean, Barbara Hutmacher. 1996. *"I Can't Do What?" Voices of Pathfinding Women*. Ventura, Calif.: Pathfinder.

Mindell, Phyllis. 1996. *A Woman's Guide to the Language of Success*. New York: Prentice Hall.

Nivens, Beatryce (ed.). 1987. *The Black Woman's Career Guide*. New York: Anchor/Doubleday.

Rousso, Harilyn. 1993. *Disabled, Female, and Proud! Stories of Ten Women with Disabilities*. Westport, Conn.: Bergin & Garvey/Greenwood.

Russell, Kathy, and Midge Wilson. 1996. *Divided Sisters: Bridging the Gap Between Black Women and White Women*. New York: Anchor/Doubleday.

Shelton, Beth Anne. 1992. *Women, Men, and Time: Gender Differences in Paid Work, Housework, and Leisure*. Westport, Conn.: Greenwood.

Spain, Daphne, and Suzanne Bianchi. 1996. *Balancing Act: Motherhood, Marriage, and Employment among American Women.* New York: Russell Sage.

Stockdale, Margaret (ed.). 1996. *Sexual Harassment in the Workplace: Perspectives, Frontiers and Response Strategies.* Thousand Oaks, Calif.: Sage.

Swiss, Deborah. 1996. *Women Breaking Through: Overcoming the Final 10 Obstacles at Work.* Princeton, N.J.: Peterson's.

Tannen, Deborah. 1994. *Talking from 9 to 5.* New York: Morrow.

Wallace, Michele. 1990. *Black Macho and the Myth of the Superwoman.* New York: Verso.

Zuckerman, Amy, and George Simons. 1996. *Sexual Orientation in the Workplace: Gay Men, Lesbians, Bisexuals, and Heterosexuals Working Together.* Thousand Oaks, Calif.: Sage.

Videos

The Double Burden: Three Generations of Working Mothers. This fifty-six-minute documentary gives a multicultural and multigenerational look at women and work. It tells the stories of Mexican-American, Polish-American, and African-American women who have always combined work with family life. Good for stimulating discussion. Available from New Day Films, Department WM, 22–D Hollywood Avenue, Hohokus, NJ 07423. Phone: (201) 652–6570.

The Impossible Takes a Little Longer. This forty-six-minute documentary was made by the National Film Board of Canada and portrays the personal and professional lives of four women with disabilities. Each woman has developed creative solutions to the frustrations she encounters in the workplace and at home. It is available for rent from Indiana University, Audio-Visual Center, Bloomington, IN 47405. Phone: (812) 855–8087.

Through the Glass Ceiling. An entertaining seventeen-minute animated film made by the BBC. It recounts the story of Princess Ella, who sets out on her a career path at the Equal Opportunities Kingdom. With her magic laptop she journeys past the Typing Pool, over the Gender Salary Gap, and through many misadventures before confronting the biggest hazard of all, the Glass Ceiling. Filmakers Library, 124 East 40th Street, New York, NY 10016. Phone: (212) 808–4980.

Union Maids. This now-classic forty-eight-minute documentary recounts the birth of the CIO (Congress of Industrial Organizations) in the 1930s by telling the stories of three women who participated in the organizing, hunger marches, unemployment, and strikes that brought it about. Nominated for an Academy Award, it is inspiring and exhilarating. Available for rental or purchase from New Day Films, Department WM, 22–D Hollywood Avenue, Hohokus, NJ 07423. Phone: (201) 652–6570.

Weirded Out and Blown Away. This forty-three-minute consciousness-raising documentary interviews four career people who have disabilities, including Sharon Greytak, the film's director. It provides insight into the personal and social relationships of men and women, the relationship between sexuality and disability, the social acceptability of physical disabilities, and issues people with disabilities encounter in job interviews. Available for rental from Cinema Guild, 1697 Broadway, New York, NY 10019. Phone: (212) 246–5522.

Organizations

American Business Women's Association (ABWA), 9100 Ward Parkway, PO Box 8728, Kansas City, MO 64114–0728. Phone: (816) 361–6621. ABWA is a professional association for women in business and professions. It organizes conferences on workplace issues and provides leadership training, education programs, and business-skills-training loans. It publishes the bimonthly magazine *Women in Business* and awards an annual scholarship to a woman student.

Council on Career Development for Minorities (CCDM), 1341 West Mockingbird Lane, Suite 412–E, Dallas, TX 75247. Phone: (214) 631–3677. The council works to heighten the awareness and employability of African-American, Latino, and Native American college students and to improve the career counseling and referral services that are offered to them. It conducts a Corporate Orientation Program, which gives sophomore-level minority students the opportunity to study actual business activities and the factors that affect their employability and chances for promotion in the business world. It grants one or two Julius A. Thomas Fellowships each year to students of color wishing to pursue graduate study.

Council on Economic Priorities (CEP), 30 Irving Place, New York, NY 10003–9990. Phone: (212) 420–1133. The Council produces the guide *Shopping for a Better World* ($17), which evaluates companies on family-friendly policies, minority hiring, environmental policy, and more. CEP also produces a student guide to shopping for a better world, which covers brand-name clothing, tapes, CDs, and so on.

ERIC Clearinghouse on Adult, Career, and Vocational Education, 1900 Kenny Road, Columbus, OH 43210–1090. Phone: (800) 848–4815, ext. 4–7886. ERIC (Educational Resource Information Center) provides information on many aspects of career development for persons with disabilities, including attitudes, self-knowledge, and specific occupational and vocational skills. It also produces many useful resource guides and bibliographies.

HEATH Resource Center, American Council on Education, One Dupont Circle, Suite 800, Washington, DC 20036–1193. Phone: (800) 544–3284. This is a national clearinghouse on postsecondary education for individuals with disabilities. It publishes many resources, including "How to Choose a Career and a Career School: Guide for the Student with a Disability" and "Career Planning and Employment Strategies for Postsecondary Students with Disabilities."

Glass Ceiling Commission, U.S. Department of Labor, 200 Constitution Avenue NW, Room C-2313, Washington DC 20210. Phone: (202) 219–7342; TDD Phone: (800) 326–2577. The Commission publishes a list of its reports about the workplace conditions women face.

Institute for Women's Policy Research, 1400 20th Street NW, Suite 104, Washington, DC 20036. Phone: (202) 785–5100. The Institute is a public policy research organization that focuses on women's issues, including pay equity, child care, and parental leave.

9 to 5, The National Association of Working Women, 238 West Wisconsin Avenue, Suite 700, Milwaukee, WI 53203–2308. Phone: (414) 274–0925; Job Survival Hotline: (800) 522–0925. 9 to 5 is an advocacy organization for working women, especially office workers. It is interested in equity in pay and advancement, sexual harassment, workplace health and safety, and abuses of electronic monitoring. It operates a Job Survival Hotline, which offers counseling on such topics as workers' rights, sexual harassment, and coping with office politics. It also publishes fact sheets, including "9 to 5 Profile of Working Women," and books on work-related issues.

National Association for Female Executives (NAFE), 30 Irving Place, 5th Floor, New York, NY 10003. Phone: (212) 477–2200 or (800) 949–6233. NAFE is the largest businesswomen's organization in the country. Its purpose is to make women aware of the need to plan for career and financial success and to help them create tools to support these goals. Members have access to a career databank, résumé service, career development conferences, and networking opportunities. The organization publishes the magazine *Executive Female* and newsletters and maintains a good Web site: http://www.nafe.com.

National Federation of Business and Professional Women's Clubs, 2012 Massachusetts Avenue NW, Washington, DC 20036. Phone: (202) 293–1100. The Federation works to improve the status of working women. It awards grants and loans, based on need, to mature women reentering the workforce or entering nontraditional fields.

National Foundation for Women Business Owners, 1100 Wayne Avenue, Suite 830, Silver Spring, MD 20910–5603. Phone: (301) 495–4975. NFWBO is a nonprofit research, leadership development, and entrepreneurial training foundation. Its goal is to support the growth of women business owners and their organizations through gathering and sharing knowledge. It is a major source of information and statistics on women business owners and their businesses, and publishes a list of research reports and monographs.

NOW Legal Defense and Education Fund (NOW LDEF). Phone: (212) 925–6635.

NOW's main office is 1000 16th Street NW, Suite 700, Washington, DC 20036. Phone: (202) 331–0066. NOW LDEF has many publications pertaining to the workplace, including the *State Index of Women's Legal Rights*, *Attorney Referral Services List*, and *Employment—Sexual Harassment*.

Wider Opportunities for Women, 815 15th Street NW, Suite 916, Washington, DC 20005. Phone: (202) 638–3143. The organization promotes equal employment opportunities for women. It conducts nontraditional skills training programs, and monitors public policy relating to jobs, affirmative action, vocational education, training opportunities, welfare reform, and pay equity.

Women's Bureau, U.S. Department of Labor, 200 Constitution Avenue NW, Washington, DC 20210. Phone: (202) 219–6667; TDD: (800) 326–2577. Work and Family Clearing House phone: (800) 827–5335. The Bureau monitors women's employment issues and sponsors workshops, job fairs, symposia, and pilot projects. It also conducts research, collects statistics, and produces publications on issues that affect working women, including: *A Working Woman's Guide to Her Job Rights*, *Preventing Sexual Harassment in the Workplace*, *Directory of Nontraditional Training and Employment Programs Serving Women*, and *Care Around the Clock: Developing Child Care Resources Before 9 and After 5*.

CHAPTER 15

Women and

Politics

SO MANY WOMEN ran for national, state, and local offices in 1992 that the media declared it The Year of the Woman in politics. Twenty-four new women were elected to the House of Representatives, increasing their number from twenty-nine to forty-seven; four new women were elected to the Senate, including the first African-American woman senator, Carol Moseley-Braun, bringing the total to six. Some analysts attributed this surge of political activity to the anger women felt over the Senate's treatment of Anita Hill and her allegations of sexual harassment during Clarence Thomas's televised Supreme Court nomination hearings. Whether or not the hearings motivated women to enter politics, they did make many women realize just how detached from their lives most male senators were and how potentially harmful to their interests a male-dominated law-making body could be.

Although women make up 51 percent of the U.S. population and about 54 percent of its electorate, in 1997 they held only 12 percent of House seats, 9 percent of Senate seats, 4 percent of governorships, and 21 percent of state senate and house seats.[1] No American woman has ever served as president, vice president, or speaker of the U.S. House of Representatives. Bella Abzug, former member of Congress and currently president of Women USA, has called on Congress to adopt its own affirmative action policy, like other sectors of the government, business, and academia. Political scientists R. Darcy, Susan Welch, and Janet Clark, authors of *Women, Elections & Representation*, have pointed out: "Women belong in the same category as social, ethnic, religious, or linguistic groups, which in a just society are to be represented in political deliberations by able individuals *of a like sort* [emphasis added]."[2]

Women have fared much better in terms of Cabinet-level presidential appointments. In 1997, women held 41 percent of all Cabinet-level appointments, up from just 14 percent in 1977. At the local level, the number of women holding public office as members of city councils, school boards, and the like has also grown substantially in the last twenty years. So has the number of women mayors. In 1997, 203 women were mayors of cities with populations of over 30,000, or 21 percent of the total. Even with this kind of progress, however, American women are still clearly underrepresented in politics. Why?

A 1994 study by the National Women's Political Caucus (NWPC) of more than fifty thousand candidates for Congress and for state legislatures found that when women run for office, they win as often as men do.[3] On the state level, incumbent women won 95 percent of their races, compared to 94 percent for incumbent men. Women running for open seats won 52 percent of their elections, compared to 53 percent for men; female challengers won 10 percent of their races, compared to 9 percent for men. A 1992 *U.S. News & World Report* poll also found that a majority of Americans (61 percent) felt that the country would be "governed better" if more women were elected, up from only 28 percent eight years earlier.[4] If this is the case, why don't more women run for political office?

The media may be partly to blame. Before the National Women's Political Caucus announced its findings, two media myths were that voters would not vote for female candidates and that women could not handle the pressures of political office. Such perceptions undoubtedly discouraged some women from becoming candidates and made it difficult for other women to obtain financial backing. Media coverage still slights women candidates and politicians. One study of twenty-six Senate races found that newspapers like the *Chicago Tribune* and the *Los Angeles Times* wrote almost nine paragraphs more each day about races that included male candidates than they did about those with women. When articles did deal with a female candidate, they tended to concentrate on her campaign resources and political viability (as if it were in question) rather than on her platform. A 1994 study by Women, Men and Media found that of the eighty-nine members of Congress interviewed on a sample of network news stories, only five were women. It also concluded that few women who made the news were political or opinion leaders. Former member of Congress Pat Schroeder was so annoyed with how she and other members of the

Congressional Caucus for Women's Issues were slighted by the *Washington Post* that she commented on it during floor discussion of the Violence Against Women Act:

> We are also sending a letter to the *Washington Post.* As we met yesterday with Hillary Clinton, they put it on the style section. That is one of the problems with dealing with the very serious issues the caucus is dealing with. When we talk about women's health, women's economic status, and violence against women, it gets put in the style section by this city's major paper, and they talk about what we wear. It is time we move those issues to the front page. It is time that they are taken seriously. And it is time that women lawmakers are given the same play in the paper with their issues that the others are by that newspaper.[5]

Traditional gender roles and expectations may also prevent some women from choosing a career in politics. Many girls grow up thinking that politics is unsuitable for women. When Democratic pollster Celinda Lake asked a sample of people to respond to men and women reading the same political script at identical decibel levels, she found that the women readers were described as more aggressive and louder than men. Many qualified women do not become candidates because traditional gender roles leave them little time or energy. Most married professional women still work a double day, returning from work to start their second job as homemaker, mother, and cook. Men are still typically freer to concentrate on their career aspirations, including politics, unfettered by family considerations. Once in office, women politicians can also pay the price for breaking gender conventions. Sociologists Nijole Benokraitis and Joe Feagin explain: "The least stereotypical women are the most likely to be criticized by the media and the general public."[6] Ann Richards, the former governor of Texas, received as much media attention for her sharp tongue as for her progressive policies. When Bill Clinton became president, Hillary Rodham Clinton was loudly criticized for her role as an advisor and policy maker. A *U.S. News & World Report* poll in 1993 found that 59 percent of respondents did not approve of her being a major advisor; 70 percent wanted her to serve as a traditional First Lady.[7] As Benokraitis and Feagin note, however, Hillary Rodham Clinton is not traditional. She chose a career over being a full-time mother and wife; as a lawyer, at one time she earned four times as much as her husband. And until her husband's presidential campaign, she had retained her own last name.

Financial backing is another problem for women candidates. Many wage-earning women do not routinely make campaign contributions. "Women still feel they ought to say thank you for their paychecks," claims former Republican National Committee cochairwoman Maureen Reagan, "so it's hard to get

CALVIN and HOBBES <small>by WATTERSON</small>

Panel 1: LET'S SEE WHAT YOU DREW FOR ART CLASS, SUSIE.

Panel 2: WELL, A TIDY LITTLE DOMESTIC SCENE. A HOUSE IN A YARD WITH FLOWERS. HOW TYPICALLY FEMALE.

Panel 3: GIRLS THINK SMALL AND ARE PREOCCUPIED WITH PETTY DETAILS. BUT *BOYS* THINK *BIG!* BOYS THINK ABOUT ACTION AND ACCOMPLISHMENT! NO WONDER IT'S *MEN* WHO CHANGE THE WORLD!

Panel 4: YEAH? WHAT DID *YOU* DRAW?

A SQUADRON OF B-1s NUKING NEW YORK.

them in the habit of making campaign contributions and doing it for more than spare change." In contrast to male-dominated corporate and defense interests, women's groups usually have much less money to contribute. This gender deficit, however, is being addressed by such successful fund-raising operations as EMILY'S List (Early Money Is Like Yeast) and the Women's Campaign Fund. Women's organizations such as the League of Women Voters, the American Association of University Women (AAUW), and Business and Professional Women also have been important springboards for many women politicians. As job conditions for women improve and the wage gap is eliminated, more women will be able to individually support the political candidates of their choice.

Our electoral arrangements also mean that there is an extremely slow rate of turnover in Congress. The majority of current officeholders are men, and incumbents generally win. Consequently, men have an automatic advantage over women challengers and their numbers remain high. "For those involved in politics, the task is to work to bring about the [institutional] change that will open and enrich our political life."[8]

Not all women automatically share the same beliefs, but as a group, they do tend to hold different political positions than men. In the November 1994, Congressional elections, for example, Democratic candidates received 8 percent more votes from women than they did from men. This was the largest gender voting gap in an off-year election since 1980.[9] As a group, women are more interested than men in economic programs that provide a safety net for the less fortunate, and they are more likely to want government to play an active role in ensuring social justice. Women are also more likely than men to be concerned about gun control, the environment, and child care, and to consider abortion a central issue when they vote.[10] Statistics show that some of the most restrictive abortion laws have been passed in the state legislatures (like Pennsylvania and Louisiana) that have the fewest women members.

Men, in contrast, are more likely to want government to play a small role in people's lives and to accept the conclusion that in a capitalist economy, some people simply lose out. A survey of fourth-year students at a prestigious Ivy League university found that women scored higher than men on issues of social conscience, and that their beliefs had changed more than men's had during their four years at college.[11] According to pollster Celinda Lake, the largest political gender split occurs among younger college-educated voters; there is frequently a twenty- to thirty-percentage-point difference between women and men on particular policies and a ten-point difference on party affiliation.

Since the breakup of the Soviet Union, American voters have been less worried about foreign affairs and defense budgets—usually identified as men's issues—and have become more concerned about social issues such as family-leave policy, day care, health, and the environment, which traditionally have been labeled women's concerns. As Pat Schroeder once quipped, "Our stereotype is finally in." Unfortunately, countertrends are always present, like the political fight for a balanced budget amendment that would result in further cuts in social programs, and the removal of more of the safety net for less-well-off Americans. The time is ripe for the new generation of women to run for office and improve the state of government and the country. The National Women's Political Caucus once calculated: "If women made up half of all open seat and challenger candidates in general elections for the U.S. House, they could make dramatic gains. Starting in 1994 and assuming 50 open seats each cycle . . . a computer simulation found that women would hold one-third of all seats in the U.S. House by the year 2000."[12]

_____ DID YOU KNOW? _____

- A survey of entering first-year students at UCLA found that only 32 percent thought that "keeping up with political affairs" was an important goal in life.
- Only twenty-three women have ever been elected heads of state. Among the world's presidents and prime ministers in 1994, 180 were men and nine were women. The United States has never had a woman head of state. This is ironic, at best, for a democratic nation that claims to lead the world in human rights and equality.
- Women are now making more strides in politics than in some other areas of American life. While there were fifty-five women in the 103rd U.S. Congress, only one Fortune 500 company was headed by a woman.
- More than a quarter of the women serving in the 103rd Congress were women of color: ten African Americans, three Latinas, and one Asian American.
- More than fifteen years ago, Loretta Glickman became the first African-American woman to head a city of over 100,000 when she was elected mayor of Pasadena, California.
- Most women politicians are Democrats. In 1994, 61 percent of the women in state legislatures, 74 percent of women in the U.S. Senate, and 75 percent of women governors were Democrats.
- Martha Wright Griffiths, a ten-term Democratic member of Congress (1955–1975), presented the argument for including "sex" in the 1964 Civil Rights Act as one of the areas in which discrimination is forbidden. She also shepherded the Equal Rights Amendment (ERA) through the House of Representatives. Shunned by her party and by organized labor, she once said, "You were supposed to take orders . . . the truth was . . . I had a brain and I could speak and I could get something done."

- The only member of Congress to ever vote twice against taking America to war (World War I and World War II) was a woman—Jeanette Rankin, who was also the first woman elected to the House of Representatives. A committed pacifist, she lost her seat in Congress each time as a result of these votes. She also led a group of women in a protest at the Capitol against the Vietnam War.

- A national park—the Women's Rights National Historical Park—is devoted to preserving and celebrating an important event in the political history of American women. Located in Seneca Falls, New York, it preserves the original Wesleyan chapel where the first women's rights conference was held in 1848. Elizabeth Cady Stanton's home and the National Women's Hall of Fame are also located in Seneca Falls.

WHAT YOU CAN DO

- Run for office!!! Participate in student government. This will give you the experience and opportunity to better decide if you are interested in pursuing a political career. It will also give you the chance to make positive changes on campus, especially for women.

- Take courses that will make you better informed. Investigate the course offerings of your college or university's women's studies program, or political science and sociology departments. Familiarize yourself with how our government works and with the social issues that affect men and women.

- Be aware. *Action Alert* is a monthly publication that provides the latest legislative news. It discusses education, health care reform, reproductive choice, and other issues critical to women's fundamental freedom and rights and tells you how to protect these rights. Write to the *American Association of University Women (AAUW) Action Alert*, PO Box 96793, Washington, DC 20090–6793 for more information. You can also call the AAUW Congressional Action Line at (202) 785–7785.

- If an issue you believe in strongly is coming up for a vote in Congress, let your legislators know your views. Call the Senate at (202) 224–3121 and the House of Representatives at (202) 225–3121. If you are not sure which congressperson represents your district, ask the main switchboard or call your local League of Women Voters or your local public library. Target the representative from your hometown.

- The most effective way to influence members of Congress is to write to them. Address mail to the senator of your choice: U.S. Senate, Washington, DC 20510; and your congressperson: U.S. House of Representatives, Washington, DC 20515. *Common Cause* suggests the following steps to make your letter effective: First, use your own words, and avoid wording that sounds as if it came from a form letter. Write your letter on personal or business (if you have it) stationery, and place your return address on the letter, since envelopes may be discarded. Clearly identify your subject and the title of the legislation you are concerned about. Briefly state why you are writing. State how you believe the legislation will affect you, your family, or the country, and what you want your legislator to do. State things reasonably. Time the arrival of your letter to reach the Capitol before the legislation is acted on in committee or on the floor. Be sure to thank your legislators if they have done something you think is right on a particular issue. Write to Common Cause, 2030 M Street NW, Washington, DC 20036 for its booklet "A Common Cause Guide to Citizen Action" for further information.

☒ Consider organizing support on campus for an issue you care about. Join or start a political action group and get more students involved in politics (see Organizations).

☒ Organize a voter registration drive on campus.

☒ Demand to see a proportional number of women commentators, reporters, and experts covering politics on television. If women don't insist on equality in public affairs programming, they can expect to continue to have women candidates treated in a diminished fashion by male-dominated media.

☒ Call the editorial desk whenever TV commentators treat the political races of female candidates differently than those of men. ABC (212) 456–7777, CBS (212) 975–4321, and NBC (212) 664–4444.

☒ Volunteer your time to help in the campaigns of local women candidates who you feel are qualified; try to encourage friends on campus to become involved.

☒ Attend a summer institute in politics or other program run for women students.

☒ *Atlanta Summer Program: Women, Leadership and Social Change* takes place at Agnes Scott College. This summer program combines classroom learning with internships in corporations and nonprofit organizations in Atlanta such as Amnesty International, Turner Broadcasting, and the Egleston Children's Health Care System. *Atlanta Summer Program*, Agnes Scott College, Director, Atlanta Semester, 141 East College Avenue, Decatur, GA 30030–3797.

☒ *Center for the American Woman and Politics (CAWP)*, located at Rutgers University, runs an annual National Education for Women's (NEW) Leadership program. This summer institute gives you the opportunity to work with women politicians, officials, and public leaders (see Organizations).

☒ *Leadership America* is an annual program focusing on educating, empowering, and advancing women leaders and linking them to an expanding network of women across the country. It is a highly competitive program geared toward women who have made professional and community achievements and have demonstrated leadership abilities. Speakers at the 1995 program included: Vice President Albert Gore, Jr., Supreme Court Associate Justice Sandra Day O'Connor, Secretary of the United States Air Force Sheila Windall, and Marian Wright Edelman, president of the Children's Defense Fund. Even if you may not have the qualifications to be accepted this year, it is a good program to keep in mind for the future. For more information contact: Leadership America, 700 North Fairfax Street, Suite 610, Alexandria, VA 22314–2040. Phone: (703) 549–1102.

⊠ *The Washington Center* sponsors an annual two-week Women as Leaders Seminar for college women in Washington, DC. Its goal is to challenge young women to realize their full potential, to help them examine their professional and personal goals, and to teach them to clearly articulate their views on issues of importance so that they will be prepared to assume leadership positions. See if the administration or a campus organization will sponsor a few women as participants. The Washington Center, Women as Leaders Seminar, 1101 14th Street NW, Suite 500, Washington, DC 20005.

RESOURCES

Books and Other Publications

Applewhite, Harriet, and Daline Levy (eds.). 1993. *Women & Politics in the Age of the Democratic Revolution.* Ann Arbor: University of Michigan Press.

Boxer, Barbara. 1993. *Strangers in the Senate.* Bethesda, Md.: National Press.

Cook, Elizabeth Adell, Sue Thomas, and Clyde Wilcox. 1994. *The Year of the Woman: Myths and Realities.* Boulder, Colo.: Westview.

Darcy, R., Susan Welch, and Janet Clark. 1994. *Women, Elections & Representation.* Lincoln: University of Nebraska Press.

Ferraro, Geraldine. 1993. *Changing History: Women, Power & Politics.* Wakefield, R.I.: Moyer Bell.

Genovese, Michael (ed.). 1993. *Women as National Leaders.* Newbury Park, Calif.: Sage.

Gill, LaVerne McCain. 1997. *African American Women in Congress: Forming and Transforming History.* New Brunswick, N.J.: Rutgers University Press.

Hardy, Gayle. 1993. *American Women Civil Rights Activists: Biographies of 68 Leaders.* Urbana: University of Illinois Press.

Kunin, Madeleine. 1994. *Living a Political Life.* New York: Knopf.

Loeb, Paul Rogat. 1994. *Generation at the Crossroads: Apathy and Action on the American Campus.* New Brunswick, N.J.: Rutgers University Press.

Margolies-Mezvinsky, Marjorie. 1994. *A Woman's Place: The Freshmen Women Who Changed the Face of Congress.* New York: Crown.

Nelson, Barbara, and Najma Chowdhury. 1994. *Women & Politics Worldwide*. New Haven, Conn.: Yale University Press.

Norris, Pippa (ed.). 1997. *Women, Media, and Politics*. New York: Oxford University Press.

Okeyo, Achola Pala (ed.). 1994. *Connecting across Cultures and Continents: Black Women Speak Out on Identity, Race, and Development*. New York: Woman Ink/United Nations.

Ries, Paula, and Anne J. Stone. 1992. *The American Women 1992–1993: A Status Report*. Special issue on women and politics. New York: Norton.

Witt, Linda, Karen M. Paget, and Glenna Matthews. 1994. *Running as a Woman: Gender and Power in American Politics*. New York: Free Press.

Video

See Jane Run: How Women Get Elected. This fifty-six-minute documentary explores how women get elected and who chooses politics as a career. It shows college women learning to be effective spokespersons and campaigners in a unique university program. Veteran women politicians also share their thoughts and stories. Banner Productions, PO Box 6595, New York, NY 10128. Phone: (212) 831–2324.

Organizations

Center for the American Woman and Politics (CAWP), Eagleton Institute of Politics, Rutgers University, New Brunswick, NJ 08901. Phone: (732) 828–2210. CAWP is a think tank and education and resource center. It works to educate the public and policy makers on issues of women's equity and conducts research on such topics as rape; domestic violence; occupational segregation; and math, science, and technology education for girls and women of color. Subscribers receive three information packets a year, containing the Center's newsletter, fact sheets, reports, reprints of articles, and other information. CAWP produces books, bibliographies, and reports on women's participation in politics, and a documentary film, *Not One of the Boys*. CAWP also acts as a clearinghouse for information on women and politics; it has an extensive library of resource material.

Center for Women Policy Studies (CWPS), 1211 Connecticut Avenue NW, Suite 312, Washington, DC 20036. Phone: (202) 872–1770. The Center is an independent feminist policy research and advocacy organization. Its purpose is to educate the public and policy makers about issues involving women's equality. It has conducted studies of rape; occupational segregation; sexual harassment; and math, science, and technology education. It operates a speakers' bureau and maintains a library with emphasis on women's issues and AIDS.

College Democrats of America (CDA), 430 South Capitol Street SE, Washington,

DC 20003. Phone: (202) 479–5189. The student arm of the Democratic Party has over eight hundred chapters on college campuses. It trains and encourages students to become active in politics.

College Republicans, 600 Pennsylvania Avenue SE, Suite 301, Washington DC 20003. Phone: (202) 608–1411. The student arm of the Republican Party.

EMILY'S List (Early Money Is Like Yeast), 805 15th Street NW, Washington, DC 20005. Phone: (202) 326–1400. The organization raises money and provides political training and resources for prochoice Democratic women candidates for federal and state political office.

The Fund for a Feminist Majority (FFM), 1600 Wilson Boulevard, Suite 801, Arlington, VA 22209. Phone: (703) 522–2214. The Fund encourages women to fill leadership positions in business, education, law, medicine, and government. It sponsors the Feminization of Power Campaign, which promotes a national feminist agenda, conducts a campus campaign (makes available organizing kits, fact sheets, videos, and books), publishes the quarterly *Feminist Majority Report*, provides internship programs, maintains a speakers' bureau, and compiles statistics. It has also set up a World Wide Web voter registration center.

MANA: A National Latina Organization, 1725 K Street NW, Suite 501, Washington, DC 20006. Phone: (202) 833–0060. It works to register voters and helps start the citizenship process for Latinas/Latinos who are not citizens.

National Council for Research on Women, 530 Broadway, 10th Floor, New York, NY 10012–3920. Phone: (212) 274–0730. The Council is a nonprofit consortium of seventy-five centers and organizations that provide resources for feminist research, policy analysis, and educational programs for women and girls. It publishes the quarterly journal *IQ*. Each issues focuses on a single topic of concern to women.

National Gay and Lesbian Task Force, 2320 17th Street NW, Washington, DC 20009. Phone: (202) 332–6483. The Task Force recently published a report on gay voters: "Power at the Polls: The Gay/Lesbian/Bisexual Vote."

National Institute for Women of Color (NIWC), 1301 20th Street NW, Suite 702, Washington, DC 20036. Phone: (202) 298–1118. The organization promotes educational and economic equity and awareness about issues and principles of feminism. It is also a networking vehicle for women of color.

National Organization for Women (NOW), 1000 16th Street NW, Suite 700, Washington, DC 20036. Phone: (202) 331–0066. In addition to its many other activities, NOW works to increase the number of women elected to public office and seeks the enforcement and passage of federal legislation prohibiting discrimination.

National Women's Political Caucus (NWPC), 1211 Connecticut Avenue NW, Suite 425, Washington, DC 20036. Phone: (202) 785–1100. The organization seeks to gain an equal voice and place for women in the political process at the local, state, and national levels. It compiles statistics, raises women's issues in elections, and supports women candidates for elective and appointed office. Joining the NWPC provides full membership in your local, state, and national organization and entitles you to receive local and state newsletters and the *Women's Political Times*, a national quarterly newsletter.

Project Vote Smart (PVS), 129 4th Street NW, Suite 204, Corvallis, OR 97330. Phone: (541) 754–2746; Voter's Research Hotline: (800) 622–SMART. PVS tracks the issue positions and voting records of more than thirteen thousand political leaders at the state and federal level. Its staff is comprised largely of college students and volunteers. A national internship program brings hundreds of students together to work at PVS's two regional offices; scholarships are available. For information, call Corvallis (541) 737–3760 or Boston (617) 373–5032. You can also contact PVS's Web site: http//www.vote-smart.org.

Third Wave, 185 Franklin Street, New York, NY 10013. Phone: (212) 925–3400. This national, multicultural organization works to initiate and facilitate young women's leadership and activism.

United Nations Development Fund for Women (UNIFEM), 304 East 45th Street, 6th Floor, New York, NY 10017. Phone: (212) 906–6400. UNIFEM promotes gender equality and women's political and economic empowerment internationally. It works within the United Nations to ensure women's participation in development planning.

The Woman Activist (TWA), 2310 Barbour Road, Falls Church, VA 22043–2940. Phone: (703) 573–8716. The Activist is a nonprofit consulting firm specializing in issues of political concern to women. It writes reports, compiles statistics, rates members of Congress on women's issues, and compares gender differences in their voting patterns on civil and social rights issues. It publishes *The Woman Activist* ten times a year.

Women's Campaign Fund (WCF), 1601 Connecticut Avenue NW, Suite 800, Washington, DC 20009. Phone: (202) 393–8164. The organization supports the election of qualified progressive women to public office, raises funds, promotes public awareness, and recruits and develops women candidates.

Women's Research and Education Institute (WREI), 1700 18th Street NW, Suite 400, Washington, DC 20009. Phone: (202) 329–7070. WREI is a policy research organization focusing on women's issues, including women's access to health care and women in the military. It sponsors Congressional Fellowships on Women and Public Policy, and offers fellowships to graduate students with a proven commitment to equity for women. It also publishes the biennial *The American Woman: A Status Report*, annual reports on the status of women, and specialized reports.

APPENDIX
_____

Safety on
_____

Campus

COMPARED TO MANY SETTINGS, college campuses appear to be tranquil, protected places. But no matter how beautiful and well maintained, a college campus is never completely safe. Campus police can only facilitate safety; they cannot ensure it. Fires, accidental injuries, and crime occur on campus just as they do elsewhere in society, whether your school is located in a small town, the suburbs, or a major urban area. What may come as a surprise is that you are more likely to be victimized by another student than by a stranger. According to Towson State University's Campus Violence Prevention Center, students perpetrate 80 percent of campus crime.

Awareness is the first step you can take toward your personal safety. Since passage of the Student Right-to-Know and Campus Security Act of 1990 (and its amendment, the Higher Education Security Act of 1992), all colleges and universities that receive federal funds must keep detailed data on reported campus crimes. Learn what crimes have occurred on your campus, and familiarize yourself with your school's security regulations and suggestions. Schools must give a copy of their federal crime report—which typically includes a description of campus security programs—to any student or prospective student who asks for it. Most campus security offices also publish pamphlets that contain information on safety equipment, the location of emergency telephones and alarms, escort services, and sound advice culled from years of working with students. Take the time to read it. Don't fall victim to everyone's worst enemy—the belief that "it can't happen to me."

Theft and Vandalism

Theft and vandalism account for the vast majority of all student crime, despite features like tamper-proof windows and state-of-the-art alarm systems in residence halls. Students have many expensive and easily portable goods like bicycles, computers, televisions, CD players, VCRs, cameras, and sports equipment, which make them attractive targets. You can protect yourself by making your apartment or room and your possessions less accessible. Remember that opportunity plays an important role in all crime. Many thefts occur because residence halls, dorm rooms, apartments, and cars are left open. So keep your doors locked and your bike and car locked, too. Park your car in a well-lighted area and keep anything tempting out of sight. Don't leave other possessions lying around unattended on campus, even in the library, student union, gym, or classrooms. As a precaution, keep a list of your most valuable possessions with brief descriptions and serial numbers if applicable, and register your bike and car with campus police.

Vandalism is a problem on most campuses. Not only does it diminish everyone's enjoyment of the university, it raises the cost of everyone's education. When expensive outdoor lights are smashed after a weekend party, the university has to replace them. When a male student gets angry and pours epoxy glue into his former girlfriend's dorm room lock, the college must replace it. When sports teams arrive on campus to begin training before classes start and some players break furniture and windows in the residence hall they stay in, the university has to pay. When a fraternity loses its college-owned house because of hazing or alcohol violations, and its members then systematically ransack the building to vent their anger, all students end up paying. The replacement costs become part of the college's operations budget and are eventually passed on to you. Even at a small college, the cost of repairs from vandalism may run into the tens of thousands of dollars each year.

Alcohol and Drugs

As discussed in earlier chapters, alcohol and other drugs are potentially dangerous. Not only can you damage your health, but other people under the influence can be dangerous to you. According to the Campus Violence Prevention Center, a research institute at Towson State University in Maryland, alcohol is related to 90 percent of violent campus crime, including physical assaults and rape.[1] Alan Lizotte, executive director of the Consortium for Higher Education Campus Crime Research at the State University of New York at Albany, says, "Rape, aggravated assault, robbery, and larceny are heavily drug- and alcohol-related. By cracking down on those sorts of things, they [universities and colleges] can reduce other crimes. And in the long run, students will get the message, and alcohol and drug crimes will go down, too."[2] Some campus police report a greater willingness among students today to report other students' drug infractions. "Students are getting tired of living next door to someone who smokes marijuana constantly," claims one security officer.

Driving under the influence is another important safety issue, especially given the amount of drinking students do and the fact that much of it takes place off campus. Fully half of all fatal car accidents in the United States involve a driver who has been drinking. Never drive when drunk or high on drugs or ride with someone who is. Call the campus escort service, a sober friend, or a taxi instead. The University of Texas at Austin dispatches free cabs on weekends to pick up drunk students anywhere in the city. Over twelve hundred students used the free program during its first ten weekends.

Smoking and Fire Hazards

A higher proportion of students smoke today than in the general population. If you smoke, do so only in designated areas and put all cigarettes (and cigars, which are now a fad on some campuses) out completely. Follow campus rules about smoking and use other combustible items—candles, incense, bottled gas appliances, and halogen-bulb lamps—carefully. In many schools the use of halogen lamps, space heaters, hot plates, and other appliances with exposed heating elements is banned in residence halls. If your school allows their use, do not leave them unattended and avoid plugging too many electrical cords into one outlet. You could easily overload the circuit. Before putting an iron or other electrical appliance away, make sure it has completely cooled. Learn where the fire alarms, extinguishers, and emergency exits are located in your building and report any blocked exits or vandalized smoke alarms, heat detectors, extinguishers, or exit lights to campus security.

Some students engage in dangerous pranks like setting fire to wastebaskets and bulletin boards and vandalizing smoke alarms and emergency exit lights. Report such incidents to campus security. They may seem trivial, but they endanger everyone. A fatal fire in a fraternity at the University of North Carolina at Chapel Hill in 1996 prompted many universities to be more vigilant about fire code violations. After a fire broke out at a fraternity at the University of Georgia that had been previously cited for eighty-five fire code violations, the president closed it and five others.

Assault

Assaults are uncommon on most campuses, but you still need to be careful whom you befriend and help. Don't let anyone you don't know into your residence hall or building, whether it's to use the phone, borrow a tool to fix a car, visit a "friend," or deliver pizza. Make the telephone call, report the car trouble to campus security, ring the student whose friend or pizza delivery has arrived, and make the stranger wait outside. Refuse entry to all salespeople; most schools prohibit them from soliciting on campus anyway. Don't worry about seeming rude or overly cautious; your safety comes first. If someone insists on or tries to coax you into letting him or her inside the building or otherwise seems suspicious, trust your gut feeling and call campus security immediately. Report to security any stranger you see entering the building.

According to campus security officers, one of the most common safety mistakes students make is leaving the door of their residence hall or apartment building propped open. Many residence halls have devices to keep ground-floor windows from being opened more than a few inches and alarms to discourage students from propping exterior doors open. Apparently, however, the convenience of doing so is too much for many students to resist. Just remember, if you can enter the building easily, so can someone who shouldn't. When you see a building door propped open, close it. If you don't, you may be compromising the safety of everyone inside. Never give your key to anyone. The person you loan it to could easily lose it, loan it to someone else, or make a copy that could be used later to gain entry for assault or theft. Lock your door and windows whenever you leave your room and at night while you sleep. Draw curtains or blinds once it gets dark, and don't dress near windows. Make sure the entrances to your residence hall or apartment are well lighted. Call campus security or your landlord if they're not.

During breaks, campuses can be particularly dangerous. Most students go home, leaving those left behind vulnerable. A decade ago Meera Anathahrishnan, a female physics graduate student from India, was murdered in her residence hall room at the University of Pennsylvania during Thanksgiving break. Unfortunately, many international students still spend their holidays on campus alone. In response to Meera's death, the University of Pennsylvania's Women's Center set up a program to encourage students and faculty to invite international students home for holidays, and each fall the Meera Memorial Women's Safety Seminar is held to help promote safety on campus.[3]

As a woman, the crime you probably fear most is rape. Although the odds are in your favor that you will never be raped, the threat exists. Even if your university reports few rapes and assaults, don't become complacent or careless. Remember that many victims do not report these crimes, and colleges are only required by law to report those crimes that occur on campus or on nearby college-controlled property. One survey of students on thirty-two campuses found that one out of six women had been raped or had been the victim of an attempted rape during the previous year.[4] Research by Towson State University's Campus Violence Prevention Center found that one in twenty-five female students had been raped. As discussed in chapter 12, most rapes and sexual assaults are perpetrated by someone the woman has met.

Acquaintance rape usually follows a pattern, with a man first invading your personal space—sitting or standing inappropriately close, touching you, or more. If you are not sexually interested in someone, make it clear from the beginning. And don't leave the group to go off with him—no matter what he says—unless you are prepared for and receptive to a sexual advance.

Many women students run and work out. But no matter how physically fit or fast you are, you are not invincible. Much of the advice that follows applies to running and walking both on campus and in nearby neighborhoods: First, never run after dark or alone (early morning is probably the safest time). If you must walk across campus at night, go with friends and use lighted pathways or else call your campus escort service and avoid shortcuts through darkened areas or parking lots. Second, never run or walk in isolated places or while wearing headphones, which isolate you from your surroundings. According to J. J. Bittenbinder, a Chicago police detective and personal safety expert, it is a dangerous practice: "They're like wearing sunglasses in the dark. I realize lots of people love them. In fact, I've had women come up to me and say, 'But I feel so confident when I'm listening to my own music.' Well, that's because you are blocking out reality. . . . When you wear those things, you may not have the extra 3– to 4–yard head start to break away, and that could be the difference between making it or not—all because you couldn't hear the bad guy approaching."[5]

Experts advise women runners to vary their routes and the exact time of day they run, to avoid allowing someone to plan an assault. When you pass people, establish brief eye contact with them rather than looking away or looking down, which signals "I'm weak" and "You intimidate me." Look back when you hear people behind you, to let them know you can't be surprised; then run in the direction of more traffic and people. If a car pulls alongside you, turn around and run in the opposite direction. If necessary, enter a busy store. If you have a dog, bring it along on your runs and walks. A dog is a deterrent, since potential attackers cannot be sure how it will react to protect you. Always carry identification and a few coins with you, so that you are able to call for help.

Many experts advise carrying a portable self-defense device in a visible place, preferably in your hand and ready for use. Several types are available, including small hand-held alarms (which can also be clipped to your waist) that give off an ear-splitting shriek. Various types of sprays are also available at many security and hardware stores; some contain ultraviolet dyes for later identification. Pepper spray is the most effective, since mace and sprays that contain tear gas have been found not to deter drug users, drunks, and psychotics. Even a whistle can help; many campus security offices and women's centers dispense them free. Some schools are also investigating the cost of purchasing personal alarms for all female students.

Should you be attacked, react *immediately with fury.* Scream, use your alarm, and fight back with full force. Although this is intimidating advice, especially if the person attacking you has a weapon, it is what police suggest. According to Sanford Strong, a twenty-year veteran with the San Diego Police Department and defense training instructor, you need to accept the fact that an attacker intends to hurt you. Your goal must be to escape in any way possible. Research on sexual assaults suggests that fighting back can stave off rape. Janice Zoucha-Jensen and Ann Coyne at the University of Nebraska at Omaha School of Social Work found in a study of 150 women who had been targets of rape that women who screamed, bit, kicked, scratched, or ran were half as likely to be raped as were women who did nothing. The first few seconds of contact between you and an attacker—whether a stranger on the street or a fellow student—are crucial because that is when he has the least control, since he doesn't know how you are going to react.

The place where you are first attacked is as good as the situation is going to get, say police experts.[6] Don't lose precious time and the element of surprise by allowing yourself to be moved to a second, more isolated crime scene because you think things will get better if you just stay calm. And try never to allow yourself to be forced into a car. "Believe me, if you get into the car, you're dead," warns Detective Bittenbinder, who believes that your odds of escape and survival are much better, even if your attacker has a weapon, if you break away and run.[7]

Consider taking a self-defense course so that you feel more confident and can react immediately rather than be paralyzed by indecision or fear. Because most assailants will wrestle you to the ground where they can pin you, many experts think that "grappling" martial arts like jiujitsu and judo are better than those that stress kicks and punches.[8] Many colleges, women's centers, and YWCAs offer self-defense courses. The University of Pennsylvania, for example, offers a twelve-hour short course called Rape Aggression Defense for a small fee. The Rape Crisis Center at the University of Wisconsin at Madison offers training in Chimera, a self-defense program that emphasizes assertiveness and awareness as well as physical responses women can use. Such courses will not make you invincible; it takes years of training to become proficient at self-defense. But they should boost your confidence, increase your agility, and help you react quickly. Researchers at Stanford University who studied one Model Mugging self-defense course and its graduates found that out of the hundreds of women who took the course, forty were later assaulted. Of these women, thirty-eight managed to escape their assailants by stunning and disabling them or frightening them off.[9]

_____ **DID YOU KNOW?** _____

- It takes only about eight seconds for someone to enter your unlocked room and steal something of value to you.
- UCLA has three hundred student community service officers who have received special training from the university police department. They patrol the campus, provide an escort service for other students, and help campus police file crime reports.
- Campus police at the University of Massachusetts at Dartmouth, the University of Washington, the University of Wisconsin at Madison, and several other schools use mountain bikes to patrol their sprawling campuses more effectively.
- Rutgers University runs a Street Smart Survival program in which student participants act as victims of crimes perpetrated by plainclothes police officers. Students do not know where or when the staged incident will occur, or what it will involve. Afterward, students discuss the incident with officers and learn how it could have been avoided or handled differently.
- Union College in upstate New York, with a student body of two thousand, provides a door-to-door escort service for students living on and off campus. The service responds to approximately twelve hundred calls each week.
- Most victims of sexual assault who fought back say their resistance helped them. Fewer than 10 percent say it made things worse.

_____ **WHAT YOU CAN DO** _____

- If your campus does not feel as safe as it could be, organize a women's campus safety audit. The Metro Action Committee on Public Violence Against Women and Children (METRAC) in Ontario, Canada, produces a detailed booklet, instructional video, and survey forms for conducting a campus safety audit (see Resources). The goal of the audit is to improve the physical environment on campus as well as campus policies and services in ways that reduce opportunities for sexual and other kinds of assaults and property crimes. The campus audit is especially designed to focus on the safety concerns of women. The teams that carry out the audit should include the perspectives of all women: young women and older women and staff, heterosexuals and lesbians, women students and staff who are able-bodied as well as those who use wheelchairs or are visually or hearing impaired. METRAC provides detailed checklists for audit members to use to evaluate campus safety that ask specific questions about lighting, sightlines, signage, isolation, possible assault sites, escape routes, and other aspects of the physical environment. The checklists also ask questions about college policies and services that affect women's safety. Many groups on campus are likely sponsors: a residence hall or floor, the women's center or a women's group, or the offices of the dean of students, campus security, or residence life.

☒ If your residence hall feels unsafe and a guard is not currently employed to monitor entry, contact the administration (usually the residence life coordinator or campus security) about assigning someone to this duty.

☒ Read the chapters in this book on sexual assault and on drinking and drug use to heighten your awareness of these topics and their safety implications, and to find suggestions for what you can do.

☒ Watch a self-defense video to familiarize yourself with defensive techniques (see Resources). Organize a campus showing and bring in a self-defense expert who can answer questions and comment on the points raised in the film.

☒ Ask a men's group on campus or a male friend to organize a showing of a video on sexual assault and acquaintance rape. (Several good choices are listed in the Resources section below; others are listed in chapter 12.) Make men on campus aware of rape myths, the effect sexual assault has on women and on the men who are accused of it, and on the ways in which the fear of sexual assault constrains women's behavior every day.

☒ Take a self-defense course to give yourself confidence and quicker reaction time. Sponsor a self-defense workshop on campus for women students. Model Mugging teaches women how to fight even on the ground and how to knock an unarmed assailant unconscious. It was started by men trained in martial arts who wanted to do something to prevent violence against women. The organization now has eighteen branches across the country, some of which offer financial assistance for its expensive five-session course. Consult your telephone book, contact the campus women's center or your local YWCA, a martial arts studio, or a health club for suggestions of qualified experts and classes. Model Mugging, PREPARE (Protection Awareness Response, Empowerment), and Impact Personal Safety can be reached at (800) 345–KICK.

☒ When walking and jogging, hold your head up and be aware of your surroundings. Make brief eye contact with the strangers you pass. Acting confident, rather than fearful and weak, may deter an assailant from selecting you. Whenever possible stay in the center of the sidewalk, and follow the other advice contained in this chapter. Trust your instincts and use common sense.

 For a small monthly fee, a service called Project Safe Run lends women trained dogs to run or walk with. The dogs are carefully trained to defend you should someone show aggression toward you while you walk or run. There may be a chapter in your area.

 Contact campus security and encourage them to look into the possibility of the college or university's purchasing personal alarms for students. If alarms cannot be distributed free, suggest making them available to interested students at a reduced cost.

 Encourage the student newspaper, radio station, and computer bulletin board to disseminate news about campus crimes. By spreading the word, you alert other students to potential danger and prevent the administration from minimizing the risk. You may also encourage witnesses and victims to come forward.

RESOURCES

Books and Other Publications

Adams, Aileen, and Gail Abarbanel. 1988. *Sexual Assault on Campus: What Colleges Can Do.* Write: Rape Treatment Center, Santa Monica Hospital Medical Center, 12225 15th Street, Santa Monica, CA 90404.

Caignon, Denise, and Gail Groves (eds.). 1987. *Her Wits About Her: Self-Defense Success Stories by Women.* New York: HarperCollins.

Keller, Daniel. 1992. *Rape Awareness, Education, Prevention, and Response.* Write: Campus Crime Prevention Programs, Box 204, Goshen, KY 40026.

Langelan, Martha. 1993. *Back Off!* New York: Simon & Schuster.

McCaughey, Martha. 1997. *Real Knockouts: The Physical Feminism of Women's Self Defense.* New York: New York University Press.

McShane, Claudette. 1988. *Warning! Dating May Be Hazardous to Your Health.* Racine, Wisc.: Mother Courage.

Parrott, Andrea. 1992. *Acquaintance Rape and Sexual Assault: A Prevention Manual.* Holmes Beach, Fla.: Learning.

Thompson, Stephen. 1993. *No More Fear.* 2nd ed. Dubuque, Iowa: Kendall/Hunt.

Wiseman, Rosalind. 1994. *Defending Ourselves: A Guide to Prevention, Self-Defense, and Recovery from Rape.* New York: Noonday.

Videos

Acquaintance Rape: The Broken Trust. This twenty-two-minute video made in 1990 provides a factual account of sexual assault and acquaintance rape. In a straightforward manner it discusses rape myths, types of assailants, prevention strategies, and options for victims. KDN Crime Check Video Library, Box 71402, Madison Heights, MI 48071. Phone: (313) 546–3385.

Dating Games: Gang Rape on Campus. This twenty-eight-minute video starts with an interview with a gang-rape survivor who tells how the attack has affected her life. It also interviews a convicted rapist, giving insight into his psyche. In a dramatic reenactment, the film shows how a party can turn into a tragedy. Filmakers Library, 124 East 40th Street, New York, NY 10016. Phone: (212) 808–4980.

Defend Yourself! For Women; *The Instant Self-Defense Guide for Women*; and *Protect Yourself: A Woman's Guide to Self-Defense.* These self-defense videos and others are available from The How to Video Source (800) 835–2246, ext. 119.

Rape Is Not Just a Woman's Problem. This crime prevention video focuses on the role and responsibility of men to stop rape on campus. It covers rape myths, types of assault, legal considerations, and the impact of rape on women as well as men accused of rape. Campus Crime Prevention Programs, Box 204, Goshen, KY 40026. Phone: (502) 228–1499.

Rape: The Boundaries of Fear. This video focuses on how the fear of rape affects women's daily lives. Survivors and other women talk about the precautions they take and the restrictions they must deal with. Self-defense classes, prevention workshops, and Men Stopping Rape are shown as ways to put an end to the crime. Barr Films, 12801 Schabarum, Box 7878, Irwindale, CA 91706–7878. Phone: (818) 338–7878.

Organizations

Metro Action Committee on Public Violence Against Women and Children (METRAC), 158 Spadina Road, Toronto, Ontario M5R 2T8, Canada. Phone: (416) 392–3135. Order the *Women's Campus Safety Audit Guide* and/or the twenty-seven-minute video *Safer for Women . . . Safer for Everyone.*

Safe Campuses Now, 337 South Milledge Avenue, Athens, GA 30605. Phone: (706) 354–1115. Safe Campuses Now is a watchdog and commercial security systems consulting group. Among other things, it has pushed for more states to pass laws requiring local police to record crime victims' status as students and to name their institutions. They hope this will make it easier to keep track of off-campus crime affecting college students.

Security on Campus, 215 West Church Road, Suite 200, King of Prussia, PA 19406–3207. Phone: (610) 768–9330. This organization was founded by the parents of Jeanne Clery, who was murdered in her dorm room in 1986. It is a non-profit watchdog group that seeks to increase awareness of campus crimes. It provides information, lobbies for better legislation, and provides legal support for victims. It also produces the semiannual *Campus Watch* newsletter.

CHAPTER 1 **What Is Feminism?**

1. Attributed to Rebecca West in Mary Biggs, *Women's Words: The Columbia Book of Quotations by Women* (New York: Columbia University Press, 1996), 137.

2. Linda Jackson, Ruth Fleury, and Donna Lewandowski, "Feminism: Definitions, Support, and Correlates of Support among Female and Male College Students," *Sex Roles* 34 (1996): 687–693.

3. Donna Henderson-King and Abigail Stewart, "Women or Feminists? Assessing Women's Group Consciousness," *Sex Roles* 31 (1994): 505–516.

4. Quoted in Dana Putnam et al. (eds.), *The Journal Project: Dialogues and Conversations Inside Women's Studies* (Toronto: Second Story Press, 1995), 155.

5. Alice Walker, *In Search of Our Mothers' Gardens: Womanist Prose* (New York: Harcourt Brace Jovanovich, 1983). See also Maggie Humm, *The Dictionary of Feminist Theory* (Columbus: Ohio State University Press, 1990), 241.

6. bell hooks, "Black Students Who Reject Feminism," *Chronicle of Higher Education* 40 (13 July 1994): A44.

7. Sue Street, Ellen Kimmel, and Jeffery Kromrey, "Revisiting University Student Gender Role Perceptions," *Sex Roles* 33 (1995): 185.

8. "In the Fraternal Sisterhood: Sororities as Gender Strategy," *Gender and Society* 9 (April 1995): 237.

9. Ibid.

10. Henderson-King and Stewart, "Women or Feminists?" 505–516.

11. Ibid., 506.

12. According to the researchers, this is "even more noteworthy in light of the greater advantage to women in adopting masculine sex-typed traits than to men in adopting feminine ones." Street, Kimmel, and Kromrey, "Revisiting University," 198.

13. bell hooks, *Feminist Theory: From Margin to Center* (Boston: South End Press, 1984), 24.

14. Quoted in Helen Zia, "How NOW?" *Ms.* 7 (July/August 1996): 50.

15. Nancy Fraser and Linda Nicholson, "Social Criticism without Philosophy: An Encounter between Feminism and Postmodernism," *Theory, Culture & Society* 5 (1988): 382.

16. Robin Morgan, *Going Too Far: The Personal Chronicle of a Feminist* (New York: Random House, 1973), 121–130.

17. Carol Hanisch, *Notes from the Second Year: Women's Liberation; Major Writings of the Radical Feminists* (New York: Radical Feminism, 1970).

18. The phrase was used by Marsha Weinman Lear in an article ("The Second Feminist Wave") in the *New York Times Magazine* in 1968.

19. Carol Sternhell, "The Tenure Battle: The Women Who Won't Disappear," *Ms.* 13 (October 1984): 94–98.

20. *Feminist Fatale: Voices from the "Twentysomething" Generation Explore the Future of the "Women's Movement"* (New York: Donald I. Fine, 1991), 1.

21. Rebecca Walker, "Becoming the Third Wave," *Ms.* 2 (1992): 39–41.

22. Barbara Findlen, ed., *Listen Up: Voices from the Next Feminist Generation* (Seattle: Seal Press, 1995), xiii–xiv.

23. Cheryl Green, "One Resilient Baby." In Findlen, *Listen Up*, 142. See also Marsha Saxton, "Born and Unborn: The Implications of Reproductive Technologies for People with Disabilities." In *Test-Tube Women: What Future for Motherhood*, ed. Rita Arditti, Renate Dvelli Klein, and Shelly Minden (Boston: Pandora Press, 1984).

24. bell hooks, *Feminist Theory*.

25. In 1995, for example, Grrl activists protested a National Women's Studies Association conference, which included a session on adolescent girls, for not involving young women in its planning and for cosponsoring the session with a psychiatric service that "pathologizes" girls and women.

26. Findlen, *Listen Up*, xiii.

27. Fraser and Nicholson, "Social Criticism," 391.

28. *Black Feminist Thought: Knowledge, Consciousness, and the Politics of Empowerment* (Boston: Unwin Hyman, 1990), 7.

29. Ibid., 8.

30. Peggy McIntosh, "Examining Unearned Privilege," *On Campus with Women* 22 (Fall 1992/Winter 1993): 9.

31. Katie Roiphe, *The Morning After: Sex, Fear and Feminism on Campus* (Boston: Little, Brown, 1993).

32. Christine Hoff Summers, *Who Stole Feminism? How Women Have Betrayed Women* (New York: Simon & Schuster, 1994).

33. Camille Paglia, *Sexual Personae: Art and Decadence from Nefertiti to Emily Dickinson* (New Haven, Conn.: Yale University Press, 1990).

34. Mary Matalin, "Stop Whining!" *Newsweek* 122 (25 October 1993): 62.

35. Susan Faludi, *Backlash: The Undeclared War Against American Women* (New York: Crown, 1991).

36. Robert Bly, *Iron John: A Book About Men* (Reading, Mass.: Addison-Wesley, 1990); and Sam Keen, *Fire in the Belly: On Being a Man* (New York: Bantam, 1991).

37. Nijole Benokraitis and Joe Feagin, *Modern Sexism: Blatant, Subtle, and Covert Discrimination* (Englewood Cliffs, N.J.: Prentice Hall, 1995), 15.

38. bell hooks, Gloria Steinem, Urvashi Vaid, and Naomi Wolf, "Let's Get Real about Feminism: The Backlash, the Myths, the Movement," *Ms.* 4 (September/October 1993): 34–43.

39. Sheila Tobias, *Faces of Feminism: An Activist's Reflections on the Women's Movement* (Boulder, Colo.: Westview Press, 1997).

40. See Mary Fainsod Katzenstein, "Feminism within American Institutions: Unobtrusive Mobilization in the 1980s," *Signs: Journal of Women in Culture and Society* 16 (1990): 27–54.

41. Lisa Handler, "In the Fraternal Sisterhood: Sororities as Gender Strategy," *Gender and Society* 9 (April 1995): 237.

42. Katha Politt, *Reasonable Creatures: Essays on Women and Feminism* (New York: Vintage, 1994), xxi.

CHAPTER 2 Sexism in the Genderless Classroom

1. Elizabeth Cady Stanton, *Eighty Years and More: Reminiscences 1815–1897* (New York: Schocken, 1971), 33–34.

2. *The Chilly Classroom Climate: A Guide to Improve the Education of Women* (Washington, D.C.: National Association for Women in Education, 1996).

3. "Letters," *Physics Today* (September 1993): 13, 15.

4. Cited in *Teaching Faculty Members to Be Better Teachers: A Guide to Equitable and Effective Classroom Techniques* (Washington, D.C.: American Association of Colleges and Universities, 1992), 14.

5. Quoted in Patricia Beard, "The Fall and Rise of the Seven Sisters," *Town & Country Monthly* 148 (November 1994): 159–175.

6. Quoted in "Taking the Campus Pulse: Student Leaders Wrestle with the Toughest Questions," *Maclean's* 107 (14 November 1994): 42–51.

7. The research was done by Pauli Murray. Cited in Patricia Hill Collins, *Black Feminist Thought: Knowledge, Consciousness, and the Politics of Empowerment* (Boston: Unwin Hyman, 1990), 8.

8. "Taking Women Students Seriously." In *On Lies, Secrets and Silence: Selected Prose 1966–1978*, by Adrienne Rich (New York: W. W. Norton, 1979).

9. "A Case in Point: Architectural Education," *Women in Higher Education* 3 (October 1994): 6.

10. Madonne Miner, "'You're Going to Be the Only Guy in There': Men's Minority Experience in Introduction to Women's Studies," *National Women's Studies Association Journal* 6 (Fall 1994): 455.

11. Women outnumber newly hired men at both liberal arts and community colleges; they make up about a third of newly hired faculty at institutions with doctoral programs ("Dramatic Increase in Women Faculty But Average Salary Still Lower," *Women in Higher Education* 5 [May 1996]: 6). In 1994, 13 percent of female faculty were women of color.

12. In 1994, Harvard University settled a six-year-old lawsuit filed by Clare Dalton, wife of Robert Reich, who served as President Clinton's Secretary of Labor. She claimed that she was denied tenure in 1987 because of her gender and her work in critical legal studies. At the time, only five of Harvard Law School's fifty-seven tenured faculty were women. She was awarded $260,000, which she used to establish a Domestic Violence Institute at Northeastern University, where she is now a tenured professor.

13. Timothy Harper, "A 'Hostile Environment' for Women," *American Bar Association Journal* 81 (May 1995): 16–17.

14. Mary Hart, "Defanging the Wolf Pack: Handling Hostile Male Students," *Women in Higher Education* 3 (September 1994): 4.

15. Reported in Lisa Guernsey, "Study Finds Sexism at Many Law Schools," *Chronicle of Higher Education* 42 (16 February 1996).

16. Research by Elissa Lewis, reported in "Student Evaluations Can Harm Women's Studies Profs," *Women in Higher Education* 4 (July/August 1995): 12.

17. Cited in Patricia Beard, "The Fall and Rise of the Seven Sisters," *Town & Country Monthly* 148 (November 1994): 159–175.

18. They drew their hypotheses from the AAC/NAWE's 1982 "chilly climate" report. Reported in "More on the Classroom Climate," *On Campus with Women* 22 (Summer 1992): 3.

19. Paula Kamen, *Feminist Fatale: Voices from the "Twentysomething" Genera-*

tion Explore the Future of the "Women's Movement" (New York: Donald I. Fine, 1991), 294.

20. Ibid.

21. Ibid.

22. Marcia Greenberger and Deborah Blake, "The VMI Decision: Shattering Sexual Stereotypes," *Chronicle of Higher Education* 42 (5 July 1996): A52.

23. Twenty-six women's colleges filed a joint supportive legal brief against VMI in which they differentiated their mission as single-sex institutions from that of VMI. The women's colleges asserted that their mission is "to dissipate, rather than perpetuate, traditional gender classifications."

24. Jayne Stake et al., "The Women's Studies Experience: Impetus for Feminist Activism," *Psychology of Women Quarterly* 18 (1994): 17–24; and Jayne Stake and Suzanna Rose, "The Long-Term Impact of Women's Studies on Students' Personal Lives and Political Activism," *Psychology of Women Quarterly* 18 (1994): 403–412. See also Miner, "You're Going to Be," 452–467.

25. I borrow this term from Mary Jo Neitz, quoted in "The Classroom Climate," *On Campus with Women* 21 (Spring 1992): 1–5, 10.

26. According to Paludi and DeFour, 30 percent of undergraduate women experience some form of sexual harassment during their four years at college. Wilson and Kraus found in the early 1980s that 9 percent of female undergraduates had been touched to the point of personal discomfort by professors.

27. F. Till, *Sexual Harassment: A Report on the Sexual Harassment of Students* (Washington, D.C.: National Academy Advisory Council on Women's Educational Programs, 1980), 7.

28. Robert O'Neill, "Protecting Free Speech When the Issue Is Sexual Harassment," *Chronicle of Higher Education* 43 (13 September 1996): B3; and Verna Williams and Deborah Blake, "Sexual Harassment: Let the Punishment Fit the Crime," *Chronicle of Higher Education* 43 (18 April 1997): A56.

29. See *Hostile Hallways: The AAUW Survey on Sexual Harassment in American Schools* (Washington, D.C.: American Association of University Women, 1993).

30. The professor's stance on this incident and her philosophy of teaching are discussed in Jane Gallop's *Feminist Accused of Sexual Harrassment* (Chapel Hill, N.C.: Duke University Press, 1997).

31. "Sex Harassers Deliberately Disregard Campus Policies," *Women in Higher Education* 5 (June 1996): 14–15.

32. "Georgia Profs Cited for Sex Misconduct," *Women in Higher Education* 5 (June 1996): 3–4.

33. Reported in "Three Tenured Profs No Longer Employed," *About Women on Campus* 3 (Winter 1994): 3.

34. Adrienne Rich, "Taking Women Students Seriously." In *On Lies, Secrets*

and Silence: Selected Prose 1966–1978 (New York: W. W. Norton, 1979), 242–243.

35. Jean O'Gorman Hughes and Bernice Sandler, *Peer Harassment: Hassles for Women on Campus* (Washington, D.C.: Project on the Status and Education of Women, Association of American Colleges, 1988).

36. Timothy Harper, "A 'Hostile Environment' for Women," *American Bar Association Journal* 81 (May 1995): 16–17.

37. "Sexist E-Mail Circulates at Cornell," *Monthly Forum on Women in Higher Education* 3 (December 1995): 8.

38. Philip Elmer-DeWitt, "Snuff Porn on the Net," *Time* 145 (20 February 1995): 69.

39. Title VII of the Civil Rights Act (1991), Common Law Tort, and many state statutes also make sexual harassment illegal. For a convenient summary of this legislation see Bernice Sandler, "Important Events in the History of Sexual Harassment in Education," *About Women on Campus* 3 (Spring 1994): 5–6.

40. The following is a modified version of guidelines developed by Mary Rowe and reproduced by Bernice Sandler in "Writing a Letter to the Sexual Harasser: Another Way of Dealing with the Problem" (Washington, D.C.: Project on the State and Education of Women, Association of American Colleges, 1982). See also a printed transcript of Mary Rowe's talk "Dealing with Harassment Concerns" (New Haven, Conn.: Office for Women in Medicine, Yale University, 1985).

41. Reported in "A Tough Call: Choosing Your Response to Sexual Harassment," *Women in Higher Education* 4 (November 1995): 9–10.

42. Linda Knopp, "Women in Higher Education Today: A Mid-1990s Profile" (Washington, D.C.: American Council on Education, Research Brief #5, 1995).

43. *Women, Minorities, and Persons with Disabilities in Science and Engineering: 1994* (Washington, D.C.: National Science Foundation, No. 94–333, 1995).

44. Marguerite Holloway, "A Lab of Her Own," *Scientific American* (November 1993): 102.

CHAPTER 3 **Language and Gender**

1. Ludwig Wittgenstein, *Tractatus Logico-Philosophicus*, trans. D. F. Pears and B. F. McGuinness (London: Routledge and Kegan Paul, 1974).

2. Nancy Henley and Barrie Thorne, "Womanspeak and Manspeak: Sex Differences and Sexism in Communication, Verbal and Nonverbal." In *Beyond Sex Roles*, ed. Alice Sargent (St. Paul, Minn.: West, 1977), 201–218.

3. Deborah Tannen, *Gender and Discourse* (New York: Oxford University Press, 1994).

4. Linda Carli, "Gender, Language, and Influence," *Journal of Personality and Social Psychology* 59 (1990): 48.

5. William O'Barr and Bowman Atkins, "'Women's Language' or 'Powerless Language.'" In *Women and Language in Literature and Society*, ed. S. McConnell-Ginet, R. Borker, and N. Furman (New York: Praeger, 1980).

6. Most students today take "Ms." for granted and do not associate it with feminism.

7. Michael Messner, Margaret Carlisle Duncan, and Kerry Jensen, "Separating the Men from the Girls: The Gendered Language of Televised Sports," *Gender & Society* 7 (March 1993): 128.

8. Ibid.

9. Jane Mills uses "weapman" for adult male person. See Jane Mills, *Womanswords: A Dictionary of Words About Women* (New York: Henry Holt, 1989), 265.

10. Ibid., 267–268.

11. Quoted in Betsy Wagner, "Struggling with Sex," *U.S. News & World Report* 117 (26 September 1994): 119.

12. Timothy Moore, Karen Griffiths, and Barbara Payne, "Gender, Attitudes Towards Women, and the Appreciation of Sexist Humor," *Sex Roles* 16 (1987): 521–531.

13. "Fraternity Songs and Writings: Coming Under Criticism," *About Women on Campus* 2 (Spring 1993): 8–9.

14. Ibid.

15. See Carol Cohn, "Wars, Wimps, and Women: Talking Gender and Thinking War." In *Gendering War Talk*, ed. Miriam Cooke and Angela Woolacott (Princeton, N.J.: Princeton University Press, 1993), 227–246.

16. Messner, Duncan, and Jensen, "Separating the Men from the Girls," 130.

17. Deborah Cameron, *Feminism and Linguistic Theory* (London: Macmillan, 1985).

18. For a good summary of the research, see Judy Pearson et al., *Gender and Communication* (Dubuque, Iowa: Wm. C. Brown, 1991). See also Mykol Hamilton, "Masculine Bias in the Attribution of Personhood," *Psychology of Women Quarterly* 15 (1991): 393–402. The novel *Egalia's Daughters: A Satire of the Sexes*, by Gerd Brantenberg, reverses male/female pronouns and nouns to comic effect. Translated from German by Louis McKay (Seattle: Seal Press, 1985).

19. A. R. McConnell and I. Gavanski, reported in Allen R. McConnell and Russell Fazio, "Women as Men and People: Effects of Gender-Marked Language," *Personality and Social Psychology Bulletin* 22 (October 1996): 1004–1013.

20. Ibid.

21. Mark McMinn et al., "The Effects of God Language on Perceived Attributes of God," *Journal of Psychology and Theology* 21 (1993): 309–314. Interest-

ingly, the researchers also found that listeners enjoyed the experiment more when a female voice described the "male" God and a male voice described the "female" or gender-neutral God than when the genders matched.

22. Wendy Martyna, "Beyond the 'He/Man' Approach: The Case for Nonsexist Language," *Signs* 5 (1980): 482–493.

23. J. Silveria, "Generic Masculine Words and Thinking," *Women's Studies International Quarterly* 3 (1980): 165–178.

24. Rebecca Merritt and Cynthia Kok, "Attribution of Gender to a Gender-Unspecified Individual: An Examination of the People=Male Hypothesis," *Sex Roles* 33 (1995): 147.

25. See, for example, Mykol Hamilton et al., "Jury Instructions: Words in the Masculine Generic." In *The Women and Language Debate*, ed. Camille Roman, Suzanne Juhasz, and Cristanne Miller (New Brunswick, N.J.: Rutgers University Press, 1994).

26. Ibid., 490.

27. Sandra Bem and Daryl Bem, "Does Sex-Biased Job Advertising 'Aid and Abet' Sex Discrimination?" *Journal of Applied Social Psychology* 3 (1973): 6–18.

28. Mark Johnson and Seana Dowling-Guyer, "Effects of Inclusive vs. Exclusive Language on Evaluations of the Counselor," *Sex Roles* 34 (1996): 407–418.

29. Quoted in "No Sexism Please, We're Webster's," *Newsweek* 117 (24 June 1991): 59.

30. In *Metamagical Themas: Questing for the Essence of Mind and Pattern*, by Douglas Hofstadter (New York: Basic Books, 1985), 159–167.

31. Catharine MacKinnon, *Only Words* (Cambridge, Mass.: Harvard University Press, 1993), 13.

32. Susan Sontag, "Third World of Women," *Partisan Review* 40 (1973): 186.

CHAPTER 4 **Women and Sports**

1. Barbara Findlen, ed., *Listen Up: Voices from the Next Feminist Generation* (Seattle: Seal, 1995), xi–xii.

2. The effect has been stunning because women athletes and coaches have turned to the courts. In 1975, the NCAA gave colleges and universities three years to comply with Title IX. Even though 95 percent of schools failed to comply, no funding was cut and no penalties were assessed.

3. In 1994–1995, women made up half the undergraduates enrolled at Division 1–A colleges, yet only a third of the varsity athletes and athletic scholarship recipients were women.

4. In 1994, 105,532 college women were playing seventeen varsity collegiate sports, compared to 189,958 men in twenty-one sports.

5. "Female Athletes Study Harder," *On Campus with Women* 19 (Winter 1990): 10.

6. M. Melnick, D. Sabo, and B. Vanfossen, "Educational Effects of Interscholastic Athletic Participation on African-American and Hispanic Youth," *Adolescence* 27 (106): 295–308.

7. Dennis Black, "Gender Equity: Not Just for Athletics Anymore . . . Or Ever," *Women in Higher Education* 3 (1994): 10.

8. "Feds: Report Gender Equity in Athletics," *Women in Higher Education* 3 (November 1994): 3.

9. "Judge Rejects Brown U's 'JV' Plan," *Women in Higher Education* 4 (October 1995): 4.

10. Jim Naughton, "Appeals Court Affirms Ruling That Brown U. Discriminated Against Female Athletes," *Chronicle of Higher Education* 43 (29 November 1996): A41–42.

11. Reported in *Women in Higher Education* 4 (April 1995): 3.

12. Task Force on Women and Girls in Sports, *Empowering Women in Sports* (Arlington, Va.: Feminist Majority Foundation, 1996).

13. Quoted in Carol Galbraith, "Title IX: It's the Law," *Women's Sport & Fitness* (January/February 1992): 29.

14. This is a result of the Moseley-Braun/Kennedy Amendment to the 1994 Elementary and Secondary Education Act.

15. "Cooperation Settles U of Penn Title IX Athletics Complaint," *Women in Higher Education* 4 (October 1995): 1.

16. Nijole Benokraitis and Joe Feagin, *Modern Sexism: Blatant, Subtle, and Covert Discrimination* (Englewood Cliffs, N.J.: Prentice Hall, 1995), 86–91.

17. "$6 Million Bias Suit by Former Coach Hits Ohio State University," *Women in Higher Education* 6 (May 1997): 1–2.

18. Task Force, *Empowering*.

19. Ibid.

20. R. Ann Casey, "Title IX and Women Officials—How Have They Been Affected?" *JOPERD* (March 1992): 45–47; and Vivian Acosta and Linda Jean Carpenter, "As the Years Go By—Coaching Opportunities in the 1990s," *JOPERD* (March 1992): 36–41.

21. Debra Blum, "2 More Coaches of Women's Teams Go to Court to Press Claims of Sex Discrimination," *Chronicle of Higher Education* 40 (1 September 1993): A47–48.

22. Quoted in "No Room at the Top," *Sports Illustrated* 77 (September 1992): 62.

23. Susan Cahn, *Coming On Strong: Gender and Sexuality in Twentieth-Century Women's Sport* (New York: Free Press, 1994).

24. Laurel Davis, *The Swimsuit Issue and Sport: Hegemonic Masculinity in Sports Illustrated* (Albany: State University of New York Press, 1996).

25. See Susan Cahn, "From the 'Muscle Moll' to the 'Butch' Ballplayer: Mannishness, Lesbianism, and Homophobia in U.S. Women's Sport," *Feminist Studies* 19 (1993): 343–368.

26. Elaine Blinde and Diane Taub, "Women Athletes as Falsely Accused Deviants: Managing the Lesbian Stigma," *Sociological Quarterly* 33 (1992): 521–533.

27. Task Force, *Empowering.*

28. "Homophobia Intimidates Women Athletes, Panel Agrees," *Women in Higher Education* 5 (July 1996): 1.

29. Task Force, *Empowering.*

30. Ibid.

31. See J. Graydon, "But It's More Than a Game," *Feminist Review* 13 (1983): 1–16; and Michael Messner, Margaret Carlisle Duncan, and Kerry Jensen, "Separating the Men from the Girls," *Gender & Society* 7 (1993): 121–137.

32. Messner, Duncan, and Jensen, "Separating the Men from the Girls," 121–137.

33. At the time of writing, they were the Women's Professional Fastpitch Softball team and an all-women professional baseball team, the Colorado Silver Bullets.

34. Nike's overseas assembly operations, for example, have come under a lot of criticism for using child labor and for paying all workers a pittance, a fraction of what American workers would earn for the same work.

35. In 1997, Kenyan runner Lameck Aguta won the marathon in 2 hours, 10 minutes and 34 seconds. The women's leader, Fatima Roba from Ethiopia, won with a time of 2 hours, 26 minutes, and 23 seconds. The record time for the course—2 hours, 7 minutes, and 15 seconds—was set in 1994.

CHAPTER 5 **Sexual Identity and Homophobia**

1. Anastasia Higginbotham, "Chicks Goin' at It." In *Listen Up: Voices from the Next Feminist Generation*, ed. Barbara Findlen (Seattle: Seal, 1995), 6.

2. W. Masters and V. Johnson, *Homosexuality in Perspective* (Boston: Little, Brown, 1979).

3. Quoted in Jeffrey Berman, *Diaries to an English Professor: Pain and Growth in the Classroom* (Amherst: University of Massachusetts Press, 1994), 215.

4. D. Martin and P. Lyon, *Lesbian-Woman* (New York: Bantam Books, 1972), 1.

5. Tamar Lewin, "So, Now We Know What Americans Do in Bed. So?" *New York Times,* 9 October 1994, E3. After examining the research findings on homosexuality, psychologist Robert Crooks and clinician Karla Baur concluded that 1 percent of American women and 2 percent of men are exclusively homosexual; 14 percent of women and 23 percent of men have had

both homosexual and heterosexual experiences; and 85 percent of women and 75 percent of men are exclusively heterosexual (cited in Crooks and Baur, *Our Sexuality* [Redwood City, Calif.: Benjamin/Cummings, 1990]).

6. Carolyn Mooney, "Attack on Homosexuality Angers Divinity Students," *Chronicle of Higher Education* 40 (11 May 1994): A38.

7. Bill Turque et al., "Gays Under Fire," *Newsweek* (14 September 1992): 35–40.

8. Ruth Sidel, *Battling Bias: The Struggle of Identity and Community on College Campuses* (New York: Viking Press, 1994).

9. Stephanie Mansfield, "Gays on Campus," *Redbook* 181 (1993): 124, 126.

10. "Changing the Climate of Gay and Lesbian Students on Campus," *On Campus with Women* 24 (Summer 1994): 4, 8.

11. Toni McNaron, "Making Life More Livable for Gays and Lesbians on Campus: Sightings from the Field," *Educational Record* 72 (Winter 1991): 19–22.

12. Jill Tinmouth and Gerald Hamwi, "The Experience of Gay and Lesbian Students in Medical School," *Journal of the American Medical Association* 271 (1994): 714–716.

13. Higginbotham, "Chicks Goin' at It," 10.

14. Sidel, *Battling Bias.*

15. Michael Messner, "Like Family: Power, Intimacy, and Sexuality in Male Athletes' Friendships." In *Men's Friendships*, ed. Peter Nardi (Newbury Park, Calif.: Sage, 1992), 215–237.

16. Elaine Blinde and Diane Taub, "Women Athletes as Falsely Accused Deviants: Managing the Lesbian Stigma," *Sociological Quarterly* 33 (1992): 521–533.

17. Amy Wahl, "Texas A&M President Criticized for Vetoing 2 Curricular Changes," *Chronicle of Higher Education* 42 (1 December 1995): A30.

18. Bonnie Zimmerman, "Lesbian Studies in an Inclusive Curriculum," *Transformations* 5 (Fall 1994): 18–27.

19. Quoted in Tinmouth and Hamwi, "Experience," 715.

20. Reported in *Chronicle of Higher Education* 43 (24 January 1997): A28.

CHAPTER 6 **Racism in the Colorblind Academy**

1. Quoted in Patricia Beard, "The Fall and Rise of the Seven Sisters," *Town & Country Monthly* 148 (November 1994): 159–175.

2. Quoted in William Tierney, "The College Experience of Native Americans: A Critical Analysis." In *Beyond Silenced Voices,* ed. Lois Weis and Michelle Fine (Albany: State University of New York Press, 1993), 311.

3. "Latino/Latina" are preferred by many Spanish-speaking Americans, although Americans of Mexican ancestry may prefer "Chicano/a" or "Mexi-

can American" and Puerto Rican students may prefer to be known as Puerto Ricans. The term "Hispanic" was created by the federal government as a census category and includes persons of Cuban, Mexican or Mexican-American, Puerto Rican, South or Central American, or other Spanish ancestry or descent.

4. Erlene Wilson, *The 100 Best Colleges for African-American Students* (New York: Plume Books, 1993), 4.

5. Scott Jaschik, "A New Philosophy and the New Style at the Office for Civil Rights, *Chronicle of Higher Education* 39 (14 July 1993): A19.

6. Quoted in Yolanda Moses, "Black Women in Academe: Issues and Strategies" (pamphlet). (Washington, D.C.: Association of American Colleges, 1989): 3.

7. Mel Elfin with Sarah Burke, "Race on Campus," *U.S. News & World Report* 114 (19 April 1993): 53–56.

8. Quoted in Gustav Spohn, "Universities Confront Bias with Programs," *National Catholic Reporter* 32 (29 March 1996): 22.

9. Quoted in Denise Mahner, "Blacks and Whites on the Campuses," *Chronicle of Higher Education* 35 (16 April 1989): A3.

10. Ibid.

11. Moses, "Black Women in Academe," 6–7.

12. Affirmative action is under attack across the country. In July 1996, the Supreme Court refused to review a U.S. Court of Appeals ruling that barred the University of Texas Law School from considering race in its admission process. Now colleges in states in the Fifth Circuit—Texas, Louisiana, and Mississippi—can no longer used race-based preferences to enhance diversity. D. Lederman, "Court Rulings Force College to Consider Ending Use of Race in Admissions Process," *Chronicle of Higher Education* 42 (19 July 1996): A27–28.

13. Kim Stosnider, "Minority Law School Enrollment Would Drop Without Affirmative Action, Study Finds," *Chronicle of Higher Education* 43 (31 January 1997): A28.

14. Farai Chideya, *Don't Believe the Hype* (New York: Plume Books, 1995), 83.

15. Ibid, 87. "Modest" refers to families earning less than $21,500 in 1991.

16. Ibid., 88. The combined figures (university and federal support) were 30 percent for African Americans, 48 percent for whites, and 74 percent for international students.

17. Higher Education Research Institute, *The American Freshman: National Norms for Fall 1996* (Los Angeles: University of California, 1997).

18. Jee Yeun Lee, quoted in Barbara Findlen, ed., *Listen Up: Voices from the Next Feminist Generation* (Seattle: Seal Press, 1995), 206–207.

19. Courtney Leatherman, "At a Black College, Race Often Takes Precedence Over Gender," *Chronicle of Higher Education* 39 (14 July 1993): A13–15.

20. Robert Blauner, *Black Lives, White Lives: Three Decades of Race Relations in America* (Berkeley: University of California Press, 1989); and "The Two Languages of Race," *American Prospect* (Summer 1992): 55–64.

21. Charles Judd et al., "Stereotypes and Ethnocentrism: Diverging Inter-ethnic Perceptions of African American and White American Youth," *Journal of Personality and Social Psychology* 69 (1995): 478.

22. Quoted in Carol Weinberg, *The Complete Handbook for College Women* (New York: New York University Press, 1994), 205.

23. Higher Education Research Institute, *The American Freshman: National Norms for Fall 1995* (Los Angeles: University of California, 1997).

24. Richard Schaefer, "Education and Prejudice: Unraveling the Relationship," *Sociological Quarterly* 37 (Winter 1996): 8.

25. Paula Rothberg, "Rural U: A Cautionary Tale," *National Women's Studies Association Journal* 6 (Summer 1994): 291–298.

26. Ibid., 293.

27. Connie Chan and Mary Jane Treacy, "Resistance in Multicultural Courses: Student, Faculty, and Classroom Dynamics," *American Behavioral Scientist* 40 (1994): 212–222.

28. For a thorough discussion of the political correctness "debate," see Nancy Baker Jones, "Confronting the PC 'Debate': The Politics of Identity and the American Image," *National Women's Studies Association Journal* 6 (Fall 1994): 384–403.

29. Ibid., 399.

30. Quoted in Amy Wallace, "Occidental College's Noble Experiment in Diversity," *Journal of Blacks in Higher Education* 11 (1996): 116–117.

31. Christopher Shea, "Wesleyan University Asks White Students Not to Live in Black Dormitory," *Chronicle of Higher Education* 42 (10 May 1996): A47.

32. A. P. Sanoff and S. Minerbrook, "Students Talk About Race," *U.S. News & World Report* 114 (19 April 1993): 57–64.

33. According to the Higher Education Research Institute's 1996 survey of first-year college students, 64 percent believe campuses should prohibit racist/sexist speech.

34. Higher Education Research Institute, *The American Freshman: National Norms for Fall 1996* (Los Angeles: University of California, 1997).

35. See Kathy Russell, Midge Wilson, and Ronald Hall, *The Color Complex: The Politics of Skin Color Among African Americans* (New York: Anchor, 1993); and Selena Bond and Thomas Cash, "Black Beauty and Body Images Among African-American College Women," *Journal of Applied Psychology* 22 (June 1992): 874–888.

36. Ben Gose, "Public Debate Over a Private Choice," *Chronicle of Higher Education* 42 (10 May 1996): A45.

37. "Sigma Gamma Rho Sorority Takes Issue with Fashion Show," *Concordiensis* (17 April 1997): 11.

38. "Final Word on Fashion Show," *Concordiensis* (24 April 1997): 15. This letter was followed by a rebuttal from a white male who wrote that his "initial reaction was to write nothing in response. If you had advanced this far in your life and education and still possessed these beliefs, what could I possibly write to enlighten your ignorant self." Conor McKenzie, "Ignorance: Rampant Among Student Body," *Concordiensis* (1 May 1997): 8.

39. "Stitching Together a Campus," *Chronicle of Higher Education* 43 (17 January 1997): A8.

40. "Students at Indiana University Demand More Minority Programs," *Chronicle of Higher Education* 43 (31 January 1997): A6.

CHAPTER 7 **Beyond the Coed**

1. U.S. Department of Education, National Center for Education Statistics, *The Condition of Education*, vol. 2 (Washington, D.C.: GPO, 1989), 44.

2. Bureau of Census, *School Enrollment—Social and Economic Characteristics of Students, October, 1993* (Washington, D.C.: GPO, 1994).

3. "Quints and College Too!" *Good Housekeeping* 214 (1992): 58.

4. Quoted in Dana Hawkins, "Older Students Make Their Mark," *U.S. News & World Report* 117 (26 September 1994): 112.

5. U.S. Department of Education, *The Condition of Education.*

6. William Giczkowski, "The Influx of Older Students Can Revitalize College Teaching," *Chronicle of Higher Education* 38 (25 March 1992): B3.

7. See Carol Keyes and Pamela Boulton, "Campus Children's Centers: Support for Children and Families," *Children Today* 23 (Fall–Winter 1995): 18–22.

8. Such programs are always vulnerable to changes in federal legislation. Welfare legislation passed in 1996 made getting an education more difficult for some women by requiring welfare recipients to perform "work activities" for at least twenty hours a week. Receiving "vocational educational training" was permitted for up to twelve months, but this would not permit a student to earn even an associate's degree. Earlier legislation had encouraged welfare recipients to attend college.

9. Quoted in Hilary Herbold, "Single Mothers on Campus," *Monthly Forum on Women in Higher Education* 1 (January 1996): 18.

10. "What Works to Retain Re-entry and Adult Women," *Women in Higher Education* 5 (April 1996): 19.

11. Karen Hube, "How Older Students Can Cut the Cost of a College Degree in Half," *Money* 25 (September 1996): 137.

1. Marsha Saxton, "Born and Unborn: The Implications of Reproductive Technologies for People with Disabilities." In *Test-Tube Women: What Future for Motherhood*, ed. Rita Arditti et al. (Boston: Pandora Press, 1984), 298.

2. Marsha Saxton and Florence Howe, *With Wings: An Anthology of Literature By and About Women with Disabilities* (New York: Feminist Press, 1987).

3. *College Freshmen with Disabilities: A Statistical Profile* (Washington, D.C.: American Council on Education, HEATH Resource Center, 1992); N. Coombs and G. P. Cartwright, "Project East: Equal Access to Software and Information," *Change* (March/April 1994): 42–44.

4. The Americans with Disabilities Act defines "disability" to mean a physical or mental impairment that substantially limits one or more of a person's major life activities. Learning disabilities are presumed to be caused by central nervous system dysfunction and vary in intensity and by area of performance for each individual. They include dyslexia (problems with reading), dysgraphia (problems with writing), dyscalculia (problems with mathematics), and other difficulties.

5. Section 508 of the amendments to the Rehabilitation Act require that all federally funded programs must make sure that all electronic office equipment and computers are accessible and usable by people with disabilities.

6. A 1992 ruling by the Department of Education suggests that universities are obligated to pay for disabled students' services, but no definitive federal ruling had been issued pertaining to study abroad. Amy Magaro Rubin, "Students with Disabilities Press Colleges to Help Them Take Part in Foreign Study," *Chronicle of Higher Education* 43 (27 September 1996): A47–49.

7. "Disabled Student Saws Off Barrier," *Women in Higher Education* 3 (October 1994): 2.

8. C. Fichten et al., "Facilitation of Teaching and Learning: What Professors, Students with a Physical Disability, and Institutions of Higher Education Can Do." In *Natcon: Special Edition—Vocational Counselling in Rehabilitation*, ed. H. I. Day and R. I. Brown, 14 (1987): 45–67. Ottawa, Canada: Employment and Immigration Canada.

9. J. Jarrow, *Title by Title: The ADA's Impact on Postsecondary Education* (Columbus, Ohio: Association on Higher Education and Disability, 1992).

10. Deborah Ellen, "Taking the Case to Court," *Connections* 3 (September 1996): 3, 11.

11. See Debra Blum, "NCAA Announces Change in the Way It Determines Eligibility of Learning-Disabled Athletes," *Chronicle of Higher Education* 42 (26 April 1996): A52; and Rubin, "Students with Disabilities Press Colleges," A47–49. Consult the Resources section of this chapter for information on a new service that arranges for study abroad.

12. C. Stovall and W. E. Sedlacek, "Attitudes of Male and Female University Students toward Students with Different Physical Disabilities," *Journal of College Student Personnel* 24 (1983): 325–330.

13. M. L. Putnam, "Postsecondary Education for Learning Disabled Students: A Review of the Literature," *Journal of College Student Personnel* 25 (1984): 68–75.

14. B. Saracoglu, H. Mindin, and M. Wilchesky, "The Adjustment of Students with Learning Disabilities to University and Its Relationship to Self-Esteem and Self-Efficacy," *Journal of Learning Disabilities* 22 (1989): 590–592.

15. Wendy Lustbader, *Counting on Kindness* (New York: Free Press, 1991), 122.

16. Patricia Long and Cheryl Fischer, "A Bright Future," *Health* 8 (March–April 1994): 52.

17. Lisa Guernsey, "Ohio High Court Affirms Medical School's Right to Reject Blind Applicant," *Chronicle of Higher Education* 42 (9 August 1996): A21.

18. Nancy Weinberg, "Another Perspective: Attitudes of People with Disabilities." In *Attitudes Towards Persons with Disabilities*, ed. Harold Yuker (New York: Springer, 1988).

19. Ibid.

20. Michelle Fine and Adrienne Asch, *Women with Disabilities: Essays in Psychology, Culture and Politics* (Philadelphia: Temple University Press, 1988).

21. Victor Florian and Nira Dangoor, "Personal and Familial Adaptation of Women with Severe Physical Disabilities," *Journal of Marriage and the Family* 56 (August 1994): 735–746.

22. Saxton, "Born and Unborn," 298–312.

23. Kristen Robillard and Catherine Fichten, "Attributions about Sexuality and Romantic Involvement of Physically Disabled College Students: An Empirical Study," *Sexuality and Disability* 6 (1983): 197–212.

24. Mary H. J. Farrell, "Silent Screams: A People Report on Sexual Assault at the Nation's Only University for Deaf Students," *People Weekly* 41 (20 June 1994): 36.

25. Ibid.

26. Ibid.

27. Quoted in Fred Pelka, "Attack of the Morally Challenged," *On the Issues* 5 (Summer 1996): 39.

28. Susan Wendell, "Toward a Feminist Theory of Disability," *Hypatia* 4 (Summer 1989): 105.

29. Barbara Hillyer, *Feminism and Disability* (Norman: University of Oklahoma Press, 1993), x.

30. C. Henderson, ed., *College Freshmen with Disabilities: A Statistical Profile* (Washington, D.C.: American Council on Education, 1992).

CHAPTER 9 **Eating and Body Image**

1. Debbie Taylor et al., *Women: A World Report* (Oxford: Oxford University Press, 1985).
2. Barbara Mangweth, Harrison Pope, and James Hudson, "Bulimia Nervosa in Two Cultures: A Comparison of Austrian and American College Students," *International Journal of Eating Disorders* 17 (1995): 403–412.
3. R. M. Raich et al., "Eating Disorder Symptoms among Adolescents in the United States and Spain: A Comparative Study," *International Journal of Eating Disorders* 11 (1992): 63–72.
4. Filmmaker Todd Haynes's movie *Superstar* tells singer Karen Carpenter's tragic story, using a cast made up entirely of Barbie and Ken dolls. Mattel originally blocked the film. Barbie's measurements recently have been changed.
5. Alexandra Rubington, "Eating Disorders: A Dietician's Perspective, An Interview with Diane Gibson, R.D.," *Developments* (HRI Hospital, Boston, newsletter) 3 (Summer 1994): 4.
6. Quoted in Jeffrey Berman, *Diaries to an English Professor: Pain and Growth in the Classroom* (Amherst: University of Massachusetts Press, 1994), 100–101.
7. Rita Teusch, "Eating Disorders and Trauma," *Developments* (HRI Hospital, Boston, newsletter) 3 (Summer 1994), 1, 5.
8. Joan Jacobs Brumberg discusses this with regard to young women in the Victorian era and today (see n. 9). Other historians have focused on women and food in earlier periods. See Rudolph Bell, *Holy Anorexia* (Chicago: University of Chicago Press, 1985); Caroline Walker Bynum, *Holy Feast and Holy Fast: The Religious Significance of Food to Medieval Women* (Berkeley: University of California Press, 1987); and Walter Vandereycken and Ron van Deth, *From Fasting Saints to Anorexic Girls: The History of Self-Starvation* (New York: New York University Press, 1990).
9. Adapted from Joan Jacobs Brumberg, *Fasting Girls: The Emergence of Anorexia Nervosa as a Modern Disease* (Cambridge, Mass.: Harvard University Press, 1988).
10. Quoted in Berman, *Diaries*, 106–107.
11. Brumberg, *Fasting Girls*, 24.

CHAPTER 10 **Women, Drinking, and Drugs**

1. Reported in "Notebook," *Chronicle of Higher Education* 43 (14 March 1997): A36.
2. Michael Kidorf et al., "Alcohol Expectancies and Changes in Beer Consumption of First-year College Students," *Addictive Behaviors* 20 (1995): 225–231.

3. Henry Wechsler et al., "Correlates of College Student Binge Drinking," *American Journal of Public Health* 85 (1995): 921–985.

4. "Notebook," A36.

5. Ibid.

6. Thomas O'Hare, "Differences in Asian and White Drinking: Consumption Level, Drinking Contexts, and Expectancies," *Addictive Behaviors* 20 (1995): 261–266.

7. H. Wechsler et al., "Health and Behavioral Consequences of Binge Drinking in College: A National Survey of Students at 140 Campuses," *Journal of the American Medical Association* 272 (1994): 1572–1577.

8. Wechsler et al., "Correlates," 921.

9. Ibid.

10. William Celis, "Drinking by College Women Raises New Concerns," *New York Times*, 16 February 1994, A18.

11. Ibid.

12. Michelle Lichtenfeld and Wesley Kayson, "Factors in College Student Drinking," *Psychological Reports* 74 (1994): 927–930.

13. Commission on Substance Abuse at Colleges and Universities, *Rethinking Rites of Passage: Substance Abuse on America's Campuses* (New York: The National Center on Addiction and Substance Abuse at Columbia University, 1994).

14. Reported in Barbara Leigh and Beatriz Aramburu, "The Role of Alcohol and Gender in Choices and Judgments About Hypothetical Sexual Encounters," *Journal of Applied Social Psychology* 26 (1996): 20–30.

15. Antonia Abbey et al., "Alcohol and Dating Risk Factors for Sexual Assualt among College Women," *Psychology of Women Quarterly* 20 (1996): 147–169; and Kelly Cue, William George, and Jeanette Noris, "Women's Appraisals of Sexual-Assault Risk in Dating Situations," *Psychology of Women Quarterly* 20 (1996): 487–504.

16. K. Fillmore, *Alcohol Use Across the Life Course* (Toronto: Alcoholism and Drug Addiction Research Foundation, 1988).

17. Wechsler et al., "Health."

18. Mary Geraghty, "How One University Responds to Drug Use with Stiff Sanctions and Student Patrols," *Chronicle of Higher Education* 43 (21 March 1997): A45.

19. Jim Naughton, "Alcohol Abuse by Athletes Poses Big Problems for Colleges," *Chronicle of Higher Education* 43 (20 September 1996): A47.

20. Ibid.

21. Reported on the *CBS Nightly News,* 5 May 1997.

22. Sharon Lerner, "If We've Come Such a Long Way, Why Are We Still Smoking?" *Ms.* 5 (May/June 1995): 22–27.

23. David Lipsky, "The Hard-Core Curriculum," *Rolling Stone* 719 (1995): 99–105.

24. Ibid., 99.

25. Ibid., 102.

26. Harrison Pope, "The Residual Cognitive Effects of Heavy Marijuana Use in College Students," *Journal of the American Medical Association* 275 (1996): 521–527.

27. Lipsky, "Hard-Core," 103.

28. Quoted in John Leland, "A Risky Rx for Fun," *Newsweek* 126 (30 October 1995): 74.

29. Kit Lively, "The 'Date Rape' Drug," *Chronicle of Higher Education* 42 (28 June 1996): A29.

30. Lipsky, "Hard-Core," 103.

31. Much of this discussion is taken from the University of California's *The Wellness Encyclopedia* (Boston: Houghton Mifflin, 1991).

CHAPTER 11 **Sexuality and Reproductive Issues**

1. "Teen Sex Is Waning, Study Says," Albany, N.Y., *Times Union,* 2 May 1997, A3.

2. The annual survey is conducted by the University of California at Los Angeles Higher Education Research Institute.

3. Karen Glover Comstock, "A Peer Educator STD Prevention Project for Women Students," *Public Health Reports* 109 (1994): 181–182; and J. R. Allen and V. P. Setlow, "Heterosexual Transmission of HIV: A View of the Future," *Journal of the American Medical Association* 266 (1991): 1695–1696.

4. David Goh, "Effects of HIV/AIDS Information on Attitudes Toward AIDS: A Cross-Ethnic Comparison of College Students," *Journal of Psychology* 127 (1994): 611–618.

5. S. Chapman De Bro et al., "Influencing a Partner to Use a Condom: A College Student Perspective," *Psychology of Women Quarterly* 18 (1994): 165–182.

6. Ibid.

7. Cited in Marilyn Elias, "More Partners, More-risky Sex," *USA Today*, 10 October 1994, D1.

8. Deborah Johnson, "Women Who Trust Too Much: What AIDS Commercials Don't Tell You," *On the Issues* 5 (Summer 1996): 26.

9. Ibid.

10. Quoted in Dianne Hales, "What Doctors Don't Know About Women's Bodies," *Ladies' Home Journal* (February 1997): 52–54.

11. Faye Ginsburg, "Procreation Stories: Reproduction, Nurturance, and Procreation in Life Narratives of Abortion Activists," *American Ethnologist* 14 (1987): 623–636.

12. Eve Powell-Griner and Katherine Trent, "Sociodemographic Determinants of Abortion in the United States," *Demography* 24 (November 1987): 553–561.

13. Ibid.

14. Katherine Trent and Eve Powell-Griner, "Differences in Race, Marital Status, and Education Among Women Obtaining Abortions," *Social Forces* 69 (June 1991): 1121–1141.

15. Christianne Esposito and Susan Basow, "College Students' Attitudes Toward Abortion: The Role of Knowledge and Demographic Variables," *Journal of Applied Social Psychology* 25 (1995): 1996–2017.

16. Reported in Alison Bass, "Abortion Demographics Detailed in New Survey," Albany, N.Y., *Times Union,* 8 August 1996, A2.

17. Donna Jackson, *How to Make the World a Better Place for Women in Five Minutes a Day* (New York: Hyperion, 1992).

18. Rachel Dobkin and Shana Sippy, *Educating Ourselves: The College Woman's Handbook* (New York: Workman Publishing, 1995), 429.

19. Willard Cates et al., "Commentary: The Quest for Women's Prophylactic Methods—Hope vs Science," *American Journal of Public Health* 82 (1992): 1479–1481.

20. Jackson, *How to Make the World a Better Place*, 94.

21. Ibid.

CHAPTER 12 **Rape and Sexual Assault**

1. Emilie Morgan, "Don't Call Me a Survivor." In *Listen Up: Voices from the Next Feminist Generation*, ed. Barbara Findlen (Seattle: Seal, 1995), 177.

2. Ruth Sidel, *Battling Bias: The Struggle for Identity and Community on College Campuses* (New York: Viking, 1994).

3. Mary Koss, Christine Gidycz, and Nadine Wisniewski, "The Scope of Rape: Incidence and Prevalence of Sexual Aggression and Victimization in a National Sample of Higher Education Students," *Journal of Consulting and Clinical Psychology* 55 (1987): 162–170. Koss and associates found that 54 percent of the women had experienced some level of sexual assault after the age of fourteen. Research by Antonia Abbey at Wayne State University in the 1990s found a very similar number: 59 percent of women had been sexually assaulted after the age of fourteen. Another national sample of college woman found that white women have a higher incidence of rape (16 percent) than do African-American woman (10 percent). A. Abbey et al., "Alcohol and Dating Risk Factors for Sexual Assault Among College Women," *Psychology of Women Quarterly* 20 (1996): 147–169.

4. Just over 7 percent of rape victims are male, according to the National Crime Survey.

5. U.S. Department of Justice Bureau of Statistics, 1988.

6. Eugene Kanin, "Date Rapists: Differential Sexual Socialization and Relative Deprivation," *Archives of Sexual Behavior* 14 (1985): 219–231.

7. Sidel, *Battling Bias*, 91.

8. Reported in *Women in Higher Education* 4 (April 1995): 19.

9. See Patricia Yancey Martin and Robert Hummer, "Fraternities and Rape on Campus," *Gender & Society* 3 (December 1989): 457–473.

10. A. Aryes Boswell and Jean Spade, "Fraternities and Collegiate Rape Culture: Why Are Some Fraternities More Dangerous Places for Women?" *Gender & Society* 10 (1996): 137.

11. Ibid., 141–142.

12. Peggy Reeves Sanday, *Fraternity Gang Rape: Sex, Brotherhood, and Privilege on Campus* (New York: New York University Press, 1990).

13. Diana Scully and Joseph Marolla, "'Riding the Bull at Gilley's': Convicted Rapists Describe the Rewards of Rape," *Social Problems* 32 (1985): 251–263.

14. At Texas A&M University, psychologists Charlene Muehlenhard and Lisa Hollabaugh found in their research that 39 percent of the 610 undergraduate women they questioned acknowledged engaging in "token resistance" at least once. The token resistance occurred when a woman wanted to have sex and planned on it, but said no to her date because she didn't want to seem too eager, felt self-conscious about her body, or was angry. The researchers concluded that the underlying reason these women engaged in token resistance was their belief that this behavior was normative for women—part of the way young women are still expected to act in American society. Charlene Muehlenhard and Lisa Hollabaugh, "Do Women Sometimes Say No When They Mean Yes? The Prevalence and Correlates of Women's Token Resistance to Sex," *Journal of Personality and Social Psychology* 54 (1988): 872–879.

15. Peggy Reeves Sanday, "The Socio-Cultural Context of Rape," *Journal of Social Issues* 37 (1982): 5–27.

16. "Duke Women Confront Fraternities," *About Women on Campus* 2 (Spring 1993): 9.

17. See Sarah Cook, "Acceptance and Expectation of Sexual Aggression in College Students," *Psychology of Women Quarterly* 19 (1995): 181–194.

18. Quoted in Sarah Glazer, "Sex on Campus: Will New Programs Cut the Sexual Assault Rate?" *Congressional Quarterly Researcher* 41 (4 November 1994): 963–979.

19. Lisa Mori et al., "Attitudes Toward Rape: Gender and Ethnic Differences Across Asian and Caucasian College Students," *Sex Roles* 32 (1995): 457–467.

20. Linda Kalof and Bruce Wade, "Sexual Attitudes and Experiences with Sexual Coercion: Exploring the Influence of Race and Gender," *Journal of Black Psychology* 21 (1995): 224–238.

21. Both cases were dismissed in 1996 by U.S. District Court Judge Jackson L. Kiser, who declared the act unconstitutional; at the time of writing his decision was under appeal. Justice Kiser had earlier upheld the Virginia Military Institute's right to remain all male, a position later rejected by the Supreme Court.

22. Quoted in Richard Jerome, "No Justice, No Peace: Both Sides Lose When Virginia Tech Tries to Settle a Rape Charge on Its Own, In Secret," *People Weekly* 45 (11 March 1996): 42–45.

23. Graham Zellick, "Discipline and Punish: Why Campus Justice Should Not Be Substituted for Criminal Prosecution," *Chronicle of Higher Education* 43 (14 February 1997): B3.

24. Spring Walton, "Date Rape: New Liability for Colleges and Universities?" *National Association of Student Personnel Administrators Journal* 31 (1994): 195–200.

25. Sarah Glazer, "Sex on Campus: Will New Programs Cut the Sexual Assault Rate?" *Congressional Quarterly Researcher* 4 (4 November 1994): 963–979.

26. James Deacon, "What Is 'Abuse'?" *Maclean's* 106 (22 February 1993): 54. See also Walter DeKeseredy, Martin Schwartz and Karen Tait, "Sexual Assault and Stranger Aggression on a Canadian University Campus," *Sex Roles* 28 (1993): 263–277.

27. These guidelines are adapted from those of the New York State Office of Crime Prevention and the National Crime Prevention Council.

CHAPTER 13 **Women in the Media**

1. Samantha Sanderson, "'You've Come a Long Way, Baby'—Or Have You?" *USA Today* 119 (November 1990): 59–62.

2. Donna Jackson, *How to Make the World a Better Place for Women in Five Minutes a Day* (New York: Hyperion, 1992), 123.

3. Jean Kilbourne, "'Gender Bender' Ads: Same Old Sexism," *New York Times,* 15 May 1994, A13.

4. Erving Goffman, *Gender Advertisements* (Cambridge, Mass.: Harvard University Press, 1978).

5. Ibid.

6. *Modern Sexism: Blatant, Subtle, and Covert Discrimination* (Englewood Cliffs, N.J.: Prentice Hall, 1995), 61.

7. Rhona Mahony, "Women at Work, Girls at Play," *Ms.* 7 (January/February 1997): 37–40.

8. Kate Pierce, "A Feminist Theoretical Perspective on the Socialization of

Teenage Girls Through *Seventeen* Magazine," *Sex Roles* 23 (1990): 491–500.

9. Ibid., 498.
10. Anastasia Higginbotham, "Teen Mags: How to Get a Guy, Drop 20 Pounds, and Lose Your Self-Esteem," *Ms.* 6 (March/April 1996): 87.
11. See Jean Kilbourne's *Still Killing Us Softly* video for these and other examples.
12. Gloria Steinem, "Sex, Lies, and Advertising," *Ms.* 1 (July/August 1990): 18–28.
13. Oscar Suris, "Mum's the Word on Subaru Ads for Gays," *Wall Street Journal,* 22 March 1996, B2.
14. Anne Carey and Marcy Mullins, "USA Snapshots: Ads Out of Touch with Women," *USA Today,* 29 January 1996, B1.
15. Stuart Elliot, "Advertising," *New York Times,* 30 July 1996, D5; and 1 May 1996, D6.
16. Nancy Signorelli, "Television and Conceptions About Sex Roles, Maintaining Conventionality and the Status Quo," *Sex Roles* 21 (1989): 341–360.
17. See Sally Steenland, "Ten Years in Prime Time: An Analysis of the Image of Women on Entertainment Television from 1979 to 1988." In *Women: Images and Realities*, ed. Amy Kesselman, Lily McNair, and Nancy Schniedewind (Mountain View, Calif.: Mayfield, 1995), 76–82.
18. Katha Politt, "The Smurfette Principle," *New York Times Magazine,* 7 April 1991, 22.
19. Ibid.
20. Sharon Silvas with Barbara Jenkins and Polly Grant, "The Overvoice: Images of Women in the Media." In *Women's Studies: Thinking Women*, ed. Jodi Wetzel et al. (Dubuque, Iowa: Kendall/Hunt, 1993), 77–87.
21. "Women of the Year: They're Gaining Power in Hollywood and Using It to Make Films that Women—and Men—Want to See," *Time* 146 (13 November 1995): 96–100.
22. Quoted in Alexandra Marks, "A Woman's Place is Behind the Camera," *Christian Science Monitor,* 8 January 1996, 12.
23. See D.E.H. Russell, "Pornography and Rape: A Causal Model." In *Making Violence Sexy: Feminist Views on Pornography*, ed. D.E.H. Russell (Buckingham, U.K.: Open University Press, 1993), 120–150; and D. Zillmann and J. Bryant, "Pornography, Sexual Callousness, and the Trivialization of Rape," *Journal of Communication* 32 (1982): 10–21.
24. E. Donnerstein, "Aggressive Erotica and Violence against Women," *Journal of Personality and Social Psychology* 39 (1980): 269–277.
25. Penny Reid and Gillian Finchilescu, "The Disempowering Effects of Media Violence Against Women on College Women," *Psychology of Women Quarterly* 19 (1995): 397–441.

26. Gloria Steinem, "Hollywood Cleans Up *Hustler*," *New York Times*, op-ed page, 7 January 1997, A17.

27. Ibid.

28. Nan Robertson, *The Girls in the Balcony: Women, Men and the New York Times* (New York: Random House, 1992).

29. Katia Hetter and Dorian Friedman, "The Animating Role of Women Pundits: Hillary Clinton Adds Her Voice to the Dialogue," *U.S. News & World Report* 119 (7 August 1995): 33–35.

30. Reported by the media watchdog group Women, Men and Media. See Judy Mann, "Newspapers and the Invisible Woman," *Washington Post,* 19 April 1996, E3.

31. *USA Today* and the *Post* had 9 percent of front-page references to women, while the *Times* had 8 percent.

32. Susan Faludi, "Where's the Feminist Conspiracy?" *The Nation* 262 (29 April 1996): 10.

33. Katha Pollitt, "Subject to Debate," *The Nation* 259 (17 October 1994): 409.

34. Judy Mann, "Women and the Powers That Be," *Washington Post,* 29 March 1996, E3.

35. Patricia Made, "Africa's Invisible Women," *UNESCO Courier,* September 1995, 21.

36. Jill Abramson, "The 'Boys' on the Presidential Campaign Bus Often Take a Backseat to Women Reporters Now," *Wall Street Journal,* 21 August 1996, A16.

37. Cited in Jackson, *How to Make the World a Better Place*, 123.

38. Ibid.

39. Steenland, "Ten Years in Prime Time," 77.

CHAPTER 14 Women and Work

1. Sara Ann Friedman, *Work Matters: Women Talk About Their Jobs and Their Lives* (New York: Viking, 1996), 129.

2. According to the U.S. Department of Labor's Women's Bureau, 59 percent of women worked either part- or full-time in 1996, making up 46 percent of the labor force.

3. Diane Harris, "How Does Your Pay Stack Up? (Salary Survey 1996)," *Working Woman* 21 (February 1996): 27–29.

4. According to the U.S. Department of Labor's Women's Bureau, women who worked part- and full-time for hourly wages earned 81 percent of what men earned in 1996. (More than half the U.S. labor force earns hourly wages.) The weekly earnings of women who were full-time wage or salary workers was 75 percent of men's; their annual earnings were 71 percent of men's.

This difference is due to women, on average, working fewer hours a week than men (40 vs. 45) and fewer weeks a year.

5. Mary Anne Wichroski, "The Secretary: Invisible Labor in the Work World of Women," *Human Organization* 53 (1994): 33–41.

6. See Joyce Beggs and Dorothy Doolittle, "Perceptions Now and Then of Occupational Sex Typing: A Replication of Shinar's 1975 Study," *Journal of Applied Social Psychology* 23 (1993): 1435–1453.

7. The minimum wage as of September 1997 was $5.15 per hour.

8. Barry Gerhart, "Gender Differences in Current and Starting Salaries: The Role of Performance, College, Major, and Job Title," *Industrial and Labor Relations Review* 43 (April 1990): 418–433.

9. Some states, like Massachusetts and Minnesota, have passed laws requiring equal pay for *comparable* work, which means that an employer must pay his or her workers the same salary for work that is different but comparable in terms of its conditions and required skills and experience.

10. Cited in Meryl Gordon, "Discrimination at the Top," *Working Woman* 17 (September 1992): 70.

11. Cited in "An Extra $11,724 for the Guys," *Working Woman* 17 (September 1992): 21.

12. David Kirkpatrick, "Women Occupy Few Top Jobs, a Study Shows," *Wall Street Journal,* 18 October 1996, A7.

13. Quoted in Nijole Benokraitis and Joe Feagin, *Modern Sexism: Blatant, Subtle, and Covert Discrimination* (Englewood Cliffs, N.J.: Prentice Hall, 1995), 105.

14. Ella Edmondson Bell and Stella Nkomo, *Barriers to Work Place Advancement Experienced by African-Americans* (Washington, D.C.: MIT/Glass Ceiling Commission, 1994).

15. Deborah Frable, "Sex Typing and Gender Ideology: Two Facets of the Individual's Gender Psychology That Go Together," *Journal of Personality and Social Psychology* 56 (1989): 95–108.

16. Deborah Tannen, *Talking from 9 to 5* (New York: Morrow, 1994).

17. Susan Sontag, "The Double Standard of Aging," *Saturday Review* 55 (23 September 1972): 29–38.

18. Discussed in Benokraitis and Feagin, *Modern Sexism.*

19. Information from the National Foundation for Women Business Owners.

20. Shelly Emling, "Family-Friendly Policies Work Both Ways," *Atlanta Constitution,* 29 July 1996, C4.

21. Trip Gabriel, "New Issue at Work: On-Line Sex Sites," *New York Times,* 27 June 1996, C1, C9.

22. Ibid.

23. Ibid.

24. Barry Meier, "When Abuse Follows Women to Work," *New York Times*, 10 March 1996, sec. 3, p. 11.

25. Juliet Schor, *The Overworked American: The Unexpected Decline of Leisure* (New York: Basic Books, 1991), 132.

26. For the woman who is married to a substantially older man—often in a second marriage—or has a substantially older partner, the issue may be balancing work with retirement rather than children. She may find that just as her career is really taking off, her partner wants to retire, slow down, spend time together, travel, take up new hobbies and sports, and perhaps relocate.

27. Benokraitis and Feagin, *Modern Sexism*, 104.

28. Alice Reid, "Too Busy to Commute by Metro," *Washington Post*, 14 April 1996, B1.

29. "My Family Leave Act," *New York Times*, 8 November 1996, op-ed, A33.

30. Anne Carey and Marcy Mullins, "USA Snapshots: Reasons for Using Flextime," *USA Today*, 9 January 1996, B1.

31. Quoted in Marie Cocco, "Unions and Women: The Time has Come," Albany, N.Y., *Times Union*, 26 February 1997, A7.

32. National Foundation for Women Business Owners' fact sheet, 1996; and "Putting Women's Issues Back on the Funding Map," *On Campus with Women* 22 (Winter 1997): 3.

33. Janet Irwin and Michael Parrault, "Gender Differences at Work: Are Men and Women Really That Different?" *Wall Street Journal*, 24 September 1996, A1.

34. Cited in Cecilia Conrad, "College Grads and Affirmative Action: Are African American Students Getting More Jobs?" *Black Enterprise* 26 (September 1995): 24.

35. Donna Jackson, *How to Make the World a Better Place for Women in Five Minutes a Day* (New York: Hyperion, 1992).

CHAPTER 15 **Women and Politics**

1. These figures are for 1997 and the 105th Congress.

2. R. Darcy, Susan Welch, and Janet Clark, *Women, Elections & Representation* (Lincoln: University of Nebraska Press, 1994), 18.

3. Jody Newman, *Perception and Reality: A Study Comparing the Success of Men and Women Candidates* (Washington, D.C.: National Women's Political Caucus, 1994).

4. Patricia Aburdene and John Naisbitt, "Going for the Gold in Political Arena," *U.S. News & World Report* 113 (28 December 1992): C1.

5. *Congressional Record*, 24 February 1993, quoted in Susan Carroll and Ronnee Schreiber, "Media Coverage of Women in the 103rd Congress." In *Women, Media, and Politics*, ed. Pippa Norris (New York: Oxford University Press, 1997), 132.

6. Nijole Benokraitis and Joe Feagin, *Modern Sexism: Blatant, Subtle, and Covert Discrimination* (Englewood Cliffs, N.J.: Prentice Hall, 1995), 6.

7. Kenneth Walsh and Thomas Toch, "Now, the First Chief Advocate," *U.S. News & World Report* 114 (25 January 1993): 46–50.

8. Darcy, Welch, and Clark, *Women, Elections,* 195.

9. Peter Brown, "Gender Differences are Felt in Voting Booth," Albany, N.Y., *Times Union,* 21 November 1994, A1.

10. Paula Ries and Anne Stone, *The American Woman 1992–1993: Women and Politics* (New York: W. W. Norton, 1992), 178–201.

11. "Does an Ivy Affect Students' Attitudes?" *Women in Higher Education* 3 (November 1994): 15.

12. Newman, *Perception and Reality,* 6.

APPENDIX **Safety on Campus**

1. Teresa Tritch, "Give a College This Safety Test," *Money* 23 (1994): 32–37.

2. Ibid.

3. "U of Penn Women's Safety Seminars Help Decrease Women's Risk," *Women in Higher Education* 4 (December 1995): 7

4. Charles Dimare and Lule Korsgen, "Rape and Sexual Assault: Civil Liability of Colleges and Universities," *Nova Newsletter* 4, 1990.

5. Quoted in A. L. Miller, "Street Smart," *Runner's World* (June 1993): 58–65.

6. See Sanford Strong, *Strong on Defense* (New York: Pocket Books, 1996).

7. Ibid., 65.

8. Tom Callos, "Grappling with the Truth," *Women's Sports and Fitness* (March 1991): 23.

9. Donna Jackson, *How to Make the World a Better Place for Women in Five Minutes a Day* (New York: Hyperion, 1992), 140.

INDEX

abortion: attitudes toward, 189–190, 190–191; facts about, 191–192; funding, 191; law, 191; statistics, 190

Abzug, Bella, 19, 255–256

Affirmative Action, 288n12

age discrimination, 238–240

alcohol, 167–172, 268–269; and course work, 169; education programs, 173; and fraternities, 173; laws, 173; and medication, 172; and sex, 169, 187; and socialization, 170; statistics, 168; and violence, 169; and women, 167–168

Americans with Disabilities Act (ADA), 135, 291n4

anorexia nervosa, 154. *See also* eating disorders

Architectural Barrier Act, 135

assault, 270; and alcohol, 268; and fraternities, 201; sexual, 200–203; statistics, 296n3. *See also* rape

athletics: and disabled, 291n11; facts about, 69–70; and homophobia, 67, 84; and media, 68–69; stereotypes, 67; and violence, 68. *See also* sports

birth control, 189

body image: and athletics, 155; dieting, 153; eating disorders, 153–154; and media, 156

bulimia, 154. *See also* eating disorders

Campus Security Act, 207

career planning, 236

child care, 244–246, 248

Civil Rights Restoration Act, 60–61

Collins, Patricia Hill, 13

crime and safety, 270–271; facts about, 273

disabilities: facts about, 140–141; new courses about, 139; types of, 134–136

Leonard Law, 104
Lifelong Learning Act, 119

masculinity, 15
media: advertisements, 217–223; facts about, 227; rock videos, 219–220; television, 223–227; and women in politics, 256
men's movement, 15
Millet, Kate, 10
Movimiento Estudiantil Chicano de Aztlan (MECdA), 104
multiculturalism: attacks on, 13–14; goals, 102

National Collegiate Athletic Association (NCAA), 60, 62
National Organization for Women (NOW), 9
Nineteenth Amendment, 9
nontraditional students, 118; attitudes toward, 122, 128; child care, 125; contributions of, 121; difficulties for, 123–124; and domestic violence, 126–127; flexibility for, 126; motivations of, 123; and sexual harassment, 123; statistics, 120; stereotypes, 120; support for, 125, 127, 290n8; and women's movement, 119

Pipher, Mary, 155
Planned Parenthood, 189
political correctness, 51–52, 103, 289n28
politics: facts about, 260–261; financial backing for women, 257, 259; and gender, 257; and women, 255–256; women's beliefs about, 259–260
profanity, 45–46

racism, 50, 53, 94–96, 100–101, 107; apathy toward, 97; in college entrance exams, 99; in financial aid, 99; and stereotypes, 98; and women's studies, 99
rape, 270–271; acquaintance, 200–203, 271; and alcohol, 203, 268; college liability, 206; date, 14; definition of,

200; and drugs, 204; facts about, 107; and fraternities, 201–203; homosexual, 205; self-defense, 272; statistics, 200–201; victim counseling, 207
Real Men, 15
Rehabilitation Act, 136, 291n5
returning students. *See* nontraditional students
Robertson, Nan, 226

safe sex, 186–188
safety: and alcohol, 268–269; on campus, 267; and drugs, 268; precautions, 268–272
self-defense, 272; courses, 272–273; devices, 271–272; precautions, 271; strategies, 272
sexism: in advertising, 217–223; in hiring of coaches, 65; in rock videos, 219–220; in television and film, 223–227; and women of color, 106; in the workplace, 235; on World Wide Web, 241
sexual assault. *See* assault
sexual freedom, 186
sexual harassment, 35–37; in the classroom, 30; facts about, 38–39; and nontraditional students, 123; in the workplace, 240–241, 247–248
sexual identity, 86–87
sexuality: and alcohol, 187; college policies, 187; double standard, 186; and relationships, 186; and sexually transmitted diseases, 186–187; statistics, 186
sexually transmitted diseases (STDs): and birth control pills, 189; and the media, 188; prevalence of, 186–187
sexual orientation, 77–78
sororities, 7
speech codes, 103
sports: administration, 64; coaching, 64; equipment, 64; facts about, 69–70; and gender roles, 65; media representation of, 66, 68; sex discrimination in, 64; Title IX, 59, 61–63. *See also* athletics

Sharon Bohn Gmelch is Director of Women's Studies and Professor of Anthropology at Union College in Schenectady, New York. She is the author of numerous academic articles and four books, including *Nan: The Life of an Irish Travelling Woman* (W. W. Norton and Waveland Press) and most recently *The Parish Behind God's Back: The Changing Culture of Rural Barbados,* co-authored with George Gmelch. She has conducted research in Ireland, Alaska, and Barbados in the areas of gender, ethnicity, and culture change.